SOFT PATRIARCHS, **NEW MEN**

✳Roles

✙ Pgs 3+4 - "3 important domains of family life" from Men: Parenting, household labor, and (emotion work) in marriage.

MORALITY AND SOCIETY SERIES   Edited by Alan Wolfe

SOFT PATRIARCHS, **NEW MEN**

How Christianity Shapes Fathers and Husbands

W. BRADFORD WILCOX

The University of Chicago Press · *Chicago and London*

W. BRADFORD WILCOX is assistant professor of sociology at the University of Virginia and a fellow of the Center for Research on Religion and Urban Civil Society at the University of Pennsylvania.

The University of Chicago Press, Chicago 60637
The University of Chicago Press, Ltd., London
© 2004 by The University of Chicago
All rights reserved. Published 2004
Printed in the United States of America

13 12 11 10 09 08 07 06 05 04   1 2 3 4 5

ISBN: 0-226-89708-7 (cloth)
ISBN: 0-226-89709-5 (paper)

Library of Congress Cataloging-in-Publication Data

Wilcox, William Bradford, 1970–
    Soft patriarchs, new men : how Christianity shapes fathers and husbands /
    W. Bradford Wilcox.
      p. cm. — (Morality and society series)
    Includes bibliographical references and index.
    ISBN 0-226-89708-7 (cloth : alk. paper) — ISBN 0-226-89709-5 (pbk. : alk. paper)
        1. Christian men—United States—Family relationships. 2. Protestants—
    United States—Family relationships. 3. Fatherhood—Religious aspects—
    Christianity. 4. Marriage—Religious aspects—Christianity. 5. Sex role—
    Religious aspects—Christianity. 6. Family—Religious aspects—Christianity.
    I. Title. II. Morality and society.

    BV639.M4 W55 2004
    261.8′358742—dc22

                                                            2003016602

CONTENTS

ACKNOWLEDGMENTS

LIKE EVERY ACADEMIC, I am deeply indebted to a wide circle of colleagues, friends, and family for the intellectual advice and moral support they have offered to me over the course of my graduate study and academic career. This book is in large part a product of their generosity over the years. My dissertation adviser, Robert Wuthnow, was a steady guide during my years at Princeton, helping me navigate the challenges of graduate life and imparting great wisdom to those of us interested in the study of religion. More than that, Bob is a gracious scholar who has never failed to encourage me.

Sara McLanahan challenged me with her wisdom on the family and with her suggestions for the methodological design of this book. She was also kind enough to furnish me with a postdoctoral fellowship at Princeton's Center for Research on Child Wellbeing in 2000–2001. Above all, I appreciate Sara's willingness to entertain unconventional ideas about the family; she is admirably open-minded on the subject.

Paul DiMaggio's classes on culture were formative in my intellectual development. His attention to theoretical and methodological issues in my empirical work is greatly appreciated, especially since he offered exceptionally detailed comments and criticisms on all of my written work. I would also like to thank Tom Espenshade and Sara Curran for serving as outside readers at my dissertation defense and for challenging me to address the larger intellectual issues that this book takes up. Finally, I appreciate the assistance I have received from Blanche Anderson, Cindy Gibson, and Pam Shebel.

While I was pursuing my graduate work at Princeton, I benefited from numerous comments given by fellow graduate students and friends. Lynn Robinson offered great insight on evangelicalism, cultural sociology, and sundry other matters during morning runs around Lake Carnegie. David Oakley kept me laughing in the midst of it all and paradoxically also helped me keep my sights on the permanent things. Jeff Finch and I commiserated about the challenges of dissertation writing. At various points, Wendy Cadge, John Evans, Dana Glei, Jacki Gordon, Kieran Healy, John Hintermaier, Erin Kelly, Man Kwok, Tania Lyon, Becky Petit, Abby Saguy, Gabby Seto, Brian Steensland, Yongjun Sun, and Steve Tepper offered helpful comments on my work.

I would like to thank Princeton University's Center for the Study of Religion, Jim Lewis and the Louisville Institute, the Institute for the Advanced Study of Religion at Yale University, the Center on Religion and Democracy at the University of Virginia, and the Pew Charitable Trusts for generous financial support of my research. The Center for the Study of Religion, the Louisville Institute, and the Center on Religion and Democracy also sponsored workshops and conferences that helped shape my thinking for this book. I also benefited from presentations and discussions regarding this project at the Brookings Institution, Harvard University, the University of North Carolina at Chapel Hill, Notre Dame University, Ohio State University, the University of Texas at Austin, the University of Virginia, and Yale University.

I am deeply grateful for the advice and support I have received from a number of sociologists. Steven Nock at Virginia read the entire manuscript and has given generously of his time and insight regarding key theoretical and methodological issues I faced in writing the book. John Bartkowski and I have shared countless phone conversations and email discussions on issues related to gender, family, and religion. Chris Ellison has been a font of wisdom on religion and family matters; he has also helped me navigate the shoals of academic publishing. Chris Smith has challenged me with his thinking about religious identity. Penny Edgell has offered helpful insights on my work on mainline Protestantism and has generously shared her ongoing research results. Darren Sherkat has never failed to amuse me with his pointed but insightful email critiques of my work. Mark Chaves generously shared his data on congregations and helped shape my thinking about the pastoral efforts of churches on family matters. I am also indebted to Kraig Beyerlein, Marcy Carlson, Joe Davis, Melinda Denton, Trenton Merricks, Jerry Park, Mark Regnerus, Wendy Sigle-Rushton, David Sikkink, Bob Woodberry, and David Yamane for intellectual, moral, and spiritual support. Finally, James Hunter's stimulating seminar on modernity prompted me to become a sociologist in the first place. His insights, encouragement, and commitment to tackling the big questions have been a great inspiration to me over the years.

I am grateful to Niall Fagan, Sarah Curran, and Elizabeth Williamson for research assistance. Niall and Sarah surveyed the *Christian Century* and *Christianity Today* for me. Elizabeth provided research assistance, ran regression models, and helped me with references; her help was particularly invaluable. Thanks also go to Alan Wolfe, the editor of the Morality and Society series, to Doug Mitchell and Tim McGovern at the University of Chicago Press, and to copyeditor Meg Cox. They offered a range of substantive and editorial suggestions that helped make this a better book. The anonymous reviewers for Chicago also provided insightful editorial and methodological feedback.

Of course, I am most profoundly indebted to my family. My mom, Daphne Wilcox, has had faith in me from the beginning; she also prodded me along with frequent queries about the status of my book and has helped take care of my sons on numerous occasions. In their own ways, my sister, Melissa Wilcox, and grandmother, Virginia Hastings, have been steady sources of love and support over the course of my life. My in-laws, William and Pamela Dunne, graciously kept questions about the progress of the book to a minimum; they have also been generous in opening their home and lives to me and my family when we have needed a break from academic life.

My wife, Danielle, made the most important contributions to the book. She helped me think through key questions, endured my prolonged absences from our home, furnished untold moral support along the way, and kept a sense of humor about having a husband who studies male familial involvement but does not always practice it. Above all, her dedication to and love for our growing family have been a constant inspiration and challenge to me as a husband and father. I also appreciate the love and affection I received from my sons, Alexander and Michael, in the midst of writing this book.

Finally, this book is dedicated to my father, Michael Wilcox, and grandfather William Bradford Turner Hastings. Their deep and abiding faith in God shaped their love for their families in countless ways—even up to their deaths. *Requiescant in pace.*

CHAPTER ONE

RELIGION: A FORCE FOR REACTION
IN THE GENDER REVOLUTION?

The primary cause of this national crisis [the decline of the family] is the feminization of the American male. . . . The first thing you do is sit down with your wife and say something like this: "Honey, I've made a terrible mistake. I've given you my role. I gave up leading this family, and I forced you to take my place. Now I must reclaim that role." Don't misunderstand what I am saying here. I'm not suggesting that you *ask* for your role back; I'm urging you to *take it back.* If you simply ask for it, your wife is likely to say, "Look, for the last 10 years, I've had to raise these kids, look after the house, and pay the bills. . . . I've had to do my job *and* yours. You think I'm just going to turn everything back over to you?" Your wife's concerns may be justified. Unfortunately, however, there can be no compromise here. . . . Treat the lady gently and lovingly. But *lead!* . . . To you ladies who may be reading this: *"Give it back!* For the sake of your family and the survival of our culture, let your man be a man if he's willing."

—Tony Evans, *Seven Promises of a Promise Keeper*

The decline of family is the feminization of the American male".

IN 1994, Tony Evans, a black evangelical pastor from Dallas, Texas, delivered variations of the message quoted in the epigraph above to more than 200,000 men across the United States who attended stadium events sponsored by Promise Keepers (PK) that year. Evans struck themes that were characteristic of this social movement, mixing a gendered diagnosis of the sources of family change in the United States with blunt calls for the reassertion of male authority and responsibility in the family. Since the 1970s, conservative Protestant churches and family-oriented organizations like Focus on the Family have devoted countless radio shows, sermons, videos, and books to the task of shoring up the American family. Promise Keepers, which enjoyed a burst of popularity from 1994 to 1997, when more than a million American men attended its events, is only the most visible expression of these recent conservative Protestant efforts to respond to dramatic changes in American family life, a recurrent theme

1

Table 1.1

Religious Traditions of Married Men with Children and All Adults (percent)

	Married Men with Children[a]	All Adults[b]
Conservative Protestant	25	34
Mainline Protestant	27	22
Unaffiliated	13	11
Roman Catholic	25	25
Jewish	3	2
Other	7	6
n	3,564	12,747

[a] National Survey of Families and Households (1987–1988).
[b] General Social Survey (1990–1998).

of which is the need for men to focus on their responsibilities as husbands and fathers.[1]

These efforts have occasioned sustained media attention, along with considerable criticism from feminist and academic circles. Observers and critics alike have raised important questions about the sources and consequences of the distinctive family-related culture produced by conservative Protestant institutions in recent years and, more broadly, about the relationship between religion and the family in the United States. How do we account for the popularity of a traditional message about gender and family in a subculture that is embraced by approximately 30 percent of the U.S. population even as the surrounding society has moved in the last thirty years to embrace an egalitarian outlook (see table 1.1)?

Is the conservative Protestant message about family life and gender connected to the everyday practice of family life for conservative Protestant men, or is it simply a mechanism for building a collective identity by asserting strong symbolic boundaries with the secular world? Is conservative Protestantism a reactionary force in American families, or does this subculture's stress on male responsibility translate into a progressive style of male familial involvement? Given the long-standing association between religion and family in the United States, is the conservative Protestant concern with family life unique to this subculture or is it also characteristic of other religious traditions in the United States, and do other religious traditions influence the family practices of men in much the same way that conservative Protestantism does? And, finally, is conservative Protestantism in the United States successfully resisting the pull of family modernization—marked by declines in the family's social functions, stability, and moral authority—which has exerted so much influence over contemporary family trends in the West?

In this book, I set out to answer these questions first by examining the family and gender ideologies produced by conservative and mainline Protestant churches in the second half of the twentieth century. I then explore how the family-related ideologies produced by these churches are connected to the attitudes of the married men with children who are affiliated with these religious bodies, and how these attitudes compare to those of married men with children who have no religious affiliation. Finally, I analyze the effects that religious affiliation, belief, and practice, along with the family-related ideologies produced and legitimated by these religious traditions, have on three domains of male familial involvement—parenting, household labor, and marriage—for these mainline, conservative, and religiously unaffiliated married men with children.

I include mainline Protestant men and churches in this study for three reasons. First, mainline Protestantism is, in many ways, the most conventional form of religiosity in the United States. By including mainline men, I am able to distinguish the distinctive effects of conservative Protestant belief and practice on men's familial involvement from the generic effects of religious participation on such involvement. Until the second half of the twentieth century, mainline Protestantism was the largest and most influential religious group in the United States. Second, in contrast to conservative Protestant churches, mainline churches have adopted a largely accommodationist stance toward the dramatic cultural and demographic changes in American family life since the 1960s. By focusing on mainline Protestant churches' response to contemporary family change, I am able to view the conservative Protestant response through a comparative lens. Third, mainline Protestantism has long played a central role in American family life, and mainline Protestants make up approximately 25 percent of the population of married men with children.

Men with no religious affiliation make up 13 percent of the population of married men with children. I included them in my empirical analyses of attitudes and family behaviors in order to determine the ways in which the mainline and conservative Protestant men I studied do and do not differ from their secular peers.

The questions addressed by this book take on particular importance in light of the fact that married men with children seem to be the primary obstacles to the complete triumph of the gender revolution that gathered steam in the second half of the twentieth century. This revolution, which is marked by the declining significance of gender in the organization of public and private life and by greater equality between the sexes, has already had a dramatic impact on the socioeconomic status of women and on popular support for gender equality.[2]

In the world of paid work, the labor-force participation rates of working-age women more than doubled in the latter half of the twentieth century, from 37 percent in 1950 to 75 percent in 1994. Even women with families have been deeply involved in this revolution. From 1970 to 1990, the percentage of married women with children working outside the home rose from 51 to 73 percent. Equally dramatic shifts have occurred in the cultural arena. The public has become much more supportive of working mothers. In 1977, 78 percent of Americans thought that preschoolers suffer if their mothers work; less than twenty years later, in 1993, only 45 percent of Americans thought so. Popular opinion has tracked even more strongly in the direction of egalitarianism with respect to the division of family labor. In 1977, 76 percent of Americans believed that it was better for the man to work outside the home and for the woman to focus on the care of the home and family. By 1993, only 37 percent of Americans took that view.[3] The gender revolution, then, made marked strides in the twentieth century.

But this revolution has not completely triumphed, in large part because men in families have not taken up an equal share of the parental, domestic, and emotional work associated with family life. Sixty-eight percent of households with children have married parents,[4] but women in these homes bear a disproportionate share of family responsibilities. Scholars such as Paula England and Arlie Hochschild point out that most gender inequality now found in the labor market and other public venues can be tied to the responsibilities women take on in the private world of the family.[5] The work that women do in the home limits their ability to devote the same level of attention and effort as men to the world of paid work and public life. These scholars also argue that investment in the "second shift" of child care and housework can take a severe toll on women's mental health and on the quality and stability of their marriages. Hochschild thinks men's reluctance to embrace gender equality in the family puts the success of the gender revolution in doubt; she goes so far as to describe the situation as a "stalled revolution."[6]

A close look at the state of gender change in the United States suggests that Hochschild's characterization is overstated. It is fairer to say that men have slowed, but not stalled, the gender revolution. This study focuses on the contributions that men make to three important domains of family life: parenting, household labor, and "emotion work" in marriage.[7] In these domains married men have not yet reached parity with their wives, but they are taking up a significantly larger share of family responsibilities than men did in previous generations.[8] A number of studies by Suzanne Bianchi and her colleagues support this conclusion. One time-diary study of married parents with children under eighteen found that married fathers spent an average of 3.8 hours a day with their children in 1998, up 36 percent from 2.8 hours in 1965. This means that family men are now spending 65 percent as much time as mothers spend with their children, up from 51 percent in 1965.[9] Another time-diary study indicates that married men have increased their weekly hours of household labor more than 100 percent, from 4.7 hours in 1965 to 10.4 hours in 1995. This means they are now doing about half as much household labor as their wives, a dramatic increase from 1965, when they did about one-seventh as much as their wives.[10]

We know less about the emotion work that men do in their marriages. Here I am referring to the effort men devote to expressing positive emotion to their wives, attending to the dynamics of the relationship and the needs of their wives, setting aside time for couple activities, and refraining from engaging in destructive forms of marital conflict, such as domestic violence.[11] There is no longitudinal research on this subject, but a 1991 study of more than three hundred couples in Connecticut found that younger husbands (under thirty-six years old) were significantly more willing to address serious issues about their marriages than were older husbands.[12] Specifically, 38 percent of wives of younger husbands indicated that it was very easy to raise marital issues, compared with only 25 percent of wives of older husbands. This finding could reflect a life-course effect in which husbands do less positive emotion work as they age, but I suspect that it instead indicates a cohort effect such that younger husbands are more progressive-minded and willing to devote greater attention to the dynamics of their relationships.

Even though men in families have moved to take up a larger share of the practical and emotional work associated with family life, they still have not come close to shouldering an equal share. Our society has taken an egalitarian trajectory in the public worlds of law, education, work, politics, and the cultural understanding of gender, but the private institution of the family has not changed as quickly as our public institutions, largely because men have failed to take on an equal portion of the responsibility for family life. Men's behavior in this regard has two important consequences: first, it contributes to gender inequality in public and private life as women's domestic responsibilities limit their public opportunities; and second, it places tremendous practical and psychological pressure on women, especially mothers who work outside the home.

Thus, as Frances Goldscheider and Linda Waite have observed, the way to an egalitarian "new family" order "will lead through men."[13]

Given the long-standing association between religion and traditional family practices, and especially the largely patriarchal vision of gender and family life advanced by conservative Protestant institutions, I explore the possibility that religion, particularly conservative Protestantism, is a central source of the gender inequality that persists in American homes. This possibility is especially important given that about a quarter of American fathers are conservative Protestants and about a quarter of them are mainline Protestants (see table 1.1).

The questions addressed by this book are also important because the contributions that men make to the family are vital to the well-being of women and children. This is especially true in the domains of parenting and marital emotion work. Paternal involvement is positively associated with the economic achievement, educational attainment, and emotional health of children. Indeed, some studies have found that the contributions fathers make to their children's well-being are almost as important as those made by their mothers.[14]

Likewise, the amount of effort men devote to being affectionate and understanding and to spending time alone with their wives is deeply important for the quality and stability of their marriages. Women report significantly higher levels of marital quality when men invest themselves in the emotional life of the marriage.[15] Indeed, men's emotion work in marriage is the most important predictor of women's evaluation of marital quality, easily surpassing other factors, such as marital commitment, participation in household labor, perceptions of equality, and the presence of children.[16] Women formally initiate most of the divorces in this country, so it is not surprising that men's positive emotion work dramatically reduces the risk of divorce.[17]

The amount of time men devote to household labor and the percentage of the household labor they perform do not play a central role in women's evaluation of marital quality or stability.[18] Surprisingly, one study even suggests that couples are more likely to divorce when men do a greater share of household labor.[19] What matters for women is not so much the precise division of labor as their perception that it is fair to them, and most women perceive the division of household labor as fair even when they are responsible for the lion's share of housework.[20] Married women who do feel that the division of household labor is unfair to them—about 30 percent of all married women— are much less happy in their marriages.[21] And it turns out that men's emotion work in marriage plays an important role in determining whether women view the division of labor as fair. Thus, the influence of conservative Protestantism, and of religion more generally, on the practical and especially the emotional work that men do in their families has a profound effect on the welfare of women and children.

CONSERVATIVE PROTESTANTISM, RELIGION, AND MEN IN THE FAMILY

This study is not the first public or intellectual effort to evaluate the relationship between conservative Protestantism, and religion more generally, and the family. Three important perspectives currently inform the debate about the nature of this relationship. The first, which might best be called the *family modernization* perspective, argues that as the family grows weaker as an institutional force in the lives of most Americans, religion is becoming increasingly marginal as an influence on the culture and practice of family life.[22] Adherents to this perspective tend to be demographers, sociologists, and historians focusing on national and international patterns of change in the family. Specifically, they argue that macro-level changes in the economy and in polity and culture—from the growing cultural power of expressive individualism to shifts in the economy in the direction of postindustrialism—are stripping the family of its functions, authority, and salience in the lives of most Americans. These changes, in turn, undercut the ability of religious institutions to exercise moral authority and offer social support to the family in ways that strengthen it as an institution.

The family modernization perspective assumes a mantle of inevitability by arguing that the ability of religious institutions to shape the culture and practice of family life in the United States necessarily becomes weaker as these larger social and cultural forces continue to exert their influence on the family. Pointing to declines in traditional family attitudes and increases in divorce, cohabitation, and out-of-wedlock births, Larry Bumpass has argued that "the aggregate consequences of the high prevalence of the new family behaviors, and demography of cohort replacement, do not make a return of conservative values seem at all likely" and that "individuation and secularization will likely continue to move family behavior away from traditional patterns."[23] Likewise, Scott Coltrane maintains that the "recent trend toward diversity in family forms is inevitable," an irreversible consequence of structural changes in the socioeconomic order; he further maintains that religious and civic efforts to "promote idealized father-headed families will have little influence on marriage rates or fathering practices."[24] Thus, the family modernization perspective would predict that conservative Protestantism's capacity to propagate a family-centered ideology will weaken as the society changes and that the effect of religious belief and practice on men's family-oriented behavior will be minimal.

A second perspective argues that conservative Protestantism is an important force for *gender reaction* in American family life because it promotes a traditional view of gender that is assumed to push men away from an active and expressive approach to family life. This perspective considers recent conservative Protestant efforts to address changes in gender and family, such as the Promise Keepers movement, to be straightforward examples of a subcultural backlash against feminism and the socioeconomic gains of women,[25] but most of the leading public actors who hold the perspective— from the media to feminist organizations to scholars who specialize in gender and family studies—have devoted no serious ethnographic or quantitative study to conservative Protestantism and family life.[26] The gender reaction perspective is largely congruent with the "culture war" thesis advanced by James Davison Hunter, which maintains that orthodox religionists are at war with modernity's egalitarian and individualistic values and that the family is the primary battleground for this conflict.[27]

Adherents to the gender reaction perspective argue that the conservative gender ideology issuing from conservative Protestant institutions and leaders has a baleful influence on the family, and especially men. Commenting on a 1998 Southern Baptist statement advocating male headship in marriage, journalists Cokie Roberts and Steve Roberts argued that this way of thinking "can clearly lead to abuse, both physical and emotional."[28] Patricia Ireland, then-president of the National Organization of Women, accused Promise Keepers of being promoters of a "feel-good form of male supremacy" intent on keeping women in the "back seat."[29] John Gottman, a psychologist and a leading scholar of the family, warns that conservative Protestantism is pushing fathers away from a warm, expressive style of parenting: "As the religious right gains strength in the United States, there is also a movement of some fathers toward authoritarian parenting in childrearing patterns of discipline."[30] Likewise, sociologists Julia McQuillan and Myra Marx Ferree contend that the "religious right" is "pushing men toward authoritarian and stereotypical forms of masculinity and attempting to renew patriarchal family relations."[31] These journalists, feminists, and scholars infer that the conservative Protestant subculture's gender traditionalism, and especially its emphasis on male authority in the family, translates into an authoritarian style characterized by low levels of positive emotion work and familial involvement along with high levels of corporal punishment and domestic violence.

A third perspective stresses the *complexity* of the relationship between conservative Protestantism and the family by noting nuances, ambiguities, and contradictions in conservative Protestant gender ideology. It points out that the family-centered ideology produced by conservative Protestantism, what I call familism, stresses male responsibility for the family and asserts that persons are not passive dupes of the ideologies they encounter in the institutions to which they belong.[32] More generally, this perspective suggests that conservative Protestantism has an ambiguous relation to late-modern forms of family culture and practice—alternately resisting, innovating, and accommodating in response to the gender and family culture it finds itself surrounded by. For the most part, this perspective is held by scholars of religion who have done extensive ethnographic work on conservative Protestant families or women. One of the most surprising findings associated with their work is that conservative Protestantism seems to have some success in domesticating men; that is, it prompts them to make greater investments in the practical and emotional dimensions of family life, especially in ways that appeal to the ideals and aspirations of their wives.[33] The complexity perspective maintains that conservative Protestantism domesticates men by linking male authority to a demanding ethic of male familial involvement. It offers men a "patriarchal bargain" that accords men symbolic authority in the home in return for their exercise of greater responsibility for the well-being of their families.[34]

The work of John Bartkowski, for instance, emphasizes the ways in which the traditional, essentialist gender discourse produced by leading conservative Protestant leaders is often moderated by an emphasis on men overcoming their weaknesses in the expressive arena of family life and contested by a small group of evangelical leaders who seek to promote an egalitarian gender agenda. This complexity perspective also suggests that the conservative Protestant subculture's commitment to familism often coexists with gender traditionalism in ways that accord high value to male involvement in the home. In Bartkowski's words, "recent years have witnessed a shift in elite support toward a neopatriarchal family model in which husbands are now urged to become servant-leaders within the home."[35] Adherents to this perspective further argue that conservative Protestant men and women draw creatively on the diverse and at times contradictory ideological resources at their disposal to construct strategies of action that may or may not conform to the ideological advice offered by the most prominent leaders. In the final analysis, the ethnographic work done from this perspective suggests that conservative Protestantism's emphasis on the family, along with its recent reinterpretation of male headship in terms of service to family, is encouraging men to devote themselves to the practical and emotional tasks associated with family life.[36]

In this book I suggest that each of these perspectives helps to illuminate distinct dimensions of the relationship between men, the family, and conservative Protantism but misapprehends other dimensions of this relationship.

Here I cast new light on this complicated relationship by adopting a comparative approach to the study of religion, men, and the family. Indeed, this is the first book to address the relationship between conservative Protestantism and the family by using nationally representative survey data to compare conservative Protestant men to mainline Protestant men and to men who are not affiliated with a religious denomination on attitudinal and behavioral outcomes. This comparative focus enables me to determine the extent to which these two branches of Protestantism responded differently to the process of family change and to evaluate the assumption that religion's influence on the family is weakening in a uniform and unilinear fashion. My comparative, quantitative study also throws into relief what is and is not distinctive about the family-related practices of the conservative Protestant subculture, allowing me to evaluate the claims of critics of the subculture who, without referring to careful empirical research, argue that it is a force for gender reaction.

With this approach I can also evaluate the more sympathetic and nuanced assessments made by scholars whose ethnographic work has focused only on conservative Protestants. I show, for instance, that in spite of the complexity, contradictions, and ambiguity of gender ideology that the ethnographic literature highlights, conservative Protestant men are consistently more likely to espouse traditional gender attitudes than mainline Protestant and unaffiliated men. But contrary to the expectations of those who adhere to the gender reaction perspective, conservative Protestant men spend more time in one-on-one interaction with their children than both mainline Protestant men and unaffiliated men.

My argument unfolds in two stages. First, relying on recent theoretical developments in cultural sociology, I explore mainline and conservative Protestant institutional responses to family change in the latter half of the twentieth century.[37] With a close reading of the secondary literature and a qualitative survey of religious periodicals over twenty years (1970–1990), I show how two religious traditions with distinctive cultural commitments, collective identities, and institutional resources responded in markedly different ways to large-scale social and cultural change.

Mainline Protestant institutions adopted a largely accommodating stance to the family and gender changes ushered in during the 1960s, whereas conservative Protestant institutions largely took on a resistant posture in regard to these changes. Mainline institutions stressed gender equality and tolerance of family diversity, while conservative institutions underlined their support for gender-role traditionalism and a familistic ideology. I argue that we can understand their largely polar responses to family modernization only by comprehending their divergent cultural orientations toward theological authority, modernity, and freedom and the distinct positions of their members in the U.S. class structure in the 1960s and 1970s. Conservative Protestantism was able to maintain its distinctive family-related culture even as its members moved toward the socioeconomic mainstream from the 1970s to the 1990s. By linking its family-related culture to its collective identity, conservative Protestantism has continued to produce largely traditional family and gender ideologies to maintain normative boundaries against a modern world that it sees as deeply sinful, especially in the domains of sexual and family ethics.

I argue that family modernization perspective presents a monochromatic and overly deterministic view of the impact that family change has on religion, overlooking the ways in which countercultural religious institutions with substantial social resources can resist society-wide trends. Conservative Protestantism has capitalized on the unease that a substantial minority of Americans have felt about the direction of family and gender change. My findings do lend some support to those who view conservative Protestantism as a force for reaction because, at least at the institutional level, this subculture is fundamentally in tension with late modernity's embrace of gender equality and family pluralism. Recent evaluations of conservative Protestant family-related culture have overemphasized the extent to which conservative Protestantism is riven by internecine ideological conflicts; conservative Protestant institutions and leaders are much more likely than their mainstream Protestant counterparts to promote conservative gender and family ideologies. Indeed, the ideological polarities I document between mainline and conservative Protestant institutions indicate that the culture war thesis has some validity, at least in the institutional domain of American religion.

In the second part of the book, I show that the distinctive family and gender ideologies produced by conservative and mainline Protestant institutions are in different ways "loosely coupled" and "closely coupled" to the attitudes and practices of their married men with children.[38] My conclusions are based on evidence taken from three nationally representative data sets: the General Social Survey (GSS), the National Survey of Families and Households (NSFH), and the Survey of Adults and Youth (SAY). I find that although conservative Protestant married men with children are significantly more traditional and familistic than their mainline and unaffiliated peers, they hold views that are more moderate than those expressed in the ideological discourse of conservative Protestant institutions and leaders. Likewise, the views of mainline Protestant men with children are not as progressive as those articulated in the institutional discourse of the intellectuals and leaders who speak for their churches. So both conservative and mainline Protestant men tend to stake out ground that is closer to the ideological center than the public discourse of their religious institutions would suggest.

I draw on insights from the family modernization perspective, the ethnographic literature on conservative Protestant families, and neo-institutional analysis to explain this loose coupling between institutional and lay culture. As the first two perspectives would predict, rising rates of education, divorce, and female labor-force participation among conservative Protestants have fostered a more progressive outlook among some men in this subculture. For mainline men, the long-standing association between family-centered living and religious practice helps to explain why some mainline men are more moderate than their institutions. Moreover, the neo-institutional perspective suggests that religious institutions and elites often produce ideologies that are more extreme than the views held by their members in an effort to assert collective boundaries against other groups and to maintain a measure of ideological consistency within their own traditions.[39]

I then turn to look at the ways in which the religious participation of conservative and mainline Protestant men and the family-related culture produced by their religious institutions influences these men's family practices, especially in comparison to men who have no religious affiliation. Here I draw on perspectives from classical and cultural sociology that address the effect that institutions and the culture they produce have on social action. Specifically, I argue that religious participation is generically associated with integration into the social order and with a family-centered logic of practice in ways that foster familial involvement for men regardless of their religious tradition. But I also argue that the tradition-specific culture associated with religious institutions plays a powerful role in influencing men's family behaviors. In particular, I focus on the ways in which the moral culture, or ideology and norms, and the practical culture, or ethos, associated with religious institutions fosters particular kinds of family behaviors among men, especially men who are strongly integrated into these institutions through frequent church attendance.[40]

The religious and family related culture found in conservative Protestantism is closely coupled with the practices of married men with children who hail from this subculture. When it comes to paternal discipline and household labor, this subculture's theological conservatism and gender-role traditionalism push conservative Protestant men in a clearly traditional direction. As critics of conservative Protestant patriarchy might predict, I find that conservative Protestant fathers are more likely than mainline and unaffiliated fathers to discipline their children by spanking them. Likewise, I also find that conservative Protestant homes have a more unequal division of household labor than nonevangelical homes.

In most domains of family life, however, conservative Protestantism is not a force for reaction in the family. Conservative Protestant married men with children are consistently more active and expressive with their children than unaffiliated men and are often more engaged with their children than mainline Protestant fathers. (To be sure, in some domains of fatherhood, mainline Protestants are about as invested in the parenting enterprise as their conservative counterparts. The two groups of fathers, for instance, are about equally likely to praise and hug their children.) Furthermore, conservative Protestant family men are more likely than unaffiliated men to do positive emotion work in their marriages and are more consistently engaged emotionally in their marriages than mainline men. So charges that conservative Protestantism fosters authoritarian and other stereotypical displays of masculinity among its family men are overdrawn. Indeed, my findings offer considerable support for the idea that conservative Protestantism domesticates men. In other words, at least when it comes to parenting and marriage, the soft patriarchs found in evangelical Protestantism come closer to approximating the iconic new man than either mainline or unaffiliated men do.

How do I account for these surprising findings, especially in light of conservative Protestant support for gender-role traditionalism? It turns out that the positive effects of high levels of theological conservatism, familism, and church attendance among conservative Protestant men more than offset the negative effects of gender-role traditionalism. Theological conservatism, which can be taken as an indicator of how much these men embrace the religious worldview produced by conservative Protestant institutions, is associated with heightened levels of paternal and marital expressiveness, as well as a strong commitment to parental supervision. Familism, which taps their beliefs about the sanctity of the family, is also important in motivating conservative Protestant men to do positive emotion work with their children and wives. This is in keeping with the increasingly therapeutic character of conservative Protestant family advice, which pays particular attention to the emotional dimension of family relationships.

Although church attendance almost uniformly promotes higher levels of paternal involvement and expressiveness among conservative Protestant family men, it does not always do so among their mainline counterparts. Church attendance integrates conservative Protestant men into a distinctive normative order where they are encouraged to give time and attention to their families, regardless of their own commitment to the family-related ideologies found in the conservative Protestant subculture. Conservative Protestant churches offer an intense, expressive ethos that provides men with an implicit model for the treatment of their wives and children. So the family-related ideologies, norms, and cultural repertoires associated with conservative Protestant institutions work in various ways to foster a soft patriarchy among its family men that is characterized by traditional practices in some domains and progressive practices in other domains.

Mainline Protestantism exerts less of an influence on the family behaviors of its married men with children than does conservative Protestantism. Some mainline men are theologically conservative and familistic in ways that make them strict disciplinarians and expressive fathers and husbands, much like their conservative Protestant peers, but a large number of mainline men hold a liberal gender-role ideology that seems instead to make them more likely to do household labor than their conservative Protestant peers. There is also some evidence that high-attending mainline Protestants are more involved with and emotionally engaged in the lives of their children and wives than their unaffiliated peers, though attendance is less consistently predictive of this active and expressive approach to family life for mainline Protestants than it is for conservative Protestants. These findings lend some credence to the notion that religious practice is generically related to a family-centered lifestyle. This link holds in spite of the deep ideological differences separating mainline and conservative Protestant churches, providing some evidence that the family-related discourse produced by mainline Protestant institutions is only loosely coupled to the practices of married men with children who are affiliated with these institutions. Still, mainline Protestantism does seem to foster among its family men many of the attributes of the iconic new man—namely, a more egalitarian division of household labor and somewhat higher levels of paternal and marital involvement and emotional engagement.

The second part of this book, then, largely vindicates the ethnographic literature on family and gender in conservative Protestantism by showing that men in this subculture are in some respects more progressive than the gender ideology of their religious institutions would suggest and, indeed, that conservative Protestantism plays a role in domesticating men. The general thrust of the conservative Protestant response to family modernization might therefore be characterized as a form of *innovative traditionalism,* a practical strategy that neither accommodates nor resists change but rather seeks to maintain the traditional strength of the family as an institution by fostering an innovative approach to men's familial involvement. Thus, in this book I argue that conservative Protestantism, and religion more generally, does not pose a central obstacle on the road to new families, but it remains to be seen what effect they will have on the well-being of families, women, and children.

THE RELIGIOUS MEASURE OF MEN

Religion is a complex social phenomenon and consequently can be measured in a variety of ways.[41] Social scientists generally classify survey respondents according to three characteristics: religious affiliation, religious ideology, and religious self-identification. Given my focus on institutions and on the effect that institutionally produced family and gender ideology has on attitudes and practices, I rely primarily upon an institutional measure—the religious affiliation that respondents report—to classify the men in this study as conservative Protestant, mainline Protestant, or unaffiliated. Table 1.1 shows that conservative and mainline Protestantism are two of three largest religious traditions in the United States (the third is Roman Catholicism), encompassing more than 50 percent of the population of married men with children. Unaffiliated men make up 13 percent of this population. Thus, this study focuses on 65 percent of the population of married men with children in the United States.

I classify all Protestant denominations and independent churches that adhere to a theologically conservative worldview as conservative. Thus, I include groups that have important differences in religious belief and practice—from Pentecostal to Baptist churches, and from Anabaptist to Reformed churches—under the broad umbrella of conservative Protestantism. It is important to note that I include churches that would define themselves as evangelical as well as those that would call themselves fundamentalist. Evangelicalism tends to stress evangelism, a willingness to engage the world, and a commitment to theological orthodoxy, whereas fundamentalism stresses doctrinal purity, separation from the world, and a very strict view of biblical inerrancy. I also include a number of predominantly black churches, such as the Church of God in Christ, and predominantly white churches, such as the Southern Baptist Convention, under this umbrella.

What evangelical and fundamentalist churches share is a high view of biblical authority, usually expressed as the view that the Bible is the literal Word of God; a belief in Jesus Christ as the sole source of salvation; and a belief that the Bible provides the primary guide to moral life. In practice, most of these churches also stress the importance of a personal experience of conversion—of being "born again," in popular parlance—and of evangelizing nonbelievers. More generally, these churches share a willingness to question key values associated with late modernity—egalitarianism, pluralism, and

Table 1.2

Religious Beliefs and Practices of Married Men with Children, by Tradition (percent)

	Conservative Protestants	Mainline Protestants	Unaffiliated	National Average
Theological conservatism				
Theologically conservative	63	31	16	36
Not theologically conservative	37	69	84	64
Church attendance				
Frequent[a]	50	39[b]	7	42
Infrequent	50	61[b]	93	58
n	898	977	446	3,564

Source: National Survey of Families and Households (1987–1988).

Note: Chi-square for all figures is significant at the .01 level.

[a] Frequent church attendance is defined as attending church several times a month or more.

[b] Chi-square for mainline Protestants is not significantly different from the national average at the .01 level.

tolerance—when the application of these values comes into conflict with the moral and religious truths they believe to be found in the Bible.

The distinctive religious beliefs and practices promoted by conservative Protestant churches are associated with an unusual level of religious vitality. Table 1.2 shows that, for instance, conservative Protestant married men with children are much more likely than their mainline and unaffiliated peers and other American men with children to attend church several times a month or more. They are also more likely to take a theologically conservative view of the Bible—with 63 percent of them agreeing that the Bible is literally true and is "the answer to all important human problems."

Conservative Protestant family men are distinctive in other ways as well. As table 1.3 indicates, their socioeconomic status—measured by income and education—is lower than that of mainline Protestants and lower than the national average (but not lower than the status of unaffiliated men). Conservative Protestant family men are also much more likely than other family men to be African American and to hail from the South. These characteristics help to account for their distinctive religious beliefs and practices. Their demographic profile, however, is less distinctive. Conservative Protestant married men with children come close to the national average in their age, the number of children they have in the home, and their biological relationship with their children.

Table 1.3

Sociodemographic Status of Married Men with Children, by Tradition (percent)

	Conservative Protestants	Mainline Protestants	Unaffiliated	National Average
Education				
Some high school or less	20	8	23	15
High school graduate	61	59	52	57
College graduate	19	33	25	28
Income				
Less than $24,000	30	19	30	24
$24,000–32,999	28	23	26	25
$33,000–49,999	23	28	22	25
$50,000 or more	19	30	22	26
Race/ethnicity				
White	73	92	82	82
African American	22	5	4	8
Hispanic	4	2	6	8
Other	1	1	8	3
Region				
Northeast	9	16[a]	19	19
North central	20	36[a]	28	27
South	59	32[a]	28	34
West	12	16[a]	25	20
Age				
18–33	36	30	36	34
34–40	33	35	33	33
41 or older	31	35	31	33
Number of children				
1	37[b]	35	42	36
2	38[b]	44	39	40
3 or more	25[b]	21	19	24
Average number of children	2.08[b]	2.05	2.01	2.15
Father's relation to children				
All biological	80	82	81	81
All stepchildren	4	4	5	4
Blended	16	14	14	15
n	898	977	446	3,564

Source: National Survey of Families and Households (1987–1988).

Note: Chi-square for all religious groups is significantly different from the national average at the .01 level, except Age and Father's relation to children.

[a] Chi-square for mainline Protestants is not significantly different from the national average at the .01 level.

[b] Chi-square for conservative Protestants is not significantly different from the national average at the .01 level.

Mainline Protestantism is noted for its accommodating stance to modernity, its status as a pillar of religious and social convention in the United States, its ongoing attempt to apply the central truths of Christianity to the changing circumstances of the day, and its tolerance of lay differences in belief. Most mainline Protestant churches are well-established in U.S. society, with historical roots going back more than a century and, in many cases, several centuries. I classify the following denominations as mainline Protestant: Methodist, Episcopal, Lutheran, Presbyterian, United Church of Christ, and a number of smaller mainline churches.[42] What these churches share is a commitment to what Nancy Ammerman calls "Golden-Rule Christianity," the idea that Christianity is essentially about loving God and loving neighbor in the way that one would like to be loved.[43]

Firm adherence to Christian orthodoxy is downplayed in most mainline churches. Instead, these churches seek to reinterpret the religious and moral teaching of the faith in light of insights derived from the contemporary world but in ways that remain consistent with what they see as the central truths of the gospel: kindness, mercy, the equal dignity of every person, and so on. Mainline churches also place a high value on social justice. In practice, mainline churches stress the importance of treating one's neighbors and children well, of adhering to the dominant social conventions of the upper-middle-class United States, and of being socially conscious in a progressive way. Mainline churches generally embrace the project of late modernity, and particularly values such as egalitarianism, pluralism, and tolerance. Most mainline Protestant married men with children do not take a theologically conservative view of the Bible, and they attend church infrequently. Indeed, compared to the national average, mainline family men are quite conventional in their theological beliefs and levels of religious attendance, though they fall slightly below the national average in theological conservatism (see table 1.2).

Table 1.3 reveals that mainline Protestant family men are more socioeconomically advantaged than their conservative Protestant and unaffiliated peers, and their socioeconomic status is higher than the national average. Mainline family men have higher incomes and levels of education, and they also are disproportionately white. They also have smaller families than the national average. However, they do not differ from the national average in terms of age, region, and family status. Thus conservative and mainline Protestant family men differ in both their religiocultural orientation and their socioeconomic profile.

The religious restructuring that has taken place in the United States since the 1950s adds an additional layer of complexity to the religious categorization of these men. In the period since the 1950s, ideological divisions have emerged within religious traditions, so theologically conservative and liberal men can now be found in both mainline and conservative Protestant denominations.[44] While it is still the case that theological conservatism is concentrated in conservative Protestant churches and theological progressivism is concentrated in mainline churches, one can find self-identified theologically conservative evangelicals in mainline Protestant churches and theologically liberal mainline believers in conservative Protestant churches.

This heterogeneity is a particularly important dynamic for mainline Protestant men because a significant minority of them identify with a conservative theology they have encountered in conservative Protestant organizations, like InterVarsity Christian Fellowship, that span denominational lines; indeed, 31 percent of mainline Protestants take a theologically conservative view of the Bible.[45] These men are influenced by the religious, family, and gender ideologies produced by conservative Protestant institutions and often identify with the religious and familial agendas of these institutions even though they are not formally affiliated with a conservative Protestant church.

In an effort to see how religious ideology mediates, contradicts, or accentuates the effects of religious affiliation, I incorporated a measure of theological conservatism, based upon respondents' views of biblical literalism and authority, into my analyses. If I found that conservative Protestant affiliation and theologically conservative ideology work in essentially the same way on men's family behavior, I would have more evidence in support of the notion that there is a connection between conservative Protestantism and family life no matter how one measures conservative Protestantism; moreover, if I found that theological conservatism accounts for some of the effects of conservative Protestant affiliation on the family behaviors of men, I would also have evidence that the theologically conservative ideology produced by conservative Protestant institutions mediates the effect of such affiliation. This measure confirms the validity of my claims about the connection between conservative Protestantism and family life.

To examine the connections between religion, ideology, and men's family attitudes and practices, I analyzed data from three different national surveys using three different types of regression techniques: ordinary least squares (OLS) regression, logistic regression, and Tobit regression. Most of the empirical analyses for this book are conducted with data from the National Survey of Families and Households (NSFH), a nationally representative survey of American adults focusing on a range of family attitudes and behaviors. The NSFH also includes data on religious affiliation and measures theological conservatism and church attendance. The NSFH surveyed more than three thousand married men with residential children eighteen and under in 1987–1988 (NSFH1) and 1992–1994 (NSFH2). To document attitudinal changes from the 1970s to the 1990s among American adults, including married men with children, I use data derived from the General Social Survey (GSS). The GSS regularly samples Americans to ask them questions about a range of topics, including religion, gender, and the family.

I also analyzed data from the Survey of Adults and Youth (SAY), which questioned more than six thousand parents and adolescents (aged ten to eighteen) around the nation in 1998–1999. SAY has two advantages: it is the first survey to offer information on religion and parenting in the wake of Promise Keepers, and it is the first parenting survey to offer detailed information on the religious identity of parents instead of merely their denominational affiliation. Thus, SAY allowed me to compare married men with children who self-identity as "evangelical" or "fundamentalist" Protestants to their counterparts who self-identify as "mainline" or "liberal" Protestants, and to compare them to men who indicate that they have no religious identity. SAY also allowed me to confirm my findings on religion and fatherhood with data collected more than ten years after NSFH1. More details about all three surveys can be found in the appendix.

Finally, to determine the nature and trajectory of elite conservative and mainline Protestant opinion on family and gender issues, I sampled issues of the evangelical Protestant magazine *Christianity Today* and the mainline Protestant magazine *The Christian Century* from 1970 to 1990 at five-year intervals, analyzing all the articles on family- and gender-related issues. With this range of survey and qualitative data, I have assembled a comprehensive picture of the relationship between religion, ideology, and the family among conservative and mainline Protestant married men with children.

CHAPTER TWO

MAINLINE AND CONSERVATIVE PROTESTANT PRODUCTION OF FAMILY AND GENDER CULTURE, 1950–1995

> The mid-century decade has been described as the most permissive ten years in our history. Is it merely coincidental that the generation raised during that era has grown up to challenge every form of authority that confronts it? I think not. It should come as no surprise that our beloved children have hangups; we have sacrificed this generation on the altar of overindulgence, permissiveness, and smother-love. Certainly, other factors have contributed to the present unsettled youth scene, but I believe . . . the central cause of the turmoil among the young must again be found in the tender years of childhood: we demanded neither respect nor responsible behavior from our children, and it should not be surprising that some of our young citizens are now demonstrating the absence of these virtues.
>
> —James Dobson, *Dare to Discipline*

IN 1970, Dr. James Dobson, then a professor of child development at the University of Southern California, introduced his first book, *Dare to Discipline*, with a provocative thesis. After cataloguing a long list of social ills afflicting the youth of the day—from dramatic increases in drug use, sexual activity, and juvenile violence to pervasive alienation from authority—Dobson argued that in large part these ills could be traced back to the "permissive" child-rearing style of the 1950s. Parents of this era "demanded neither respect nor responsible behavior from [their] children," and the consequence, in short, was the 1960s. Dobson then went on to offer the antidote to parental permissiveness: his own blunt, homespun advice about parenting, in general, and the need for a strict regime of parental discipline, in particular.

Dare to Discipline proved enormously popular, selling more than three million copies, and helped launch Dobson's career as a conservative family expert and advocate. In 1977 he founded Focus on the Family, which has since grown into a $100-million Christian family ministry.[1] The success of *Dare to Discipline* can be attributed to a number of factors, including the fact that it struck a chord among Americans, especially conservative Protestants, who were disturbed by the tidal wave of cultural and familial change—from the antiwar movement to the dramatic increase in divorce—that swept the United States in the 1960s and 1970s.

The way Dobson connected his parenting advice to a broader critique of the counterculture is indicative of the manner in which conservative Protestantism linked the larger cultural conflicts taking place in the 1960s and 1970s to specific cultural and demographic shifts also taking place in the family in this period. In particular, Dobson asserted that the larger conflicts then dividing the nation were rooted in part in lax and inattentive parenting styles that had turned young people into prideful, alienated, and delinquent citizens. More generally, his comments are suggestive of the ways in which conservative Protestantism, acting as a distinctive subculture in the United States, adopted a strategy of resisting and innovating response to particular developments associated with modernity—especially secularism and cultural liberalism. The family became one of the most central crucibles for this strategy.[2]

Dobson's observations call into question a crucial assumption entertained by some of the leading scholars of the family: namely, that modernization is associated with macrostructural and macrocultural developments that lead to a decline in the functions, authority, and strength of the institution of the family and to a decline in familistic culture across all sociocultural sectors.[3] The basic tenets of this approach, which I call the family modernization perspective, run as follows:

Increased social differentiation associated with industrialization and the expansion of the state, along with higher rates of female labor-force participation, mean that more functions of the family—for example, education, leisure, food preparation—and more authority are delegated to state and market spheres. These developments, in turn, diminish the strength and authority of the family as an institution, thereby reducing the incentives and dependencies that once fostered high levels of commitment to and investment in the family. Moreover, developments in the cultural arena, which are seen to have an elective affinity with these social-structural transformations, tend to promote secularization, increased individualism, and a desire for personal fulfillment. These cultural developments, of course, also undercut the values and virtues associated with family-centered living. To the extent that the family continues to play a meaningful role in the lives of individuals, its functions are increasingly focused on a narrow range of expressive tasks—for example, affection, psychological support, and companionship. In conjunction with this expressive focus in family life, the interpersonal relations in families are also more likely to be governed by a therapeutic ethic that emphasizes the psychological well-being of parents and children as the summum bonum of family living.

Larry Bumpass's presidential address to the Population Association of America captures the general thrust of this view:

> Family relationships occupy an important but ever shrinking space in our lives. . . . This is the continuation of a long-term process and is not confined to one country. Trends in cohabitation, marriage, fertility, and marital disruption are widely shared across Western industrial societies. To my mind, major causes include the individualizing tendency of participation in our economy and cultural values of individualization that both facilitate this participation and are reinforced by it. There is no reason to think that these processes are exhausted or are likely to reverse.[4]

While the general narrative advanced by the family modernization perspective captures important dynamics at work in society and the family, the perspective suffers from a monochromatic and overly deterministic view of social life. The larger issues raised by Dobson's commentary suggest that this theory has overlooked ways in which particular groups accommodate, resist, or innovate in response to modernization, in general, and to family modernization, in particular. Recent work in the sociology of culture and the sociology of religion has taken modernization theory to task, showing how macrocultural and macrostructural forces can impact groups differently depending upon their sociocultural position and their strategic response to these forces.[5] In other words, collectivities often mediate the effects of modernization on the cultural commitments and behavioral patterns of their members.

Two developments in the sociology of culture help explain how this mediation takes place. First, Robert Wuthnow's articulation theory shows how communities may produce markedly different ideologies in response to similar developments in their social environment, especially when they acquire institutional resources that allow them to articulate ideologies that are independent of or critical of that environment.[6] These ideologies are symbolic systems that incorporate a vision of the good life, critiques of alternative systems, and specific guidance about the normative ordering of social relations.[7]

Second, work on cultural identity by Pierre Bourdieu and Christian Smith indicates that groups can generate considerable collective solidarity and power by asserting strong cultural boundaries against social out-groups and the cultural ideals they represent.[8] Smith's subcultural identity theory posits that groups that articulate countercultural ideologies—including those that incorporate critiques of elements of modern life—and construct "distinct identity boundaries vis-à-vis outgroups will produce more satisfying morally orienting collective identities and will, as a consequence, grow in size and strength."[9] Taken together, these developments in the sociology of culture suggest that groups can rely on institutional resources, distinctive ideologies, and cultural boundaries to exert a measure of collective agency, even in directions that are orthogonal or contrary to the general social and cultural forces associated with modernization.

This is not to say that collectivities have complete autonomy from the larger social environment—including modernizing influences. To survive and flourish, groups must articulate their ideologies in ways that address salient contours of the larger social environment they find themselves in.[10] Moreover, the ideologies and norms that groups produce to orient social behavior must be linked to resources in such a way that "they mutually imply and sustain each other over time."[11] Thus, to remain vital, groups must engage the cultural and social forces they encounter in their social environment—either accommodating, innovating, or resisting in response to them. Attempts to retreat wholesale from the larger social environment generally cuts collectivities off from the resources they require to maintain themselves and can lead to collective stasis and decline. Among other things, this means that even groups that retain antimodern ideologies or practices will often accommodate or adapt some elements of cultural and structural modernity as they seek to legitimate themselves in the eyes of their members, potential recruits, and influential elites.[12]

How do these observations about culture and collective identity speak to the family modernization perspective? Taking religion as one expression of collective identity, one could imagine religious groups responding in markedly different fashion—depending upon their institutional resources, ideological commitments, and cultural boundaries—to trends in the family, including its structural and cultural modernization. Mainline and conservative Protestantism have articulated—in many areas—distinctly different ideological responses to key developments in American family life. Mainline Protestantism has adopted a largely accommodationist stance toward family modernization while conservative Protestantism has generally resisted it. Their disparate stances on issues like familial authority, abortion, and family structure can only be understood with reference to the distinctive institutional resources, ideological commitments, and cultural boundaries that inform these religious traditions.

Of course, it is possible that the family strategies of religious groups are more symbolic than real; in other words, there may be little difference between the social behavior of conservative and that of mainline Protestants even though their family culture is in some ways quite different. Pointing to Catholic divorce rates that parallel those of the population at large even though the Catholic Church opposes divorce, Bumpass has argued that ideological resistance to contemporary family trends does not necessarily impact the basic dynamics of family modernization.[13] In this chapter I outline the family-related culture produced by mainline and conservative Protestants and account for the cultural and social sources of the distinctive ideological approaches to the family advanced by these two traditions. In chapters 4, 5, and 6 of this book, I will take up the question of what, if any, impact the family-related culture produced by mainline and conservative Protestantism has upon the family behaviors of married men with children.

THE CULTURAL AND SOCIAL SOURCES OF CONSERVATIVE AND MAINLINE PROTESTANT FAMILY IDEOLOGY

We can understand mainline and conservative Protestant ideologies of family life only by exploring the outworking of the decisive encounters of these two religious traditions with the dramatic cultural and social shifts of the late 1960s and the 1970s. Their strategic responses to this era have structured the contemporary family discourse of mainline and conservative Protestantism along the lines of two cultural logics: respectively, Golden Rule liberalism and expressive traditionalism. The mainline logic of Golden Rule liberalism combines a progressive emphasis on tolerance of family diversity, egalitarian gender roles, and child autonomy with a familistic emphasis on a Golden Rule ethic of caring, especially in the family. The conservative Protestant logic of expressive traditionalism stresses the importance of patriarchal and parental authority, traditional sexual morality, and an ethic of familial duty, but softens these ideals with an expressive interpersonal ethic that suggests personal fulfillment can be found through adherence to traditional social and moral conventions. Golden Rule liberalism is more accommodating of family modernization, while expressive traditionalism is more resistant to the developments associated with family modernization.

These distinct cultural logics emerged from the dynamic encounters between the social transformations of the late 1960s and the 1970s and the religiocultural traditions that orient mainline and conservative Protestantism. The tradition of mainline Protestantism is marked by a posture of openness to the world: it self-consciously seeks to adjust its teachings—including some of its theological and moral teachings—to developments in the world around it. This posture is rooted theologically in a basic confidence in human nature and in the belief that God is at work and is powerful enough to do a "new thing" in the world. It is also indebted to an Enlightenment faith in the power of human reason—especially reason exercised in universities, seminaries, and the professions—to discern truth as it unfolds in different ways in new social contexts and to revisit old assumptions in light of new intellectual discoveries.[14]

In practical terms, this progressive Enlightenment orientation has three important consequences. First, the theology produced by mainline churches and especially seminaries tends toward rationalism, abstraction, and complexity; it also admits of a certain indeterminacy and universalism, which is reflected in efforts to downplay the particularity of classical Protestant claims and to highlight moral truths that are noncontroversial and held throughout society.[15] Second, the mainline's moral compass, while flexible, does point in a discernable direction. Drawing on prophetic strands found in the Old Testament and on the works of early twentieth-century social gospel thinkers, the mainline consistently articulates a commitment to social justice. It interprets Jesus Christ's life, as recorded in the New Testament, as a template for a pastoral ethic of love and acceptance that can, if necessary, lead to the overturning of social norms that have come to be seen as outmoded and legalistic.[16] Third, the mainline's comparatively high cultural status in the U.S. religious field, along with its posture of openness to the world, has meant that it has been a crucial carrier of middle- and upper-class convention, acting as both a guardian of social convention and a legitimating agent for changes in social convention advocated by cultural elites. The establishmentarian character of mainline religion has also meant that its worship style is formal and liturgical and that its cultural style stresses civility and tolerance of pluralism.[17] Because its establishmentarian liberal cultural style runs contrary to the cultural style found in evangelical and fundamentalist churches, mainline Protestantism has asserted symbolic boundaries against its conservative counterpart.

While conservative Protestantism shares with the mainline historical roots in the Reformation, it differs in central ways at the levels of theology, cultural orientation, social status, and practice. Theologically, conservative Protestantism views the Bible as the inerrant Word of God and the sole authority for religious and moral truth. In interpreting the Bible, conservative Protestantism draws on a common-sense epistemology rooted in the Scottish Enlightenment, which asserts that the Bible can be read in a straightforward fashion to determine religious and moral truths and that these truths exist apart from the exigencies of history.[18] This biblical faith embraces a particularistic religious vision that stresses salvation through personal faith in Jesus Christ, the need to restore Christianity to the purity and authenticity of the apostolic church, and a firm conviction that God's sovereignty extends to the life of every person. On the other hand, although conservative Protestantism professes an antimodern faith in an unchanging, exterior, authoritative text and a particularistic narrative, its emphasis on the individualistic character of faith is more in keeping with the tenor of modernity.

Conservative Protestantism's religious outlook is connected to the social world in three ways. First, the theological vision produced in conservative churches and seminaries produces a paradoxical mix of moral individualism and authority-mindedness. On the one hand, the conservative Protestant emphasis on a transformative religious experience and a deeply personal faith lends itself to subjectivism and a preoccupation with personal moral and spiritual behavior, especially personal evangelism. On the other hand, its focus on biblical authority and divine sovereignty translate into a concern for order and authority in society (Romans 13).

Second, in keeping with its restorationist religious impulse, conservative Protestantism has held up a vision of "Christian America" that both seeks a return to the nation's allegedly religious roots and legitimates American liberty and prosperity as a divine favor that must be cultivated continuously by the religious and moral reform of the citizenry.[19] This view is associated with an approach to social reform that stresses the importance of religious revival and changes in the moral fabric of society; through much of this century, this approach has also been marked by a "personal influence strategy" that prioritizes evangelizing one's friends, seeking religious and moral purity in one's own life, and leading a good family life.[20]

Third, after evangelical Protestantism lost its religious hegemony in the late nineteenth century, its successors—fundamentalism and evangelicalism—occupied a low-status position in American religion for most of the twentieth century. The particularistic religious and moral message and the expressive piety associated with conservative Protestantism have not been attractive to the cultural establishment. For most of the past century, conservative Protestantism has found its strongest traction instead among Americans who are at some remove from the carriers of cultural modernity—Southerners and working- and lower-class Americans.[21] The subcultural status and distinctive religious ideology have also meant that conservative Protestantism erects strong cultural boundaries against the secular world and other religious groups.[22]

DIVERGENT RELIGIOUS RESPONSES TO THE REVOLUTIONARY CHANGE OF THE 1960s AND 1970s

Many of these religiocultural divisions between mainline and conservative Protestantism were not salient in the culturally conservative 1950s. During that most familistic decade of the century, the fertility rate peaked, an almost century-long increase in the divorce rate stopped, and the age at first marriage declined to its century low.[23] The cultural side of this familistic orientation was visible in the emphasis on bourgeois domesticity, which was fueled in part by a growing middle class.[24] Rates of religious attendance and membership surged as a result not only of familism, but also of broader political and cultural developments that fostered interest in churchgoing. The Allied victory over the Nazis, the U.S. contest with the Soviet Union, and the unparalleled prosperity of the decade heightened the collective belief that the United States stood as a bulwark and beacon of freedom, opportunity, and religious faith. These developments were also connected to heightened levels of adherence to the American civil religion—the sense that the American nation and way of life are an expression of God's divine purposes—and to a concomitant confidence in authority and institutions, from the government to the church.[25] Thus, while mainline and conservative Protestantism retained distinctive religious outlooks through the decade, the generally conservative, conformist ethos of the 1950s meant that accommodationist mainline and countercultural conservative Protestants shared an essentially common moral outlook.

The late 1960s and the 1970s ushered in a series of political and cultural shocks that upended this consensus. A host of movements—for civil rights, against the Vietnam war, for women's liberation—appeared on the scene, calling into question the legitimacy of the American way of life and dividing adherents of the American civil religion into two camps: those who maintained a particularistic 1950s view of the United States as a chosen nation, and those who judged the nation by more universalistic standards of peace and justice and found her wanting.[26] This legitimation crisis, the rise of the counterculture, and dramatic increases in levels of education and affluence all fueled a spirit of anti-institutionalism, freedom of choice, and expressive individualism that permeated large sectors of society—especially among the baby boomers, who came of age in this era. As a consequence, organized religion lost much of its privileged status as a central player in U.S. society and a key arbiter of the nation's spiritual and moral life.

These cultural and religious developments, along with the widespread avail-ability of the Pill, occasioned the rise of a new morality that left decisions in the arena of sexuality and the family to the desires of the individual rather than the authoritative voice of religion or tradition. This new morality was evidenced in the liberalization of attitudes regarding premarital sex, abortion, divorce, and ho-mosexuality, especially among boomers.[27] Taking a cue from the Civil Rights movement and the era's interest in personal fulfillment, the women's liberation movement, exemplified in books like Jessie Bernard's *The Future of Marriage* (1972), voiced concerns about gender inequality, the relegation of women to the private sphere, and the burdens marriage and motherhood pose to women.[28]

Feminist critiques of the traditional family, the popularity of the new mo-rality, and the rise of expressive individualism combined to erode the cultural foundations of obligation, fidelity, and self-sacrifice (especially for women), and the more encompassing ideology of familism that had undergirded the institu-tion of the family.[29] These cultural trends were both cause and consequence of dramatic changes in family-related behavior in the 1960s and 1970s: female labor-force participation rose from 38 to 52 percent, the divorce rate more than doubled, the number of persons cohabiting increased threefold to 1.5 million, and the percentage of households with children declined from 49 percent to 38 percent.[30] Thus, the changes of this era pushed society away from a familistic focus on bourgeois virtues, a heavily gendered lifestyle, and the child-centered family and toward an adult-centered, individualistic world where personal ful-fillment, sexual freedom, and gender equality were more valued.

The accommodationist posture of mainline Protestantism, combined with its elites' commitment to the social gospel, meant that many mainline institutions and leaders and many young boomers moved in an isomorphic institutional and intellectual direction toward the movements for social justice in the 1960s and 1970s.[31] Turning on the Americanist civil religion of the 1950s, these mainline institutions and their members questioned the nation's under-standing of itself as a global beacon of freedom, prosperity, and righteousness. They pointed to racial injustice and poverty at home and U.S. involvement in the Vietnam War abroad as evidence of the nation's failure to live up to the universalistic standards of justice that had been gaining currency. The main-line's newfound concern about issues of equality, democracy, and inclusion also extended to its internal life, as many denominational bureaucracies were restructured to promote greater racial, ethnic, and gender diversity and to encourage decision-making processes that were more participatory.[32]

The mainline was more ambivalent about embracing the new morality, which challenged the substance and spirit of classical Protestant moral teachings head-on. Nonetheless, some leading mainline intellectuals, such as theologian Joseph Fletcher, noted for his *Situation Ethics* (1965), gave the new morality explicit support, arguing that acts like premarital sex and abortion could be justified if they advanced the well-being of the affected parties. More importantly, the mainline's commitment to a pastoral ethic of love and acceptance in the private sphere and to pluralism and civility in the public sphere led to the tacit or explicit acceptance of many of the normative changes associated with the new morality. In the congregational setting, clergy did not raise their voices against most of the practical manifestations of the new morality, and as public policy debates erupted over moral questions in the 1970s, mainline denominations, in the name of tolerance for religious and moral pluralism, often supported liberalization.[33] The mainline's encounter with the progressive spirit of the 1960s and 1970s was important in shaping its approach to the host of family-related issues that also emerged in this period.

Conservative Protestants reacted to the legitimation crisis of the 1960s and 1970s in profoundly different ways from their mainline counterparts. They argued that the United States was indeed in the midst of a crisis but that the crisis had to do with the nation's drift away from its biblical moorings and toward the shoals of social disorder, moral permissiveness, and state socialism. Influenced by Americanism, a biblically based respect for authority, and a strong suspicion of statism, conservative Protestantism saw much of the counterculture's critique of U.S. institutions as naive and as corrosive of an American way of life that, while flawed, was infinitely better than the available alternatives around the globe.

Evangelicals and fundamentalists viewed the social unrest of the era— war protests, drug use, race riots, and so on—as portents of the potential collapse of American civilization.[34] This is not to say, however, that conservative Protestants were of one mind about the unrest. Many evangelicals supported the Civil Rights movement and eventually came to oppose the Vietnam War.[35] Nevertheless, to the extent that they saw social reform as necessary, most evangelicals and fundamentalists sought to advance this reform through evangelization and revival rather than through social action or state policy. To do otherwise would be to fall captive to the social gospel that had distracted liberal Protestants from the central purposes of Christian faith, namely, knowing Christ personally and following his command to evangelize.[36]

Conservative Protestants viewed the rise of the new morality, and the concomitant increases in premarital sex, divorce, abortion, and open homosexuality, with the greatest alarm. The new morality was seen as the effective deinstitutionalization of Christian morality and, along with the declining fortunes of organized religion, was considered a sure sign that "secular humanism" was on the verge of national triumph.[37] Unlike mainline Protestants, who tended to see social justice as the yardstick of Christian ethical purity, conservative Protestants took biblical texts dealing with sexual conduct as key guides to virtuous Christian living. Not only was the sexual revolution profoundly unsettling to evangelicals and fundamentalists, the new morality's embrace of a contextual, individualistic, and self-consciously progressive approach to ethics was viewed as an assault on the conservative Protestant position that the Bible reveals timeless, absolute truths. Finally, the federal government's efforts to officially separate itself from Christian belief and morality—exemplified in Supreme Court decisions prohibiting school prayer (1963) and liberalizing abortion (1973)—were judged to be telltale signs of a retreat from the biblical faith and morality that had made America great.

This pervasive apprehension that conservative Protestant faith and morality had come under attack led to a strong reaction in the late 1970s with the mobilization of the new Christian Right.[38] Although the public dimensions of this reaction have received the most media and scholarly attention, conservative Protestantism also devoted a great deal of effort to addressing the pastoral consequences of this era for its own religious and moral life—especially in family-related matters. The defensive posture and hermeneutic of suspicion that many evangelicals and fundamentalists adopted in relation to the social changes of the 1960s and 1970s proved decisive in structuring the conservative Protestant approach to public and pastoral family-related issues in subsequent years.

Thus, after their encounter with the tumultuous 1960s and 1970s, the cultural orientations of mainline and conservative Protestantism were decisively reconfigured in ways that left the mainline generally progressive and accommodating to the cultural modernity of the period and conservative Protestantism largely resistant. This outcome can be understood partly in cultural terms as a consequence of the ways in which the divergent religiocultural logics of mainline and conservative Protestantism either fit with or contradicted the basic cultural trajectory of this period.

SOCIAL-STRUCTURAL SOURCES OF POLARIZATION

There are other important sociocultural sources of this ideological polarization. In terms of socioeconomic status, mainline Protestants enjoyed significantly higher levels of education than conservative Protestants in the 1970s,

Table 2.1

Sociodemographic Status of Protestant Adults in the 1970s, by Tradition (percent)

	Conservative Protestants	Mainline Protestants
Education		
Some high school or less	46	27
High school graduate	46	56
College graduate	8	17
Region		
Northeast	6	21
North central	22	37
South	58	27
West	14	15
n	2,322	3,065

Source: General Social Survey (1972–1978).

Note: Chi-square for religious group differences in education and region are significant at the .01 level.

and most conservative Protestants lived in the poorest region of the country, the South (see table 2.1). In that decade 73 percent of mainline Protestants had at least a high school education, compared to only 54 percent of conservative Protestants. Moreover, only 27 percent of mainline Protestants lived in the South, while 58 percent of conservative Protestants lived there. Thus, in terms of region and class, conservative Protestantism was "located furthest from the institutional structures and processes of modernity" while mainline Protestantism, whose adherents had the highest level of educational attainment of any Christian group in the United States, was closest to the forces of cultural modernity.[39]

As Bourdieu might argue, the tendency toward modernism and antimodernism characteristic of mainline and conservative Protestant religious culture, respectively, in the 1970s might also be seen as a collective effort to mark off cultural boundaries and to legitimate the social practices that made up adherents' everyday lifestyles.[40] Comparatively affluent, educated, and cosmopolitan mainliners were more inclined to embrace an "ethic of liberation" that modeled their experience of economic choice and social power and distinguished them from the fundamentalists with their conformist morality.[41] The average working-class, less-educated, and Southern conservative Protestant was more likely to embrace an ethic of moral order that modeled an experience of economic limitation and social domination and suited a Southern culture that relied on its religious identity to distinguish itself from other regions—especially the Northeast, which was known for its religious liberalism and cultural elitism.[42]

ACCOMMODATING ELEMENTS OF MODERNITY

While it is true that ideological polarization was the primary consequence of this era for the two religious traditions, it is important to note that there were some developments associated with cultural and structural modernization that affected mainline and conservative Protestantism along largely similar lines. This is not surprising for the mainline, given its fundamentally open posture to the world, but it is perhaps surprising that conservative Protestantism accommodated and adapted particular practices and cultural ideologies, often with quite modern results. This strategy is in keeping with the observation that groups often incorporate some of the practices and ideological schemas of their social environment as they seek to attract new members and retain the allegiance of current members, and to extract social, material, and cultural resources from that environment.

For instance, by the 1970s both mainline and conservative Protestantism largely embraced a therapeutic ethic that valorized personal psychological well-being and an expressive, egalitarian approach to interpersonal relations. For the mainline, this was most evident in the rise of pastoral counseling. Heavily influenced by the humanistic psychology of Carl Rogers and Abraham Maslow, pastoral theologians like Princeton Theological Seminary's Seward Hiltner stressed an empathic, client-centered approach to counseling that discouraged moralizing and encouraged personal growth, even if that meant condoning behavior that broke with social convention.[43] The institutionalization of this movement was signaled by the founding of the American Association of Pastoral Counselors in 1963, an ecumenical group dominated by mainline members.[44] By the 1970s, the mainline approach to pastoral care meshed well with growing interest in pop psychology and self-fulfillment, particularly because much of this popular therapeutic discourse incorporated religious imagery and themes, as evidenced by the subtitle to M. Scott Peck's best-selling *The Road Less Traveled: A New Psychology of Love, Traditional Values, and Spiritual Growth* (1978). The pastoral discourse and practice of the mainline increasingly endorsed the larger cultural trend toward self-realization and an approach to ethical action that privileged personal experience and feelings, not objective moral standards.[45]

Although evangelicals and especially fundamentalists were skeptical about the value of psychology prior to the 1960s, in the 1960s and 1970s, an increasing number of well-educated evangelicals began to argue that many of the ideas associated with psychology were consonant with biblical teaching—humanistic psychology's "unconditional positive regard," for instance, appeared to mirror the unconditional love of Christ.[46] Furthermore, the individualistic thrust of the therapeutic ethic—its concern with the self, relationships, and expressive living—was homologous with individualistic elements of the evangelical tradition—its emphasis on an individuated faith, a personal relationship with Jesus Christ, and an emotional worship style. Thus, as psychology and the therapeutic ethic gained currency in the culture at large, conservative Protestants thought it appropriate to incorporate therapeutic elements into their faith tradition.[47]

The founding in 1965 of the first department of psychology at a major evangelical seminary, Fuller Theological Seminary, was one sign of the therapeutic ethic's ascendancy.[48] A content analysis of *Christianity Today,* the leading conservative Protestant periodical, suggests that this ascendancy crested at the end of the 1970s. Specifically, William Smith found, beginning in the late 1970s most articles covered psychological topics positively and without reference to theological criteria of evaluation—in other words, the therapeutic acquired independent cultural authority among conservative Protestants in that decade.[49]

Thus, much like that of mainline Protestantism, the pastoral discourse of conservative Protestantism evinced increased interest in self-fulfillment and expressive interpersonal relations—concerns that stood in tension with classical Protestant emphases on self-sacrifice and hierarchical authority.[50] However, unlike mainliners, evangelicals and fundamentalists suggested that fulfillment would ultimately be found by loving God and obeying his moral law. Conservative Protestant leaders differed from mainliners also in drawing more heavily from behaviorist elements in the psychological tradition that seemed consonant with the legacy of Puritanism.[51] In more theoretical terms, homologies in the ideological substance of psychotherapeutic culture and conservative Protestantism, combined with the growing popularity and cultural authority enjoyed by psychotherapeutic ideas and practices, paved the way for the adoption of an ethic that restructured the character of conservative Protestantism along more therapeutic lines.[52]

Another way conservative Protestantism accommodated itself to its social environment was in its effort to adapt the values and practices now associated with public reason to legitimate its vision of morality in the public and pastoral spheres. Particularly as conservative Protestants sought to vindicate their moral claims in the public debates about morality and politics that began in the late

1970s, they drew on polling data, social scientific research, and the work of experts with significant educational credentials.[53] This strategy was designed to engage the increasingly democratic, naturalistic, and social scientific nature of public discourse that obtained in the late-twentieth-century United States, largely as a consequence of increased religious and cultural pluralism, higher levels of education, and the declining legitimacy of theistic civil religion. The increased popularity of parenting experts like James Dobson, who has traded on the knowledge and credentials he earned through his medical and psychological training as a child development specialist, is but one sign of the significance of this new approach.[54] The moral authority of public reason was making itself felt in this subculture partly because even conservative Protestants were being exposed to the social forces—mobility, mass media, and public education—that undercut religious and other traditional sources of moral authority.[55]

Of course, given its openness to modernity, the mainline is quite comfortable with public reason. Thus, in wide-ranging pronouncements on social issues, including family-related matters, in the 1960s and 1970s, mainline denominations were quick to draw not only on specific research findings but also on the social-structural approach to social problems favored by academics and liberal policy advocates, which helped to frame their basic approach to fundamental questions of social justice.[56] More importantly, since most mainline Protestants have a more privatized view of religious faith than do conservatives, they are more likely than conservative Protestants to rely on the secular experts—pediatricians, academics, therapists, and media commentators—who play such a prominent role in shaping the nation's family culture.[57]

Thus, the sociocultural transformations ushered in by the 1960s and 1970s impacted mainline and conservative Protestantism in ways that are more complex than a cursory glance at the history of the era might suggest. On the one hand, the mainline embraced new expressions of a progressive ideology: increased levels of tolerance, greater commitment to social equality, and a more flexible, experiential moral ethic. Conservative Protestantism, meanwhile, assumed a reactionary posture indicated by deep concern over the counterculture's assault on the American way of life, a renewed commitment to public and pastoral efforts for moral reform and evangelization, and a sense that a godly moral ethic could be found only in the unchanging and absolute truth of the Bible. On the other hand, both religious traditions largely accommodated themselves to the therapeutic tenor of the 1970s and to the increasing cultural authority of public reason. From that era on into the 1990s, the mainline took an essentially modern approach, and conservative Protestantism's traditionalist approach to family issues was tempered by modern elements.

PROTESTANTISM AND FAMILISM

In some ways, the 1950s were the apogee in the United States of the ideology of familism, the "set of both cognitive and normative assertions that interpret the family as *the* crucial social institution, both for the individual and for society as whole."[58] For the individual, this ideology, which began to take hold in the seventeenth and eighteenth centuries, depicts the family as the most important arena for the fulfillment of individual needs for emotional expression, nurture, companionship, and meaning; for society, it portrays the family as a central civilizing force that integrates its members, especially men and children, into the social order.

Familism is organized around the logic of what I call sentimental domesticity, a logic that endows the expressive functions associated with marriage, childbearing, and especially motherhood with a sense of sacredness. At the same time, due to its concern for social order and the fragility of bonds based only on emotion, familism has stressed the importance of commitment and sacrifice on behalf of the family. It is organized around a selfless ethic of service to spouse and children, in opposition to the profane, selfish world of the market and the public sphere.[59] Moreover, since the rise of industrial capitalism and a Victorian separate-spheres ideology in the nineteenth century, familism has been heavily gendered, with women taking primary ownership of the logic of sentimental domesticity in the private sphere and men taking responsibility for an instrumental provider role that embraces the logic of self-interest and assertion found in the public sphere, especially the market.

Because familism invests the family with a sense of sacredness and with a lead role as a civilizing force in society, it also stresses sexual fidelity in marriage, chastity for the unmarried, an intensive child-rearing ethic that includes a strong assertion of parental authority, a commitment to a lifelong marital covenant, and a high level of expressive interaction between all members of the family. The demographic trends, cultural tenor, and conventionally religious character of the 1950s gave familistic ideology a great deal of cultural authority and plausibility. In the 1950s the mainline largely embraced familism in its discourse and practice. The Episcopal Church added a morning service where children could, for the first time, join their parents in worship,[60] and the 1956 Methodist General Conference called the family the "bulwark of Christian faith" and celebrated rising birthrates and increased family togetherness, while expressing concern about the church's failure to prevent the marital break-ups that had left more than two million adults divorced since World War II.[61]

Conservative Protestantism, which had maintained a familistic orientation throughout the first half of the century, stepped up its celebration of domestic life, and it highlighted its traditionalist approach to familism even as society began to distance itself from the more conservative assertions of family authority, as evidenced by the popularity of Dr. Benjamin Spock's child-centered and permissive child-rearing advice.[62] Conservative Protestant leaders, such as the dean of Dallas Theological Seminary, pointedly insisted that "women are to be subject to their husbands" and that children will learn the importance of "self-control, reverence, and obedience to authority" if their parents frequently rely on corporal punishment.[63] Mainline and conservative Protestants were united, however, in their desire to put religious practice and discourse in the service of more stable, expressive, selfless, and pious homes.

The easy bond between the hearth and the altar that obtained in the 1950s was upset by the cultural and social shifts of the 1960s and 1970s, when dramatic increases in divorce, female labor-force participation, and premarital sex, as well as declines in fertility, undercut the logic of practice that made familism plausible. Concomitant shifts in the culture toward the new morality, expressive individualism, and anti-institutionalism also challenged the legitimacy of many of the virtues and values associated with familism. Moreover, the movement for women's liberation—exemplified in books from Betty Friedan's *The Feminine Mystique* (1963) to Germaine Greer's *The Female Eunuch* (1970) questioned the value of domesticity, called attention to the disproportionate familial burdens women had to bear in the name of self-sacrifice, lauded the sexual revolution, and embraced divorce when it was an occasion for a woman's personal growth. These social and cultural factors had reinforcing, reciprocal effects on one another as they simultaneously undercut the ideological and economic foundations of familism.[64]

EMBRACING FAMILY CHANGE

The mainline Protestant response to the disestablishment of familism was clearly shaped by the religiocultural strategy it adopted in relation to the developments of the 1960s and 1970s. In the 1970s and 1980s, the mainline moved to distance itself from some of its previous familistic positions and to embrace many of the changes that had taken place in family-related practices and values. Its stance on family-related matters was shaped by five cultural factors that had come to shape mainline Protestantism in the 1960s and 1970s: a progressive orientation to social change; a commitment to inclusiveness in the midst of heightened racial, ethnic, and moral pluralism; a tendency to view public issues through a social-justice prism; a therapeutic pastoral ethic that stressed the importance of personal fulfillment over adherence to traditional moral strictures; and support for an egalitarian brand of feminism. The influence of these factors can be seen in the mainline's approach to family pluralism and marital ethics, sex-related issues, child socialization, and gender roles. (I discuss gender roles later in the chapter because, at least at the analytical level, gender-role ideology must now be treated as distinct from the ideology of familism; indeed, the two ideologies seem to be moving in orthogonal directions from one another.)[65]

A 1976 pronouncement of the General Conference of the United Methodist Church—the largest mainline denomination, known for its theological and cultural moderation—is suggestive of the tack the mainline took to accommodate dramatic increases in divorce and in family pluralism generally:

> We understand the family as encompassing a wider range of options than that of the two-generational unit of parents and children (the nuclear family), including the extended family, families with adopted children, single parents, couples without children. We urge social, economic, and religious efforts to maintain and strengthen families in order that every member may be assisted toward complete personhood. . . . In marriages where the partners are, even after thoughtful reconsideration and counsel, estranged beyond reconciliation, we recognize divorce and the right of divorced persons to remarry, and express our concern for the needs of the children of such unions. To this end we encourage an active, accepting, and enabling commitment of the Church and our society to minister to the needs of divorced persons.[66]

The first sentence of the pronouncement indicates that the Methodist Church has put aside its previous valorization of the child-centered nuclear family and, in a spirit of openness to social and cultural change, has accepted the notion that shifts in family structure and practice should be viewed not through a declensionist lens but through the positive prism of "changing families" that acquired cultural authority in the 1970s. The second sentence relies on a social justice frame that suggests that social-structural or institutional measures are the way to help families; no mention is made anywhere in the statement about individual family members' responsibility to "maintain and strengthen" their families.

The third sentence retains a traditional expression of concern for the children of divorce but recognizes a right to remarry. Prior to the 1960s the United Methodist Church had, on avowedly biblical grounds, allowed for remarriage only in the case of adultery or abandonment, but with successive liberalizations of its divorce policy in 1964 and 1976, the church adopted a completely tolerant posture toward divorce.[67] The fourth sentence of the pronouncement suggests two reasons the Methodist Church took this direction: first, the revised pastoral policy was viewed as more inclusive, or accepting, than the older policy; and, second, a policy of tolerance was more in keeping with the church's commitment to a therapeutic pastoral ethic of enabling and being respectful of the needs of divorced Methodists. Thus, this statement suggests that therapeutic and political categories had largely displaced theological and familistic categories of normative evaluation for marriage, divorce, and remarriage.

Similar themes emerge in contemporary mainline pastoral discourse on family-related matters. In *Christian Marriage and Family* (1988), for instance, pastoral theologians John Patton and Brian Childs argue that the structure of a family is not important; instead, they embrace a pluralistic model of family life, writing that "there is no ideal form for the Christian family toward which we should strive." Their approach is indebted to liberal conventions about tolerance and inclusion: "The stress on the structure of the nuclear family . . . contributes to the ignoring of others in less traditional family structures."[68] More importantly, they view the pastoral enterprise as fundamentally oriented to therapeutic ideals of personal growth, interpersonal authenticity, and emotional support. Accordingly, they do not think that clergy should stand up for marriage as an institution, or structure, when it gets in the way of these ideals:

> Pastoral care and counseling exist to care for persons, not to preserve structures. Certainly, structures are necessary for a fully human life, but they are not ends in themselves. They are, rather, a means for facilitating full human living. . . . Although the marriage relationship provides an informative paradigm for other relationships, we do not understand it theologically as an enduring structure to be preserved for itself. Rather, it endures and fulfills its purpose when the human capacity for caring is continually expressed and developed through it.[69]

Survey research suggests that Patton and Childs's ideal of tolerant acceptance of family pluralism is representative of the views of a large proportion of mainline clergy. One national survey found that 73 percent of mainline Presbyterian pastors think that the church should be "tolerant of family changes (divorce, remarriage, same-sex couples) now taking place."[70] Another recent survey of clergy in upstate New York found that more than 85 percent of mainline clergy believed that "God approves of all kinds of families."[71]

This emphasis on tolerance of family diversity allows mainline Protestants to mark off an important cultural boundary with their conservative counterparts. One ethnographic study of clergy in metropolitan Milwaukee found, for instance, that mainline pastors queried about family issues were quick to highlight their distaste for the family program of the religious right, which they accused of being "intolerant" and "reactionary."[72] Another study of a prominent mainline Presbyterian church in Chicago found that its family-related pastoral discourse contrasted the religious right's focus on "family values" with Jesus Christ's ministry of inclusion.[73] Thus, the mainline's affirmation of family pluralism allows it to signal that it has embraced critical aspects of cultural modernity: tolerance, inclusion, and the therapeutic quest for personal growth.

But this ethic of tolerant acceptance also is associated with and contributes to an inability to articulate a clearly defined vision of what family life should look like or even to focus much at all on the family itself. Because the mainline has rejected the family-problem frame associated with the religious right and seeks to be tolerant of most family configurations, clergy often sidestep controversial family issues or struggle to articulate a constructive family ethic that provides specific guidance to its members on topics like marriage and divorce, and the unique stresses associated with single parenting. The aforementioned Presbyterian church in Chicago favors "conversation" rather than "definitive guidance" in its dealings with family matters,[74] and almost half of the mainline clergy who participated in one survey in upstate New York rejected the term "family ministry" as exclusionary, signaling their unwillingness to think in terms of familistic categories.[75] The mainline clergy interviewed in metropolitan Milwaukee who expressed vocal opposition to the religious right's family agenda also expressed discomfort in speaking about controversial family issues.[76]

These trends are even more pronounced at the level of elite discourse, where attention to "public" matters like social justice receive greater priority than "private" matters like the family, largely because the 1960s commitment to "peace and justice" has been institutionalized in denominational seminaries and bureaucracies.[77] My survey of the *Christian Century*, the leading voice of mainline Protestantism, found that more than 30 percent of the articles from

1970 to 1990 focused on social justice topics while less than 5 percent focused on family-related issues.[78]

Moreover, to the limited extent that the mainline has turned its collective attention to family-related issues it has focused to a large degree on matters related to human sexuality—especially abortion and homosexuality. Of all the family-related articles in the *Christian Century* from 1970 to 1990, 68 percent were devoted to sex-related matters. Since 1970, mainline denominations have produced more documents on sexual relationships, abortion, and homosexuality than at any comparable period in their history. Throughout the 1970s and early 1980s, heterosexual ethics and abortion occupied most of the attention in these news and opinion articles in the *Christian Century;* in the late 1980s and the 1990s, homosexuality took center stage.[79]

Mainline clergy, intellectuals, and denominational leaders have generally taken stands on these issues that advance a progressive "ethic of liberation" from conservative standards of sexual morality. Regarding abortion, mainline leaders have been strongly influenced by their commitment to tolerance and gender equality, as well as by concerns about the religious right's growing influence in American life, to take a vigorously pro-choice stand. Writing about a 1980 Supreme Court abortion decision, James Wall, editor of the *Christian Century,* argued that what was at "stake was a *religious* definition of the point at which life begins." He suggested that such definitions could not be the law of the land in a nation characterized by profound religious pluralism. He went on to add that the "New Right . . . has seized the theological issue of abortion and is now using it as a front for pushing right-wing political causes and candidates."[80] The pro-choice orientation of the mainline is seen also in numerous denominational pronouncements on the issue of abortion, as well as in the generally pro-choice attitudes reported by mainline clergy and laity.[81]

The mainline's commitment to the liberal virtues of tolerance, inclusion, and equality, in addition to therapeutically motivated concerns about personal fulfillment and interpersonal authenticity, has structured mainline discourse on sexuality, including homosexuality, along liberationist lines. One prominent example of this liberationist tendency in mainline thinking is the Presbyterian (U.S.A.) report *Keeping Body and Soul Together* (1991), which was drafted by a committee of leading clerics, seminary professors, denominational officials, and laypersons.[82] In the name of "inclusive wholeness" and "justice-love," the report argues that a range of sexual relationships—from homosexual relationships to sexual friendships to heterosexual marriages—can embody the types of equality and sexual and emotional intimacy that meet its liberal and therapeutic standards of legitimacy.[83] While this report and most proposals dealing with homosexuality have been rejected by church-wide legislative assemblies that are not yet ready to revise traditional Christian understandings of marriage, they do represent the thinking of key elites in the mainline and of a substantial minority of clergy and laity.

Thus, the mainline's embrace of elements of cultural modernity—tolerance, gender equality, the impulse to inclusion, and the therapeutic ethic—has led it to reject key dimensions of 1950s familism. Its acceptance of unconditional divorce and remarriage and its affirmation of family pluralism contradict the familistic idealization of the nuclear family and lifelong marriage. The mainline positions on sex-related matters have pushed the churches in a liberationist direction that, symbolically at least, stands in tension with the familistic values of sexual restraint and, in the case of abortion, the mother-child bond. The mainline's commitment to social justice to the exclusion of family matters, its focus on sex-related issues, and its desire to highlight its tolerant acceptance of all families have diminished its capacity to speak clearly to the everyday concerns and moral quandaries that confront all manner of families.

This is not to say that the mainline has entirely jettisoned familistic logic. The Bible is replete with familial stories and imagery, and much of this biblical material makes its way into mainline sermons. God is depicted as a friend, father, mother, and lover, and as a supernatural being who loves each and every person. As one mainline Presbyterian pastor put it: "God's love has no strings attached to it. It cannot be earned. It cannot be shut off, deterred. It cannot be escaped. God loves us as we are. God loves us for what we are and in spite of what we are. There is nothing we can do to make God love us less. God loves us when no one else does. God loves us when we are unlovable. God loves us when we cannot stand ourselves."[84] This kind of discourse is both a model of and a model for the kind of sentimental domesticity that the ideology of familism associates with family life. The love of God, like the love of a parent, is unconditional—there are "no strings attached"—and unmerited—it "cannot be earned." God's love is a source of safety and security that extends even to people whom "no one else" loves and who "cannot stand" themselves. This love provides a "sacred canopy" of transcendent meaning that helps mainline Protestants deal with the challenges, joys, and stresses associated with important moments in their lives—unemployment, sickness, birth, death.[85] Thus, mainline churches supply a comforting sense of the sacred that comprehends and legitimates family-centered living.

The mainline also promotes a range of noncontroversial values that lend strength to the ethic of moral obligation that undergirds familism. Nancy

Ammerman's extensive ethnographic study of mainline churches indicates that many of them foster a "Golden Rule Christianity" in which noncontroversial values—honesty, kindness, and caring—are given social and supernatural sanction. The values associated with Golden Rule Christianity fit well with the expressive character of contemporary family life. Moreover, mainline discourse about these values tends to anchor them in the context of family life, especially child rearing. In fact, one of the key reasons mainline Protestants attend church is to expose their children to religious and moral precepts that will lend meaning and purpose to their lives.[86]

This child-centered focus is evident in a number of other ways. More than 70 percent of mainline churches offer worship services specially designed to incorporate children into the corporate worship of the church—for example, some have a biblical "story time" just before the main sermon.[87] This new interest in children's worship is indebted to a new emphasis on inclusion in mainline churches, along with insights derived from developmental psychology. According to Christian educators David Ng and Virginia Thomas, "God's Kingdom is for all, and . . . God's love draws all together. . . . Children and adults worshiping together make the statement of faith."[88] Virtually all mainline churches also offer Sunday school programs that impart basic religious and moral truths to children. In keeping with an egalitarian, child-centered ethos, children are generally exposed to these truths in ways that encourage them to think of themselves as autonomous moral agents. In the survey of upstate New York clergy, 56 percent of the respondents reported that their churches "teach kids to think for themselves."[89]

Thus, the rituals and discourse associated with mainline churches signal their allegiance to the more permissive school of child rearing that assumes that children are naturally good, that they should be reasoned with in ways that respect their autonomy, and that they need not defer to the authority of adults.[90] This skepticism about authority, of course, is also linked to a theological worldview that rejects classical Protestant understandings of God as an omnipotent sovereign and righteous judge who must be obeyed.

In sum, the mainline's embrace of cultural modernity in the 1960s and 1970s led it to reject key aspects of 1950s familism, especially the notion that the "traditional" nuclear family is the cornerstone of a decent society, even as it has retained a Golden Rule ethical orientation and a child-centered focus that are largely congruent with the familism of the 1950s. This is why the mainline approach to the family can be said to exemplify the logic of Golden Rule liberalism.

The conservative Protestant reaction to the disestablishment of 1950s familism—structured as it was by deep concern about the social and cultural consequences of the events of the 1960s and 1970s, as well as by the subcultural orientation of conservative Protestantism—took a markedly different tack with family-related issues than did the mainline. The dramatic increases in divorce, premarital sex, abortion, and cohabitation, to name just a few of the social and demographic trends associated with the era, were seen as evidence that the nation had taken a turn for the worse. Evangelical and fundamentalist leaders viewed this disestablishment with alarm, and they set out to defend and strengthen the "traditional family" both in the political arena and in their churches and homes.

RESISTING FAMILY CHANGE

The conservative Protestant effort to rehabilitate familism in the last three decades of the twentieth century has been shaped by a number of factors, some of which emerged or gained new salience as a result of the sociocultural changes associated with the 1960s and 1970s: a commitment to a morality rooted in the absolute truth of the Bible, an Americanist desire to return the nation to its Christian foundations through righteous family living, concern about social disorder and disrespect for authority, worry about secular humanism and the threat it poses to faith, a therapeutically shaped belief that personal fulfillment can be found through biblical living, and a willingness to use the cultural tools associated with public reason to advance the cause of the family. The conservative Protestant effort to defend the traditional family is visible in its discourse on family pluralism and divorce, sexuality, abortion, parenting, and gender roles.

The family-related demographic and cultural shifts of the 1960s and 1970s were associated with the larger social-breakdown frame with which conservative Protestant leaders had come to view the era. In 1970, *Christianity Today* ran a lead editorial asking if the nation needed a "new Gibbon to write *Decline and Fall of the United States of America*" in light of "signs of decay": namely, social division, crime, porn, sexual license, racism, and abortion.[91] A decade later the magazine was still expressing concern about "moral decline in our society" evidenced by the "breakdown of the family, the rise of secular humanism, dishonesty in government, the onslaught of pornography, homosexual practice, free and easy abortion, social injustice, [and] the exploitation of minorities and the poor."[92] By 1980, the declensionist frame that dominated evangelical and fundamentalist thinking in the 1970s had come to be linked to a panoply of family-related matters.

Thus, unlike their mainline counterparts, conservative Protestant leaders of family ministries, political organizations, and most conservative Protestant churches viewed departures from the ideal of the intact, heterosexual nuclear family—in other words, increasing family pluralism—with great concern. One indication of this concern is the large number of organizations that emerged in the late 1970s to defend the traditional family—from political organizations like Jerry Falwell's Moral Majority and Beverly LaHaye's Concerned Women for America to pastoral organizations like James Dobson's Focus on the Family.[93] These groups were almost entirely led by conservative Protestants; they also drew the vast majority of their members from the ranks of conservative Protestantism.

Another indication of conservative Protestant alarm over growing family pluralism is found in the elite discourse of the 1980s and 1990s. Falwell linked the family issue to wider concerns about relativism and departures from the absolute moral code of the Bible: "Children are taught . . . that the traditional home is one alternative. Homosexuality is another. Decency is relative."[94] Dobson taps other themes as he expresses concern over divorce:

> Come on, America. Enough is enough! We've had our dance with divorce, and we have a million broken homes to show for it. We've tried the me-philosophy and the new morality and unbridled hedonism. They didn't work. Now it's time to get back to some old-fashioned values, like commitment and sacrifice and responsibility and purity and love and the straight life. Not only will our children benefit from our self-discipline and perseverance, but we adults will live in a less neurotic world, too![95]

Dobson signals his regard for the common good—"a million broken homes"—and his Americanist orientation: notice he addresses America rather than the church. He also highlights symbolic boundaries against the "new morality" by associating it with selfishness and hedonism. His invocation of "old-fashioned values" suggests that the answer to America's family problems can be found in individual moral reform, which fits the individualistic evangelical social-reform strategy. It also implies that people who divorce are essentially immoral. Dobson concludes by promising that conformity to an ethic of lifelong marriage is not only best for the children, but also good for the psychological well-being of adults.

Dobson and Falwell rely on a range of cultural tools, one of them consistent with the spirit of the 1960s and 1970s and others developed in tension with the era, to critique the rise of family pluralism and to signal to the world that they have not accommodated themselves to the values of cultural modernity. In this regard, their production of the "crisis in the family" frame is largely consistent with the views of most conservative Protestant clergy. None of the evangelical and fundamentalist pastors who responded to the survey of upstate New York clergy said they believed that "God approves of all kinds of families"; this is in dramatic contrast to the more than 85 percent of mainline clergy who expressed the belief that God approves of family pluralism.[96]

The sexual revolution and its fruits have received a great deal of consistently negative attention from conservative Protestantism, both because they are seen leading contributors to family breakdown and because they serve as symbolic markers of the kind of unbridled hedonism that conservative Protestant leaders consider to be the antithesis of 1950s familism and, more importantly, biblical morality. The conservative Protestant world has devoted a great deal of its family-oriented attention to matters related to sex—especially abortion and homosexuality. My survey of *Christianity Today* revealed that 58 percent of its family-related news articles and editorials from 1970 to 1990 were devoted to topics related to sex.[97] In the early 1970s, the bulk of the magazine's sex-related articles critiqued the sexual license associated with the era. After *Roe v. Wade* (1973) and the rise of the gay rights movement in the late 1970s, the magazine's attention shifted to the most visible consequences of the sexual revolution: the increase in the number of abortions and the growing acceptance of homosexuality.

Surprisingly, the conservative Protestant opposition to abortion is not based on the commonsense reading of Scripture that has helped guide most evangelical social engagement in the last three decades. The Bible does not directly condemn abortion. Moreover, some Old Testament passages suggest that the fetus is not accorded the full status of personhood (for example, Exod. 21: 22–25; Lev. 27:6). Nonetheless, throughout the 1970s, with some prompting from the Roman Catholic Church and evangelical leader Francis Schaeffer, conservative Protestant leaders began to turn strongly against abortion for a number of biblical, theological, and moral reasons. They took passages in the New and Old Testaments (Matt. 1:18–20; Jer. 1:4–5; Ps. 139:13–16) to suggest that life begins at conception and came to see abortion as the murder of a person. They also insisted that humankind should not usurp God's power to create new life.[98]

Conservative Protestant leaders came to see "abortion on demand" as a sign and consequence of the excesses of an immoral sexual revolution. Falwell's comments are illustrative: "For six long years Americans have been forced to stand by helplessly while 3 to 6 million babies were legally murdered through abortion on demand. . . . When a country becomes morally sick, it becomes sick in every other way."[99] The leaders saw abortion also as an assault on a core value of familism: the sentimental bond between mother and child.[100] For all these reasons, the vast majority of conservative Protestant leaders and churches had swung into the pro-life camp by the 1980s. The Southern Baptist Convention, for example, moved from a moderately pro-choice position in 1971 that supported legal abortion in cases where the "emotional, mental, and physical health of the mother" was at risk to a pro-life position in 1980 that supported legislation banning all abortions except those necessary to save the life of the mother.[101]

Similar themes emerged in conservative Protestant discussions of homosexuality, though their position on this issue had much stronger biblical foundations. The relevant biblical passages (for example, Lev. 18:22; Rom. 1:27; 1 Tim. 1:9–10) were invoked frequently as conservative Protestant leaders voiced their objections to homosexuality. A lead editorial in a 1980 issue of *Christianity Today* asked, "What does Scripture teach? *Heterosexuality is the biblical norm.* . . . Throughout the whole of Scripture, heterosexuality is both assumed and affirmed as God's order of creation."[102] The language about creation signals the way in which homosexuality was framed as abnormal, as a lifestyle unintended by God; this language also suggests that the child-centered nuclear family is the divinely ordered model of moral living. A 1980 Southern Baptist resolution conveyed a similar message: it deplored the "homosexual lifestyle" and any move to make "it equally acceptable to the biblical heterosexual family life style."[103]

Homosexuality and abortion implicated a range of religious, moral, and cultural issues of concern to evangelicals and fundamentalists. In particular, the attention and passion that these issues generated in the conservative Protestant world must be understood partly in light of the fact that abortion and homosexuality were both seen as symbolic assaults on the sentimental, child-centered nuclear family around which familism is organized. The focus on these issues must also be seen as an indication of the antipathy this subculture had developed for the outworking of the new morality, which was seen as utterly unbiblical and decadent.

Given the clear and overwhelming opposition to homosexuality and abortion, conservative Protestant discourse regarding divorce and remarriage is characterized by a striking level of ambivalence and dissensus—especially considering the fact that divorce poses a more direct threat to familism than either homosexuality or abortion. Although evangelical and fundamentalist leaders are not inclined to look at divorce as morally neutral, as do some prominent mainline clergy and theologians, they do express a surprising range of opinions on the subject.

A small minority of conservative Protestant leaders take the position that divorce is totally impermissible; for instance, a 1980 poll of Southern Baptist clergy found that 16 percent believed that "divorce should be avoided under any circumstance."[104] However, most leaders cluster around two more permissive positions. The more conservative of these positions, adopted by figures like Dobson, attempts to hew closely to the guidance regarding divorce and remarriage found in specific biblical texts.[105] It holds that Christ's condemnation of divorce (for example, in Matt. 19:6–9 and Mark 10:9–12) means that divorce and remarriage are not permissible for Christians except on the "biblical grounds" of adultery (Matt. 19:9) or the desertion of an unbelieving spouse (1 Cor. 7:15). According to the 1980 poll, 36 percent of Southern Baptist pastors took the position that "remarriage after divorce is acceptable only in cases of desertion or adultery."[106] Nevertheless, many proponents of this position perform elaborate hermeneutical maneuvers to apply the desertion exception in the broadest possible sense to any Christian who has been divorced against his or her will:

> In some cases there will be two believers who are having problems with their marriage, and one of the believers refuses to return to his/her spouse. If there is no reconciliation, then it is right for the church to declare the wrong partner an unbeliever (according to Matt. 18:15–20) and then act under the principles of 1 Corinthians 7. . . . Then the person seeking the unrealized reconciliation is free and the other has sinned by refusing to become reconciled.[107]

The more liberal position, held by a sizable minority of conservative Protestant leaders, dispenses entirely with the effort to follow the letter of New Testament teachings on divorce. This position views divorce as sinful but, much like the mainline Protestant position, invokes the spirit of Christianity to argue that remarriage should be open to divorced Christians regardless of the reason they divorced. In this argument, biblical motifs of compassion, forgiveness, and second chances are set against a "legalistic" response to divorce. Sometimes this view is coupled with the idea that church leaders should have the authority to decide if such a remarriage serves God's purposes.[108]

Thirty-six percent of Southern Baptist pastors approved of this approach, according to the 1980 poll.[109]

The plurality of views regarding divorce and remarriage found among conservative Protestant leaders, and the willingness of a large minority to dispense with the letter of New Testament teaching, is particularly striking in light of the historic opposition to remarriage that once prevailed among conservative Protestant churches. In 1904, for instance, the Southern Baptist Convention held that remarriage was acceptable only in the case of adultery. The more permissive stand on divorce taken by a majority of Southern Baptist clergy is but one indication that the drive to defend and shore up the traditional family in this subculture is not relentless or entirely consistent. Some accommodations have been made to family modernization. Still, for the most part conservative Protestantism depicts divorce as a sin and a failure; in this regard, evangelical and fundamentalist leaders and churches remain more conservative than their mainline counterparts. Moreover, regardless of their particular position on divorce and remarriage, their sense that the family is in crisis motivates them to devote more attention, at least rhetorically, to the task of building happier and stronger marriages than mainline churches and leaders do.

The themes that animate conservative Protestant concern over the family are also apparent in the subculture's discourse on parenting—and this subject elicits none of the ambivalence characteristic of evangelical and fundamentalist discourse on divorce and remarriage. Pervasive concern that the destiny of the nation, the health of American Christianity, and society's moral fiber have been threatened by the outworking of the events of the 1960s and 1970s—especially secular humanism, family breakdown, and the new morality—motivates calls for an ethic of intensive family living. The idea is that better family living and Christian parenting in particular will help return the nation to its avowedly Christian roots, in terms of both religious belief and biblical morality, and restore divine favor to the American experiment. As one conservative Protestant leader put it, "If we are to rebuild our nation we must first strengthen our homes and make sure that they are Christ-centered. Husbands and wives must assume the full responsibilities of Christian parents so that children may walk in the ways of the Lord."[110]

The Christian home is also viewed as the primary arena where parents can cultivate the logic of sentimental domesticity in a world where authentic, biblical love seems in danger of disappearing. Thus, parenting is depicted as a way of building an "enclave of loving authority and godly guidance and truth" in a harsh, selfish, and godless modern world.[111] Sentiment and piety commingle in conservative Protestant discourse on parenting as children and child rearing are endowed with sacredness. Children are to be viewed as a blessing from God (Psalm 127), and parents are asked to convey the love of God to their children so that they may bring them to eternal salvation. The comments of Charles Swindoll, a prominent evangelical pastor, are illustrative: "So whatever He [Christ] gives to you comes from His love. It's what I call a 'domestic love transfer.' You are entrusted with the title deed to His property when your child is born. . . . Children are assigned by God, His property, delivered to you as a loving reward for you to carry on the process [of salvation] He began."[112]

This sentimental approach is also linked to a therapeutic view that parents must do positive emotion work to promote self-esteem and good behavior in their children. James Dobson, who holds a doctorate in child development, frequently resorts to psychological language when he offers parenting advice, despite his protestations that he is only passing on the timeless parenting "wisdom of the Judeo-Christian ethic." His advice draws on both the humanistic and behaviorist traditions in psychology: "Children and adults of all ages seek constant satisfaction of their emotional needs, including the desire for love, social acceptance, and self-respect. . . . As a result, verbal reinforcement can be the strongest motivator of human behavior."[113] Taken together, these beliefs fuel a commitment to the sacred vocation of parenting that is heightened by concerns that contemporary parents are not devoting enough time to their children. Thus, when it comes to parenting, conservative Protestantism seeks to be a bulwark of child-centered familism.

However, evangelical and fundamentalist leaders do not cultivate the permissive brand of child-centered familism that occupies center stage in much of the wider society's parenting discourse.[114] One reason they reject it is that they view the popularity of the counterculture among baby boomers raised in upper-middle-class homes as an indictment of Dr. Spock–style parenting. Recall, for instance, the way James Dobson, in *Dare to Discipline,* ridicules the "permissiveness" of the 1950s that led to the youth culture of the 1960s.[115] Concern about the social disorder associated with the 1960s and 1970s motivated efforts to establish parental authority and strict discipline on a firm footing.

The Bible, which has much to say about parenting, is depicted as a primer for authority-minded parenting among virtually all conservative Protestant parenting experts. In *What the Bible Says about Child Training,* Richard Fugate invokes the Fourth Commandment (Exod. 20:12) and a range of other Bible verses (for example, Eph. 6:2–3; Col. 3:20) to argue that children must learn to respect and obey their parents: "Contrary to the popularly accepted teaching of child psychology, your child needs a leader—not a pal, buddy, big sister, or big brother. . . . Parents are the symbol and representative of God's authority to their children."[116]

The conservative Protestant commitment to authority is manifested in support for a strict, controlled disciplinary style that seeks to shore up obedience and good behavior through frequent applications of corporal punishment, which is justified by numerous texts from Scripture (for example, Prov. 22:15, 29:15; Heb. 12:6). However, evangelical and fundamentalist experts strongly counsel against yelling and against abusive forms of corporal punishment, since these behaviors are depicted as counterproductive: "Chastisement is not a tongue lashing, threats or screaming fits of anger; in other words, adult temper tantrums. These things do nothing but support the child's disrespect for his parents' authority and demonstrate the parents' inability to rule."[117] Instead of yelling at or hitting children when they are disobedient or misbehaving, conservative Protestant family experts generally advise, parents should deliver a firm but calm spanking. Another indication of the emphasis conservative Protestant leaders place on this strict, authority-minded approach to child rearing comes from the survey of upstate New York clergy. More than 90 percent agreed that they "teach kids to trust, obey parents/teachers/pastors." Less than 50 percent of mainline clergy affirmed this statement.[118] Thus, at least when it comes to parenting, the familism of conservative Protestantism retains a distinctively traditional regard for authority and discipline.

In sum, the disestablishment of familism that took place in the 1960s and 1970s has largely been met with resistance from conservative Protestant leaders and churches. This resistance is tied to preexisting cultural commitments to biblical literalism and the traditional nuclear family and to pervasive concerns that shifts in family-related behavior and practice are associated with secular, hedonistic, and amoral trends that threaten the nation's moral fiber and Christian faith. In some ways the conservative Protestant discourse on family-related matters can be viewed as a symbolic rejection of cultural modernity. At the same time, however, this rejection is tempered by ambivalence and dissensus about divorce and remarriage, phenomena that are intimately associated with cultural and structural modernity. Moreover, conservative Protestant leaders appear quite willing to adopt peculiarly modern cultural tools— therapeutic techniques and ideas—in their effort to defend and strengthen the traditional family. Taken together, these elements make up an approach to the family best described as expressive traditionalism.

Regardless of how conservative Protestant discourse on family-related matters is understood to relate to modernity, the subculture's concern about the state of the family has resulted in a concerted emphasis on the family, at least at the level of discourse. My surveys of the leading magazines of conservative and mainline Protestants revealed that the proportion of articles and editorials devoted to family-related issues by *Christianity Today* was nearly four times that of the *Christian Century*—19 percent versus 5 percent from 1970 to 1990. Moreover, the historical trends in these two publications indicate that interest in family-related matters has increased in conservative Protestant circles while it has remained fairly constant among mainliners.[119]

Because conservative Protestant leaders and churches reject tolerant acceptance of family pluralism and instead embrace a familistic ethic, they are more likely to articulate a normative vision of family life and to highlight difficulties associated with parenting, marriage, and divorce than are mainline leaders and churches. One study of churches in metropolitan Chicago found that the more theologically conservative churches were more likely to have developed a "*culture of openness* in talking about marriage and the family . . . [that] can address both family ideals and frailties."[120] This pattern can also be seen in mainline and conservative Protestant ministers' differing levels of comfort with the concept of family ministry. While almost 50 percent of mainline clergy surveyed in upstate New York rejected the term *family ministry* as exclusionary, only 13 percent of conservative Protestant clergy rejected the term.[121] Evangelical and fundamentalist leaders have thus devoted a great deal of attention, at least discursively, to the task of defending and strengthening a host of values and virtues related to the child-centered nuclear family. In this way, they resist the disestablishment of familism, which they associate with the broader discontents of late modernity.

PROTESTANTISM AND GENDER-ROLE IDEOLOGY

For much of the history of Christianity, the symbolic and social structure of the church has been organized along patriarchal lines, with God the Father standing symbolically at the apex of the Trinity, and with men occupying the primary positions of social authority and power. The patriarchal character of the Christian faith bears not only on the discrete relations of men and women, but also on a wider complex of cultural and social matters—not to mention believers' understanding of the relationship between God and humanity. For instance, gendered depictions of the Godhead have been linked in Christianity to cultural understandings of sexual difference in order to render the relation between Creator and creature meaningful, with the masculine gender of God signifying transcendence, initiative, and sovereignty and the feminine gender of the person signifying worldliness, receptivity, and obedience. Efforts to signal adherence to biblical or traditional canons of orthodoxy have led to ecclesiastical policies that reserve particular church offices—for example, the priesthood or pastorate—for men only. The right ordering of church and society has, in turn, been linked to the proper ordering of social relations between men and women. In these ways and more, gender has been intimately bound up with the symbolic and social organization of Christianity.

Given the links between gender and Christianity, it should come as no surprise that Protestantism was a key carrier of the separate-spheres gender-role ideology that was institutionalized in the nineteenth century among the middle and upper classes.[122] This ideology divided family work along gendered lines, with men focusing on breadwinning and women on child rearing; established men's preeminence in the workplace and women's preeminence in the home; and institutionalized a gendered division between paid employment and unpaid domestic labor. Women's newfound preeminence in the home was guided by the logic of sentimental domesticity.[123] The expressive, pietistic character of the Second Great Awakening that swept across large sectors of U.S. society in the middle of the nineteenth century meant that many women "infused these roles with a sense of Christian vocation."[124] Not surprisingly, given the strong ties between the family and the church, women's domestic focus was paralleled by feminine numerical dominance in the religious arena. Protestant women took the lead in educating and nurturing their children in the Christian faith at home, heightening the sacralization of domesticity.

This pattern obtained in the worlds of mainline and conservative Protestantism up through the 1950s. Both traditions gave religious and moral sanction to the separate-spheres ideology in this decade of bourgeois domesticity. But the cultural and structural shifts of the 1960s and 1970s—especially the women's liberation movement and dramatic increases in women's labor-force participation and education—undercut societal support for traditional gender roles and for norms of patriarchal authority.[125] As with so many other things, mainline and conservative Protestant churches and leaders responded quite differently to the disestablishment of gender traditionalism—both because of discrete concerns about men's and women's roles and because gender is bound up with, in the words of Joan Wallach Scott, "the concrete and symbolic organization of all social life."[126]

ACCOMMODATING THE GENDER REVOLUTION

Responding to the rise of feminism in the late 1960s and early 1970s, the mainline made a number of moves to signal its accommodation to the

newly egalitarian ethos of the wider culture. Partly because the women's movement had come to be seen as a logical extension of the civil rights movement,
mainline churches were early and ardent supporters of key feminist goals like
the Equal Rights Amendment and universal child care.[127] Perhaps more importantly, under pressure from internal feminist movements, mainline churches
also reformed their internal life to promote greater gender equality. By 1976,
all mainline churches had adopted policies in support of women's ordination,
and the percentage of women in mainline seminaries surged more than 100
percent in the 1970s. By 1987 women accounted for one-third of the student
population in mainline Presbyterian seminaries. This effort also extended to
efforts to diversify mainline denominational and institutional leadership: starting in the 1970s, women were elected to head mainline entities like the United
Presbyterian Church and the National Council of Churches.[128]

This egalitarian commitment also led mainline denominations to issue
statements in support of gender equality in the home. Beginning in 1972 the
United Methodist Church passed a series of resolutions seeking the elimination
of gender-role stereotypes in work and family life.[129] In 1988 Methodist resolutions affirmed "shared responsibility for parenting by men and women" and
rejected "social norms that assume different standards for women than for
men in marriage."[130] The results of the survey of upstate New York clergy
suggest that this egalitarian ethic is also shared by mainline ministers: less
than 10 percent of those surveyed agreed with a separate-spheres ideology—
"It's better for all if the man earns the money and the woman takes care of
home/children"—or an explicitly patriarchal ideology—"It's God's will that the
man is spiritual head of the family."[131]

This egalitarian drive in mainline Protestant churches has also led to
scrutiny of the symbolic center of the Christian faith. The patriarchal tradition
of historic Christianity has been steadily deconstructed since the 1970s. Linguistic shifts in the world of mainline Protestantism signal the dramatic
changes that have taken place in theology and pastoral practice. Mainline
churches are now much more likely to use gender-neutral language and to
incorporate images of God as mother into Sunday worship and everyday spirituality.[132] For instance, in 1979 the Episcopal Church incorporated gender-
neutral language into its *Book of Common Prayer* and eliminated scriptural
references to the subordination of women from its daily lectionary. More recently, the United Methodist Church added rites using gender-neutral language,
such as "God, our Father and Mother," to the 1992 edition of its *Book of
Worship,* and the Presbyterian Church (U.S.A.) eliminated all use of masculine
pronouns in reference to God in the 1994 edition of its *Book of Common*

Worship.[133] Thus, the mainline has gone to great lengths to establish, symbolically at least, its commitment to gender equality.

Three cultural factors help account for this commitment. First, the mainline has long maintained a self-conscious effort to adapt to important social changes. In this case, mainline leaders believed that the dramatic increase in women's status and labor-force participation meant that they had an obligation to recast the faith along egalitarian lines. In the words of mainline social ethicist Max Stackhouse: "The rapid inclusion of women in the work force demands fresh attention to women's rights, to new patterns of shared responsibility in family life, and especially to those values which can guide women's newly discovered sense of extrafamilial vocation."[134] Second, the mainline's commitment to a therapeutic ethic of self-realization and expressiveness has led it to reject gendered roles and hierarchies that might constrain the self or its interaction with others. This therapeutic emphasis can be seen in the Presbyterian report *Keeping Body and Soul Together,* in which egalitarian marriages are affirmed for their capacity to "enhance individual identity in the midst of deepening intimacy and interpersonal encounter."[135] Third, and most fundamentally, the mainline's egalitarian stance flows from its commitment to the liberal project of modernity, especially the "notion that individuals have distinctive moral standing *qua individuals* and not as members of 'natural' groups . . . that possess certain 'natural' rights and functions."[136] Thus, once gender came to be framed as an illiberal and arbitrary criterion for discrimination in the broader society during the 1970s, the mainline moved to recast its family-related gender discourse and its very symbolic foundations to signal its adherence to the canons of cultural modernity.

RESISTING THE GENDER REVOLUTION

By contrast, the conservative Protestant response to the gender revolution in social practice and ideology of the 1960s and 1970s was largely hostile. Many conservative Protestant leaders viewed the women's movement as a threat to the values and virtues associated with the traditional family and as part and parcel of a broader cultural revolt against authority, religion, and morality. Addressing an audience of Christian husbands about feminist critiques of homemaking, James Dobson wrote: "It is high time you realized your wives are under attack today! Everything they have been taught from earliest childhood is being subjected to ridicule and scorn. Hardly a day passes when the traditional values of the Judeo-Christian heritage are not blatantly mocked and undermined."[137] In Jerry Falwell's more succinct formulation, "Feminists are saying that self-satisfaction is more important than the family."[138] As they confronted the social disorder that seemed to be enveloping the nation and the family, conservative Protestant leaders became all the more resolved to shore up order in the family along traditional lines. To resist the perceived excesses of feminism and the dangers associated with disorder in society and the family, they highlighted their support for patriarchal authority in the church and home, as well as their commitment to the separate-spheres ideology.

In the public and ecclesial spheres, conservative Protestant leaders, churches, and special-purpose groups have generally opposed efforts to advance gender equality. Special-purpose groups that represent the most conservative wing of this subculture, such as the Moral Majority and Concerned Women for America, have led fights against the political and cultural objectives of feminist groups. In the 1970s and early 1980s they spearheaded political resistance to the Equal Rights Amendment and universal child care, measures they saw as threats to women's distinct and God-given roles as mothers.[139]

Most conservative Protestant churches have resisted efforts to ordain women, partly because they seek to draw attention to a gendered order in the social world and partly because they believe that the Bible prohibits the practice. A 1984 Southern Baptist resolution on the matter conveys this dual concern:

> WHEREAS, We . . . recognize the authority of Scripture in all matters of faith and practice; . . . and . . . WHEREAS, The Scriptures attest to God's delegated order of authority . . . distinguishing the roles of men and women in public prayer and prophecy (1 Cor. 11:2–5); and . . . WHEREAS, While Paul commends women and men alike in other roles of ministry and service (Tit. 2:1–10), he excludes women from pastoral leadership (1 Tim. 2:12) to preserve a submission God requires because the man was first in creation and the woman was first in the Edenic fall (1 Tim. 2:13ff.).[140]

The resolution legitimates this gender order by reference not only to divine will, but also to the created order, that is, to the very nature of things. Needless to say, most conservative Protestant churches have not entertained any efforts to recast the heart of their faith along gender-neutral lines. On pietistic grounds, leaders worry that such efforts would deny believers access to a personal God who makes himself known in the persons of the Father and Son. Conservative Protestant churches and leaders also view such efforts as a threat to their commitment to biblical inerrancy because they see the biblical witness as unambiguously patriarchal, at least in terms of its depiction of the triune God. Most importantly, they see the move to recast the symbolic structure of the Christian faith along egalitarian lines as the most egregious example of the mainline's idolatrous habit of adapting the transcendent to the desires of the human heart.[141]

Conservative Protestants have also sought to draw clear distinctions in the family on the basis of gender. This effort is, in part, a consequence of the drive to assert divinely constituted order in a disorderly era. Writing at the height of the counterculture movement, family expert Larry Christenson asserted the importance of a "Divine Order" in which Christ is the head of the father, the father is the head of the wife, and the parents exercise headship over the children; he then argued that "God has made the well-being and happiness of the family absolutely dependent upon the observance of His divinely appointed order."[142] Christenson's comments suggest how naturalistic and therapeutic assumptions orient conservative Protestant thinking in this area. Because they believe the world reflects the intentions of the Creator (or the "Divine Order"), family experts in this subculture are quick to legitimate their views on gender differences by incorporating the naturalistic standards of public reason. Leaders like Dobson marshal an array of psychological, physiological, anthropological, and sociological research in their efforts to support the notion that "differences between the sexes" are deeply rooted in nature.[143] Moreover, as Christenson's comments indicate, conservative Protestant discourse holds out a therapeutic vision of well-being for men and women who accept these divinely ordained gender differences.

This divinely sanctioned gender order in the family has two central components: patriarchal authority and a division of family labor based on the separate-spheres ideology. Throughout much of the twentieth century, the conservative Protestant discourse on authority has assumed that God has ordered the family along patriarchal lines, with the man directing the affairs of the family and the woman submitting to her husband's leadership.[144] Leaders employed therapeutic and naturalistic arguments as they responded to the feminist challenges to patriarchal authority of the 1960s and 1970s. One of the most prominent defenders of gender-role traditionalism, Elisabeth Elliot, had this to say about women's acceptance of their place in the divine order: "It is in the willing and glad submission rather than grudging capitulation that the woman in the Church . . . and the wife in the home find their fulfillment."[145] Likewise, Dobson has sought to legitimate patriarchal authority by pointing to psychological and cross-cultural anthropological research that indicates that men tend to be more dominant, aggressive, and competitive.[146]

But the driving force in the conservative Protestant defense of male authority has been the doctrine of biblical inerrancy. Most evangelical and fundamentalist leaders have taken passages asserting that "the head of a woman is her husband" (1 Cor. 11:3, Revised Standard Version), commanding that "wives also be subject in everything to their husbands" (Eph. 5:24, RSV; see also 1 Peter 3:1), and denying women "authority over men" (1 Tim. 2:12, RSV) as clear evidence that the Bible commands patriarchy. Moreover, they have viewed the biblical stories chronicling the creation and fall—which report that man was created first, that woman was created second as a "helpmeet," and that woman sinned first (Gen. 2–3)—as a narrative framework for this patriarchal order. In their view, the fact that man was created first suggests that God intended male primacy, and woman's lead in initiating the fall suggests the dangers of violating this order.[147]

Conservative Protestant leaders have felt duty bound to uphold patriarchal authority in order to signal their willingness to submit themselves to the principle of biblical inerrancy and to the broader principle of divine authority, and the fact that the doctrine is subject to widespread attack has convinced them of the need to stand fast.[148] This desire to maintain a countercultural commitment to biblical inerrancy is one of the reasons the Southern Baptist Convention recently amended its core statement of faith, the *Baptist Faith and Message,* to include a pronouncement on the family. Backed up by more than forty biblical citations, it affirms—among other things—that a "wife is to submit herself graciously to the servant leadership of her husband even as the church willingly submits to the headship of Christ."[149]

By contrast, the conservative Protestant defense of separate spheres has been more tentative, in part because the scriptural warrant for this ideology is weaker. For the most part, conservative Protestant family experts have relied upon an expansive reading of the passage in Genesis where God designates woman as man's "helpmeet" (Gen. 2:18)—in other words, companion and helper—to argue that women should focus on homemaking and child rearing, while men need to focus on breadwinning. They also point to Titus 2:3–5, where older women are told to instruct young women to be "sensible, chaste, domestic, kind, and submissive to their husbands" (RSV). But neither of these two passages offers a plan for the division of household labor.

Given the slender biblical warrant for separate spheres, conservative Protestant elites tend to use other strategies to legitimate this bourgeois ideology. One common approach is to assert that gender-role specialization is an integral part of the Christian tradition. Recall that Dobson asserts that feminists are attacking the "traditional values of the Judeo-Christian heritage." As James Davison Hunter has observed, "this association of traditional with bourgeois constitutes the implicit assumption of virtually all Evangelical family specialists."[150] This assumption is problematic, of course, because separate-spheres ideology is a nineteenth-century innovation that has no long-standing ties to either the Jewish or the Christian tradition. Moreover, the notion that an ideology merits obedience because it is traditional is curious in light of the fact that the vast majority of conservative Protestant churches and leaders have not hesitated to dispense with other values that are deeply rooted in tradition— for example, racism—but have lost cultural legitimacy since the 1960s.

So what is really going on here? The conservative Protestant support for this "traditional" gender-role ideology seems to be shaped, more than anything else, by the fact that it is the only widely available approach for organizing the social order along clearly gendered lines. In other words, the embrace of separate spheres is motivated by the conservative Protestant commitment to order, especially in the family, and the assumption that gender is a divinely created distinction between persons. This desire to assert a gendered order, especially in the face of the social disorder associated with the 1960s and 1970s, is evident in this observation by Dobson: "Traditional concepts of masculinity and femininity have been battered and ridiculed for more than twenty years, creating confusion for both men and women . . . [and] awkwardness in the relationships between the sexes."[151] And Peter Blitchington, author of the aptly titled *Sex Roles and the Christian Family,* has this to say about gender distinctions: "Sex roles cannot be easily switched around without grave damage to family stability. The reason is simple: God made each sex with certain biological propensities toward one role or another."[152] Conservative Protestant family experts' attachment to separate spheres is also shaped by familism, which leads them to worry that egalitarian alternative models of family life—especially the dual-full-time-career model—threaten the ethos of sentimental domesticity, which is marked by intensive emotional and temporal investments in family living.

The elite defense of gender-role traditionalism and patriarchy has not gone unchallenged among conservative Protestants. Starting in the 1970s, a growing feminist movement in evangelicalism has sought to position itself between secular feminists and conservative supporters of patriarchy by asserting that gender equality in authority and social roles is rooted in a proper understanding of the Bible. Sounding like mainline Protestants in their insistence that the Bible must be "interpreted holistically and thematically," groups like Christians for Biblical Equality, founded in 1987, have argued that biblical passages that assert the equal dignity of the genders (for example, Gal. 3:28: "There is neither Jew nor Greek, there is neither slave nor free, there is neither male nor female; for you are all one in Christ Jesus" [RSV]) can be used to interpret the Bible in such a way as to evacuate other texts of their patriarchal character.[153] Although evangelical feminists remain a minority within the world of elite conservative Protestantism, they have mounted serious intellectual and organizational challenges to the hegemony of patriarchal and separate-spheres thinking—especially because these feminists hail disproportionately from intellectual centers of evangelicalism like colleges, Christian publishing, and the evangelical media.

This burgeoning feminist movement and the dramatic increase in conservative Protestant female labor-force participation since the 1970s have had two primary consequences among conservative Protestants.[154] First, since the 1980s the discourse on patriarchy has softened, and men are being urged to act as expressive "servant leaders" committed to serving their wives and children.[155] According to conservative Protestant family experts, a husband should not "bully his wife" or "exercise tyranny" over his family; in making decisions about the family, he should take his wife's "opinions as seriously as he regards his own."[156] Most importantly, husbands are being exhorted to do significant emotion work as they seek to meet their wives' psychological needs—to be "cherished," "comforted," "praised," and understood.[157]

More recently, psychologist Mary Stewart Van Leeuwen has argued, the Promise Keepers movement, which enjoyed a burst of popularity from 1994 to 1997, has "embraced a rhetoric of *both* servanthood and soft patriarchy." Conservative Protestant leaders who have been involved with Promise Keepers tend to stress an active and expressive style of men's familial involvement and to emphasize a style of male leadership in the home that is oriented to the family's well-being, especially its spiritual well-being.[158] In *What Makes a Man?* (1992), a volume of essays compiled by Promise Keepers leader Bill McCartney, the husband is encouraged on the one hand to be the "real decision-maker" in the family, and on the other hand to dedicate himself to a romantic style of marital love characterized by "attention and admiration," "because God made women to be loved."[159]

Second, conservative Protestant elite support for the separate-spheres ideology has eroded significantly. In his best-selling book *If Only He Knew: What No Woman Can Resist,* originally published in 1979, marital specialist Gary Smalley explicitly addresses men married to "career women" and urges all his male readers to revisit their assumptions about gender roles: "We as men need to take a close look at our traditional roles and choose what is best based on genuine love and the commitment to cherish our mates."[160] One sign of this shift is that while in the late 1990s 91 percent of upstate New York conservative Protestant pastors endorsed the idea that the "man is the spiritual head of the family" only 78 percent thought it better for men to focus on breadwinning and women to focus on taking care of the home and children.[161] Thus, conservative Protestant discourse about gender has become increasingly tentative about the separate-spheres ideology even as it has tried to retain some kind of patriarchy, albeit of a strikingly soft, denuded form.

Still, conservative Protestantism sends off strikingly traditional signals about gender. While mainliners have enthusiastically embraced many of the egalitarian goals of the feminist movement that emerged in the 1970s, conservative Protestants have expressed reservations about and resistance to those goals. Because both traditions were focusing on women's roles and status in theology, the church, and the family, for most of the last three decades of the twentieth century public and pastoral discourse in pursuit of egalitarian or traditional goals has not as often targeted men.[162] It was only with the arrival of Promise Keepers in the mid-1990s that conservative Protestant churches and parachurch groups began to make a significant effort to target men in their pastoral discourse. And here the discourse on gender has linked its traditional emphasis on male authority to a new emphasis on an active and expressive style of male familial involvement.[163] This focus is, of course, consonant with the conservative Protestant logic of expressive traditionalism.

MAKING SENSE OF PERSISTING POLARITIES IN FAMILY DISCOURSE: IDENTITY AND INSTITUTIONS

The contemporary differences—over family pluralism, parental authority, abortion, sexuality, and gender roles—that mark the family-related discourse of mainline and conservative Protestantism cannot be understand simply as artifacts of socioeconomic factors or of proximity to modernity. While it is true that real sociodemographic differences between the two groups remain, these differences narrowed dramatically in the last thirty years of the twentieth century. In the 1990s, 79 percent of conservative Protestants had a high school degree or more, for example, compared to 54 percent in the 1970s, and they were closing the educational gap with mainline Protestants, 88 percent of whom had a high school education or more in the 1990s, compared to 73 percent in the 1970s. Also in the 1990s, for the first time in the century, 50 percent of conservative Protestants lived outside the South (see tables 2.1 and 2.2).

Table 2.2

Sociodemographic Status of Protestant Adults in the 1990s, by Tradition (percent)

	Conservative Protestants	Mainline Protestants
Education		
Some high school or less	21	12
High school graduate	63	58
College graduate	16	30
Region		
Northeast	8	18
North central	26	30
South	50	35
West	16	17
n	3,459	2,562

Source: General Social Survey (1990–1998).
Note: Chi-square for religious group differences in education and region are significant at the .01 level.

But the cultural gap over family matters has remained large. Indeed, the largest conservative Protestant denomination, the Southern Baptist Convention, has become *more* conservative on family-related matters (for example, patriarchal authority and abortion) even as its members have made considerable gains in socioeconomic status. How can this be explained? The social-structural position of these two religious traditions did play an important role at the outset. The religiocultural logics that oriented mainline and conservative Protestant responses to the cultural shifts of the 1960s and 1970s were initially strongly linked to socioeconomic factors, especially region and class, that helped position the two traditions in very different positions vis-à-vis modernity and, especially, ideologies and practices associated with the family. Nevertheless, the ongoing influence of these cultural dynamics cannot entirely account for the fact that conservative Protestant churches and leaders have not accommodated themselves more to liberal family conventions in the last decades of the twentieth century, especially given the fact that conservative Protestant socioeconomic mobility has put them into closer contact with the engines of cultural modernity: higher education, the professions, elite media, and so on. The persistence of a distinctive conservative Protestant family-related discourse must be viewed also as a consequence of the unique character of the conservative Protestant institutional field and of ongoing efforts to assert a distinctive collective identity.

CONSERVATIVE PROTESTANT FAMILY DISCOURSE AS IDENTITY WORK

I turn first to a consideration of the way that this discourse functions as a kind of identity work. Christian Smith has argued that religious subcultures often thrive on "distinction, engagement, tension, conflict, and threat" and that "the evangelical movement's vitality is not a product of its protected isolation from, but of its vigorous engagement with pluralistic modernity."[164] The distinctive character of conservative Protestant discourse about matters like abortion, family pluralism, and parental authority allows leaders and adherents to draw cultural boundaries with the larger secular culture, to assert their moral superiority, and to establish an atmosphere of fateful conflict between good and evil, all in ways that strengthen collective identity.

Consider, for instance, a guest editorial in the *New York Times* written by R. Albert Mohler Jr., president of Southern Baptist Theological Seminary, to defend the Southern Baptist Convention's stands on male headship, homosexuality, and abortion: "Southern Baptists are engaged in a battle against modernity, earnestly contending for the truth and authority of an ancient faith. To the cultured critics of religion, we are the cantankerous holdouts against the inevitable. But so far as the Southern Baptist Convention is concerned, the future is in God's hands. If faithfulness requires the slings and arrows of outraged opponents, so be it."[165] The language of battle locates conservative Protestants in a deeply meaningful conflict for their nation and faith, not to mention civilization itself, against modernity's dark side. Cultural boundaries are delineated against a powerful other, the corrupting "cultured critics of religion," marking evangelicals and fundamentalists as righteous defenders of "the truth and authority of an ancient faith." The family-related matters that are depicted as central battlegrounds in this struggle have been intimately connected to the identity work that conservative Protestantism does to retain its subcultural status and institutional vitality. This helps to explain why the cultural distinctiveness of conservative Protestantism on family-related matters has continued to a large degree even as this subculture has come closer to the engines of modernity and has come to occupy a social-structural position that is ever more similar to that of the mainline.

THE INSTITUTIONAL CONTEXT OF CONSERVATIVE PROTESTANT FAMILY IDEOLOGY

Conservative Protestantism's ideology is also shaped by its unique institutional context. Wuthnow's articulation theory demonstrates that collectivities can acquire a measure of independence from their social environment when they control institutions that articulate distinctive ideologies and shape social practices while they maintain their access to key socioeconomic resources.[166] Conservative Protestantism has an array of institutional resources—more than four hundred colleges and seminaries, a billion-dollar publishing industry, more than one hundred thousand congregations, and hundreds of special-purpose organizations—that enable it to maintain some distance from its social environment.[167]

The specific character of an institutional field—that is, the field's legitimate organizational practices and ideological structures, as well as the sociocultural forces impinging upon it—shapes the ends and means that its constituent organizational actors and elites pursue.[168] Three features associated with the institutional field of conservative Protestantism are of particular interest in accounting for the uniqueness of its family-related discourse.

First, the vitality of conservative Protestant organizational life is without parallel in American religion. Because of their subcultural status and the salience of their religious faith, conservative Protestants devote more of their time, money, and talent to congregations, parachurch organizations, and church-centered social networks than any other major religious group in the United States. At the congregational level, this is reflected in higher levels of per capita giving, stronger social ties, and greater levels of participation in church-sponsored activities within and outside of worship.[169] Conservative Protestants focus on what Robert Putnam calls bonding social capital—that is, inwardly directed reciprocal social interaction—rather than bridging social capital—more encompassing patterns of interaction with heterogeneous groups.[170] Special-purpose groups, including parachurch groups and civic organizations, are able to tap into this religious vitality to accumulate significant levels of social, economic, and cultural capital, which they can then spend on various cultural and political projects. For instance, Focus on the Family, which has a budget exceeding $100 million dollars, employs approximately 1,300 people, broadcasts a syndicated radio show on over 2,900 stations in North America, and reaches its more than 2.3 million members through magazines, videos, and books.[171] This organizational vitality means that conservative Protestantism can draw upon both face-to-face and virtual communities that lend plausibility to its family ideology,[172] and it furnishes conservative Protestant elites with the social and cultural resources—money, social networks, and a distinctive religious worldview—necessary for the production of a conservative family ideology that cuts against the grain of conventional wisdom.

Second, most of the key culture-forming organizations in the world of conservative Protestantism are located in regions that are sympathetic to a conservative religious and cultural agenda. Special-purpose organizations, seminaries, and "megachurches" (congregations with more than nine hundred regularly attending adults) tend to be concentrated in the South, the Midwest, and the Rocky Mountains. Major seminaries like Dallas Theological Seminary, Moody Bible Institute, Southern Baptist Theological Seminary, and Trinity Evangelical Divinity School are located in the Midwest and the South. More than 70 percent of the largest megachurches, whose pastors exercise strong cultural leadership in the world of conservative Protestantism, are also located in the South and Midwest.[173] Moreover, groups of organizations are often clustered around particular cities or towns. In the 1980s Jerry Falwell's various enterprises—the Moral Majority, Liberty University, and his television show— were headquartered in Lynchburg, Virginia. A decade later, his successor as the standard-bearer of the religious right, Pat Robertson, had centered his media (Christian Broadcasting Network), educational (Regent University), and po- litical (Christian Coalition) empires in Virginia Beach, Virginia. Focus on the Family is located in Colorado Springs, Colorado, which also hosts a range of prominent Christian organizations like the Navigators, Youth with a Mission, and the International Bible Society.

The geographic distribution and local clustering of evangelical and funda- mentalist organizations has two key consequences. Because the organizations are located in regions where culturally conservative views have greater legiti- macy, employees have greater social support for their religiocultural world- view. This is especially the case in places like Colorado Springs, where thou- sands of paid employees of conservative Christian organizations live and work in close proximity to one another. Also, the geographic location of these organizations means that their employees are distant from societal centers of cultural production; accordingly, they are less likely to encounter liberal- minded intellectuals, professionals, artists, and so on. Thus, the geographic composition of the conservative Protestant organizational field helps its culture-producing institutions maintain their cultural distinctiveness, including the distinctiveness of their family ideology.

Third, the organizational field of conservative Protestantism has a distinctly entrepreneurial character. This field is largely made up of non- hierarchical denominations and independent churches, as well as membership- supported special-purpose organizations with small endowments. As a consequence, conservative Protestant organizations and their leaders, particularly at the special-purpose level, have a great deal of autonomy in pursuing their objectives. At the same time, because they do not have strong financial support from denominations and endowments, they must meet their organizational objectives through their own efforts. This combination means that pastors and leaders of special-purpose organizations both can and must incorporate innovative cultural strategies that elicit the attention and the personal and financial support of new and old members.

The disestablishment of familism and gender-role traditionalism in the broader society ironically presented an opportunity for pastors and special-purpose group leaders who had an interest in family-related matters. They could use the pervasive concern and confusion among conservative Protestants about the nature and state of the traditional family—both in society at large and in the subculture itself—to produce a family-focused ideology that elicited, and continues to elicit, tremendous personal and financial support for their organizations. Not surprisingly, many of these elites moved quickly to capitalize on the concern and confusion. The 1970s witnessed the founding of groups the Moral Majority, Focus on the Family, and Concerned Women for America (CWA). The Moral Majority has since been supplanted by the Christian Coalition, but Focus on the Family and CWA translated concern about the family into organizations with more than 2.8 million members and multimillion-dollar budgets in the mid-1990s.[174] Groups like these have a vested interest both in maintaining a "crisis in the family" frame and in offering a distinctive political, cultural, and pastoral family ideology that sets them apart from mainstream family-related groups.

THE INSTITUTIONAL CONTEXT OF MAINLINE PROTESTANT FAMILY IDEOLOGY

The nature of a religious tradition's collective identity and the features of its institutional field have also influenced mainline Protestantism's embrace of Golden Rule liberalism. Three features of mainline Protestantism's institutional field are particularly influential in shaping the character and quantity of its family discourse. First, mainline Protestantism has less religious vitality than its conservative counterpart; mainliners see their religious identities as weaker, more provisional, and more compartmentalized. This is reflected in lower levels of church attendance, social network closure, and participation in church-related activities.[175] Consequently, mainline organizations elicit less personal and financial support from their members, and there are fewer special-purpose organizations in the mainline Protestant world and no large, nationwide organizations dedicated to serving the family. Accordingly, mainline Protestant discourse on the family has fewer organizational conduits, and mainline Protestants are less likely to be exposed to family discourse from religious organizations. Another consequence of the more sedate, conventional status of mainline religiosity is that mainline Protestants are less likely to attend church if their family status is unconventional (if they are single, cohabiting, childless, or divorced), because they feel less comfortable with a conventional congregational ethos or because they do not have children who could benefit from the religious and moral messages offered by Sunday churchgoing. This means that mainline churches are disproportionately dependent upon nuclear families, which helps account for the high congregational focus on child-centered rituals and discourse.[176]

Second, the regional distribution of mainline culture-producing organizations has historically been concentrated in the Northeast, a center of cultural liberalism. Although a number of mainline denominations moved their offices out of New York City in the 1980s, partly because laity had expressed concern about geographic influences on denominational thinking, the most prestigious mainline seminaries still tend to be located in urban centers or college towns in the Northeast. For instance, Union Theological Seminary is located in New York City (next to Columbia University); Princeton Theological Seminary is in Princeton, New Jersey (next to Princeton University); and Harvard Divinity School is in Cambridge, Massachusetts (and is affiliated with Harvard University); and Yale Divinity School is in New Haven, Connecticut (and is affiliated with Yale University). Thus many of the most prestigious mainline educational institutions are located in close proximity to organizational producers and social networks of cultural liberalism. As a consequence, seminarians and seminary professors are likely to encounter greater social and organizational support for a progressive family ideology, and mainline clergy and leaders are more likely to embrace this ideology in part because they have encountered or are enmeshed in geographically based plausibility structures that make it seem commonsensical.

Third, the inclusive ethos of the organizational culture associated with mainline denominations lends itself to a progressive orientation. Starting in the 1970s, many denominations reorganized their bureaucratic structures along more professional and participatory lines. In his history of Presbyterian managerial culture, Richard Reifsnyder argues that the Presbyterian Church in the United States (one of two ecclesial forerunners of the current Presbyterian Church [U.S.A.]) deliberately set out in 1972 to make its organizational structure and processes more "inclusive and participatory." In this new organizational environment, managers with strong administrative skills and a collegial outlook pushed charismatic former pastors out of denominational bureaucracies as "process and procedure were elevated over strong, dominating, visible personalities."[177] Moreover, the mainline Presbyterian church also made strong efforts to ensure that its governing bodies and committees promoted, in the words of the church's *Book of Order,* "diversity and inclusiveness" along the lines of race, ethnicity, gender, marital status, age, and theology.[178] This inclusive managerial ethos is most strongly embedded in national and regional church bureaucracies, but it has also made its way into many of the midsized and large suburban churches that now dominate most mainline denominations.[179] This new approach, which stresses process, collegiality, and efficiency, suits the managerial and professional employment experience of many active mainline members. Its logic of practice and ideological commitment to diversity is consonant with the mainline's discursive support for an inclusive approach to family diversity, making an inclusive family ideology seem not only plausible but entirely appropriate.

MAINLINE PROTESTANT FAMILY DISCOURSE AS IDENTITY WORK

With respect to collective identity, the mainline sees itself as a sedate steward of the religious and moral life of its members and generally pursues a left-leaning but conventional cultural strategy of "engagement-without-distinction."[180] Because it has long functioned as a bulwark of conventional civic and cultural life in the United States, the mainline generally legitimates cultural developments that have attained a measure of respectability in the professions, the academy, and other elite centers of cultural production; such legitimation is likely when the developments in question are consistent with the mainline's normative commitments to inclusion, tolerance, and egalitarianism.[181] Thus, the mainline's collective identity is a religious form of establishmentarian liberalism, so the mainline's identity efforts do not require the level of intensity, commitment, and boundary work required in conservative Protestantism. Still, the mainline does engage in boundary work to highlight its mainstream and modern colors.

For instance, *Christian Century* editor James Wall argued that a 1980 voting guide for Christians that evaluated candidates on a range of conservative issues including, in Wall's words, "restricting freedom of choice on abortion" was emblematic of a "far right" drive to impose an overly ideological agenda on the U.S. political scene: "The demand for purity on single issues, or more precisely, clusters of emotion-laden issues, is a dangerous trend in American politics—not for ideological reasons, but because government suffers if voters ignore overall records and refuse to acknowledge the need for trade-offs in the political arena. And certainly the Christian faith should not be used by either the left or the right to demand purity in situations where purity is an impossibility."[182] His language suggests that religious conservatives are far-right extremists, emotional, naive, and untutored in the ways of democratic give and take. By implicit contrast, Wall's mainline readers come off as progressive stewards of political moderation.

Or consider a recent review essay on homosexuality by Sally Geis, director of the Iliff Institute at the Methodist Iliff School of Theology in Denver: The authors whose work Geis reviewed "name and describe contemporary gatekeepers who, like the Pharisees of old, pass judgments on others and deny them full participation in the community of faith. . . . In a time when churchgoers are deeply divided over the meaning of homosexuality, I doubt that any Christian could read either of these books without being moved to deep sadness as well as serious reflection over what gatekeeping means in our time."[183] Although the substance of Geis's review indicates that homosexuality is still being debated in mainline circles, her language conveys a message that resonates with many mainline elites: she suggests that opponents of homosexual practice are intolerant, judgmental Pharisees intent on excluding homosexuals from the church and implies that such opponents are unfeeling and unreflective. This pattern, in which mainliners use the ethic of tolerant acceptance to do boundary work against religious conservatives, has also been documented in ethnographic literature on the family discourse of mainline pastors.[184] Thus, for both mainline and conservative Protestant churches and elites, differences in family-related discourse persist in part because these distinctions allow the two religious groups to assert their unique collective identities.

Looking at mainline and conservative Protestant discourse on family-related matters through the prism of identity helps us to make sense of the disproportionate focus on matters touching on human sexuality—especially abortion and homosexuality. This focus on sexuality is especially paradoxical since abortion and homosexuality are issues that do not personally confront Protestant churchgoers nearly as much as do issues associated with marriage, parenting, and divorce. The vast majority of conservative and mainline churchgoers are heterosexuals who are married and have children, and abortion is relatively infrequent among the white, married, churchgoing Protestant women who make up the vast majority of female attendees at conservative and mainline churches.[185] By contrast, this demographic makeup indicates that Protestant churchgoers frequently face issues related to parenting, marriage, and divorce. This disjunction suggests that Protestant discourse on family-related matters has as much to do with identity as it does with governing family-related behavior. Stances on issues like abortion allow mainline and conservative Protestant churches and elites to signal their stance vis-à-vis cultural modernity and its concomitants—inclusiveness, tolerance, the new morality, egalitarianism, and the disestablishment of familism. Moreover, the comparatively high level of emphasis on sex-related matters suggests that conservative and mainline leaders are focusing on symbolic issues that make for safer targets because they do not impinge directly on the lives of most of their churchgoers.

MAKING SENSE OF CONTRADICTIONS, AMBIVALENCE, AND AMBIGUITY IN RELIGIOUS FAMILY DISCOURSE

How do we make sense of the contradictions, ambivalence, and ambiguities that work their way into conservative and mainline family-related discourse? Many conservative Protestant churches and leaders dispense with a commonsensical reading of inerrant Scripture and with the larger project of resisting cultural modernity when it comes to matters related to gender roles and to divorce and remarriage. Likewise, the mainline remains remarkably committed to offering child-centered rituals and discourse and surprisingly divided over homosexuality for a religious tradition that has recently begun to stress an ethic of tolerant acceptance of family diversity that encompasses "a wider range of options than that of the two-generational unit of parents and children."[186]

These disjunctions between the general thrust of religiocultural ideologies and positions on particular issues exist primarily because the social practices and resources that would sustain total ideological purity and organizational survival are not available. As William Sewell has observed, ideologies and social resources cluster together in "*structures* only when they mutually imply and sustain each other over time."[187] The conservative Protestant ambiguity and disagreement on divorce and remarriage can largely be explained by the fact that divorce rates are just as high among conservative Protestants as they are in the population at large.[188] Thus, given that the divorce rate more than doubled from 1960 to 1990, conservative Protestant churches and pastors may be adjusting their views on divorce to the social practices they confront in pews and pulpits.[189] Likewise, conservative Protestant women now work outside the home at almost the same rate as their nonconservative peers, and a majority of them are in the workforce.[190] This development is related to conservative Protestant women's gains in higher education and to the decline in the socioeconomic resources that once sustained separate-sphere practices: the percentage of jobs that paid enough to support a single-breadwinner family of five in minimal comfort shrank from 40 percent of all jobs in 1976 to 25 percent of all jobs in 1987.[191] Thus, the movement of conservative Protestant women into the workforce has undercut the practical basis for the traditional gender-role ideology that has played a prominent role in the religiocultural system of conservative Protestantism.

Mainline Protestant culture's retention of a strong focus on children and child-centered rituals and its deep divisions over homosexuality are probably tied to the fact that mainline churches are bastions of nuclear families headed by heterosexual couples. Despite their avowed commitment to an ethic of inclusive tolerance, on any given Sunday mainline churches actually have a smaller share of single parents and childless adults than either conservative Protestant churches or the population at large.[192] Given this demographic composition, mainline churches and leaders face strong and fairly uniform internal pressure to offer child-centered discourse and rituals, and they face resistance to prohomosexual measures from a slim majority of the laity, who view homosexuality as a symbolic threat to the nuclear family lifestyle. Thus, mainline and conservative Protestant family-related discourse is not without its own ironies: modernity has exacted a price from conservative Protestantism as it has moved in accommodationist directions on two of the more consequential family issues, divorce and gender roles, while the mainline's long-standing dependence on the nuclear family has hindered its efforts to live up to its own impulse toward total acceptance of family pluralism.

CONCLUSION

Students of contemporary family change have tended to view modernization as pressing almost inexorably on the culture and behavior of the family. The idea has been that traditional patterns of authority, sexual restraint, gender asymmetry, marital stability, and family institutional capacity are giving way both behaviorally and culturally to more egalitarian, individualistic, and fragile family patterns. Because the key sociocultural forces behind this transformation are seen to be operating at the macro level, scholars have assumed that these forces are pushing all sociocultural sectors of society in the direction of family modernization even though the various sectors presently differ in their level of accommodation to family modernization.[193]

However, family modernization is not pressing inexorably across all sectors of society, at least at the cultural level. Various groups are responding quite differently to these dramatic shifts in family life. Mainline Protestant institutions have largely pursued a deliberate strategy of accommodation to these shifts, while conservative Protestant institutions have generally maintained their resistance to key dimensions of family modernization. These findings are particularly interesting because the gap in sociocultural status between mainline and conservative Protestants narrowed dramatically between the 1970s and the 1990s. Thus, the differences in the type of family culture produced by these two groups cannot be viewed as the epiphenomenal effect of underlying social-structural factors. Rather, the differences in their orientations to modernity in general, in their ideological commitments, and in their institutional resources and contexts have played key roles in structuring their distinct responses to family modernization. Identity maintenance has also played a central role, especially for conservative Protestantism, as central institutional actors have used family-related discourse to assert cultural boundaries, generate an atmosphere of collective conflict, and shore up a sense of common purpose. In all these ways communities exert agency as they resist, innovate, or accommodate in response to larger sociocultural forces—in this case, family modernization and the concomitant cultural shifts that marked the last thirty-five years of the twentieth century.

One of the ironic consequences of the dramatic family modernization in the United States at the end of the millennium is that it may have actually strengthened conservative Protestantism as a whole, and in particular some of the more conservative cultural elites within the subculture. The rapid pace of change and the new morality's repudiation of classical Protestant sexual morality created a cultural climate in which many conservative Protestants, as well as a significant minority of other Americans, felt confused and alarmed. In theoretical terms, these dramatic cultural changes amounted to the kind of "unsettled times" that Ann Swidler notes can prompt collectivities to take a more self-consciously ideological approach to issues.[194] Conservative Protestant groups have capitalized on this alarm and confusion by building organizations that now play a significant role in resisting many of the developments associated with family modernization. The Southern Baptist Convention, the largest conservative Protestant denomination in the United States, has grown more conservative, at least institutionally, on family-related issues like patriarchal authority and abortion. There is also some evidence that mainline Protestants, Catholics, and Jews who have been affected by the trends associated with family modernization—divorce, premarital sex, single parenthood, and so on—have abandoned religion entirely or have sought out a vital form of community by joining a conservative Protestant church.[195] Thus, family modernization, especially when it takes place rapidly, can fuel a backlash among groups who have the cultural and institutional resources to resist it.

Nevertheless, it would be false to paint an overly Manichean picture of family-related ideology in the mainline and conservative Protestant worlds.

Although mainline and conservative Protestant institutions tend toward accommodation and resistance of family modernization, respectively, there are also signs of ambiguity, dissensus, and contradiction in their approach to family-related issues. The mainline is more focused on families with children and more divided over homosexuality than its inclusive discourse would suggest. Conservative Protestantism is more ambivalent and divided over gender-role ideology and divorce than its antimodern, biblically focused discourse would lead one to expect. These institutional inconsistencies appear to be largely a consequence of practical organizational exigencies—the prevalence of nuclear families in mainline churches and high rates of female labor-force participation and divorce among conservative Protestants. These inconsistencies suggest that institutions must pick their battles as they follow through on an ideological program and avoid issues that might unduly upset their core constituencies.

The basic logic of conservative Protestant family-related ideology may be characterized, then, as an expressive traditionalism in which efforts to shore up the family have led to an intensive approach to family living for men *and* women. This leaves open the ironic possibility that in spite of their gender-role traditionalism conservative Protestant men may take an active and expressive approach to family life that makes them, in some ways, more progressive than their nonconservative peers. At the same time, the conventional character of Golden Rule liberalism, which is the guiding logic of mainline Protestantism's family-related ideology, may result in a selectivity effect in which the most conventional and family-oriented but liberal men attend mainline churches, making the mainline unexpectedly child-oriented and ambivalent on issues like homosexuality.

CHAPTER THREE

FAMILY AND GENDER ATTITUDES AMONG MAINLINE AND CONSERVATIVE PROTESTANTS

AS LATE AS THE 1990s, the Southern Baptist Convention (SBC), the largest conservative Protestant denomination in the United States, issued a series of statements underlining its commitment to familism and gender-role traditionalism and its ability to defy, at least symbolically, the logic of family modernization. After describing the family as "the foundational institution of human society," the SBC went on to argue in 1998 that marriage is a "covenant commitment for a lifetime" and that husbands and wives have unique roles in the family: the husband has a "God-given responsibility to provide for, to protect, and to lead his family," and the wife has a "God-given responsibility" to submit graciously to her husband and "to serve as his helper in managing the household and nurturing the next generation."[1]

By contrast, starting in the 1970s the United Methodist Church, the largest mainline Protestant denomination in the United States, embraced an inclusive and egalitarian approach to families that largely accommodated the logic of family modernization. In various statements, the United Methodist Church defined the family expansively as "encompassing a wider range of options than that of the two-generational unit of parents and children (the nuclear family)"; called for an "an active, accepting, and enabling" ministry to divorced persons; and stressed the importance of egalitarian decision making and practice in families, explicitly rejecting "social norms that assume different standards for women than for men in marriage."[2]

These statements from the Southern Baptist and United Methodist churches are emblematic of the ways in which mainline and conservative Protestant institutions produced markedly different family and gender ideologies in response to the demographic, social, and cultural developments of the late twentieth century. But how connected are these institutional ideologies to the family and gender attitudes of men and women in mainline and conservative Protestant pews? Often, as Mark Chaves has argued, the formal ideological positions of religious institutions are only "loosely coupled" to the attitudes and practices of their members.[3] In this case, institutional family and gender ideologies may be produced more for the sake of establishing a particular type of collective identity, for maintaining fidelity to a particular dimension of each group's religious tradition, and for appeasing important internal and external constituencies than for the purpose of guiding the beliefs and practices of average church members. Religious denominations and parachurch organizations and their elites may issue statements on family and gender that are not regularly reinforced in the pulpit, in church groups, and in the religiously inspired media consumed by mainline and conservative Protestants. Furthermore, as we have seen, these institutional messages sometimes display inconsistencies, as exemplified by conservative Protestant discourse on divorce.

Even when religious institutions produce clear and consistent messages regarding family and gender, these messages are not likely to be completely accepted by their adherents. Work in the sociology of culture has shown that persons are not oversocialized dopes who simply internalize the culture of the institutions with which they are associated; rather, the extent to which persons internalize or adopt the collectively produced culture they encounter depends upon a range of sociocultural factors.[4] Such factors include whether persons have the practical competencies—the disposition, skills, and habits—to enact an ideology, the extent to which they have the requisite socioeconomic resources, and the degree to which they are integrated into the institution producing the ideology. And even when persons do internalize the ideology and norms produced by an institution, they often do so in a selective, ambiguous, and inconsistent fashion, accepting some elements of a particular institutionally produced ideology and its attendant norms and rejecting other elements.

Still, the ideologies and norms produced by religious institutions can and do influence the attitudes of their members. This influence is especially likely in a time when ideals and practices in particular domains are unsettled, leaving many people looking to religious institutions for guidance in these domains. Given their institutional vitality and their symbolic stress on family life, conservative Protestant institutions are likely to exert especially strong influence on their members in the unsettled domains of family and gender.

RECENT HISTORICAL TRENDS IN FAMILY AND GENDER ATTITUDES

Since 1972, the General Social Survey (GSS) has tracked national trends in religious affiliation and in public attitudes on a range of topics, including family- and gender-related issues.[5] In this section I focus on the 24,099 GSS respondents who answered family- and gender-related questions in surveys conducted from 1972 to 1998 (see the appendix for additional GSS details). I relied on a standard religious categorization scheme to assign GSS respondents to conservative or mainline Protestantism on the basis of the theological and broader religious orientation of their denomination.[6]

I concentrate on two measures of familism and two measures of gender-role traditionalism to illustrate general ideological trends. The two measures of familism, one dealing with divorce and the other with premarital sex, tap the extent to which respondents endow the institution of marriage with a high measure of moral significance. The two measures of gender-role traditionalism, one assessing attitudes toward a gendered division of family labor and the other assessing attitudes toward working mothers, tap the extent to which respondents embrace a traditional gender ideology. For each of these measures, I conducted two sets of multivariate logistic analyses to determine the influence of religious affiliation and active religious participation on these family and gender attitudes, and to account for the social and cultural sources of mainline and conservative Protestant attitudes over these three decades.[7]

The first set of statistical models compare the family and gender views of mainline and conservative Protestants to those of unaffiliated respondents, controlling for a range of sociodemographic factors such as education, race, and region. (To ensure that I have a nationally representative sample, I also included respondents from other religious backgrounds. But I generally do not report these religious effects because they are beyond the scope of this book.)

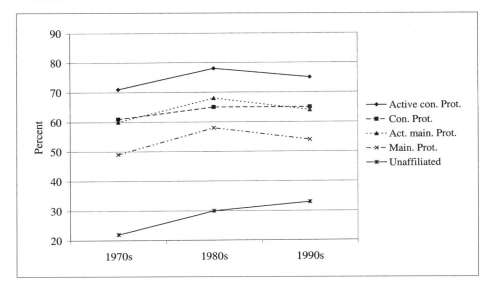

Figure 3.1 Respondents who agree that divorce should be more difficult to obtain

Source: GSS (1974–1998).

In these models, I also examine the effect on these outcomes, net of the controls above, of active religious participation, defined as attending church several times a month or more, versus nominal religious participation, defined as attending church once a month or less. In a second, ancillary set of regressions, I focus specifically on two subsets of the GSS population—conservative Protestants and mainline Protestants—in an effort to determine how period (measured in years), educational, racial, gender, and regional factors influenced attitudes within these two groups.[8]

ATTITUDES TOWARD DIVORCE AND PREMARITAL SEX

The twilight of the second millennium was marked by dramatic declines in familism in the United States, as evidenced by indicators ranging from decreased rates of fertility to increased rates of nonmarital births.[9] But figure 3.1 shows that attitudes toward divorce among mainline and conservative Protestants, as well as among unaffiliated Americans, moved in a slightly more familistic direction from the 1970s to the 1990s, with a higher percentage of GSS respondents reporting at the end of the century than in the 1970s that divorce should be "more difficult to obtain."[10] Of course, divorce laws were liberalized in the 1970s, so some of this movement may be a reaction to specific legal developments,[11] but given that most Americans do not keep abreast of changes in family law, this turn against divorce across all three groups suggests that the public has become more familistic over the last three decades, at least when it comes to divorce.

In the 1970s, 61 percent of all conservative Protestants and 49 percent of all mainline Protestants thought that divorce should be more difficult to obtain. By the 1990s, these figures had risen to 65 and 54 percent, respectively. Not surprisingly, opposition to divorce was higher among conservative and mainline Protestants who attended church several times a month or more than among their nominal counterparts, and it was lowest among Americans with no religious affiliation. By the 1990s, 75 percent of active conservative Protestants and 64 percent of active mainline Protestants, compared to just 33 percent of unaffiliated Americans, supported tougher divorce legislation. Over this period, the attitudinal gaps among the various groups remained quite consistent. Statistical analyses confirm these observations. Logistic regression models controlling for a range of socioeconomic factors also indicate that conservative and mainline Protestants were more likely than unaffiliated Americans to support toughening divorce laws. Moreover, in these models, active conservative Protestant religious participation is the most important factor associated with this attitude toward divorce, surpassing education, race, education, and gender. These trends suggest that religious affiliation and church attendance are positively associated with this measure of familism. (See table A3.2 in the appendix for complete details.)

My second set of statistical models indicates that among both conservative and mainline Protestants, period effects—unmeasured factors associated with the passage of time—account for much of the growing familism in these religious groups. This suggests that both groups have been affected by a more general society-wide reaction against divorce at the end of the last century. Interestingly, over this time period education is associated with more liberal attitudes toward divorce among mainline Protestants, as the family modernization perspective would predict, but this is not so for conservative Protestants, for whom education was initially nonsignificant. Moreover, a model interacting period and education for conservative Protestants indicates that education became positively associated with opposition to divorce starting in the 1980s.

At least when it comes to divorce, then, the familistic ideology produced in conservative Protestant churches seems closely coupled to the attitudes of men and women affiliated with these churches, especially those of frequent churchgoers. From the 1970s to the 1990s, a majority of conservative Protestants, and a commanding majority of active conservative Protestants, thought divorce laws should be toughened. And their views have become more familistic over time, especially among educated conservative Protestants, who may have been the most inclined and able to pick up the familistic cues offered by their institutions. As one evangelical woman from Georgia said, "Getting a divorce is easier than [terminating] a contract to fertilize your lawn. That's wrong. In a country where it is easier to break up a family than to get out of a business arrangement, that's wrong. The family has not been given the place that it needs to have."[12] Thus, despite the fact that we see some ambiguity and inconsistency in institutional conservative Protestant discourse about divorce, at the grassroots level most conservative Protestants connected the familistic ideology produced in this subculture to an individual concern about easy divorce. Nonetheless, conservative Protestants' support for toughening divorce laws did not increase at faster rate than that of people in mainline and unaffiliated circles. This suggests that conservative Protestant attitudes regarding divorce have also been influenced by larger societal concerns about divorce.

By contrast, the inclusive family ideology produced by mainline Protestant institutions is only loosely coupled to the attitudes of mainline Protestants, particularly those who attend church frequently. In the 1970s, a slim majority of mainline Protestants did not support tougher divorce laws. By the 1990s, the tables had turned, and a slim majority took a more familistic position on the issue.[13] Moreover, throughout the last three decades of the twentieth century, a clear majority of active mainline Protestants supported tougher divorce laws. All of this suggests that many men and women in mainline pews do not identify with the inclusive ideology offered by their religious institutions. The most educated mainline Protestants were the most likely to identify with the liberal approach endorsed by these institutions.

We see a somewhat different story when we turn to another indicator of familism: attitudes toward premarital sex. From the 1970s to the 1990s, as figure 3.2 indicates, attitudes toward premarital sex became more liberal among both conservative and mainline Protestants. In the 1970s, 51 percent of conservative Protestants and 30 percent of mainline Protestants reported the view that sexual relations before marriage are "always wrong."[14] By the 1990s, only 45 percent of conservative Protestants and 21 percent of mainline Protestants held this view. Opposition to premarital sex remained fairly constant among unaffiliated Americans, moving from eight to seven percent over this period of time. Thus, familism declined modestly among most Americans, including both conservative and mainline Protestants, in the domain of sexual morality.

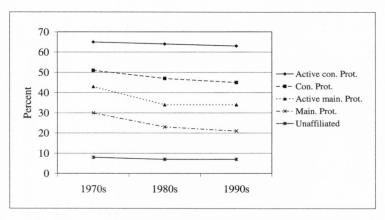

Figure 3.2   Respondents who agree that premarital sex is always wrong

Source: GSS (1972–1998).

Active conservative and mainline Protestants were more likely to take a familistic stand than their less active counterparts in this area. In the 1990s, for instance, 63 percent of active conservative Protestants and 34 percent of active mainline Protestants expressed disapproval of premarital sex. Moreover, the likelihood of disapproval barely budged among active conservative Protestant churchgoers, while it dropped markedly among active mainline Protestant churchgoers. In fact, the gap in sexual attitudes between active conservative Protestant and active mainline Protestant respondents grew from approximately 20 percentage points to about 30 percentage points in this three-decade period. The gap between mainline and conservative Protestants as a whole also grew slightly. Thus, while modest liberalization occurred in each group's attitude toward premarital sex, frequent church attendance and conservative religious affiliation appear to be linked to higher levels of familism in this domain. My statistical models indicate that these findings are not artifacts of other, unmeasured factors. The effect of conservative Protestantism on public attitudes exceeds that of period, education, gender, and age. They also reveal that active conservative Protestant religious participation exceeds a range of socioeconomic factors in its effect on public attitudes for this measure of familism. (See table A3.3 in the appendix for details.)

What accounts for these attitudinal trends regarding premarital sex? Among both conservative and mainline Protestant populations, period effects were associated with the liberalization of attitudes. This suggests, as the family modernization perspective would predict, that both communities were affected by society-wide increases in support for sexual freedom and experimentation. However, this liberalization was less pronounced in the conservative Protestant world, especially among active churchgoers, than among mainline Protestants. One reason for this is that education had different effects on sexual attitudes in these two communities. Education was associated with greater acceptance of premarital sex among mainline Protestants and in the population at large, but with greater opposition to premarital sex among conservative Protestants. The interaction between education and time period is positive and significant among conservative Protestants, indicating that this distinctive educational effect among conservative Protestants became stronger over the years.

In the domain of sexual morality, conservative Protestants' attitudes are only loosely coupled to the familistic ideology promoted by their religious institutions. It is striking that almost 40 percent of active conservative Protestants reject the idea that premarital sex is always wrong, thus opposing a position that has unanimous support among conservative Protestant elites. Still, the facts that conservative Protestants were much more likely than members of any other group to oppose premarital sex and that opposition to premarital sex increased among educated conservative Protestants over this period suggest that conservative Protestant institutions had some success in resisting family modernization in the domain of sexual morality.

Mainline Protestants were much less likely to oppose premarital sex. By the end of the twentieth century, only one-third of active mainline Protestants and one-fifth of all mainline Protestants opposed premarital sex. Thus, in this domain of familism, there seems to be a close coupling between the inclusive and accepting family ideology produced by mainline Protestant institutions and the attitudes of the men and women who identify with the mainline tradition. Nevertheless, the fact that opposition to premarital sex is higher among the mainline Protestants who are most integrated into the life of their religious institutions suggests that regular church attendance continues to be a mark of moral traditionalism for some in the mainline.

In sum, then, modest declines in familism have occurred on some issues and modest gains on others. Also, society-wide trends in familism affect Americans from a range of religious and nonreligious backgrounds. Neither conservative nor mainline Protestant populations are immune from the influence of broader societal trends against divorce and for sexual liberalism. Nevertheless, we see that in the last three decades of the twentieth century, religious affiliation and church attendance were consistently associated with higher levels of familism. Some of these effects are probably due to selection: men and women who endow the family, and marriage in particular, with greater moral

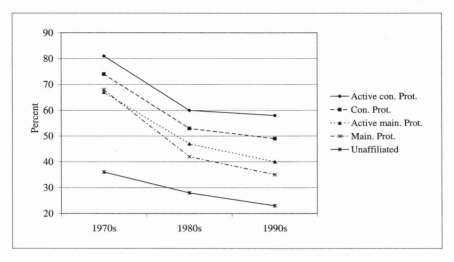

Figure 3.3   Respondents who agree that men should be breadwinners and women should be homemakers

Source: GSS (1977–1998).

significance are more likely to adopt a religious identity and to seek social support for their familism through regular church attendance. But given that religious factors—especially a conservative Protestant affiliation—powerfully and consistently predict higher levels of familism and that conservative Protestant institutions have pushed family issues to the fore since the 1970s, undoubtedly one of the reasons that conservative Protestants are much more likely to report familistic views is that they have been influenced by the familistic ideology they encounter in their churches, on radio and television programs, and in parachurch ministries.

ATTITUDES TOWARD GENDER ROLES AND WORKING MOTHERS

The last three decades of the twentieth century in the United States marked the triumph of a gender revolution that dramatically altered, among other things, public attitudes about gender roles for men and women. Support for one measure of gender traditionalism, the gendered division of family labor, declined dramatically among both mainline and conservative Protestants from the 1970s to the 1990s (see figure 3.3).[15] In the 1970s, 74 percent of conservative Protestants and 68 percent of mainline Protestants agreed that it is better if "the man is the achiever outside the home and the woman takes care of the home and the family." Thirty years later, only 49 percent of conservative Protestants and 35 percent of mainline Protestants held this view. Support for a traditional gender-role ideology also dropped among active conservative and mainline Protestants—from 81 to 58 percent and from 67 to 40 percent, respectively. Even in the 1990s, a majority of active conservative Protestants maintained their support for separate-spheres ideology. Moreover, the attitudinal gap between conservative and mainline Protestants grew over this time period to about 15 percentage points among both average and active adherents. Thus, church attendance and religious affiliation, especially conservative Protestant affiliation, are tied to the persistence of gender traditionalism.

My regression models indicate that these trends hold up even after a range of socioeconomic factors are controlled for. In the population at large, conservative Protestantism is the third most important predictor of gender attitudes, after educational and period effects. Interactions between affiliation and period confirm that the growing attitudinal gap between conservative and mainline Protestants in general and between active conservative Protestants and active mainline Protestants in particular is statistically significant. So men and women who attend church frequently and who hold a religious affiliation—especially a conservative Protestant one—are significantly more likely to hold traditional gender-role attitudes, even after factors such as gender, education, and region have been controlled for. (See table A3.4 in the appendix for complete details.)

Models designed to account for trends within conservative and mainline Protestantism indicate that both groups became more liberal in their views regarding the gendered division of labor because of gains in education among their adherents and societal changes in gender attitudes. Specifically, education and period effects were negative for both groups. Women in both groups were also more likely than men to reject a traditional division of family labor. However, educational and period effects exerted more of an influence on mainline than on conservative Protestant attitudes, which helps explain why the attitudinal gap between mainline and conservative Protestants grew over this time. In other words, even though conservative Protestants were affected by changes in the broader society and by their own advances in socioeconomic status, they were not affected as much by these changes as mainline Protestants were.

The fact that by the 1990s only a slim majority, 58 percent, of active conservative Protestants continued to believe that men should be breadwinners and that women should be homemakers in families indicates that the attitudes of active conservative Protestants are only loosely coupled to the gender ideology produced by conservative Protestant institutions in this domain. Nevertheless, conservative Protestant institutions have had some success in maintaining gender-role traditionalism among their members. Conservative Protestants are significantly more likely than other Americans to support a separate-spheres view of the division of family labor. One newly married evangelical man from Texas drew on the traditional and biblical claims he had heard articulated in his church, contending that it is "clearly the man's role to be the primary breadwinner through life" and that the wife should be "a 'help-mate' to her husband. . . . Her primary role would be to be a support and encouragement to her husband."[16]

This kind of talk is not likely to be found in mainline Protestant circles, especially among younger people. The views of average mainline Protestants, of whom only 35 percent endorsed a traditional division of labor in the 1990s, is somewhat more closely coupled to mainline Protestant gender ideology. But it is curious to see that, once again, active mainline Protestants are more conservative than nominal mainline Protestants. This means that mainline Protestants who go to church regularly are less likely than nominal churchgoers to identify with the official gender ideology of the churches they attend. Again we are seeing evidence that a significant minority of mainline churchgoers are more conservative than the leaders of their denominations.

Americans have also become more accepting of working mothers, though they now have more reservations about working mothers than about an egalitarian division of work and family responsibilities (see figure 3.4). Specifically, in the 1970s, 69 percent of conservative Protestants and 70 percent of mainline Protestants believed that a "preschool child is likely to suffer if his or her mother works."[17] By the 1990s, only 52 percent of conservative Protestants and 44 percent of mainline Protestants held this view. Concern about mothers of preschoolers working also dropped among active conservative and mainline Protestants, though at a lesser rate. By the 1990s conservative Protestants, especially active conservative Protestants, were clearly more concerned about working mothers of preschoolers than were their mainline and unaffiliated peers; their move toward gender liberalism in this domain had stalled in the 1980s. Not surprisingly, from the 1970s to the 1990s, the gap between conservative and mainline Protestants on this measure grew to approximately ten percentage points, and that between conservative Protestants and unaffiliated Americans grew to twenty percentage points.

Statistical tests of the importance of religious affiliation indicate that a conservative Protestant affiliation, but not a mainline Protestant affiliation, is associated with this dimension of gender traditionalism from the 1970s to the

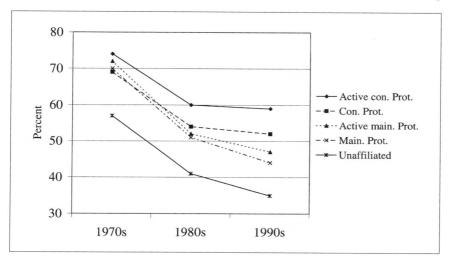

Figure 3.4   Respondents who agree that preschool children suffer if their mothers work

Source: GSS (1977–1998).

1990s. Mainline Protestants are slightly more traditional than unaffiliated Americans in this case largely because of the fact that they tend to be older than unaffiliated Americans. Additional tests confirm that active mainline Protestants and especially active conservative Protestants were more likely than their less active peers to believe that preschool children are harmed if their mothers work. Indeed, active conservative Protestants were significantly more likely to oppose working mothers of preschoolers than active mainline Protestants. (For more details, see table A3.5 in the appendix.)

Statistical models looking at trends within conservative and mainline Protestantism suggest that period effects account for much of the liberalization of attitudes in these two religious traditions. In other words, both Protestant populations seem to have been influenced by increasing levels of societal acceptance of working mothers of preschoolers. Women in both groups are less likely than men to express concern about working mothers. Education, on the other hand, seems to function differently for each group; it is associated with lower levels of concern among mainline Protestants and higher levels of concern among conservative Protestants. Indeed, the interaction of education and period effects is statistically positive. This means that in recent years highly educated conservative Protestants have become more likely than their less-educated peers to adhere to a traditionalist position on this issue. Here we have additional evidence that advances in education do not necessarily lead to declines in familism and gender-role traditionalism among conservative Protestants.

Thus, the attitudes of both mainline and conservative Protestants are loosely coupled to the gender ideologies produced by their institutions. In the 1990s, more than 40 percent of conservative Protestants believed that preschool children are not hurt if their mother works; their views are in tension with the sacralization of motherhood found in this subculture. At the same time, more than 40 percent of mainline Protestants did express concern about working mothers of preschoolers, even though their churches have underlined their support for working mothers in recent years. But this does not mean that religious institutions have had no influence on their adherents in this domain. Conservative Protestant institutions in particular appear to have nearly halted the decline in this form of gender-role traditionalism among their active adherents since the 1980s.

Both mainline and conservative Protestants, then, have become less traditional in their orientation toward gender issues in the last three decades of the twentieth century. Thus, we have some evidence that conservative Protestants have accommodated themselves to the logic of family modernization, at least when it comes to gender-role ideology. Nevertheless, a slim majority of active conservative Protestants continue to espouse a traditional gender ideology, and liberalizing trends among them in this domain have slowed dramatically since the 1980s. In fact, the attitudinal gap in gender ideology separating conservative Protestants from both unaffiliated and mainline Protestants grew during the last three decades of the twentieth century. Furthermore, regression models indicate that an active conservative Protestant affiliation is the strongest sociocultural predictor of gender-role traditionalism in the United States. For all these reasons, and because conservative Protestant churches and parachurch ministries are the only large institutional actors in the United States promoting a conservative gender ideology, we can conclude that conservative Protestantism has been an important force in delaying the complete ideological triumph of the gender revolution.

This analysis of family- and gender-related attitudinal trends from the 1970s to the 1990s suggests five conclusions. First, mainline and conservative Protestant attitudes remained fairly stable when it came to familism; with respect to gender-role traditionalism, however, they moved in a markedly egalitarian direction. Second, their movement on gender-role traditionalism provides evidence in favor of the family modernization perspective, especially insofar as conservative Protestant trends in this area appeared to be influenced by society-wide trends. But, third, we also have evidence that conservative Protestant institutions have had some success in resisting the ideological manifestations of family modernization in the last thirty years: conservative Protestants, and especially active conservative Protestants, are consistently more familistic and traditional than mainline Protestants and unaffiliated Americans; the ideological gap over family and gender issues appears to be growing between conservative Protestants and these other groups; and education does not have a consistently liberalizing effect on conservative Protestant attitudes. Fourth, conservative Protestant success in these areas gives some credence to feminist concerns that conservative Protestantism is a force for gender reaction. And finally, the widening attitudinal gap between conservative Protestants and others also provides some evidence in favor of the culture war thesis that posits a growing ideological divide in the United States between religious traditionalists and religious and secular progressives over family-related issues.

RELIGIOUS AND FAMILY-RELATED IDEOLOGIES AMONG MARRIED MEN WITH CHILDREN

To study the influence of religious affiliation and theological conservatism on familism and gender-role traditionalism among married men with children, I relied on nationally representative data from the 1987–1988 wave of the National Survey of Families and Households (NSFH1). This wave surveyed more than thirteen thousand primary adult respondents and a large group of secondary respondents who were married to or cohabiting with the primary respondents. My analyses in this section focus on a subsample of primary and secondary respondents from NSFH1: 3,539 men who were married and had children (ages eighteen and under) at home. All of the NSFH analyses used for this book are based on weighted data and adjusted for oversamples of African Americans, Puerto Ricans, Mexican Americans, and families with stepchildren. (See the appendix for additional methodological details.)

THEOLOGICAL CONSERVATISM AMONG MARRIED MEN WITH CHILDREN

Before turning to the question of how religion is connected to familism and gender-role traditionalism among married men with children, I must first discuss a key religious factor, theological conservatism, which mediates the effect of religious affiliation upon these two family-related ideologies and on the family behaviors discussed in chapters 4, 5, and 6. Theological conservatism, the guiding religious ideology of the conservative Protestant world, is measured here by two survey items tapping biblical literalism and authority: "The Bible is God's word and everything happened or will happen exactly as it says," and "The Bible is the answer to all important human problems." Men who indicated agreement with both of these items were coded as theological conservatives.

There is a substantial amount of ideological heterogeneity in both conservative and mainline Protestant churches, in part because religious adherents often are selective in their adoption of the ideologies and norms they encounter in their religious institutions. In 1988, 31 percent of mainline Protestant men who were married with children identified with the conservative religious ideology produced by conservative Protestant churches and parachurch institutions like InterVarsity Christian Fellowship (see table 1.2 in chapter 1). At the same time, 37 percent of conservative Protestant men who were married with children did not identify with conservative religious ideology, even though it is produced primarily in their churches and in conservative Protestant parachurch ministries.

Nevertheless, religious institutions do exert a powerful influence on the probability that a married man with children is a theological conservative. Logistic regression models predicting theological conservatism on the basis of religious affiliation and a range of sociodemographic factors indicate that a conservative Protestant affiliation is the strongest predictor of theological conservatism. Conservative Protestant married fathers are over seven times more likely than their unaffiliated counterparts to be theological conservatives, and they are significantly more likely to be theological conservatives than their mainline Protestant peers. Still, even mainline Protestants are more than twice as likely as unaffiliated men to be theological conservatives.

Not surprisingly, statistical models that seek to tap institutional effects of religious affiliation by comparing men who attend church several times a month or more to men who attend fewer than several times a month provide even stronger evidence for the positive effect of an active conservative Protestant affiliation on the odds of being a theological conservative. Frequently attending conservative Protestants are the most likely to be theologically conservative (78 percent), followed by frequently attending mainline Protestants (49 percent), infrequently attending conservative Protestants (48 percent), and finally, infrequently attending mainline Protestants (20 percent). These findings indicate that both conservative Protestantism and frequent church attendance are strongly associated with theological conservatism among married men with children. (See table A3.6 in the appendix for details.)

Thus, although conservative Protestant churches foster a theologically conservative outlook among married men with children, especially those who attend church frequently, married men with children who are active churchgoers may be inclined to identify with a conservative theological outlook regardless of the church they attend. Given the extensive presence of conservative Protestant parachurch ministries in print, radio, and television media and the fact that some mainline Protestant churches are more theologically conservative than others, even mainline men who are attracted to theologically conservative ideology can find institutional reinforcement for such an outlook. All this suggests that the dominant religious ideology produced by conservative Protestant churches and parachurch ministries is closely coupled to the religious outlook of married men with children who frequently attend conservative Protestant churches. By contrast, the dominant liberal religious ideology produced by mainline Protestant institutions seems only loosely coupled to the religious outlook of married men with children who frequently attend mainline Protestant churches. These findings are important because married men with children who are theological conservatives have distinctive family-related attitudes and a distinctive approach to familial involvement.

FAMILISM AMONG MARRIED MEN WITH CHILDREN

Familism is an ideology that sacralizes the obligations that individuals have toward their family members—children, spouse, and parents—and takes a highly sentimental view of family life. I constructed an index that measures this ideology by averaging responses to seven questions dealing with the value of marriage and childbearing, the importance of adult children caring for elderly parents, and the appropriateness of unhappy couples with children divorcing (see table A3.1 in the appendix for complete details). These questions tap the two key dimensions of familism, familial obligation and sentimental domesticity, which are discussed at greater length in chapter 2. Men who indicated that they believe that it is better to go through life married than unmarried, that children should let their elderly parents live with them if they are unable to live by themselves, that divorce for parents of preschool children should be avoided even if the couple is unhappy, and so on score high on the familism index.

Religious affiliation, church attendance, and theological conservatism apparently foster familism among married men with children. A summary of results from ordinary least squares (OLS) regression models appears in figure 3.5. Compared to men with no religious affiliation, conservative Protestant men score about one-half of a standard deviation higher and mainline Protestant men score about one-third of a standard deviation higher in familism. These

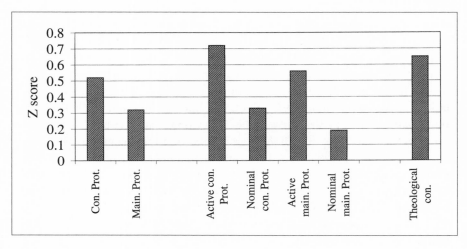

Figure 3.5   Familism of married men with children

Source: NSFH1 (1987–1988).
Note: The comparison category for all religious affiliation effects is Unaffiliated, and for theological conservatives it is Non–theological conservative.

findings represent strong and moderate effect sizes, respectively. The effect of
conservative Protestantism is more significant than that of mainline Protestantism, and it surpasses the effects of age, education, race, and region on this
measure. (See table A3.7 in the appendix for complete details.)

Frequently attending conservative Protestant men are exceptionally familistic: their score is almost three-quarters of a standard deviation higher than
that of unaffiliated men. Their score is also higher than that of active mainline
Protestant men, which is a little more than one-half of a standard deviation
higher than that of unaffiliated men who are married with children. Both
groups of active Protestant men are significantly more familistic than their
nominal peers. For example, 57 percent of active conservative Protestant men
opposed divorce in cases involving unhappily married couples with preschool
children, compared to 42 percent of active mainline Protestant men and 30
percent of unaffiliated men.

Theological conservatism helps to explain the association between religious affiliation, especially active religious affiliation, and familism. Adding
theological conservatism to the model reduces the association between active
conservative Protestantism and familism by one-half and the association between active mainline Protestantism and familism by forty percent. Men who

are theological conservatives are two-thirds of a standard deviation higher in familism than men who are not theological conservatives; this is a large effect size (see figure 3.5).

These findings suggest that conservative Protestant institutions play an important role in fostering familism among married men with children, especially men who attend church frequently and who identify with the guiding religious ideology of this subculture, namely, theological conservatism. But a substantial minority of mainline Protestant men also embrace a familistic outlook, especially theologically conservative and churchgoing men in this religious tradition, and support for familism is not unanimous among conservative Protestant men who are married with children. A substantial minority even of conservative Protestant men do not hold familist views.

Nevertheless, my models indicate that religious factors—especially a conservative Protestant affiliation and theological conservatism—are the most important predictors of familistic attitudes among married men with children. This may be in part a consequence of selection effects: family-oriented men may be attracted to conservative Protestant churches and a theologically conservative outlook. But given the attention that conservative Protestant institutions have devoted to the family since the 1970s, it also seems safe to assume that these effects are a consequence of conservative Protestant institutions' substantial efforts to persuade men to focus on their families.

GENDER-ROLE TRADITIONALISM AMONG MARRIED MEN WITH CHILDREN

Gender-role traditionalism is an ideology that valorizes women's roles as mothers and stresses the value of dividing the economic, child-rearing, and household tasks associated with family life along gendered lines. Using NSFH1, I constructed an index of gender-role traditionalism based on respondents' attitudes regarding male breadwinning and female homemaking, mothers of preschoolers working outside the home, and the importance of sharing housework equally when both spouses work full-time (see table A3.1 in the appendix for details). Men in the sample who believed that men should focus on breadwinning and women should focus on homemaking, who disapproved of full-time work by mothers of preschool children, and who did not believe in sharing household labor equally scored high on this index of gender traditionalism.

Results of OLS regression models indicate that conservative Protestant married men with children are almost a third of a standard deviation higher in their gender traditionalism than their unaffiliated counterparts, and significantly

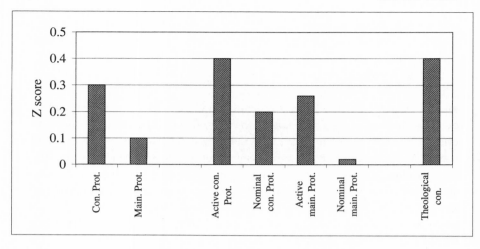

Figure 3.6 Gender-role traditionalism of married men with children

Source: NSFH1 (1987–1988).
Note: The comparison category for all religious affiliation effects is Unaffiliated, and for theological conservatives it is Non–theological conservative.

more traditional than mainline Protestant married men with children as well. Respondents in the latter group are slightly more traditional than their unaffiliated counterparts, but the difference between these two groups is not statistically significant. Although conservative Protestant affiliation has only a moderate effect size here, it surpasses that of income, education, and race (see figure 3.6).

Active conservative Protestant men in this group, not surprisingly, are the most traditional. They are four-tenths of a standard deviation higher in their gender traditionalism than unaffiliated men, and they are also significantly more traditional than active mainline Protestant men, whose score is one-quarter of a standard deviation higher than that of unaffiliated men. Active conservative Protestant men are also significantly more traditional than nominal conservative and mainline Protestant men. In statistical terms, these effect sizes are moderate. (For more details on these statistical models, see table A3.8 in the appendix.)

How do these results translate into specific views on gender? Among active conservative Protestants, 58 percent of married men with children believe that it is "much better for everyone if the man earns the main living and the woman takes care of the home and family," compared to only 44 percent of active mainline Protestant men and 37 percent of unaffiliated men who are married with children. There is more parity between the groups when it comes to concerns about working mothers. Fifty-six percent of active conservative Protestant men in this group and 53 percent of active mainline Protestant men, compared to 45 percent of unaffiliated men, believe that "preschool children are likely to suffer if their mother is employed."

The relationship between religious affiliation, especially an active religious affiliation, and gender-role traditionalism is mediated in part by theological conservatism. Adding theological conservatism to the model reduces the effect of active conservative and mainline Protestant affiliation by half. This means one of the primary reasons active mainline and conservative Protestant men tend to be more traditional in their gender views is that many of them subscribe to the guiding religious ideology of conservative Protestantism. Indeed, theologically conservative married men with children are four-tenths of a standard deviation higher on gender traditionalism than men who are not theologically conservative.

Thus, conservative Protestant institutions play an important role in fostering gender traditionalism among married men with children. Men who are active churchgoers in this subculture and who identify with its theologically conservative outlook are particularly likely to hold a traditional gender ideology. Of course, we also have evidence that a substantial minority of active mainline Protestants take a more traditional view on gender. Given the fact that theological conservatism mediates much of the active mainline effect, these men probably have access to conservative Protestant media and parachurch institutions that promote a traditional view of gender as part and parcel of their larger religious and cultural agenda. Undoubtedly, some of the results documented in this section are also a consequence of selection effects: traditional men are the more likely to gravitate toward conservative Protestant churches and toward active churchgoing. Nevertheless, given that conservative Protestant institutions are probably the only major institutional proponent of gender traditionalism in the United States and that an active conservative Protestant affiliation is more strongly associated than any other sociodemographic factor with gender traditionalism, we can conclude that conservative Protestantism plays a signal role in fostering gender traditionalism among married men with children.

MAKING SENSE OF GENDER AND FAMILY ATTITUDES AMONG MAINLINE AND CONSERVATIVE PROTESTANTS

A recurring theme in recent ethnographic research on conservative Protestantism is that academic, feminist, and media stereotypes that suggest monolithic support for gender-role traditionalism and familism in this sub-culture overlook the considerable ideological heterogeneity among ordinary conservative Protestants. Research conducted by Christian Smith and John Bartkowski, for instance, shows that although most evangelical Protestants take a traditional view of gender that encompasses support for a gendered division of labor and for male headship, a substantial minority of evangelicals take an explicitly egalitarian view of family relations or qualify their support for gender traditionalism in important ways.[18]

My findings confirm those of the ethnographic research: a substantial minority—40 percent, more or less, depending on the specific issue—of active conservative Protestants, including married men with children, do not subscribe to the familistic and traditional gender ideologies generally promoted by conservative Protestant institutions and elites. The inverse is true of active mainline Protestants, about 40 percent of whom do subscribe to familistic and traditional gender ideologies—which are not supported by the dominant institutions and elites in mainline Protestantism. Thus, ideological heterogeneity can be found in the pews of both conservative and mainline Protestant churches.

How can we account for the heterogeneity in attitudes across both of these religious traditions? First, conservative Protestants have not been im-mune to the social and cultural forces influencing the rest of the society. Since the 1960s they have been affected by at least four factors—declining real wages for men; dramatic increases in education, employment, and income among women; falling birthrates associated with the introduction of the Pill; and the rise of feminism—that have undercut the ideological and practical bases of the strongly gendered view of family life that has been idealized in this subcul-ture. Rising rates of divorce and expressive individualism among conservative Protestants have also eroded the practical and ideological bases for familism.

Second, mainline Protestants continue to be subject to the force of the long-standing ties binding mainline churches to the nuclear family in the United States. To this day, the conventional character of mainline religiosity has meant that a disproportionate percentage of active mainline Protestants are married with children (including grown children).[19] Many of the mainline men and women in these families have a traditional lifestyle marked by high maternal investment in children, strong emotional ties among family mem-bers, and a gendered division of labor in which the husband earns all or most of the family income—a lifestyle that provides a strong social and cultural basis for familistic ideology and a traditional gender outlook. A large share of the men and women in this group may attend mainline churches to reinforce their family lifestyle.

Indeed, my findings consistently show that frequent church attendance is associated with higher levels of familism and gender-role traditionalism among mainline Protestants, even though we might expect that closer integration into the egalitarian, inclusive world of mainline Protestantism would have the opposite effect. The presence of a traditional, family-oriented group within the mainline may also help explain why the NSFH results indicate that a substantial minority of mainline Protestants are theologically conservative. It is possible that theologically conservative mainline Protestants identify with and seek out the family and gender discourse offered by conservative Protestant media and parachurch organizations and incorporate that discourse into their own thinking about family life. Finally, a substantial minority of mainline churches, especially in the South, are theologically conservative and have ties to evangelical parachurch institutions, including evangelical family ministries. The presence of these churches may help to explain why theologically conservative and frequently attending mainline Protestants are more familistic and traditional than expected.

But this heterogeneity should not obscure a truth that at least partially vindicates the views of feminist, media, and academic critics of conservative Protestantism and qualifies the family modernization perspective: namely, that conservative Protestantism may well be the most important institutional force behind the ideological persistence of gender traditionalism and familism in the United States. A conservative Protestant affiliation, especially among frequent churchgoers, is generally the strongest predictor of profamily and traditionalist attitudes in the population at large and among married men with children. The NSFH1 results suggest that theological conservatism plays an important role in mediating the positive relationship between religious affiliation and the ideologies of familism and gender-role traditionalism; indeed, theological conservatism is a significant predictor of familism and traditionalism among married men with children in its own right. Furthermore, although neither the GSS nor the NSFH poses questions about male headship, the results of the 1996 Religious Identity and Influence Survey, which looks specifically at the issue of male headship in the population at large, lend further credence to the notion that conservative Protestantism fosters gender traditionalism. The 1996 survey reveals that about 85 percent of conservative Protestants endorse male headship, compared to approximately 65 percent of mainline Protestants and 25 percent of unaffiliated Americans.[20]

There are also indications that conservative Protestant institutions have at least partially succeeded in resisting the effects of family modernization. First, in the last decades of the twentieth century education was much more likely to be positively associated with familism and gender-role traditionalism among conservative Protestants than among mainline Protestants. Second, the gap between the family-related attitudes of conservative Protestants and those of mainliners and unaffiliated Americans grew from the 1970s to the 1990s. Third, declines in familism and gender-role traditionalism generally came to a halt in the late 1980s in the conservative Protestant subculture. Finally, a clear majority of active conservative Protestants continue to express familistic attitudes on issues like divorce, and traditional attitudes on issues like the gendered division of family labor. Taken together, these findings suggest that conservative Protestant institutions fostered a significant level of resistance to the cultural dimensions of family modernization among men and women who were able to pick up and internalize the institutions' family-related messages as a consequence of their frequent church attendance, theological conservatism, or education.

The unique effects of education on family-related attitudes among conservative Protestants are particularly noteworthy. They suggest that the vitality of conservative Protestant institutions has enabled them, at least at the cultural level, to forge a family path that amounts to a kind of innovative traditionalism. That is, a distinctive sense of collective identity, tight social networks, the substantial institutional presence of conservative Protestant churches and parachurch institutions, and the ample family media produced by these institutions have all helped conservative Protestants—especially the well-educated and frequently attending conservative Protestants who are the most attuned to the messages produced by conservative Protestant elites—to maintain a subcultural identity that is defined, at least in part, by countercultural family beliefs.

To be sure, the meaning that conservative Protestants ascribe to these family-related ideologies has softened in recent years in ways that may make men and women more inclined to pay attention to the responsibilities rather than the privileges of men in their patriarchal vision of family life. But the reality is that a majority of active conservative Protestants in the United States still believe that men should be the primary breadwinners in their families, and a clear majority of conservative Protestants continue to affirm the principle of male headship in marriage. The next three chapters take up the question of what, if any, impact the gender traditionalism and familism fostered in this subculture has upon conservative Protestant married men with children, and of how such men compare to their mainline and unaffiliated counterparts.

CHAPTER FOUR

SOFT PATRIARCHS, NEW FATHERS: RELIGION, IDEOLOGY, AND FATHERHOOD

THE LAST TWO DECADES have witnessed increased public support for a "new fatherhood" ideal, according to which men take an active and expressive role in the lives of their children. The irony of the current situation, however, is that this iconic new father is often in short supply; scholars note a significant gap between the "culture" and "conduct" of fatherhood.[1] For instance, although the amount of time fathers devote to child rearing increased 170 percent from twenty-one minutes a day in 1965 to fifty-seven minutes a day in 1998, fathers now contribute only 35 percent of the total parental time devoted to child rearing.[2] In other words, mothers continue to spend the lion's share of time with children. Mothers also continue to do most of the emotional work associated with parenting.

One of the central questions suggested by the gap between contemporary fatherhood culture and practice is whether religion—and conservative

Protestantism in particular—is pushing men toward or away from a new fatherhood style. Given the long-standing link between traditional behavior and religious practice, and conservative Protestant support for gender traditionalism, it could be that religious institutions and culture—especially conservative religious institutions and culture—are pushing men away from this new fatherhood style. One prominent family psychologist, John Gottman, has suggested the "religious right" is behind "strong trends away from fathers being involved with their children's emotions."[3] Sociologists Julia McQuillan and Myra Marx Ferree argue that the "religious right" is "pushing men toward authoritarian and stereotypical forms of masculinity and attempting to renew patriarchal family relations."[4] On the other hand, the generally familistic orientation of religious institutions, especially conservative Protestant ones, and the progressive gender-role ideology supported by mainline Protestant institutions may translate into higher levels of paternal involvement and expressive behavior on the part of men affiliated with conservative and mainline Protestant churches.

In this chapter I also address another central question: whether the conservative Protestant emphasis on parental authority and discipline translates into an authoritarian or an authoritative fathering style. An authoritarian style of parenting is marked by harsh and abusive discipline, excessive levels of parental control, frequent parental resort to corporal punishment and yelling, minimal expressions of affection, and low levels of parental support in the form of everyday involvement, praise, and guidance. Needless to say, this style has a detrimental effect on children's well-being.[5] An authoritative parenting style, on the other hand, is characterized by moderately high levels of parental control and high levels of parental support, has been linked to positive outcomes for children and adolescents.[6] Authoritative parenting typically incorporates clear rules and expectations, consistent penalties for misbehavior, high levels of parent-child interaction, and frequent displays of praise and affection. (A permissive approach to parenting, characterized by high levels of parental support and low levels of parental control, is the primary alternative to authoritarian and authoritative parenting styles; this approach is also associated with negative outcomes for children, such as higher levels of antisocial behavior and impulsiveness.)

Critics of conservative Protestant parenting have charged that this subculture's approach is authoritarian. In a provocatively titled 1991 presidential address to the Society for the Scientific Study of Religion, "Religion and Child Abuse: Perfect Together," Donald Capps argued that conservative Protestant parenting is abusive and authoritarian. He said that children are "betrayed, exploited, and abused in the name of religion"—a religion that draws on notions of divine sovereignty and human sinfulness to prescribe corporal punishment as a valuable form of parental discipline.[7] Gottman and other leading scholars of the family, such as historian Philip Greven and sociologist Murray Straus, have made similar charges.[8] But these charges have been made without careful recourse to empirical data and without careful consideration of the range of parenting practices conservative Protestants engage in.

Understanding the links among religion, culture, and paternal involvement is also important in light of recent research that indicates that the extent and style of paternal engagement is strongly associated with the well-being of children. Paternal involvement is linked to pro-social behavior, educational attainment, and psychological well-being among children.[9] Indeed, after conducting a study that took into account the effects of both maternal and paternal involvement, sociologist Paul Amato somewhat surprisingly concluded that "fathers are about as important as mothers in predicting children's long-term outcomes."[10] One of the reasons that the style and extent of paternal involvement is so crucial to child well-being is that maternal investment in children tends to be consistently high while paternal investment varies a great deal. By exploring the connections among religion, culture, and paternal involvement using data from NSFH1 (1987–1988) and SAY (1998–1999), I offer some insight into the relationship between paternal religious involvement and child well-being.

RELIGION AND FAMILY BEHAVIOR: A BRIEF THEORETICAL EXCURSUS

This study takes place against the backdrop of a larger theoretical debate about the influence of religion on the family. Much of the recent work in this area has argued that generic religiosity is the most salient determinant of family behavior and that the distinctive religious and family culture associated with particular religious traditions no longer plays a key role in influencing such behavior.[11] Other new research focusing on conservative Protestantism suggests, however, that the distinctive religious and family ideologies produced in this subculture can and do have significant independent effects on child-rearing behavior, apart from the effects of generic religiosity.[12] In this section I review the central claims made by proponents of each perspective to develop a theoretical framework that integrates the contributions of both views; in the next section I then apply this framework to the subject of religion and fatherhood.[13]

Why might generic religiosity—defined as any kind of participation in group religious activities; any kind of individual meditation, prayer, or reflection on religious themes; and any kind of belief derived from the theological and moral ideology of a religious tradition—have fairly uniform effects on family life? Émile Durkheim argued that religion fosters the collective good by inculcating "a certain number of beliefs and practices common to all the faithful, traditional and thus obligatory. . . . The details of dogmas and rites are secondary. The essential thing is that they be capable of supporting a sufficiently intense collective life."[14] In other words, the cultural content of particular religious activities, beliefs, and practices is not overly important in promoting pro-social behavior; what is important is that religious institutions promote beliefs and practices that bind individuals to a common way of life that affords them a sense of purpose, solidarity, and self-control and that makes them embrace the duties attendant to social institutions such as the family. Thus, religion's primary function is to integrate persons into the social and normative structure of society.

A number of mechanisms may account for generic associations between religion and family life. First, most major religious systems—from Hinduism to Roman Catholicism—foster religious and moral beliefs that have direct and indirect effects on family life. These institutions endow family relations, including conjugal and parental relations, with a measure of transcendent significance.[15] They also encourage specific moral norms about marriage, parenting, and a range of other family-related behaviors and legitimate them with theological claims.[16] Religious institutions also support generic moral norms, such as the Golden Rule, that foster ethical behavior in a wide range of social domains, including the family.[17] Finally, religious beliefs often help persons cope with stressful events, such as unemployment or the death of a loved one, that might otherwise cause them to withdraw from family life or to adopt a harsh and punitive pattern of relating to their family members.[18] Consequently, as a number of studies suggest, men and women who have strong religious beliefs bring the sacred into their secular spousal and parental roles by investing more time and emotional effort in these roles.[19]

The second set of mechanisms involves the family-centered rituals and ethos associated with religion. Religious institutions offer rituals—from bar mitzvahs to baptisms—that mark important stages in the life course and imbue family roles with religious significance. Worship services also provide families with regular opportunities to spend time together, and family programming— couples retreats, youth groups, family camps, and so on—offers spouses, parents, and children opportunities to deepen their relationships with family members. More generally, religious institutions tend to foster a family-centered ethos characterized by a range of explicit and implicit norms that reinforce a family-centered lifestyle. For all these reasons, individuals who participate regularly in the life of a religious institution are more likely to have strong, positive relationships with family members than are those who do not.[20]

The social ties found in religious institutions and their family-centered character and functions are the third set of mechanisms accounting for generic associations between religion and family behavior. Observers of the contemporary U.S. religious scene, such as Penny Edgell, note that regardless of their ideological stripe religious institutions often embrace familism at the level of practice, even when their denominational elites and clergy explicitly endorse a liberal, inclusive family ideology.[21] This means, at least at the congregational level, that most religious institutions continue to offer rituals, generic moral messages, and, to some extent, family-specific messages that appeal to nuclear families composed of married couples with children. Consequently, religious institutions in the United States attract a disproportionate share of their active adult members from the ranks of parents in nuclear families who seek out religious participation in part because of the religious and moral significance they attach to family life.[22]

Accordingly, the social networks found in religious institutions tend to offer more family-related social support and social control than any other institution except for the extended family. Parents can seek support from their place of worship and their fellow congregants in the form of advice, free childcare, and emotional and financial support in times of crisis. The family-centered character of these social networks exposes them to implicit and explicit norms that make family life a priority; they legitimate a family-centered lifestyle in a society that often emphasizes work, leisure, and consumption in ways that compete with family life. Finally, religious social networks can exercise social control over adults who depart from community family norms in one way or another. Actions that threaten family life—such as physical abuse, child neglect, excessive devotion of time to work, and extramarital sexual activity—can lead to formal and informal sanctions from the religious community. For all these reasons, the social ties found in religious institutions can reinforce, affirm, and deepen congregants' commitment to family life.

The presence of these three sets of mechanisms would lead us to expect that individuals who are religiously active are generically more involved and expressive with members of their family. But there are two important caveats to the expectation that religiosity has such generic effects on family behavior. First, norms and behaviors regarding parenting, marriage, and other family relations are more likely to be universally cultivated by religious institutions, both explicitly and implicitly, if they are held throughout much of the society. Second, as Durkheim's work suggests, religious institutions must have a minimum level of collective vitality to influence the beliefs and behaviors of their members. Specifically, only those religious institutions that have a "sufficiently intense collective life" are likely to provide the level of social integration associated with pro-social behavior, including higher levels of practical and emotional investment in family life.[23] Religious institutions that do not enjoy sufficiently high levels of religious vitality are less likely to foster familistic beliefs, practices, and networks.

These caveats are suggestive of the ways in which particular religious institutions can have distinctive effects on family behavior. Three additional sets of mechanisms explain why some religious institutions exert a distinctive, and not just a generic, influence on family life. First, religious institutions that enjoy particularly high levels of religious strength—as measured by group participation, salience of faith, adherence to beliefs, and retention and recruitment of members—are better able to cultivate an "intense collective life" that secures high levels of social integration.[24] Such institutions tend to cultivate strong ideological assent, exert a large measure of social control, and generate high levels of solidarity among their members. This high level of integration, in turn, makes members particularly resistant to succumbing to the anomic pressures of contemporary life; to life stresses such as unemployment, poverty, and illness; and to the challenges associated with family life. Thus, because they are more resilient than other adults amid the stresses that can harm family life, adults in strong religious communities should be better parents and partners.[25] The high level of social integration in strong religious institutions also means that individuals are exposed to higher levels of family-related social support and control, as well as to the family-related and generic moral norms typically promoted in religious institutions. For all these reasons, we should expect that individuals whose religiosity is tied to a highly vital religious institution will invest more time and emotional energy in family life.

Second, insofar as particular religious institutions promote a distinctive symbol-laden "logic of practice" and a distinctive normative-ideological outlook, these institutions may also have distinctive effects on family behavior, for good or ill. In terms of the logic of practice, to use Bourdieu's formulation, the type of rituals and the broader ethos found in religious institutions may have implications for family life.[26] Particular types of rituals can serve to communicate, clarify, and reinforce particular types of family behaviors and norms both for those who directly participate in the rituals and for those who witness them.[27] Religious traditions that incorporate a particularly solemn wedding ceremony, for instance, may reinforce the sense of sanctity with which newlyweds view their marriage; they may also revive the marital commitment of onlookers at the ceremony. More generally, the broader ethos—be it liturgical or informal, individualistic or communitarian—of a religious institution may shape the style of interaction that family members have with each other. Religious congregations that have a formal, liturgical approach to worship, for example, may foster less expressive familial behavior than congregations that have an informal, charismatic approach. Taken together, the ethos associated with a particular religious institution and the specific symbol-laden logic of practice embodied in its ritual action may foster distinctive patterns of familial practice among men and women who encounter this logic through regular religious practice.

Third, and perhaps most importantly, religious institutions can produce distinctive family-related ideologies that influence family behavior in unique ways. Particularly in "unsettled times" when family ideals and norms have lost their taken-for-granted character, religious institutions often produce ideologies that can guide family behavior and dramatize the moral obligations and ends associated with family life by situating them within a coherent and compelling worldview.[28] These ideologies can then motivate individuals to imbue their family roles with heightened significance. The emphasis that religiously rooted familism places on the mother-child bond, for instance, may lead a new mother to accord her maternal role great social and religious import.

Religious institutions can also promote distinctive family-related norms, especially when these norms are associated with an ideology that plays a salient role in the lives of adherents to a particular religious tradition. Thus, the Mormon theological belief that "parents have a sacred duty to rear their children in love and righteousness" and that they "will be held accountable before God" for their parenting is associated with the weekly Family Home Evening, where the family gathers to worship and discuss the teachings of the Church of Jesus Christ of Latter-Day Saints.[29] The effect of religiously produced family-related ideologies and norms on behavior should be particularly strong for individuals who identify with these ideologies and norms and who are integrated into the life of their religious community through regular religious practice.

But even individuals who do not fully accept the family-related culture produced by their religious institutions can be influenced by this culture if they are integrated into the life of their religious community. Religious institutions that are strongly committed to a specific family-related ideology or norm and enjoy substantial religious vitality can exert an especially large measure of social influence on their members to reinforce the benefits of adherence to their family culture, and when necessary can apply formal sanctions to foster normative conformity among active religious adherents who do not necessarily accept the ideology or norm. In such situations, as Ann Swidler has argued, "culture's power" can be "independent of whether or not people believe in it."[30]

The cultural content of particular religious activities, beliefs, and practices, then, can matter for family behavior. Variations in religious strength, the religious logic of practice, and family-related ideologies and norms may be associated with distinctive levels of familial involvement and patterns of familial interaction. Religious institutions that have a substantial measure of religious vitality, distinctive congregational practices and style of religious worship, and a countercultural family worldview are especially likely to have a distinctive effect on the family life of their members. In turn, individuals who identify with the religious and family-related ideologies produced by their religious institution or who are integrated into the life of that institution will probably be more influenced in their family behavior by the cultural content of their religion.

In sum, we can expect religion to have a *generically* pro-social effect on family behavior insofar as most religious institutions enjoy a modicum of vitality, promote social integration, and foster rituals and norms that endow aspects of family life with heightened significance. But we can also expect particular religious institutions to have a *distinctive* effect on family life, for better or worse, depending upon their vitality, religious ethos, and the specific family-related ideologies and norms they promote.

RELIGIOUS PARTICIPATION, IDEOLOGY, AND FATHERHOOD

Religious participation is an indicator of religiosity that may influence paternal behavior in at least five ways. First, the discourse that fathers encounter in churches—from Father's Day sermons to homilies on the Prodigal Son—typically underlines the importance of family ties in general and father-child ties in particular. Similarly, churches legitimate moral norms, such as kindness, that have universal social appeal and consequently may foster family-centered behavior on the part of men. Second, the family-centered ethos and rituals—from baptisms to father-daughter dances—found in religious institutions can endow fatherhood with a sense of transcendent meaning and provide an implicit model of authoritative, active, and affectionate parent-child interaction that influences male familial involvement.

Third, by offering educational programs, worship services, and social activities for families, churches provide regular opportunities for fathers to spend time with their children in activities that are often freighted with religious and moral meaning. Fourth, the family-centered social networks that fathers typically find in religious institutions offer them child-rearing advice and encouragement, opportunities to learn about child-centered activities in the local community, and sanctions against behavior that is viewed as abusive and neglectful.[31] Finally, by erecting a "sacred canopy" over everyday life and over stressful events such as paternal unemployment, religious participation can provide a buffer against challenges that would otherwise harm father-child relations.[32]

For these reasons, we may see a generic religiosity effect in which more religious fathers are more authoritative, active, and expressive with their children. If so, church attendance should be associated with greater paternal involvement; warm, expressive fathering; and a firm disciplinary style because the church supplies cultural tools that promote family-focused behaviors among married men with children. A small body of literature does suggest that religious participation is associated with greater paternal involvement.[33]

But there are reasons to suspect that the specific cultural content and institutional vitality of particular religious institutions matter for the level and style of paternal involvement as well. Thus, we now turn to a consideration of the distinctive cultural messages that conservative and mainline Protestant institutions convey to their adherents regarding fatherhood.

In chapter 2, I explained that conservative Protestant institutions, especially parachurch organizations like Focus on the Family, responded to the dramatic changes in family practice and culture of the 1960s and 1970s by articulating a largely antimodern family ideology that mixed religious, Americanist, and familist themes. At the same time, however, conservative Protestant institutions have been strategic, whether unwittingly or not, in adopting a therapeutic approach to family life that has allowed them to appropriate the quintessentially modern means of a psychological style of language and practice in pursuit of a traditional end: strengthening the quality, functions, and stability of the family. These themes are readily apparent in the discourse related to fatherhood that has been produced by conservative Protestant leaders and family experts.[34]

The conservative Protestant subculture is known for its high view of the Bible and for its stress on having a personal relationship with God. Accordingly, in their discussion of human fatherhood conservative Protestant leaders and family experts have been particularly attentive to the analogical power of biblical symbols of divine fatherhood. For instance, in her book *How to Develop Your Child's Temperament* (1977), Beverly LaHaye, chair of Concerned Women for America, admonishes fathers to remember that they are their children's "first image" of their "Heavenly Father": "He learns of God's love by watching you. He learns of God's mercy and forgiveness by watching you. Be sure you are giving him an honest picture of what he can expect from his own Heavenly Father."[35] Thus, biblical symbols serve as models for the general orientation and specific practices of fatherhood—in this case, love, mercy, and forgiveness. But the conservative Protestant stress on God's sovereignty and his justice is linked to more severe models of fatherhood, as suggested by a passage from Larry Christenson's *The Christian Family* (1970): "A spanking combines the twin aspects of love and fear, and in this it is patterned after our relationship to the Heavenly Father."[36] Conservative Protestant theological assumptions about the nature of God the Father and of Jesus Christ thus give shape to a model of human fatherhood that encompasses, on the one hand, love, abiding concern, and mercy, and on the other, authority, justice, and sufficient severity to engender fear in a child.

What gives this model particular moral power is that conservative Protestant elites suggest that the successful performance of the father role can play an integral role in the securing of a child's salvation. In his own reflections on fatherhood, James Dobson, president of Focus on the Family, wrote, "*my number one responsibility is to evangelize my own children.*"[37]

The conservative Protestant discourse about fatherhood is also shaped by the pervasive strains of Americanism and familism found in this subculture. Many conservative Protestant elites view the sociocultural trends of the last three decades of the twentieth century as manifestations of the social disorder that threatens the health and stability of the family and the American experiment in ordered liberty. Thus, conservative Protestant family experts legitimate assertions of paternal authority by arguing that post-1960s increases in juvenile delinquency, premarital sex, and cultural rebellion were caused by declines in the assertion and acceptance of paternal authority.[38] In their effort to give homage to the sacrosanct character of family life, they also argue that men need to avoid the financial and status temptations associated with excessive work and that fathers should devote more time to their families.[39] They tie their focus on male investment in family life to concerns about family stability, arguing that "the breakdown of the family is directly related to the absence of a man's involvement in his home, especially as a servant leader."[40] The sentimental character of conservative Protestant familism also comes through in the elite discourse regarding fatherhood: for instance, Dobson's books on family living are replete with descriptions of him weeping over his children, professing his "tenderness" for his family, and "speaking from" his "heart."[41]

Conservative Protestant discourse on parenting and fatherhood also draws heavily from therapeutic approaches to family living. In a humanistic vein, family counselors Gary Smalley and John Trent advise parents that they need to give their children "words of encouragement, love, and acceptance" to boost their sense of self-esteem, and they argue that such words of love and encouragement should be offered regardless of a child's behavior.[42] In a behaviorist vein, many of these experts stress the importance of rewarding good behavior with praise and punishing bad behavior with corporal punishment.[43] This therapeutic advice is legitimated by references to the authors' psychological training and knowledge, as well as to parenting studies conducted by researchers at institutions like Harvard, Princeton, Purdue, and UCLA.[44] These therapeutic approaches allow conservative Protestant elites to connect with their audience on terms that are widely comprehensible and that have a high measure of credibility in the society at large. The irony is that many of these experts, including Dobson, present themselves as Christian guides to family living who rely only on the timeless wisdom of the Bible; their extensive use of therapeutic techniques and terminology, however, reveals that in important respects they are quite modern.[45]

How do these general themes translate into specific family behaviors for fathers? First, conservative Protestant family ideology stresses the importance of paternal involvement with and supervision of children. The family experts deride the conventional notion that "quality time" can make up for deficiencies in the quantity of time that parents, including fathers, spend with their children; accordingly, they exhort men to spend as much time as possible with their children. They also stress the father's role in supervising the behavior, choice of friends, and broader social environment of his children.[46] At the same time, many of these elites also present a conservative approach to gender roles that stresses the father's traditional role as the primary breadwinner.[47] Sociologists have often argued that men's commitment to the breadwinner role stands in tension with their extensive family interaction;[48] indeed, there is empirical evidence that gender-role traditionalism is linked to lower levels of one-on-one father-child interaction.[49] If the familist ideology associated with evangelicalism guides the behavior of conservative Protestant men, we should expect to see that they are more involved with their children than unaffiliated men are with theirs. Conversely, if the gender-role traditionalism associated with this subculture does indeed reduce male investments in parenting, it may be the case that conservative Protestant men spend less time with their children than other fathers do.

Second, for the most part, conservative Protestant family ideology is connected to the warm, expressive style of fatherhood that scholars deem important to positive outcomes for children. There are a number of ways that this ideology connects theological, familistic, and therapeutic rationales to the "emotion work" associated with this style of fathering.[50] Popular Christian pastor and writer Charles Swindoll mixes theological and familistic reasoning in his advice to fathers. He urges men to remember that their children have been assigned to them by God and that they should therefore make "domestic love transfers" from God to their children. The sentimental side of conservative Protestant familism is in full view in his advice: "Your boy must be very aware that *you love him* . . . When is the last time you took him in your arms and held him close so no one else could hear, and you whispered to him how happy you are to have him as your son?"[51]

This affirmative style is also advocated on therapeutic grounds. Invoking both humanistic (a "child's need for self-esteem and acceptance")[52] and behaviorist logic (rewarding good behavior with a "positive comment"),[53] conservative Protestant experts exhort fathers to bless their children, to praise them, and to be affectionate toward them. Thus, judging by the prescriptive advice of its family discourse, there appears to be little evidence that conservative Protestantism is pushing men to the kind of remote, stoic, or indifferent emotional style that some scholars have associated with religious conservatism.[54] Indeed, by linking an array of religious, cultural, and therapeutic moral objects to positive parental emotion work, conservative Protestant family ideology probably pushes conservative Protestant men to be more expressive with their children than unaffiliated men are.

However, fathers are not encouraged to be warm and expressive all the time. Although in most circumstances the "framing rules" supplied by conservative Protestant ideology guide the emotion work of these parents in the direction of a warm, expressive style,[55] in situations in which the father deems a child's behavior unwise, immoral, or disobedient, conservative Protestant family experts exhort the father to adopt a traditional approach to discipline largely in keeping with a classical Protestant disciplinary style.[56] It is true that behaviorist thinking colors the conservative Protestant approach to discipline, but theological notions of human sinfulness and divine sovereignty remain paramount.

Because they view children as inherently sinful, these experts view discipline as a positive process that teaches children to develop a respect for divine justice, to learn that there are consequences for misbehavior, and to turn away from sin. Drawing on numerous passages from the Bible (for example, Exod. 21:15, 17; Deut. 21:18–21; and Prov. 13:24, 19:18, 22:15, and 30:17), conservative Protestant commentators argue that parents, especially fathers, need to model the swift and powerful nature of divine justice by taking strong action— up to and including corporal punishment—in response to misdeeds.[57]

Swindoll, for example, relies on Proverbs 13:24 ("He who spares his rod hates his son, but he who loves him is diligent to discipline him" [RSV]) to argue that corporal punishment used "correctly and consistently" can deliver the "soul" of a child from evil.[58]

Conservative Protestant family experts treat children's disobedience with particular concern because they view parental authority as analogous to divine sovereignty, and they believe that obedience to parents prepares a child to obey God as an adult. Dobson explains: "If a little child is taught to disrespect the authority of his parents, systematically from the tender years of childhood—to mock their leadership, to 'sass' them and disobey their instructions, to exercise extreme self-will from the earliest moments of awareness—then it is most unlikely that this same child will turn his face up to God, about twenty years later, and say humbly, 'Here I am, Lord; send me!' "[59] Accordingly, deliberate disobedience is treated as a particularly heinous form of misbehavior and is framed as most worthy of corporal punishment.[60] Given the unique stress on paternal authority in this subculture, one would expect that conservative Protestant fathers are more likely than other fathers to resort to corporal punishment.

It is important to note, however, that conservative Protestant family ideology erects fences around the exercise of paternal discipline, furnishing fathers with framing rules that guide their emotion work and their conduct in disciplinary situations. These fences are justified on theological and therapeutic grounds. First, the conservative Protestant stress on paternal authority is connected to an emphasis on self-control in disciplining children. Second, fathers are exhorted to discipline their children in a respectful spirit, bearing in mind that their sons and daughters are made in the image of God (Ps. 139: 13–16; Gen. 1:26–27) and that abusive discipline hurts children's self-esteem.[61] Conservative Protestant elites link both concerns to prohibitions of negative emotion work, or yelling, which is depicted as emotionally abusive to children and a clear sign that the father has lost control.

Conservative Protestant family experts specifically tell parents not to punish their children in an angry or abusive manner. LaHaye warns her readers to "first get victory over their own anger and hot tempers" before disciplining a child, and she insists that "there are right and wrong spankings. A wrong spanking would be a cruel, sadistic beating that is given in rage."[62] Family experts also invoke behaviorist tenets in advising against yelling. According to these specialists, controlled corporal punishment administered promptly in the face of willful child disobedience is a more effective alternative to yelling. In this therapeutic vein, Dobson claims that "parents often use anger to get action instead of using action to get action. . . . Trying to control children by screaming is as utterly futile as trying to steer a car by honking the horn."[63] In light of the unique religious and therapeutic rationales against yelling presented in conservative Protestant ideology, conservative Protestant fathers probably yell at their children less than other fathers.

In sum, conservative Protestant family ideology draws upon theological, familistic, and therapeutic moral objects to construct a neotraditional model of fatherhood that encompasses extensive paternal involvement, positive emotion work, and a strict, controlled disciplinary style. This model is progressive in its insistence on an active and expressive approach to fatherhood and traditional in its high view of paternal authority and its endorsement of corporal punishment. In keeping with its commitment to the logic of expressive traditionalism, then, conservative Protestantism holds up a model of fathers as soft patriarchs who balance their patriarchal commitment to authority and control with an equally powerful commitment to a newer, softer, more active and expressive style of fatherhood. However, given the gap between fatherhood culture and fatherhood conduct, it remains to be seen whether this model is realized in the conduct of conservative Protestant married men with children. I turn to that question in the next section.

There is considerably less research on family-related culture in mainline Protestantism—in part because since the 1970s mainline churches and institutions have generally not devoted as much symbolic and pastoral attention to family life as have conservative Protestant churches and institutions. Mainline Protestantism also does not have the kind of large, family-oriented parachurch ministries that are closely connected to conservative Protestantism.[64] Accordingly, mainline Protestantism is not likely to address issues related to fatherhood with nearly the frequency or depth that conservative Protestantism does.

Nevertheless, many mainline churches continue to foster a Golden Rule Christianity centered around an ethic of care for family, friends, and community members.[65] This brand of Christianity sidesteps contested moral and sexual matters and does not offer guidance on specific aspects of family living, but it does stress a universal ethic of love that often incorporates familistic messages and images—especially child-centered ones.

A recent survey of members of mainline Presbyterian churches found that almost 80 percent of them had heard a sermon preached on family issues in the past year.[66] Moreover, qualitative research suggests that mainline sermons often depict God as a father who befriends, comforts, and loves his flock in an unconditional fashion. One Presbyterian sermon conveys the general tenor of this sermonic discourse: the minister explained that "the moral" of the parable of the Prodigal Son "is as clear as its outcome. When you have done wrong and you know it, you don't have to come crawling back to God. All you have to do, someone said, is to stop running from Him long enough to let Him reach out and gather you safely in his arms."[67] This discourse on divine fatherhood sends an implicit message to fathers that they should be active and emotionally supportive of their children. It may also be an indication of the explicit message that mainline churches give fathers about their role in the family. While the one study that has been done on mainline family-related sermonic discourse does not mention fathers, it does suggest that parents are called to "reflect the love of Jesus" in their family life.[68] Thus, even though the message about fatherhood that mainline men hear is probably delivered less emphatically and frequently than the message conservative Protestant fathers encounter, we might also expect mainline men to be more involved with their children than unaffiliated men are.

However, mainline Protestantism does not produce a religious or family ideology associated with strong assertions of paternal authority and discipline. Theologically it does not articulate a strong sense of God's sovereignty; nor does it stress God's righteousness in such a way as to suggest that human sin is punished by God. The religious ideology produced by mainline Protestantism generally presents a nonauthoritarian vision of a God who loves persons in an indiscriminate fashion. One Presbyterian pastor's comments turn the thrust of the famous sermon by the eighteenth-century evangelist Jonathan Edwards upside down: "Perhaps all of us can cease to see ourselves as sinners in the hands of an angry God and know that we are children held in the arms of a loving Father—a Father who seeks to throw a party in our honor."[69]

Not surprisingly, this religious ideology is associated with an orientation to parenting that emphasizes the development of autonomy in children. Qualitative research on parenting programs in mainline churches reveals that these programs stress nonauthoritarian, democratic parenting practices.[70] Similar findings have been reported in survey research. In response to a survey of upstate New York clergy, more than 55 percent of mainline clergy reported that they "teach kids to think for themselves," while approximately 40 percent said they "teach kids to trust and obey parents, teachers, and pastors." Remarkably no conservative Protestant clergy who responded to this survey reported that they would teach kids to think for themselves, and more than 90 percent of them said that they teach kids to trust and obey.[71]

Previous research links autonomy-building, nonjudgmental, and affirmative religious and family ideologies like these to markedly lower levels of support for corporal punishment.[72] Thus, mainline fathers should be significantly less likely to use corporal punishment than conservative Protestant fathers. Moreover, given the general trajectory of U.S. attitudes toward parenting for autonomy and away from support for corporal punishment,[73] we should expect to find that mainline fathers do not use corporal punishment any more than unaffiliated fathers do. However, given that parental yelling is not addressed in mainline Protestant parenting discourse, mainline fathers should be no less likely to yell at their children than unaffiliated fathers are. In sum, in keeping with the logic of Golden Rule liberalism, mainline fathering should approximate a new fatherhood style characterized by high levels of involvement and positive affect and should steer clear of the strict, controlled discipline style favored by conservative Protestant fathers.

Finally, the ideological influences on mainline and conservative Protestant fathers should largely be complemented by the religious ethos and institutional vitality characteristic of these two traditions. Since the 1970s, the ethos of conservative Protestantism has become increasingly expressive—marked by charismatic worship; a focus on authentic and intimate relationships with Christ, friends, and family; and a ready reliance on therapeutic language.[74] This expressive ethos probably increases the likelihood that conservative Protestant fathers are warm and affectionate with their children. The ethos in mainline Protestant churches, by contrast, tends to more reserved and less expressive. Mainline churches still have formal, liturgical Sunday worship services, and the expression of faith in mainline Protestant churches is more reticent and impersonal than that found in conservative Protestant churches. This reserved ethos is less likely to foster an expressive parenting style on the part of mainline fathers.

Conservative Protestantism displays more religious vitality than mainline Protestantism. For instance, 50 percent of conservative Protestant married fathers attend church several times a month or more, compared to 39 percent of mainline Protestant married fathers. These differences in religious vitality suggest that conservative Protestant fathers will be more like than their mainline counterparts to be influenced by the family-related ideologies and norms fostered by their churches.

PATERNAL INVOLVEMENT

The 1987–1988 National Survey of Families and Households (NSFH1) and the 1998–1999 Survey of Adults and Youth (SAY) allow us to see how religious affiliation, religious participation, and the distinctive religious and family-related ideologies promoted by mainline and conservative Protestant institutions are associated with the extent and style of paternal involvement of married men with children. My research on paternal involvement is based

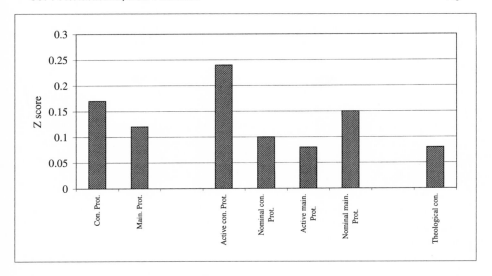

Figure 4.1   Paternal involvement in one-on-one interaction with children

Source: NSFH1 (1987–1988).
Note: The comparison category for all religious affiliation effects is Unaffiliated, and for theological conservatives it is Non–theological conservative.

on NSFH1 interviews with 2,548 married men with school-age children and
SAY interviews with 2,309 married fathers of youth ages ten to eighteen. (For
methodological details see the appendix.) For the first domain, paternal
involvement, I focus specifically on three measures of paternal involvement:
one-on-one interaction (NSFH1), one-on-one activities (SAY), and youth-related
activities (NSFH1). These measures are all dimensions of parental supportiveness, a central characteristic of authoritative parenting.

ONE-ON-ONE INTERACTION

The index of one-on-one interaction, which is derived from NSFH1, is
based on fathers' reports of involvement in four activities with their children:
going on outings, playing at home, having private talks, and helping with reading or homework (see table A4.1 in the appendix for additional details). The
associations between one-on-one interaction and religious affiliation, religious
participation, and theological conservatism are depicted in figure 4.1. Both
conservative and mainline Protestant fathers are more involved in one-on-one
activities than unaffiliated fathers, but results from ordinary least squares

(OLS) regression models indicate that only the conservative Protestant effect is statistically significant. The mean difference between conservative Protestant and unaffiliated fathers is one-sixth of a standard deviation, a modest effect size. (See table A4.2 in the appendix for complete details.)

Statistical analyses comparing active Protestants to unaffiliated fathers reveal that active conservative Protestants, but not active mainliners, are significantly more likely to engage in these one-on-one activities than unaffiliated fathers. As figure 4.1 indicates, the difference between active conservative Protestant fathers (who attend church several times a month or more) and unaffiliated fathers is moderate, representing about one-quarter of a standard deviation. These fathers have more one-on-one interaction with their children than their nominal and mainline counterparts. Surprisingly, nominal mainline Protestants are more involved than their active mainline peers, and they are significantly more involved than unaffiliated fathers; their mean involvement score is almost one-sixth of a standard deviation higher than that of unaffiliated fathers. This pattern of results suggests that conservative Protestant churches foster higher levels of paternal interaction, especially among their active attenders, but mainline churches do not. It also suggests that religious participation does not have a generic effect on this measure of paternal involvement.

Married fathers who identify as theological conservatives—that is, those who take the Bible literally and accord it a high degree of moral authority—are slightly more involved with their children than men who do not, but this effect size is not statistically significant. Nevertheless, adding theological conservatism to my equations reduces the effect of active conservative Protestant affiliation by about one-fifth. Thus theological conservatism explains some of the effect of conservative Protestantism on paternal involvement. Adding familism to the model does not influence the conservative Protestant effect; nor is it significant in its own right. By contrast, as might be expected, gender-role traditionalism has a negative effect on paternal involvement. Moreover, once gender-role traditionalism is controlled for, the positive effect of theological conservatism increases to statistical significance. All of this suggests that conservative Protestant fathers, especially the most theologically conservative ones, would be slightly more involved than they already are were it not for their gender-role traditionalism.

ONE-ON-ONE ACTIVITIES

The SAY poses a series of questions about the one-on-one activities respondents engage in with their children. Married fathers were asked how often they helped their children with homework and how often they attended social events, did volunteer work, played sports or games, and read or discussed books with their children. I relied on these reports of involvement to create an index of paternal involvement in one-on-one activities (see table A4.1 in the appendix for details).

The measure of religion in SAY is different from that in NSFH. Whereas NSFH determines religious identity on the basis of denominational affiliation (e.g., Southern Baptists are coded as conservative Protestants and Methodists are coded as mainline Protestants), SAY determines religious identity by self-identification. Specifically, in SAY, Protestants were asked if they were fundamentalist, evangelical, mainline, liberal, or "other" Protestants. Self-identified fundamentalists and evangelicals are coded as conservative Protestants and self-identified mainline and liberal Protestants are coded as mainliners. Compared to the NSFH religious classification scheme, that of SAY provides a better estimate of where respondents situate themselves religiously; however, it does not allow us to determine whether respondents attend mainline or conservative Protestant churches. For instance, a father who self-identified as evangelical and attended a mainline Protestant church would be classified as a conservative Protestant in SAY. Thus, SAY results are more indicative of a father's religious ideology than his religious affiliation.

My statistical analyses of the SAY data indicate that married men with children who identify as conservative Protestants are significantly more involved with their children than men who indicate that they have no religious identity A mainline Protestant identity is not associated with statistically higher levels of one-on-one engagement. Self-identified conservative Protestant fathers are almost one-fifth of a standard deviation more involved than unaffiliated fathers—a modest effect size. (See table A4.3 in the appendix.)

For this data set, however, frequent religious attendance is associated with higher levels of paternal involvement in one-on-one activities for both conservative and mainline Protestant married men. Active Protestant fathers are more involved with their children compared to both unaffiliated fathers and than their nominal Protestant peers. Specifically, both groups of active Protestant fathers have involvement scores that are about one-fourth of a standard deviation higher than that of unaffiliated dads. These are moderate effect sizes, but standardized coefficient tests reveal that these religious effects surpass those of region, employment, and income and are comparable to those of race, ethnicity, and education. In other words, active religious participation is one of the more important sociocultural sources of paternal involvement studied in SAY.

For this outcome, then, religious participation does have a generic effect on paternal involvement in one-on-one activities. Indeed, it would seem that one of the reasons a conservative Protestant identity but not a mainline Protestant identity is associated with higher levels of paternal involvement in one-on-one activities is that conservative Protestant fathers attend church more often than do mainline fathers. If fathers who identified as mainline Protestants were as likely to attend church as those who identified as conservative Protestants, the SAY data suggests that mainline fathers would be almost as involved as their conservative Protestant counterparts. Nonetheless, the SAY results regarding one-on-one involvement parallel the NSFH1 findings in one respect: the conservative Protestant effects on paternal involvement in both data sets are consistently larger than the mainline Protestant effects, even though the differentials are not statistically significant.

YOUTH-RELATED ACTIVITIES

The final measure of paternal involvement is father involvement in youth-related activities. Fathers were asked how many hours they spent in an average week as a participant, advisor, coach, or leader in school activities, community youth groups such as scouting programs, sports activities, and religious youth groups. I summed the responses to these four items to measure weekly paternal involvement in youth-related activities (see table A4.1 in the appendix for more details).

Figure 4.2, which is based on Tobit regression models, indicates that conservative Protestant fathers spend about 2.0 hours and mainline fathers about 1.3 hours more per week in youth-related activities than unaffiliated fathers. Only the conservative Protestant effect is statistically significant. The figures for active Protestant fathers are higher: 3.8 more hours and 2.1 more hours than unaffiliated fathers for conservative Protestant and mainline men, respectively. Over the course of a year, the average active conservative Protestant father will spend approximately 197 more hours in youth-related activities than the average unaffiliated father; the average active mainline Protestant father will spend about 109 more hours in such activities than the average unaffiliated father. Both of these effects are statistically significant. Active conservative and mainline Protestant fathers are also significantly more involved in youth-related activities than their nominal Protestant peers. (See table A4.4 in the appendix.)

For this outcome, none of the ideological factors—theological conservatism, familism, or gender-role traditionalism—exert an independent influence on involvement in youth-related activities; nor do they mediate the effect of an active

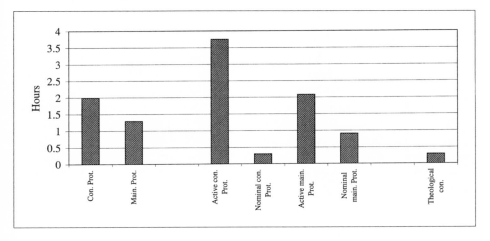

Figure 4.2   Paternal involvement in youth-related activities

Source: NSFH1 (1987–1988).
Note: The comparison category for religious affiliation is Unaffiliated, and for theological conservatives it is Non–theological conservative.

religious affiliation. Given the consistent effect of an active religious affiliation,
these results suggest that the link between religion and paternal involvement in
youth-related activities is in part a consequence of the family-oriented strategy
associated with generic religiosity.[75] Still, my findings indicate that conservative
Protestant fathers are consistently the most involved. The distinctive emphasis
that conservative Protestant churches place on family life, their family-centered
ethos, and the numerous opportunities they provide for fathers to get involved
in the religious formation of youth probably account for the results.

    This review of the links between religion, ideology, and paternal involve-
ment in three different areas suggests four conclusions. First, we have some
evidence that religious participation in both mainline and conservative Protestant congregations is linked to higher levels of paternal involvement with
school-age children. Thus, by offering common ethical advice, a religious nomos, access to family-focused networks of advice and support, and a family-
centered ethos, congregations of various religiocultural ideological stripes have
a generic influence on paternal involvement. Second, only conservative Protestantism is consistently associated with higher rates of involvement. Given that
attendance appears to be more salient than ideology in accounting for the conservative Protestant effect, the family-centered ethos and the high levels of
religious vitality found in this subculture probably account for the uniformly

positive influence of conservative Protestantism on paternal involvement. Third, the relationship between religion and the amount of paternal involvement is not mediated or confounded in any significant way by the ideologies of theological conservatism, familism, and gender-role traditionalism. Thus, contrary to the assertions of some scholars, the gender-role traditionalism associated with conservative Protestantism is not consistently linked to lower levels of paternal involvement. In sum, religiously affiliated fathers—especially conservative Protestant fathers—are more involved with their children than unaffiliated fathers, and the gender-role traditionalism of some religious fathers does not much dampen their commitment to spending time with their children.

PATERNAL STYLE

What role, if any, do religion and ideology play in shaping the style of fathers' interaction with their children? I turn first to three dimensions of father-child interaction—praise and hugging, corporal punishment, and yelling—then to three measures of paternal control—setting rules for television watching, knowing children's whereabouts, and establishing a regular bedtime. All of these measures except for the bedtime one are derived from NSFH1.

PRAISING AND HUGGING

The NSFH1 survey asked respondents how often they praised their school-age children and how often they hugged them. Because the outcome was skewed in the direction of high reports of praise and affection, these two measures were combined into one binary measure of positive emotion work. Fathers who indicated that they both praise their children "very often" and hug them "very often" were coded as highly expressive, and those who did not consistently report such high levels of praise and affection were coded as less expressive.

Figure 4.3 shows the association between paternal praise and affection and religious affiliation, religious participation, theological conservatism. To construct the figure, I calculated the predicted values from logistic regression models that I adjusted for a range of controls (see table A4.5 in the appendix for the complete models). My findings indicate that conservative and mainline Protestant married men with children are significantly more likely than their unaffiliated counterparts to praise and hug their children very often. Specifically, after adjusting for control variables, 44 percent of conservative Protestant

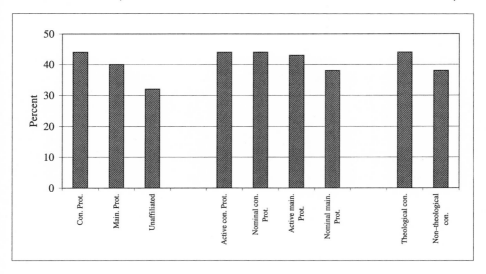

Figure 4.3   Fathers who praise and hug their children very often

Source: NSFH1 (1987–1988).

fathers and 40 percent of mainline fathers, compared to 32 percent of unaffiliated fathers, praise and hug their children very often.

Turning to patterns based on church attendance, we see that active mainline Protestant fathers are almost as affectionate as active conservative Protestant fathers. My findings indicate that 44 percent of active conservative Protestant fathers and 43 percent of active mainline Protestant fathers praise and
hug their children very often. Nominal conservative Protestant fathers are as
expressive as their active peers, while nominal mainline fathers are less expressive than their active peers, though the difference between the latter two
groups is not statistically significant. This pattern suggests that generic religiosity is associated with higher levels of paternal positive emotion work.

Married fathers who are theologically conservative are more likely to
praise and hug their children very often than fathers who are not: the figures
for these two groups are 44 percent and 38 percent, respectively. Theological
conservatism accounts for almost one-third of the relationship between active
conservative Protestantism and paternal expressiveness and for one-sixth of
the relationship between active mainline Protestantism and paternal expressiveness; it also renders both of these factors nonsignificant. These results

suggest that the distinctive religious ideology promoted by conservative Protestant institutions fosters higher levels of paternal expressiveness, accounting for a substantial portion of the conservative Protestant effect and a modest portion of the mainline Protestant effect.

Additional analyses indicate that familism is strongly associated with higher levels of paternal expressiveness and gender-role traditionalism is strongly associated with lower levels of paternal expressiveness. The most familistic fathers are 135 percent more likely than the least familistic fathers to praise and hug their children very often. The fathers who are the most traditional when it comes to gender attitudes are 70 percent less likely than the most egalitarian fathers to be this expressive. Familism accounts for one-third of the effect of theological conservatism on paternal involvement, rendering theological conservatism nonsignificant. This suggests that theologically conservative fathers are more expressive in part because they hold family-centered beliefs that motivate them to praise and hug their children. Gender-role traditionalism, however, has only a negligible effect on the relationship between theological conservatism and paternal expressiveness.

The high levels of church attendance, theological conservatism, and familism associated with the conservative Protestant subculture all help to account for the fact that these fathers consistently score the highest when it comes to positive emotion work and that the gender-role traditionalism found in this subculture does not dampen their emotionally supportive paternal behavior. Mainline Protestant fathers are also more likely than unaffiliated fathers to praise and hug their children. This can be attributed in large part to church attendance, but also to the fact that a substantial minority of active mainline fathers identify with a theologically conservative and familistic worldview.

CORPORAL PUNISHMENT

In the NSFH1, fathers were asked how often they "spank or slap" their children, with responses ranging from never to very often (see table A4.1 in the appendix for details). Figure 4.4 indicates that conservative Protestant fathers are significantly more likely than unaffiliated fathers to resort to corporal punishment. Surprisingly, they also indicate that mainline fathers are significantly more likely to spank or slap their children than are their unaffiliated counterparts. On this measure conservative Protestant fathers score one-fifth of a standard deviation higher than unaffiliated fathers, and mainline fathers one-sixth of a standard deviation higher, indicating modest effect sizes.

For the use of corporal punishment, conservative Protestant fathers who

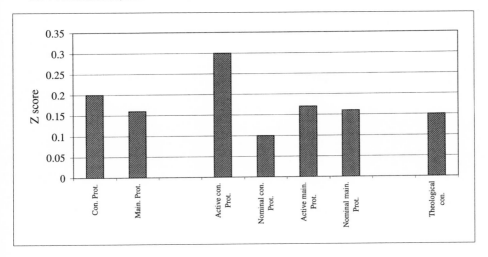

Figure 4.4   Paternal use of corporal punishment

Source: NSFH1 (1987–1988).
Note: The comparison category for all religious affiliation effects is Unaffiliated, and for theological conservatives it is Non–theological conservative.

attend church several times a month score almost one-third of a standard deviation higher than unaffiliated fathers, which is a moderate effect size. They are also significantly more likely to spank their children than nominal conservative Protestant fathers. Frequency of church attendance does not seem to make much difference for mainline Protestant levels of corporal punishment; both active and nominal mainline Protestant fathers are about one-sixth of a standard deviation higher than unaffiliated fathers on this measure (see table A4.6 in the appendix for details). Thus, religious participation does not have a generic effect on rates of corporal punishment; rather the effect of religious participation depends on the Protestant tradition which the father is identified. Though the effect size is moderate, standardized coefficient tests reveal that an active conservative Protestant affiliation surpasses education, income, race, ethnicity, and region in its predictive power for this outcome.

   Theologically conservative fathers are also more likely to spank their children than are theological liberals and moderates. The effect size here is modest, but when I add theological conservatism to the regression models, it reduces the effect of an active conservative Protestant affiliation by almost one-third and renders the active mainline Protestant coefficient statistically insignificant. Familism and gender-role traditionalism do not influence the likelihood that a father will use corporal punishment; nor do they affect the relationship between the various religious factors and such punishment. Thus one of the reasons that active Protestant fathers are more likely to spank their children is that they identify with a religious ideology that encourages fathers to respond to child misbehavior with corporal punishment.

These results suggest that conservative Protestantism plays an important role in fostering the use of corporal punishment among married fathers in the United States. It provides a traditional theological rationale for corporal punishment (the need for parents to curb children's sinfulness), a cultural rationale (most parents are overly permissive), and a congregational context in which this practice is legitimized.

YELLING

The NSFH1 survey also asked married men with school-age children to report how often they yell at their children (for more information, see table A4.1 in the appendix). The data reveal that there are no statistically significant differences between unaffiliated fathers and conservative Protestant fathers or between unaffiliated fathers and mainline Protestant fathers. However, conservative Protestant fathers are less likely to yell at their children than mainline Protestant fathers. (See table A4.7 in the appendix for complete details.)

Additional regression analyses comparing frequently attending mainline and conservative Protestant fathers to their infrequently attending counterparts indicate that both groups of active churchgoers are less likely to yell at their children than their nominal mainline Protestant peers. Active conservative Protestant fathers are about one-fourth of a standard deviation less likely and active mainline Protestant fathers are about one-fifth of a standard deviation less likely to yell than nominal mainline Protestant fathers. Neither group of active Protestant fathers differs from nominal conservative Protestant fathers on this measure. These results suggest that religious participation is associated with somewhat lower levels of yelling, especially among active conservative Protestants.

Models incorporating theological conservatism indicate that although theologically conservative fathers are less likely to yell at their children, the effect is not significant. However, theological conservatism does reduce the effects of frequent church attendance by about one-third. Familism and gender-role traditionalism do not influence paternal yelling. Thus, consistent with the literature review, we have modest evidence that conservative Protestantism encourages fathers to approach disciplinary situations in a spirit of self-control that leads them to reject yelling as an appropriate parental behavior.

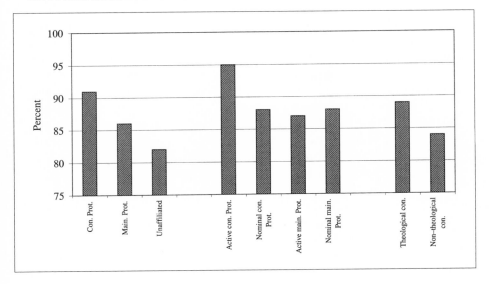

Figure 4.5 Fathers who supervise their children's television viewing

Source: NSFH1 (1987–1988).

TELEVISION RULES

Parental control encompasses a range of strategies, from setting rules that guide children's behavior to supervising their activities in and outside the home. One indicator of parental control from the NSFH1 survey is whether or not parents set rules for their children's television watching. Respondents were asked whether they restrict the amount of television their children watch; they were also asked if they restrict the types of program their children view. Married men with school-age children who answered in the affirmative to either of these questions were coded as television rule-setters (see table A4.1 in the appendix for details).

Figure 4.5, which is based on predicted values derived from logistic regression equations that include a range of sociodemographic controls, indicates that conservative and mainline Protestant fathers are more likely than unaffiliated fathers to report that they have rules governing their children's use of television. Specifically, 91 percent of conservative Protestant fathers, 86 percent of mainline fathers, and 82 percent of unaffiliated fathers report having such rules. However, the differences between these groups of fathers is statistically significant only for conservative Protestant men.

Similar patterns obtain regarding religious participation and theological conservatism. Active conservative Protestants are significantly more likely to set television rules than active mainline Protestant fathers, with 95 percent of active conservative Protestant fathers and only 87 percent of active mainline Protestant fathers setting such rules. Active conservative Protestants are also significantly more likely to set television rules than their nominal and unaffiliated peers. Indeed, logistic regression models indicate that active conservative Protestant affiliation surpasses a range of sociodemographic factors—including region, race, family structure, education, and income—in its influence on television rule setting. Fathers who indicate that they are theologically conservative are also more likely to set such rules, compared to fathers who are not. Adding theological conservatism to the logistic regression models reduces the effect of active conservative Protestantism by almost one-fifth. This indicates that one of the reasons active conservative Protestant fathers are more likely to set television rules for their children is that they identify with the theologically conservative worldview—and its attendant beliefs about human sinfulness and parental authority—fostered by conservative Protestant institutions. The measures of familism and gender-role traditionalism are not significantly associated with the likelihood that a father sets rules for his children's television viewing, although familism does account for about one-sixth of the relationship between theological conservatism and television rule setting. (See table A4.8 in the appendix for details.)

Thus, it appears that the family-centered conservative Protestant congregational culture, as reflected by the distinctive effect of active religious participation for this group, and the theologically conservative ideology produced and legitimated by evangelical and fundamentalist institutions both help to account for the high levels of paternal rule setting regarding television among conservative Protestants. These results suggest that the classical Protestant emphasis on patriarchal authority, combined with contemporary concern about protecting children from at least some elements of the popular culture, leads to higher levels of paternal control when it comes to monitoring children's television viewing.

CHILDREN'S WHEREABOUTS

Similar patterns are apparent when we look at the relationship between religion and ideology and paternal supervision. The NSFH1 survey asked parents if their children are supposed to let them know where they are at all times when away from home (see table A4.1 in the appendix). When

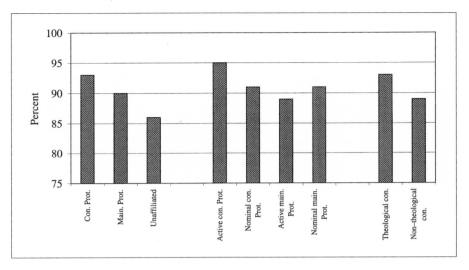

Figure 4.6 Fathers who know their children's whereabouts

Source: NSFH1 (1987–1988).

probabilities are adjusted for all controls, both conservative Protestant and mainline fathers are more likely to know their children's whereabouts than unaffiliated fathers, though only the effect of conservative Protestantism is statistically significant (see table A4.9 in the appendix for complete details). Specifically, 93 percent of conservative Protestant fathers indicated that their children are supposed to let them know their whereabouts at all times, compared to 90 percent of mainline fathers and 86 percent of unaffiliated fathers (see figure 4.6).

Models that break out the effect of religious affiliation by frequency of church attendance indicate that active conservative Protestants are significantly more likely to expect their children to inform them of their whereabouts than their unaffiliated counterparts; their level of supervision also surpasses that of all other groups of Protestant fathers, none of whom are significantly more likely than unaffiliated fathers to attend to their children's whereabouts. Figure 4.6 shows that 95 percent of active conservative Protestant fathers always know their child's whereabouts, compared to 89 percent of active mainline Protestant fathers. Thus, religious participation does not have a generic effect on paternal supervision; only conservative Protestant fathers who regularly attend church are exceptionally likely to stay abreast of their children's whereabouts. Logistic regression models indicate that the effect size of an active conservative

Protestant affiliation surpasses that of a range of other sociodemographic factors, such as race, education, income, and family structure.

Fathers who are theologically conservative are also significantly more likely to supervise their children closely than fathers who are not. Specifically, 93 percent of theologically conservative fathers, compared to 89 percent of fathers who are not theologically conservative, expect to know their children's whereabouts at all times. Furthermore, theological conservatism explains about one-fifth of the association between an active conservative Protestant affiliation and paternal supervision. Familism and gender-role traditionalism are not significantly related to paternal supervision, but familism does account for about one-sixth of the relationship between theological conservatism and paternal supervision.

Taken together, these results suggest, once again, that the congregational environment and theologically conservative ideology fostered by conservative Protestant institutions promote patriarchal authority, manifested here by particularly high levels of interest among conservative Protestant fathers in the whereabouts of their children.

REGULAR BEDTIME

The final indicator of paternal control comes from the Survey of Adults and Youth, which asked parents of youth age ten to eighteen if their children have a regular bedtime. The data indicate that conservative Protestant, but not mainline Protestant, fathers are 65 percent more likely than unaffiliated fathers to report that their children have a regular bedtime (see table A4.10 in the appendix for details). (Recall that in SAY religion is measured by self-identification rather than by denominational affiliation.)

Models that focus ons religious identity and religious participation reveal that active conservative Protestant fathers are 125 percent more likely than unaffiliated fathers to have a regular bedtime for their children. They are also significantly more likely than all of the other groups of Protestant fathers to set a regular bedtime (probably in concert with their wives). Thus, paternal religious participation does not appear to be generically related to the setting of children's bedtimes. The effect of active conservative Protestantism on this measure is large and surpasses that of other sociodemographic factors, including race, region, education, income, and family structure. Thus, the SAY results parallel those for paternal control found in NSFH1, lending further credence to the notion that the conservative Protestant subculture is particularly dedicated to encouraging parental control among its fathers (and mothers).

Collectively these results indicate that the level of paternal control is shaped more by the distinctive culture associated with conservative Protestantism than by the generic effects of religious participation. Conservative Protestant fathers have a distinctive approach to discipline that encompasses high levels of corporal punishment, somewhat lower levels of yelling, and high levels of parental control. A theological commitment to parental authority; a strong desire to cultivate an intense, wholesome family life; and a congregational context that supports a strict parenting regime all help explain why conservative Protestant married fathers are particularly likely to adopt a patriarchal approach to discipline. But the findings also indicate that conservative Protestant patriarchy is softened by these fathers' propensity to praise and hug their children and to spend substantial time with them. Their theological conservatism and their familism apparently motivate these fathers to be unusually expressive with their children in nondisciplinary settings.

Mainline Protestant married fathers of school-age children are also more likely than unaffiliated fathers to praise and hug their children, but not as much as conservative Protestant men are. Among mainline Protestants, the fathers who attend church frequently are most likely to praise their children, in part because many of them identify with the theologically conservative and familist ideologies that are associated with higher levels of positive emotion work on the part of fathers. Somewhat surprisingly, given the official commitment of their clergy to an ethic of childhood autonomy and parental support, mainline Protestant fathers are somewhat more likely than unaffiliated men to spank their children. Here, the lingering effects of the classical Protestant commitment to parental authority and strict discipline hold on despite official rhetoric to the contrary.

CONCLUSION

In this chapter I have posed three central questions: What role, if any, does religion play in pushing men toward a new-fatherhood approach characterized by active involvement and positive emotion work? Are religious effects on fathers tradition-specific or generic? And do conservative Protestant fathers exhibit an abusive and authoritarian parenting style?

With respect to the first question, I find that both mainline and conservative Protestant fathers come closer than unaffiliated fathers to approximating the new-fatherhood ideal celebrated in society at large. Both groups of fathers are more involved with their children than unaffiliated men, although conservative Protestants consistently score the highest on all three measures of involvement, as they do on the three measures of parental control. My findings also indicate that mainline and conservative Protestant fathers are significantly more likely than unaffiliated fathers to be emotionally supportive of their children. Thus, despite cleavages between the family-related ideologies produced by mainline and conservative Protestant institutions, married men with children who are affiliated with both of these traditions are more likely to be active and expressive fathers than unaffiliated men.

Religious participation has generic effects on some aspects of men's parenting behaviors: it is generically associated with higher levels of praise and affection, more one-on-one interaction and involvement in youth-related activities, and lower levels of paternal yelling. These findings suggest that the kinds of social and cultural influences men encounter in churches—advice and support from family-oriented social networks, a religious nomos that makes sense of stressful events, and rituals that sacralize family relations—encourage child-centered behavior. These generic effects are also probably a consequence of the fact that supportive fathering behavior receives widespread normative support in society at large, support that is reinforced by these religious traditions. In any case, the role that church attendance plays in structuring supportive fatherhood practices lends some support to the claims made in much of the literature on religion and the family that generic religiosity is more important than the unique cultural influences associated with particular religious traditions.[76]

Of course, the direction of causality could run the opposite way: that is, it may be that fathers who are more committed to a family-focused lifestyle are more likely to believe that church attendance is important for their families. A number of scholars have pointed out this causal reciprocity.[77] It could be that there is a conventional habitus that encompasses family-oriented living, civic engagement, and church attendance and that men who have grown up within this habitus are more likely to reproduce it in their adult life. Indeed, there is a good deal of historical evidence that supports the notion that such a habitus reached its zenith in the 1950s and continues to shape family practices to this day.[78] However, since neither NSFH nor SAY supplies detailed longitudinal data on the activities of fathers' families of origin, I am unable to evaluate this hypothesis.

Although in some ways the relationship between religion and fatherhood appears to be generic, my findings also indicate that the relationship is on some points tradition-specific. In particular, the distinctive family-related culture produced and legitimated by conservative Protestant institutions is associated with a unique approach to discipline. This disciplinary strategy has garnered a great deal of popular and scholarly criticism as one element of an authoritarian or abusive approach to parenting. Consistent with earlier research, my findings do indicate that conservative Protestant fathers are more likely to report using corporal punishment.[79] However, an authoritarian or abusive approach to parenting is also characterized by low levels of parental support and high levels of negative emotion, as indicated, for instance, by frequent yelling, and my findings show that conservative Protestant fathers are more likely to praise and hug their children and less likely to yell at them than are mainline Protestant and unaffiliated fathers.

Conservative Protestant fathers' neotraditional parenting style seems to be closer to the authoritative style—characterized by moderately high levels of parental control and high levels of parental supportiveness—that has been linked to positive outcomes among children and adolescents.[80] In any case, the accusations about authoritarian and abusive parenting by conservative Protestants appear overdrawn. The findings paint a more complex portrait of conservative Protestant fathering that reveals a hybrid of strict, puritanical and progressive, child-centered approaches to child rearing—all in keeping with the logic of expressive traditionalism guiding this subculture.

Ideology mediates some of the effects of active religious affiliation on fathering—especially on the style of paternal interaction. Theological conservatism, which is a significant predictor of paternal affection, the use of corporal punishment, and the level of paternal control in its own right, reduces the effect of an active religious affiliation, especially a conservative Protestant one. Familism is also a significant predictor of fathers' positive emotion work with their children, mediating the effect of theological conservatism on this outcome and on the level of parental control. This suggests that familism's emphasis on the sentimental and sacred character of family life translates into both higher levels of emotionally supportive behavior and more supervision on the part of fathers. Although gender-role traditionalism is associated with lower levels of paternal involvement and expressiveness, it does not much influence the relationship between religion and fatherhood.

Why is it that tradition-specific religious factors influence one domain of fathering—the style of paternal engagement—more than another domain of fathering—the amount of paternal engagement? Perhaps this is because paternal involvement receives almost uniform normative support from society while the strict parenting style championed by conservative Protestant institutions is not widely popular. Thus, men who attend any kind of major religious institution receive cultural and social support for heightened levels of involvement but not necessarily for a particular approach to disciplining and otherwise interacting with their children. It would seem that men adjust the style of their fathering behavior according to the extent to which they identify with the ideologies of familism, theological conservatism, and, to a lesser extent, gender-role traditionalism. Thus, from a theoretical perspective, the findings suggest that religious traditions can have a distinctive effect on the family behaviors of their adherents when they endorse norms that run counter to societal conventions.

It is important to note that while the magnitude of the difference between their parenting style and that of mainline fathers varies, conservative Protestant fathers are consistently the most involved, expressive, and controlling fathers in this study. The religious vitality and family-centered ethos found in the conservative Protestant subculture helps to explain these men's commitment to fathering: the frequency of their religious participation is associated with every outcome discussed in this chapter, and this is not so for mainliners.

How might these associations between religion, ideology, and fathering be significant for children's well-being? The literature on fathering indicates that an active and expressive style of paternal engagement is positively associated with a range of beneficial outcomes for children.[81] Accordingly, religious affiliation, regular church attendance, and familism may be indirectly linked to positive outcomes as well. These positive outcomes may be mitigated for conservative Protestant children, who are more likely to experience corporal punishment, which research on child well-being links to social and psychological problems.[82] On other hand, a number of studies indicate that the negative outcomes associated with corporal punishment do not obtain when parents balance spanking with higher levels of parental support,[83] and my findings show that conservative Protestant children do experience higher levels of involvement and positive affect from their fathers. In all likelihood, then, the distinctively neotraditional approach to parenting that characterizes conservative Protestant fathering is associated with some unique child outcomes. Perhaps conservative Protestant children, for instance, are more obedient but less creative than children raised in other contexts.

Strikingly, this study and previous studies have not documented a consistent effect on paternal involvement for gender-role ideology,[84] which is the prime cultural factor that fatherhood research has focused on up to this point. In all likelihood, the institutional power that religious congregations can bring to bear on their members is one reason religious participation and ideology appear to be more powerful predictors of paternal involvement than gender-role ideology does. Another irony is that religious institutions with markedly different family and gender ideologies seem to be showing some success in closing the gap between new-fatherhood culture and conduct.[85]

Both mainline and conservative Protestant fathers are more likely than unaffiliated men to embody the new fatherhood style Frank Furstenberg attributes to "Good Dads," but this appellation does not adequately describe the conservative Protestant fathers studied in this chapter.[86] While conservative Protestant fathers have adopted many attributes of the new man, they have also retained a more puritanical emphasis on authority and strict discipline, a style that allows them both to signal their distinctive sense of identity and to remain faithful to their religious ideology. Evangelical and fundamentalist men signal their disagreement with wider parenting norms, stem the tide of cultural decay, and teach their children the importance of obeying divinely instituted authority by expecting obedience from their children, spanking them when they misbehave, and monitoring their friends and television viewing. Accordingly, conservative Protestant married men with children might better be described as soft patriarchs who balance their traditional, authority-minded approach to parenting with a large measure of involvement and affection.

Conservative Protestant men's active and expressive approach to fathering would seem to be largely a consequence of the family-focused norms and ethos found in conservative Protestant institutions. This approach must also be seen, however, as a response to the dramatic socioeconomic mobility of evangelicals and fundamentalists and the changing status of conservative Protestant women since 1970. This mobility; the changes needs of wives, who are now more likely to work outside the home; and the family focus in conservative Protestantism have positioned evangelical and fundamentalist men to be as supportive of their children as their better-educated and generally more progressive mainline peers. Thus, despite the ideological and disciplinary differences that separate them, the soft patriarchs and the new fathers who hail, respectively, from conservative and mainline Protestantism have both taken the ideologies and cultural tools offered by their religious institutions to forge an active and expressive style of fathering.

CHAPTER FIVE

DOMESTIC RITES AND ENCHANTED RELATIONS: RELIGION, IDEOLOGY, AND HOUSEHOLD LABOR

> Even the most trivial transactions of everyday life may come to be imbued with profound significance.
>
> —Peter Berger and Thomas Luckmann, *The Social Construction of Reality*

> Emotion work is often all that stands between the stalled revolution on the one hand, and broken marriages on the other.
>
> —Arlie Hochschild, *The Second Shift*

HOUSEHOLD LABOR is about taking care of the basic necessities of everyday life—from cooking dinner to taking out the trash. But it is also about more than this production and consumption of household goods and services. Especially when it is situated in the institution of the family, household labor is about the production and consumption of cultural meaning. The practices associated with domestic labor—from husbands cleaning toilets to wives making apple pie from scratch—have ritual content. They send important signals to the individuals themselves, to their family members, and to their communities about the "moral order" of family life: the ideals that guide the relations between family members and the ends the family seeks to realize.[1]

In the United States, household labor has been connected in three ways to the bourgeois moral order that has shaped American families, to varying degrees, since the nineteenth century. First, the *division* of household labor between men and women is integral to one component of moral order, the "production of gender."[2] Gender is important to the order insofar as it structures the spousal and parental practices of men and women within the institution of the family.[3] The emotional and physical *attention* given to household labor sends important signals about another dimension of moral order, the extent to which the family conforms to the ideology of familism. This ideology grew out of the sacralization of family life that took hold in the nineteenth century, especially among the middle and upper classes; it is organized around a family-centered ethic of care and obligation that is explicitly opposed to the selfishness associated with the market and the public sphere more generally.[4] Finally, *norms* governing the reciprocal exchange of household labor and gratitude between a wife and a husband—an integral part of what Arlie Hochschild calls the "economy of gratitude"[5]—can play a central role in cementing the marital relationship and in legitimating the moral order itself, especially when families identify with the ideology of familism.

This bourgeois order has been challenged by the revolutionary shifts in the social and cultural status of women. The women's movement and the steady rise in women's paid employment since World War II have dramatically undercut the social and cultural bases of the separate spheres model of family life, which reached its apogee in the 1950s. The labor-force participation of mothers with children under age six went from 44 percent in 1970 to 68 percent in 1990; this surge means, among other things, that women now have less time to devote to domestic tasks and caregiving.[6] This employment shift, along with feminism, has occasioned a marked cultural turn toward gender-role egalitarianism.[7] In the 1970s almost 70 percent of Americans believed that men should be the primary breadwinners and women should be the primary homemakers; less than 40 percent held that view in the 1990s.[8]

Nevertheless, a stable moral order organized around more egalitarian new-family ideals has not yet emerged to replace the old order, largely because men's family practices have not shifted enough to match the changes brought by women's new role in the labor force.[9] One of the most important dimensions of what Hochschild calls the "stalled revolution" at home is that men have not increased their household labor to keep pace with women's increased participation in the labor force.[10] Currently, married men with children perform approximately one-third of the housework completed by the couple.[11] This means that married men with children are doing about half the amount of household labor their wives do.

This gendered asymmetry in the organization of household labor is important for a number of reasons. First, many women end up being burdened with a "second shift": they come home from their paid jobs and put in the equivalent of another work shift maintaining the home and caring for the children. Second, a large minority of married women think their household labor is unappreciated or unfair, which has significant consequences for their emotional well-being, and for marital quality and stability.[12] Finally, this asymmetry contributes to gender inequality both within the family and society at large: children reared in asymmetrical homes are more likely to internalize traditional gender-role orientations; because of their housework married women are not likely to pursue paid employment as vigorously as their husbands; sex segregation in the labor force is reinforced as employers tend to segregate women in lower-status and lower-paying jobs because of their family responsibilities; and women have less power in their marriages because their greater investment in household labor reduces their comparative earnings—a key source of marital power.[13]

This asymmetry in the home is perplexing because cultural understandings of manhood, as well as most men's attitudes, have tracked in a consistently egalitarian direction in the last three decades.[14] One of the reasons men's practices have not kept pace with their avowed egalitarianism may be that their participation in other institutions—from their place of employment to their church—encourages them either to resist investing themselves in household labor or to value the strongly gendered division of labor associated with the traditional family order. Given the long-standing ties between religion and the bourgeois family order,[15] it is possible that religious institutions push men away from active participation in household labor, even though they clearly do not push men away from being involved fathers. The housework gap between men and women may also be a consequence of some women's commitment to religious or familistic ideologies that valorize domesticity, motivating them to do more housework than other women. These possibilities are especially plausible in light of religion's long-standing legitimation of familism and traditional gender roles, a tradition that continues to be championed in much of the conservative Protestant world. On the other hand, mainline Protestant churches have moved in a decisively egalitarian direction in recent years, relying upon moral suasion and programmatic change to elevate the status of women. Thus, it is also possible that some religious institutions are pushing men in the direction of greater involvement in domestic labor.

In an effort to determine the role that religious institutions, as well as the family and gender ideologies they produce and legitimate, play in influencing men's involvement in housework, I examine the statistical links between religion, ideology, and household labor among unaffiliated and Protestant married men with children. Moreover, because the marital economy of gratitude has become a crucial determinant of marital happiness and stability in the midst of the stalled revolution, I also examine the links between religion, ideology, and men's expressed appreciation of their wives' household labor. I thereby paint a portrait of the role that religion and ideology play in structuring the practical and emotional work men do regarding household labor.

REVISITING STANDARD ACCOUNTS OF THE STALLED REVOLUTION

Despite the close ties between household labor and the moral order associated with the family, the sociological literature on domestic work—especially the literature on male contributions to it—has generally offered social-structural or undertheorized cultural accounts of the determinants of and the expressions of gratitude for such labor. Structural accounts of household labor generally focus on three microstructural determinants: (1) time availability, that is, how labor force demands on time influence availability for household labor;[16] (2) relative resources, or the influence of marital differences in income, education, and other sources of social status (occupation, looks, and so on);[17] and (3) how practical competencies regarding work, marriage, and child rearing structure the family orientations and labor patterns of men and women.[18] These micro-level explanations are then linked to macro-level political and economic forces—for example, gender-stratified labor-force patterns—to account for the ways in which macrostructural and microstructural factors jointly push women to do most of the household labor.[19] Some structural accounts even go so far as to suggest that culture does not play a significant role in shaping male household behavior.[20]

The increased prevalence and predictive utility of the "gender perspective"[21] in the study of household labor has opened the housework literature up to the ways in which gender and gender-role ideology—seen here as cultural products[22]—influence men's domestic work.[23] For instance, Julie Brines has shown how gender organizes male household labor in ways that run contrary to the theoretical claims of social-structural explanations. Specifically, she finds that in an effort to salvage their masculinity employed and unemployed men do less household labor when their wives earn substantially more than 50 percent of the household income;[24] this finding contradicts both the relative-resources and the time-availability hypotheses. Other research indicates that a progressive gender-role ideology is related to greater male involvement in household labor.[25] Thus, recent quantitative research attentive to the ways that gender and gender-role ideology influence male household labor suggests that culture does shape male family behavior.

Although this quantitative literature has highlighted the cultural influence of gender and gender-role ideology on household labor, its focus on the ways in which household labor is integral to the cultural production of what Sarah Fenstermaker Berk calls the "gender factory" has eclipsed discussions of the influence of other cultural factors on practices associated with domestic work.[26] As indicated above, household labor is not simply a way of producing gender; it is also a domestic rite. Insofar as family life is endowed with a sense of sacredness as the primary arena for the production and consumption of care and a range of related values (e.g., religious faith, solidarity, romance),[27] household labor may serve as a marker of a family's commitment to familism. Thus, the extent to which a family identifies with this ideology may influence the extent to its members invest emotional and physical labor in household upkeep. Because women, in their roles as wives and mothers, have been the primary proprietors of familism, their household labor probably varies more according to their identification with this ideology than does men's household labor. Accordingly, the ideology of familism should increase the gendered asymmetry in household labor—especially for households of married couples who have children. Moreover, given the close ties between religious institutions (especially theologically conservative ones) and the family-related ideologies of familism and gender-role traditionalism, it is also possible that a religious affiliation and theological conservatism foster inequality in the division of household labor.

To the extent that scholars of the family—especially scholars relying on quantitative methods—have acknowledged the influence of culture on household labor, they have tended to conceptualize it as an unmediated force that acts on individuals irrespective of their sociocultural location.[28] Thus, some of the best work on men's household labor addresses the influence of gender-role ideology but does not consider how this ideology may be produced, legitimated, or mediated by a particular social context.[29] These approaches overlook the ways that discrete sociocultural factors like race, class, and religion may help account for the link between household labor and broader cultural forces—for instance, gender norms, gender-role ideology, and familism.

In this chapter I address this theoretical gap by considering the ways in which religious effects are mediated by both familism and gender-role traditionalism, and by looking at the direct effects of these family-related ideologies on the amount and the share of household labor conducted by married men with children. As we have seen, religious institutions—especially those associated with conservative Protestantism—are arguably the most important institutional sources for the production and legitimation of these two ideologies in the United States.[30] Indeed, in chapter 3 I show that religious affiliation is linked to familism and gender-role traditionalism, and an active conservative Protestant affiliation is the most significant predictor of married men's adherence to these ideologies.

CULTURAL DETERMINANTS OF "ENCHANTED" ECONOMIES OF GRATITUDE

Religious institutions and the ideologies they produce and legitimate may also influence the reciprocal exchange of male gratitude for female household labor, especially in these unsettled times of gender transformation. As noted above, married women currently do approximately two-thirds of the household labor even though a majority of Americans believe that household labor should be shared. Hochschild argues that one of the most important consequences of this gap between practice and ideology is that a mismatch can develop in a couple's "economy of gratitude"—the exchange of material and symbolic gifts that foster solidarity within marriage.[31] In her words: "When couples struggle, it is seldom over who does what. Far more often, it is over the giving and receiving of gratitude."[32] Because the cultural baseline for the economy of gratitude has moved in a decisively egalitarian direction in recent decades, many women now view their disproportionate share of household labor as something extra—something beyond what husbands are legitimately entitled to expect from their wives.[33] In other words, household labor now seems to many women like a gift they give their husbands. Accordingly, many wives now expect some sign of gratitude from their husbands in return for their household labor.

Moreover, this dynamic is enormously consequential because a couple's economy of gratitude is, as Hochschild suggests, usually more important for the quality and stability of their marriage than their division of paid and unpaid labor.[34] From an institutional perspective, marriage is not generally organized in the United States around explicitly political or economic logics of power or self-interest. That is, husbands and wives—especially if they are happily married—do not see their unions as appropriate venues for the naked assertion of domination or self-interest, and they also do not expect their partners to act according to such a strategy; accordingly, most married persons are not inclined to seek a perfectly equal division of labor that would protect them from a spouse's domineering or self-interested behavior.[35] To a large degree the institution of marriage is organized around a cultural logic of sentimental solidarity that encompasses a range of expressive and instrumental support that partners give to one another (the next chapter develops this idea in further detail). This logic grows out of the increasingly expressive character of modern family life; it is itself a product of the family's sociocultural position in the private sphere.[36] Seen in the light of this logic, the health of a couple's economy of gratitude, not their division of household labor, is one of the key indicators of whether they are living up to the ideal of sentimental solidarity.

Hochschild's notion of a marital economy of gratitude is indebted to a larger literature on gift exchange.[37] The solidaristic character of marriage, along with its distance from the cultural logic of the market, suggests that the theoretical lens of gift exchange is indeed a helpful tool for looking at the contemporary institution of marriage. Following Marcel Mauss, Pierre Bourdieu has argued that the logic of gift exchange may be distinguished from the logic of market exchange in three ways.[38] First, the good-faith economy of gift exchange operates along solidaristic lines among individuals related by ties of kinship, friendship, or status, while market exchanges tend to take place between strangers.[39] Second, as opposed to the calculated, deliberate, and self-interested exchanges that take place in the market, gift exchanges presuppose a measure of uncertainty, improvisation, and excess. Of course, the uncertain and improvisational nature of gift exchange means that gifts are not always reciprocated. Finally, unlike market exchanges, gift exchanges are often marked by symbolic displays of gratitude by gift recipients that are meant to acknowledge both the gift's status as something extraordinary and the solidaristic tie fostered by the gift.

Although the logic of gift exchange is associated with solidaristic social ties, this does not mean that it leaves no room for the exercise of power or self-interest. Indeed, Bourdieu goes so far as to argue that domination and self-assertion undergird patterns of gift giving that are "misrecognized" as expressions of solidarity, obligation, or altruism. In this vein, he argues that symbolic displays of gratitude are particularly important for intimate relations of inequality that are far from the "cash nexus" of the market. For, in his view, inequality in close relationships must "be disguised under the veil of enchanted relations" so as not to threaten the ties of sentiment and solidarity that bind intimates together.[40] Although Bourdieu's view of gift exchange needlessly reduces all gift-giving behavior to a form of self-assertion, it is helpful in signaling the fact that solidarity and self-interest often commingle in reciprocal exchanges, even exchanges between intimates.[41]

These theoretical insights from the literature on gift exchange illuminate the ways in which household labor is tied to the marital economy of gratitude. Household labor performed within the institution of marriage is an important aspect of the good-faith economy that obtains between husband and wife. Because the good-faith economy in marriage depends upon voluntary responses to gifts given by one spouse to another, husbands may or may not reciprocate their wives' gifts of household labor with gifts of their own. But husbands who do not reciprocate their wives' disproportionate household labor with a gift of their own will call into question their commitment to the solidaristic logic of marriage, thereby impoverishing the marital economy of gratitude. On the other hand, husbands who reciprocate with symbolic displays of gratitude rather than an equal share of household labor are enriching the marital economy of gratitude even as they reinforce relations of inequality in the home. To borrow Bourdieu's evocative phrase, their gratitude casts a "veil of enchanted relations" over the inequality in their division of household labor.

Thus, one way for men to reciprocate a wife's "gift" of a disproportionate share of household labor is to display gratitude. Such a display can enrich the economy of gratitude that lies at the heart of most successful contemporary marriages.[42] Although there has not been any quantitative work on this subject, Hochschild's qualitative study of California married couples is suggestive in this regard. She argues that one of the key cultural determinants of a healthy marital economy of gratitude is whether a couple shares a common gender ideology and acts in accord with that ideology.[43] So, for instance, an egalitarian couple in which the husband willingly does half the household labor and affirms his wife's work is likely to have a rich economy of gratitude. By contrast, a couple that espouses egalitarian ideas of marriage but has asymmetrical patterns of household labor that the wife has tried and failed to equalize is likely to have an impoverished economy of gratitude. Hochschild also argues that the health of the marital economy of gratitude is determined by the couple's pragmatic and historical referents. That is, on a pragmatic basis married persons will evaluate their spouse according to the available alternatives, and from a historical perspective married persons will evaluate their spouse in comparison to a parent or grandparent.[44] Thus, much like the theorists of household labor, Hochschild combines a structural focus on resources (how one's spouse compares to the alternatives) with a cultural focus on gender ideology (and history).

However, like the theorists of household labor, Hochschild does not systematically consider how cultural factors other than gender-related ones may influence the economy of gratitude. This is a curious omission in light of one of the vignettes she offers in her research.[45] She describes a couple, Frank and Carmen Delacorte, whom she views as representative of couples with a traditional gender-role ideology and a "rich economy of gratitude."[46] Their economy of gratitude is rich partly because Frank reciprocates Carmen's gendered gifts—domestic labor, including baking his favorite pie—with gendered gifts of his own—symbolic displays of gratitude, including the occasional gift of roses. In this way, they conform to Hochschild's model of gender ideology. However, Hochschild also notes, without attributing much significance to it, that Frank's displays of gratitude are connected to the larger religious context of traditional Hispanic Catholicism: "For him, it was a point of male honor to show loving consideration toward one whom God had given a subordinate role in marriage."[47]

This aside suggests that there may be other important cultural determinants of "enchanted" or rich economies of gratitude besides gender-role ideology. Specifically, Frank's symbolic displays of gratitude appear to be motivated not only by his traditional gender-role ideology but also by his theologically conservative religious faith. His faith imbued his symbolic displays of gratitude with heightened meaning and also legitimated his traditional view of the division of family labor. Moreover, his faith was linked to a familist commitment to showing "loving consideration" to his wife. Thus, this vignette suggests—in keeping with the results documented in chapter 3—that religion plays a role in legitimating the ideologies of gender-role traditionalism and familism. It also suggests that religious factors and familism—not just gender-role ideology— are associated with male displays of gratitude for household labor.

Religion and ideology may be related to men's symbolic displays of gratitude for their wives' household labor in several ways. First, insofar as religious institutions provide family-oriented messages, social support for families, and rituals that sacralize family life, religious participation among married men with children may be associated in a generic fashion with higher levels of gratitude for the household labor performed by their wives.

Second, in keeping with Hochschild's analysis, gender-role ideology should play an important role in structuring the marital economy of gratitude. Because most marriages are marked by gender asymmetries in the performance of household labor, more egalitarian men may increase their emotion work to make up for their inability or unwillingness to do an equal share of household labor. Alternatively, men who abide by a more conservative gender-role ideology may increase their emotion work to legitimate the asymmetries in their households.

Third, men who are particularly committed to the ideology of familism may display more gratitude to their wives in return for the household labor they perform. This type of emotion work would be in keeping with the sentimental ethic of this ideology. Moreover, as familism, as well as its typically gendered practices, is challenged symbolically by the egalitarian claims of feminism and practically by the demands placed on women by their entry into the workforce, men who value family life may increase their displays of gratitude to shore up the marital economy of gratitude. This kind of emotion work is particularly important because, as Bourdieu argues, unequal reciprocal exchanges between intimates must be veiled by an aura of enchantment. Before turning to an empirical analysis of the relationship between religion, ideology, and the marital economy of gratitude, I briefly outline the distinctive role that tradition-specific religious factors may play in influencing men's household labor and their displays of gratitude for their wives' household labor.

CONSERVATIVE AND MAINLINE PROTESTANTISM ON THE GENDERED DIVISION OF HOUSEHOLD LABOR

Patriarchy is pervasive, at least symbolically, in the world of conservative Protestantism. God the Father stands at its Trinitarian core, transcending heaven and earth. He is all-powerful, all-wise, and all-beneficent. This is the center of the theologically conservative symbolic system that informs conservative Protestant notions of gender. Incorporating images and texts from the Bible, the dominant conservative Protestant family ideology asserts that men participate, however imperfectly, in the fatherhood of God. They are domestic patriarchs, charged with exercising divinely ordained authority in the home in a way that models the love, wisdom, and power of the heavenly Father. This perspective on men in the family is coupled to conservative Protestant teachings about the link between divinely ordained order and anthropology. Specifically, God is depicted as creating men with sex-specific qualities—logic, assertiveness, emotional distance—that correspond to their family responsibilities.[48] Thus, the theologically conservative ideology produced in conservative Protestantism provides an important intellectual framework for the familist and traditional gender ideologies that may influence the housework-related practices of men.

This theologically grounded framework is linked to the ideologies of familism and gender-role traditionalism in ways that articulate a vision of family life that is family centered and strongly gendered. In keeping with familist and theologically conservative tenets, men are supposed to sacrifice for their families. One way that they should do this, according to conservative Protestant family experts, is by loving their partners and their children. However, in keeping with the conservative gender-role ideology that influences this subculture, men are also supposed to take the lead in breadwinning, as well as exercise spiritual and moral leadership in their families. Proper male role performance ensures that wives can fulfill their God-given role as "helpmeets" focused primarily on the domestic duties that make for a bright and cheerful home.[49]

Thus, the most dominant strains of conservative Protestant ideology endorse a family moral order that is strongly gendered and characterized by a large measure of sentimental domesticity. In this order, women perform the lion's share of household labor to signal their femininity, or in more theoretical terms, to "do gender"; women also do more household labor than their mainline Protestant peers to signal their commitment to the family. These themes are found in the advice offered by many female conservative Protestant leaders and writers, from Beverly LaHaye to Marilee Horton.[50] For example, drawing on a text from the New Testament (Titus 2:3–5), Horton writes: "The conclusion that I have come to is that God would have me encourage young Christian mothers to choose to be keepers of the home, to take care of their children and to trust God to take care of their financial and other needs."[51]

At the same time, the stress on sentiment in the domestic arena— sentiment motivated both by theological beliefs about divine love and by a familistic appreciation for the sentimental character of family life—might motivate men to express appreciation to their wives for the housework they do. Here prominent male conservative Protestant leaders are emphatic in their exhortations to men to display gratitude to their wives for domestic work.[52] Gary Smalley, a family counselor and the author of a number of top-selling Christian books on marriage, advises husbands to "verbalize" their "thoughts of appreciation" and specifically mentions household labor as something for which men should express that appreciation. Smalley recounts how his criticism of his wife's sandwich making resulted in his wife's decision to stop making sandwiches for him. He then changed his tactics and restored the moral order in his family: "I sowed criticism and reaped an empty plate. I am happy to say that after that experience I began praising every sandwich she made for me, and now she unhesitantly makes them for me."[53] Although the explicitly instrumental character of Smalley's discussion is not characteristic of most elite advice on this subject, his discussion does signal the fact that conservative Protestant men may be—consciously or not—relying on symbolic displays of gratitude to shore up a bourgeois moral order in their homes.

This vision of domestic order is particularly salient for conservative Protestants given their broader preoccupation with the "traditional family," a preoccupation that has been especially powerful since the 1970s.[54] This preoccupation means that practices associated with household labor may furnish conservative Protestants with a means of doing boundary work against culturally defined out-groups. Feminism, which is seen as antifamily and antiwoman in many sectors of conservative Protestantism, is a central cultural actor against which conservative Protestant ideology positions itself.[55] The practices associated with the conservative Protestants' vision of domestic order may also be a means of putting symbolic distance between themselves and feminism. Thus, for both ideological and identity-related reasons, conservative Protestant women have considerable motivation to invest more time in the domestic rites associated with the home; likewise, conservative Protestant men should invest more emotion work in the displays of marital gratitude that give additional legitimation to those rites.

However, this picture of conservatism Protestantism—and the potential links between household labor and religion and ideology—is complicated by two factors. First, the social resources that have made a separate-spheres model of family life possible are disappearing. In the last twenty years, the stagnation of male income, the dramatic migration of women—including mothers with young children—into the workforce, and shifting cultural norms have combined to make the male breadwinner/female homemaker model increasingly unworkable for conservative Protestant couples, and conservative Protestant rates of female employment are closing in on national averages.[56] In a related development, an egalitarian brand of feminism has begun to make inroads in conservative Protestantism since the mid-1980s, especially among highly educated conservative Protestants. This egalitarian feminism, as articulated by evangelical Protestant intellectuals such as Rebecca M. Groothuis and Mary Stewart Van Leeuwen, counsels gender-role flexibility and domestic task sharing.[57]

Although the qualitative and quantitative research on conservative Protestants detailed in chapters 2 and 3 do not suggest that a majority of conservative Protestants have adopted a thoroughgoing gender-role egalitarianism, a shift in their understanding of patriarchy appears to be under way. My findings indicate that conservative Protestants are increasingly likely to express egalitarian attitudes about the public, economic and political roles of women, as well as greater openness to mothers working outside the home.

As a consequence, conservative Protestant patriarchy is moving in the direction of being more symbolic than practical. Conservative Protestants still overwhelmingly endorse male headship but this headship appears to be more of a salve for men's threatened manhood than a license for them to exercise authority over their wives or demand that they stay at home. Melinda Lundquist Denton found that although conservative Protestants endorse male leadership in the family, they do not make family decisions any differently than other American couples.[58] The qualitative evidence suggests that women in this subculture are trading symbolic leadership for greater male emotional and practical involvement in the home.[59] These discursive shifts from male headship to "servant-leadership" also suggest that a softened patriarchy has taken hold.[60]

If this shift in conservative Protestant ideals of patriarchy is having a marked impact on household labor practices, conservative Protestant men may be exercising greater involvement in household labor than their peers. Soft patriarchy would also predict higher displays of gratitude from men—especially since conservative Protestant men may be even more appreciative of their wives' domestic labor now that threats to patriarchal authority are being issued not only from outside but from within their religious subculture.

The gender-role-related messages that mainline Protestant institutions issue differ from conservative Protestant ones in a number of important ways. Since the 1970s, the symbolic patriarchy historically associated with Christianity has been steadily been deconstructed in mainline Protestant churches. Linguistic shifts signal the dramatic changes that have taken place. Churches in the mainline traditions are now much more likely to use gender-neutral language, and they are also more likely to incorporate images of God as mother into Sunday worship and everyday spirituality.[61]

These theological shifts have been paralleled by and are in some ways the product of similar shifts in mainline Protestant attitudes toward the position of women in the church, the public arena, and the family. Since the 1960s, mainline Protestant churches have taken a number of positions that indicate their support for egalitarian gender ideals in the church and the world. All mainline denominations have adopted policies in support of women's ordination, and mainliners were visible proponents of the Equal Rights Amendment. As Mark Chaves observes, the mainline's egalitarian stance toward gender in the contemporary era is of a piece with its embrace of a "broader liberal agenda associated with modernity and religious accommodation to the spirit of the age."[62]

The accommodationist spirit of the mainline has had crosscutting effects on the mainline's witness on behalf of gender equality. On the one hand, this spirit has led mainline denominations to issue strong statements in support of gender equality in the home. For instance, since 1972 the United Methodist Church has passed a series of resolutions seeking the elimination of gender-role stereotypes in the church and home.[63] Most recently, the 1996 *Book of Discipline of the United Methodist Church* said, "We affirm women and men to be equal in every aspect of their common life. We therefore urge that every effort be made to eliminate sex-role stereotypes in activity and portrayal of family life."[64] Moreover, the mainline affirmation of gender-role egalitarianism is often connected to boundary work against the "sexist" and "reactionary" gender program of Protestant fundamentalism.[65] As a consequence, mainline Protestants consistently express more egalitarian attitudes regarding the family than conservative Protestants do.

On the other hand, this accommodationist spirit has weakened the ability of mainline churches to speak forcefully on the family. Since the early 1980s, mainline churches have made a determined effort to be inclusive of all family types and have accordingly become more hesitant about offering prescriptive advice about appropriate conduct regarding the family. As Phyllis Airhart and Margaret Lamberts Bendroth have observed, "In the mainstream Protestant churches . . . toleration is the watchword, and the frequent result is a loss of consensus and an inability to speak with one voice."[66]

As a consequence, it is unlikely that mainline Protestants receive frequent and specific exhortations from their religious institutions to connect the egalitarian family vision of the mainline to specific practices—including practices associated with household labor. Moreover, the institutional weakness of mainline churches, which is related to their accommodationist position, probably limits the ability of any prescriptive household discourse to influence men's behavior. Mainline men are less likely to attend church and to grant their churches moral authority in directing their lives,[67] and, according to one study examining the influence of religion on the work-family connection mainline men were unable to make connections between their faith and work decisions—overtime, job changes, travel, etc.—that impacted their families.[68] Thus, the direct effect of the institutional support for gender-role egalitarianism upon mainline Protestant men's household labor is probably weak.

Of course, the institutional weakness of mainline Protestantism is also related to its strength in attracting well-educated Americans with a liberal social orientation and a provisional spiritual outlook.[69] Mainline churches are attractive to conventional middle- and upper-class couples who seek religious socialization for their children but who do not approve of the strong theological claims and gender-role traditionalism associated with conservative Protestant churches. These are precisely the men and women who may have the resources—higher education and dual income—that make egalitarian household labor patterns workable.[70] Thus, on balance, we should expect to find that mainline Protestant family men do slightly more household labor than family men with no religious affiliation. Finally, because the conventional character of mainline religiosity is linked to higher expressions of support for familism among mainline married men with children, these men may be more likely to express appreciation to their wives for the household labor they do.

DOMESTIC RITES

In the contemporary context, household labor for married couples has at least two forms of ritual content. First, the amount of household labor a couple performs is indicative of the extent to which they value sentimental domesticity. Second, the husband's share of household labor is suggestive of his commitment to gender equality in the family.

HUSBANDS' WEEKLY HOURS OF HOUSEHOLD LABOR

Christopher Ellison and John Bartkowski, who have conducted the only study on religion and household labor, found no evidence that conservative Protestant affiliation or theological conservatism influenced male household labor.[71] However, their sample is slightly different from mine: they examine all married men, while I focus on married men with children at home. Given the fact that gender-role segregation is highest among families with children, the effects of conservative Protestantism may be stronger for this population. Ellison and Bartkowski also did not explore the effects of mainline Protestant affiliation and familism on household labor.

I measured husbands' weekly hours of household labor using data from NSFH1 (1987–1988). On the NSFH survey, household labor includes nine different types of activities: meal preparation, washing dishes, cleaning the house, laundry, shopping, driving family members, paying bills, lawn care and household maintenance, and auto care. On average, married men with school-age children in my sample reported that they did 17.52 hours of household labor a week (see table A5.1 in the appendix).

Figure 5.1, which is based on regression models that control for a range of sociodemographic factors, indicates that conservative Protestant married men with children spend almost one and a half hours per week less on household labor than their unaffiliated peers, and that mainline Protestant married men with children spend about one-third of an hour per week more on household labor than their unaffiliated peers. Note, however, that neither of these differences is statistically significant. What is statistically significant is the difference between mainline and conservative Protestant husbands; mainline men spend about one and three-quarters more hours a week on household labor than their conservative Protestant peers. (See table A5.2 in the appendix for complete details.) These results also indicate that the softening of conservative Protestant patriarchy has not resulted in conservative Protestant family men doing more household labor than their peers, as I thought it might.

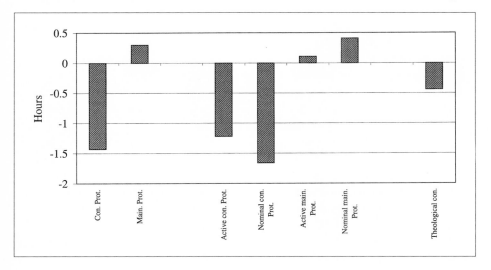

Figure 5.1 Difference in husband's hours of household labor

Source: NSFH1 (1987–1988).
Note: The comparison category for all religious affiliation effects is Unaffiliated, and for theological conservatives it is Non–theological conservative.

Religious participation does not have consistent effects on the household labor of married men with children. As figure 5.1 indicates, active conservative Protestants do slightly more household labor than nominal conservative Protestants, while active mainline Protestants do slightly less household labor than nominal mainline Protestants. These differences, however, are not statistically significant, and neither are the differences between members of any of these religious groups and unaffiliated family men. The only statistically significant difference is between nominal conservative Protestants and nominal mainline Protestants, who differ by about two hours in the amount of time they devote to household labor each week.

Theological conservatism is associated with slightly lower levels of household labor for family men, but this effect is not significant, and theological conservatism does not mediate the effects of religious affiliation. Familism, however, is associated with lower levels of housework on the part of men. Husbands with the highest familism scores spend five hours less each week on household labor than husbands with the lowest familism scores.

Gender-role traditionalism is also associated with lower levels of housework for married men with children, and it reduces the effect of familism by about one-half, to nonsignificance. It also reduces the gap between nominal mainline and nominal conservative Protestant family men to nonsignificance. The most traditional family men spend about six hours less on household labor each week than the most egalitarian family men. The negative effect of a husband's gender-role traditionalism is partly explained by his wife's employment status and income. Specifically, additional regression models indicate that half of the effect of gender-role traditionalism is accounted for by the number of hours the wife works outside the home and by the percentage of the couple's income that she earns. This means that one of the reasons more traditional husbands do less household labor is that their wives are more likely to be at home and to be earning a smaller percentage of the family's income compared to the wives of more egalitarian men.

These findings indicate that conservative Protestant family men are less dedicated to household labor than their more egalitarian mainline Protestant peers. However, these tradition-specific effects do not appear to be a consequence of the ideological cues that conservative and mainline Protestant men get at church. Frequently attending conservative and mainline Protestant men are not significantly different from one another or from unaffiliated men on this measure. Instead, the results suggest that nominal mainline Protestants identify with an egalitarian gender-role ideology that helps to explain why they are more likely than their peers to perform household labor. The results also suggest that married men's family orientation—measured here by familism—is associated with less involvement in housework, largely because men who hold profamily attitudes tend to be gender traditionalists. Finally, insofar as conservative Protestant institutions promote familism and gender-role traditionalism among their members and among mainline Protestants, they play a modest indirect role in fostering lower levels of male housework.

HUSBANDS' PERCENTAGE OF HOUSEHOLD LABOR

To measure equality in housework, an important dimension of the gendered character of marriage, I explored the effect of religion and ideology on husbands' percentage of household labor using data from NSFH1. This variable was calculated by dividing husbands' reports of total weekly household labor by the couple's total household labor. On the basis of this calculation, I estimate that married fathers in my sample perform approximately 32 percent of the couples' household labor (see table A5.1 in the appendix).

My findings indicate that conservative Protestant married men with children perform a slightly smaller share of household labor than their unaffiliated

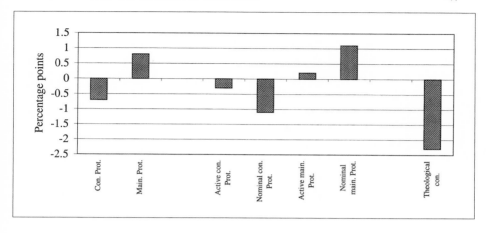

Figure 5.2   Difference in husband's share of household labor

Source: NSFH1 (1987–1988).

Note: The comparison category for all religious affiliation effects is Unaffiliated, and for theological conservatives it is Non–theological conservative.

peers and that mainline Protestant married men with children perform a slightly larger share of household labor than their unaffiliated peers. These differences are not statistically significant. Once again, however, mainline family men do perform a significantly higher share of household labor than their conservative Protestant counterparts—about one and a half percentage points more. Furthermore, when we turn to religious participation, we find that, as with weekly hours of household labor, the only significant difference is between nominal mainline and nominal conservative Protestant family men. Specifically, nominal mainline men perform a share of household labor that is about two percentage points greater than that of nominal conservative Protestant men. Although these differences are statistically significant, they amount to modest effect sizes (see figure 5.2). (See table A5.3 in the appendix for additional details.)

Theologically conservative married men with children do a share of household labor that is about two percentage points lower than that of family men who are not theologically conservative. The effect of theological conservatism is statistically significant and eliminates the effect of religious affiliation. Familism is also associated with greater inequality in the division of household labor. The most familistic men do about a share of the couple's household labor that is nine percentage points lower than that of the least familistic men. But the negative effect of familism is almost entirely eliminated by the addition of gender-role traditionalism to the regression models. This suggests that the only reason familism is associated with greater housework inequality is that men who hold familistic views also tend to hold traditional gender views.

Gender-role traditionalism is strongly associated with greater inequality in the division of household labor. The share of housework taken up by the most traditional family men is about 18 percent less than the share taken up by the most egalitarian family men. Models that add the wife's work hours and the percentage of income the wife earns reduce the effect of gender-role traditionalism by about 40 percent. This means that one of the reasons traditional family men do a substantially smaller share of the household labor is that their wives work outside the home for fewer hours and earn a smaller share of the family's income than the wives of egalitarian family men. Another reason the housework share of traditional family men is smaller than that of their peers is that their wives spend more time doing household labor than other wives. Ancillary analyses indicate that the most traditional wives do about twenty more hours of household labor each week than the most egalitarian wives.[72] In sum, the results for this outcome parallel those for husbands' hours of household labor, except that here we have evidence that a husband's theological conservatism is associated with greater inequality.

Taken together, the results for both these outcomes suggest that conservative Protestantism is modestly associated with greater inequality in the division of labor in households with children. But they also suggest that the religious and family-related ideologies produced and legitimated by conservative Protestant institutions—especially gender-role traditionalism—also play a role in fostering inequality when it comes to housework. Thus, conservative Protestant institutions seem to play a modest direct and perhaps a more substantial indirect role in fostering gender inequality in this domain. These findings also show that men's familism does not lead them to devote themselves more to household labor, contrary to my expectations. Finally, the results indicate that the slightly greater egalitarianism in mainline households is not a product of the message that family men hear in their churches. For it is the nominal, not the active, mainline family men who are the most committed to doing their share of the housework. It may be that egalitarian family men who have a conservative Protestant or Catholic heritage come to self-identify as mainline Protestants because they perceive mainline Protestant churches as the most egalitarian option among the major Christian traditions.

ENCHANTED RELATIONS

WIVES' REPORTS THAT HOUSEHOLD LABOR IS APPRECIATED

Because most married couples with children continue to have markedly asymmetrical divisions of household labor, the effort husbands make to display gratitude bears on marital happiness and stability.[73] Accordingly, I examine the link between husbands' displays of gratitude and religion and ideology. Here I rely on wives' reports that they feel their household labor is appreciated (see table A5.1 in the appendix). I rely on this methodological strategy because the NSFH does not ask respondents to report how much they display gratitude to their spouses. There are disadvantages and advantages to this strategy. On the one hand, wives' reports of gratitude may be inaccurate measures of husbands' displays of gratitude because these reports may be biased by women's differential expectations of shows of appreciation. On the other hand, this strategy is not vulnerable to self-report bias, and given that the vast majority of household labor is negotiated and performed by husbands and wives,[74] it is logical to assume that women's sense of being appreciated for household labor is largely driven by their husbands' displays of gratitude. Recent research that finds a significant link between wives' sense of being appreciated and their sense that the marital division of household labor is fair lends prima facie support to this assumption.[75]

Figure 5.3 is derived from regression models that control for a range of sociodemographic factors (see table A5.4 in the appendix). It shows that the wives of both conservative and mainline Protestant married men with children are slightly more likely to report that their household labor is appreciated, compared to wives of unaffiliated family men. These effects, however, are statistically insignificant. But my findings do show larger effects in the case of active conservative and mainline Protestant affiliations, both of which are statistically significant. Wives of active conservative Protestant family men have appreciation scores that are about one-quarter of a standard deviation higher than the those of women whose husbands are unaffiliated—a moderate effect size. Their scores are also significantly higher than the appreciation scores for wives of nominal mainline and nominal conservative Protestant family men. The appreciation scores for the wives of active mainline Protestant family men are one-fifth of a standard deviation higher than those of wives of unaffiliated family men—a modest effect size. They are also significantly higher than the appreciation scores for wives of nominal Protestant family men, both

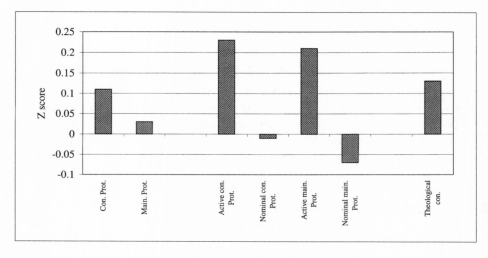

Figure 5.3   Wife's perception that she is appreciated

Source: NSFH1 (1987–1988).
Note: The comparison category for all religious affiliation effects is Unaffiliated, and for theological conservatives it is Non–theological conservative.

mainline and conservative. These results suggest that religious participation has a generic positive effect on husbands' displays of gratitude for household labor.

Theological conservatism is also associated with significantly higher scores for appreciation. The effect, however, is modest—about one-eighth of a standard deviation. Nonetheless, the addition of theological conservatism reduces the effect of active conservative Protestantism by one-third (to non-significance) and the effect of active mainline Protestantism by one-fifth (to nonsignificance). This suggests that one of the reasons wives of active conservative and mainline Protestant family men report higher levels of appreciation is that their husbands are also theologically conservative. In other words, the family-centered theologically conservative worldview promoted by conservative Protestant institutions seems to be linked to higher displays of gratitude for household labor among married men with children.

The familism of married men with children is also associated with wives' higher reports of appreciation. In fact, wives of the most family-oriented men report appreciation scores one-half of a standard deviation higher than the appreciation scores of wives of the least family-oriented men—a large effect size. Standardized coefficient tests indicate that the effects of familism surpass the influence of sociodemographic factors such as education, income, region, and family structure. Familism also reduces the effect of theological conservatism to nonsignificance, which lends further credence to the notion that theological conservatism is associated with husbands' displays of gratitude in part because of the strong family orientation associated with this religious ideology.

By contrast, family men's gender-role traditionalism is not independently associated with wives' reports of appreciation; nor does it have much of a mediating effect on the religious and familism factors. However, the addition of an interaction term for familism and gender-role traditionalism to my models renders gender-role traditionalism strongly negative and statistically significant. By contrast, the interactive effect of familism and gender-role traditionalism on wives' reports of appreciation is positive and statistically significant. This means that familistic men who are gender-role conservatives have rich economies of gratitude. By contrast, men who are gender-role conservatives but are not familistic have comparatively impoverished economies of gratitude. These findings call into question Hochschild's categorization of economies of gratitude along the lines of gender-role ideology alone.[76] They also indicate that religious factors and familism play an important role in determining whether couples with a conservative approach to gender roles have a rich or impoverished economy of gratitude.

Although these findings do not provide direct evidence about husbands' displays of gratitude for their wives' household labor, they do provide strong prima facie evidence in favor of the theory that husbands who value family life are responding to gender asymmetries in their households by displaying heightened levels of gratitude compared to other husbands. There are two alternative explanations for the results documented here. First, it could be that men who are more familistic are generally married to women who are also more familistic and who, as a consequence, have lower expectations of their husbands' gratitude either because they derive intrinsic pleasure from household labor or because they seek to convince themselves that their husbands appreciate their household labor in order to avoid facing the fact that their husbands are not shouldering a substantial share of the housework. Hochschild calls the latter response the "family myth" solution.[77] Second, given the fact that active religious affiliation is associated with higher levels of familism, it could be that men who are more familistic are generally married to women who are also actively affiliated with a church. Such women might get their appreciation of their household labor from church peers rather than their husbands.

In an effort to test these alternative explanations, I ran two sets of additional analyses.[78] In the first analysis, I compared couples who both scored above the median on the familism index and couples with heterogeneous familism scores to couples who both had scores below the median on the familism index. Only in couples where both husband and wife had high familism scores did wives indicate high levels of appreciation. This means that dyadic familism is important, but it doesn't tell us exactly why. It could be that husbands the most gratitude in a supportive, family-centered dyadic environment. Alternatively, wives may be more willing to imagine—to construct a family myth—that their husbands are grateful when they know that their husbands have a strong normative commitment to the family.

In the second analysis, I compared couples in which both attended religious services frequently with couples who had heterogeneous attendance scores. Once again, I found that attendance is related to higher reports of appreciation only when both husband and wife are frequent churchgoers. While this result indicates that my findings regarding wives' reports of appreciation are not a consequence of the affirmation wives receive from church peers, it reinforces the point that the economy of gratitude is closely tied to the dyadic normative environment, but the reasons for this are not yet clear. In sum, the results suggest that churchgoing, theologically conservative, and especially familistic married men with children—particularly those who share faith and a commitment to familism with their wives—are making a strong effort to reciprocate their wives' "gift" of extra household work with the "gift" of displays of gratitude.

CONCLUSION: THE ENCHANTMENT OF HOUSEHOLD INEQUALITY

From these findings we can draw three broad conclusions—one theoretical and two substantive. First, theoretically speaking, the gender perspective on household labor should be extended to account for the sociocultural sources of gender norms and ideologies that foster asymmetrical divisions of household labor. In this case, conservative Protestant institutions influence household labor directly by fostering somewhat lower investments in housework from men, and indirectly by producing and legitimating the ideology of gender-role traditionalism, which is tied to greater asymmetries in the division of household labor. In this chapter I move beyond the gender perspective by demonstrating that a range of cultural factors, from theological conservatism to familism, influences the practical and emotion work that gets done regarding household labor. We see that housework-related practices are about more than the production of gender; they also dramatize other dimensions of the family's moral order—for example, the extent to which husbands are motivated by familism to display gratitude to their wives for their household labor. Indeed, it is the dramaturgic function of these housework-related practices in relation to the family's moral order that explains why religion, familism, and gender-role traditionalism are linked to the household division of labor and the economy of gratitude. In other words, respondents' "world images" of God, the family, and marriage—as well as gender—guide their practical and emotional conduct in relation to housework.[79]

Second, men's commitment to familism makes them more likely to do positive emotion work. In this case, I speculate that wives' reports of appreciation for household labor are an accurate assessment of the degree to which their husbands display gratitude. Remarkably, of all the domains discussed in this chapter and chapter 4, familism is consistently related only to positive emotion work. In other words, familism is not related to the amount of time married men invest in their children's lives or, once gender-role traditionalism is controlled for, to the amount of time they devote to household labor, but it is consistently and powerfully related to the positive emotion work they do in their families. Thus it would seem that familism, which valorizes family life and attendant norms of obligation and care, leads men to focus on the emotional dimension, but not necessarily on other dimensions, of their family life. In any case, these findings provide further evidence that familism plays an important role in pushing men to the kind of expressive approach to family life associated with the new man ideal.

Third, this chapter also casts light on the ways in which religion influences contemporary household labor arrangements and the ways in which couples understand these arrangements. Critics of conservative Protestantism have argued that this subculture is a force for gender reaction. In the domain of household labor, they have a point. We see that a conservative Protestant affiliation and theological conservatism are associated with slightly lower levels of male housework and with slightly greater inequality in the division of household labor. Conservative Protestant institutions also foster inequality indirectly through their support for gender-role traditionalism, which is consistently and powerfully associated with gendered asymmetries in the division of household labor. Thus, we have evidence that conservative Protestantism plays a modest role in fostering gender inequality at the level of practice.

But perhaps the more important role conservative Protestantism, and religion more generally, plays in fostering inequality is at the cultural level, in the way couples come to see the division of household labor. Social scientists continue to find that a majority of married women report "fairness" in the division of household labor even though most women perform the lion's share of the domestic work.[80] One clue to this puzzle is that women are significantly more likely to report that the division of household labor is fair if they believe that their household labor is appreciated.[81] We have seen that religious factors, especially religious participation and theological conservatism and the familism that they produce and legitimate, play a key role in enriching the marital economy of gratitude surrounding the division of household labor—judging by wives' reports of being appreciated. If I am right to infer that wives' reports of appreciation are indicative of husbands' actual displays of gratitude, the results reported in this chapter indicate that religiously active, theologically conservative, and familistic husbands—especially those whose wives share their commitment to faith and family—are indeed shoring up their marital economy of gratitude with these displays. As Hochschild notes, "Emotion work is often all that stands between the stalled revolution on the one hand, and broken marriages on the other."[82]

For all these reasons, the marital emotion work done by churchgoing, theologically conservative men, according to this study and a number of qualitative studies,[83] may play a key role in legitimating inequality in the family and in the public sphere. After all, women who are on the receiving end of heightened displays of gratitude may be less likely to challenge the inequalities they confront at home and in the labor force. Ironically, the tremendous symbolic and practical challenges to gender inequality that have been mounted in the contemporary era appear to have had more of an impact on the emotional work of relatively traditional, religious family men than on that of more progressive, secular family men. The former group of men seem willing to devote greater attention to the emotional welfare of their wives in part because they wish to shore up the stability of their families. Indeed, the findings I discuss in chapter 6 provide more evidence that churchgoing, theologically conservative men are more devoted to the emotional lives of their wives than are unchurched and theologically liberal men.

These developments are in keeping with Bourdieu's observation that the legitimation of inequality, especially when such asymmetry is being contested, "requires constant labour in the form of care and attention devoted to making and maintaining relations; and also major investments, both material and symbolic. . . . The 'great' can least afford to take liberties with the official norms and they have to pay for their outstanding value with exemplary conformity to the values of the group."[84] In this case, it would seem that conservative Protestant men have paid for their symbolic patriarchy with the currency of heightened levels of emotion work. Such are the costs of living in a world of enchanted relations.

CHAPTER SIX

TENDING HER HEART: RELIGION, IDEOLOGY, AND EMOTION WORK IN MARRIAGE

MARRIAGE USED TO be about many things: raising a family, securing a living, seeking sexual release and a measure of companionship, and—for the fortunate—finding true friendship. Now, for more and more Americans, marriage has become primarily a matter of the heart, a vehicle for a rich and rewarding emotional relationship between husband and wife.[1] A number of developments have combined over the last century to elevate the emotional dimension of married life. The rise of feminism and dramatic increases in women's labor-force participation have heightened women's interest in sharing the emotion work of family life with their husbands.[2] Because many of the family's traditional functions—economic production, child rearing, leisure, and religious devotion—have lost ground to the state and market, people have come to see emotional expression and fulfillment as one of the primary purposes of family life.[3] Also, the rising tide of expectations for individual fulfillment that washed across the United States in the postwar era made people expect more from their marriages emotionally and less inclined to accept cultural ideals regarding marital permanence and sacrifice.[4] Thus, marital emotion work—and spousal assessments of the quality of such work—is increasingly the tie that binds together contemporary marriages.

Indeed, research on marital quality shows that the marital emotion work men do—expressing positive emotion to their wives; attending to the dynamics of the relationship and to the needs of their wives; setting aside time for couple activities; refraining from destructive forms of marital conflict, such as domestic violence—is the most important predictor of marital quality for women. On average, women rate the emotional quality of their marriages as more important than factors like financial security, the presence of children in the home, or the division of domestic labor.[5] Women have long carried the primary burden of managing the emotional life of families, including marriages, and have thus become particularly invested in the emotional quality of the marital relationship.[6] This helps to explain why the emotion work their husbands do plays a signal role in shaping their assessment of marital quality and, indeed, their global personal happiness.[7]

Moreover, because the expressive functions of marriage have come to overshadow its institutional functions, marital emotion work also plays a central role in predicting marital stability.[8] Men's marital emotion work is particularly important for marital stability because women, who judge the quality of their relationships in large part on the basis of the amount and kind of emotion work done by their husbands, initiate the majority of divorces in the United States.[9] Furthermore, men's emotion work in marriage probably has an indirect effect on children, who experience higher levels of psychological well-being when their parents are happily married.[10]

As with men's household labor, one thing is clear about men's marital emotion work: it has not increased in recent years nearly as much as women might like; nor has it come close to reaching parity with the emotion work that women do in marriage.[11] Here again it seems that men are holding up the transition to the institutionalization of new family norms. But what are the social and cultural factors holding them back? Family and gender scholars like Julia McQuillan and Myra Marx Ferree have argued that religious conservatism is one key force "pushing men toward authoritarian and stereotypical forms of masculinity and attempting to renew patriarchal family relations."[12] They argue that the conservative gender ideology produced by the religious right, and especially by organizations linked to conservative Protestantism, is associated with unequal marriages characterized by lower levels of male emotion work.

Indeed, many family and gender scholars, Christian feminists, and critics of conservative Protestantism argue that the gender ideology produced by conservative Protestant institutions fosters a particularly disturbing form of negative emotion work in marriage: domestic violence.[13] They contend that the patriarchal ideology associated with conservative Protestantism creates a climate of male domination and female subservience that discourages men from being expressive with their wives, makes wife abuse more likely, and legitimates such abuse. Sociologists R. Emerson Dobash and Russell Dobash make the general theoretical point that "the seeds of wife beating lie in the subordination of females and their subjection to male authority and control," which are characteristic of the patriarchal family. The patriarchal family, in turn, is legitimated by a religious belief system that "makes such relationships seem natural, morally just and sacred."[14]

James Beck, a psychologist and Christian feminist, contends that "the underlying power differential in a marriage sanctioned by a traditional under-standing of Scripture is [related] to the abuse of that power that characterizes some Christian homes."[15] James and Phyllis Alsdurf, Christian feminists and family counselors, make a similar point in their aptly named book *Battered into Submission:* "By sowing the seeds of patriarchy and hierarchy, we have reaped the fruit of divisiveness within the Christian home."[16] And recall that journalists Steven and Cokie Roberts claim that conservative Protestant gender ideology "can clearly lead to abuse, both physical and emotional."[17]

However, these scholars and journalists have not considered the possibility that conservative Protestantism, and religion more generally, may be associated with other cultural and social factors that foster marital emotion work on the part of men—or that reduce women's expectations of emotion work in marriage, thereby making them more inclined than secular women to take a positive view of what emotion work their husbands do. Conservative Protestant-ism promotes a familistic approach to marriage that valorizes norms like fidelity and sacrifice and fosters negative attitudes toward divorce.[18] Because these norms and attitudes are associated with higher levels of marital investment,[19] a conservative Protestant affiliation may lead to higher levels of emotion work in marriage on the part of men. Furthermore, the heightened attention that conservative Protestant institutions devote to gender and family issues may provide conservative Protestant couples with a map for marital interaction that helps them avoid the shoals of role confusion that wreck many marriages in these times of gender transformation. In addition to these tradition-specific fac-tors, religion may have generic effects on men's marital emotion work. Most religious institutions offer religious and moral messages that promote the

Golden Rule and family-oriented social networks that may provide men with the encouragement they need to do more emotion work with their wives.

It is also possible that religious women have lower expectations of marital emotion work on the part of their husbands, whereas secular women are more likely to take an egalitarian view of marriage that may inflate their expectations regarding marital emotion work.[20] This inflation of marital expectations may cause egalitarian women to view their husbands' emotion work through a more critical lens than their less egalitarian peers—especially since men generally perform only a fraction of the emotion work associated with family life.[21] Also, because of their commitment to the institution of marriage, religious women may be more likely to create what Arlie Hochschild calls a "family myth": they may make themselves believe that their husbands do a great deal of marital emotional work so as not to confront the alternatives to putting up with low or moderate levels of emotion work from their husbands.[22] Thus, ceteris paribus, religious women may view their husbands' emotion work more favorably than their secular peers do the emotion work of their own husbands.

EQUALITY, COMMITMENT, AND EMOTION WORK

Family and gender scholars such as Pepper Schwartz, Paula England, and John Gottman have argued that egalitarian marriages are more likely to be characterized by the kind of emotion work that makes for high-quality, stable marriages in an era when companionate marriage is the ideal.[23] This might be called the companionate theory of marriage, and it is predicated on three assumptions about the links between egalitarianism and marital emotion work. First, role homophily, in which spouses share similar work and family responsibilities, is supposed to increase the quality of emotion work in marriage. Such homophily provides husbands and wives with common experiences and interests around which they can build conversations, empathetic regard, mutual understanding, and so on.

Second, the elimination of gendered hierarchies of authority and power is seen as a key mechanism for promoting marital intimacy. Classical social theory has long noted the tensions between intimacy and authority or power.[24] The exercise of authority and power is usually associated with social distance, and marital theorists have argued that one of the reasons men are less expressive in marriage is that they seek to protect their traditional dominance by limiting their expression of affect. Likewise, women's dependence and relative powerlessness in marriage, at least historically, have pushed them to develop a deferential strategy of marital emotion work. That is, women's financial dependence on marriage has led them to cater to the emotional needs of their mates and to the emotional dynamics of the marital relationship in an effort to maintain the security of their marriages and to elevate their status within marriage. Likewise, women have been socialized to minimize the expression of their own thoughts, desires, and feelings—especially negative ones—for fear that they will otherwise jeopardize their unions.[25] The companionate theory of marriage predicts that, by contrast, marriages characterized by an ethic of equal regard and by equal access to the labor force will have higher levels of male emotion work and interpersonal honesty. In such marriages women should feel free to speak their minds, and men should feel a greater responsibility to shoulder their share of the necessary emotion work.

Third, egalitarian-minded men are supposed to be more open to a "counterstereotypical" masculinity conducive to marital emotion work.[26] Traditionally, masculinity has been defined in opposition to all things feminine, including attentiveness to relationship dynamics and ready and frequent expression of emotion, affection, and vulnerability.[27] By contrast, men who identify with the ethos of egalitarianism should embrace a counterstereotypical masculinity, "a style of manliness that is not afraid to accept influence from women, to recognize and express emotion, and to give cognitive room to the marriage relation as such."[28]

For all these reasons, the companionate theory of marriage would predict that egalitarian relationships are characterized by more "interpersonal closeness, trust, communication, and mutuality" than relationships that are not egalitarian.[29] In other words, this theory suggests that egalitarian marriages are more likely to generate the kinds of experiences and emotional skills that foster marital emotion work on the part of men.

The fact that contemporary marriages are indeed more equal than they used to be, with men and women sharing work and family responsibilities, has led scholars like Andrew Cherlin, Paula England, and Shelly Lundberg to emphasize the increasingly contractual nature of marriage.[30] Noting the deinstitutionalization of gender roles in marriage that has occurred since the 1960s, they argue that husbands and wives increasingly act as agents with independent interests who bargain over their respective roles. Moreover, the contractual model assumes that spouses bargain in a utilitarian fashion to maximize their self-interest, renegotiating the terms on an ongoing basis to suit their interests, abilities, and power in the relationship. When one or both spouses determine that the relationship is no longer in their self-interest, they will seek to exit the relationship.

But this contractual emphasis overlooks the extent to which many Americans conceptualize their marriages along more communitarian lines.

Many Americans see marriage as a sacred institution in the sociological sense: they accord the union extraordinary value. Hence, the marital relationship is supposed to trump the individual interests of the partners and to call forth virtues like fidelity, sacrifice, and mutual support. In this setting, exchanges between marital partners are often conducted according to an enchanted cultural logic of gift exchange in which partners give one another gifts that vary in value, may or may not be reciprocated, and often have some kind of symbolic meaning above and beyond their immediate instrumental value.[31] Thus, in what I call an institutional theory of marriage there is a continuum between the two models, with some couples falling closer to an individualistic, contractual approach and other couples falling closer to a collectivist, communitarian model.[32]

For a number of reasons, I predict that men who adopt a more communitarian approach to marriage will do more positive marital emotion work than those who do not. First, one of the central norms of modern marriage is that married people provide emotional support to one another. Now more than ever, marriage is about meaningful conversation, empathy, affection, and the spending of leisure time together. Nevertheless, such emotion work is often particularly difficult for men, who have traditionally been socialized to be less expressive.[33] However, men who are committed to the institution of marriage will feel a greater moral responsibility than other men to signal their belief in the sanctity of marriage by respecting the expressive norms now associated with the institution. The positive marital emotion work done by men committed to the institution of marriage serves the symbolic function of indicating— both to themselves and to their wives—that they are good husbands in a normative sense.

Second, men who are strongly committed to marriage are likely to have relationships with third parties who have a vested interest in the success of their marriages. Margaret Brinig has noted that marital commitment is often linked to cultural norms fostered and reinforced through communal ties, religious participation, and extended family networks.[34] The interested parties represented in these social networks—from friends to God—can bring social and religious pressure to bear on husbands and can provide social and religious rewards in an effort to encourage them to focus on the emotional well-being of their wives. Men who think that their friends, family, or God want them to stay happily married will be more motivated to invest themselves emotionally in their unions.

Third, men who are more committed to marriage are likely to be in unions that are qualitatively different from relationships characterized by lower levels of commitment to the marital institution. One way to think about this is to compare marriage to other romantic relationships. Scholars from Émile Durkheim onward have noted that one of the advantages associated with the institution of marriage, compared to other forms of relationships, is that it is more likely to discipline human impulses and desires in ways that benefit both partners.[35] In Durkheim's words: "By forcing a man to attach himself forever to the same woman, marriage assigns a strictly definite object to the need for love, and closes the horizon. . . . Being unable to seek other satisfactions than those permitted, without transgressing his duty, he restricts his desires to them. The salutary discipline to which he is subjected makes it his duty to find his happiness in his lot, and by doing so supplies him with the means."[36]

The disciplinary function that Durkheim attributes to marriage is probably most likely to be realized today in marriages in which spouses are very devoted to the institution itself—especially given the high contemporary rates of marital instability and the high levels of variance in adherence to marital ideals of permanence and fidelity.[37] Because of their dedication to the principles of sexual fidelity and lifelong commitment, men who are highly committed to marriage are more likely to avoid other romantic opportunities and to see their relationships in terms of a long-term time horizon. Their expectations of security and permanence, in turn, provide them with more incentives to devote themselves to their wives by—among other things—doing positive marital emotion work. To put this in terms of organizational theory, by foreclosing the exit option of adultery or divorce, such men are more likely to pursue the loyalty option of investing highly in their relationship in an effort to form and maintain a happy marriage.[38]

Finally, intimate relationships characterized by high levels of trust are more conducive to the cultural logic of gift exchange that most Americans associate with marriage. Men who are deeply committed to the institution of marriage are more likely to trust their wives and to engender greater trust from their wives, in large part because of their commitment to the ideals of marital fidelity and permanence. This marital trust enables them to make investments in their marriage without worrying about maintaining an ongoing account of the goods and services exchanged in the relationship.[39] Thus, they are able to conduct their marriages according to the enchanted logic of gift exchange, according to which gifts can be given even when there is no immediate expectation of reciprocity and partners avoid keeping an explicit accounting of the pattern of exchange for fear of dissipating the spirit of enchantment that permeates the intimate relationship.[40] In this type of trusting or enchanted environment, men who are more committed will feel more comfortable giving valuable gifts—that is, gifts that exceed what is expected in the normal course of marriage.[41] Men's positive emotion work represents perhaps the most important gift they can give in contemporary marital relationships, precisely because in general they have not come close to shouldering an equal share of the emotion work associated with family life.

How, then, does this institutional theory of marriage stand with respect to the companionate theory of marriage? In some ways the two theories are orthogonal to one another. There are egalitarian men who are very committed to the institution of marriage just as there are men who hold a traditional orientation to gender but are not committed to the institution of marriage. However, for a variety of reasons, egalitarian men tend to be less committed to the institution, and men who are committed to the institution tend to be traditional in their orientation toward gender. Some of these reasons are religious and historical; for instance, religious institutions have generally produced a family ideology that links familism with gender-role traditionalism. Conversely, contemporary cultural liberalism has, for the most part, sought to dispense with earlier conventions regarding both gender and marital commitment. But is the usual opposition between marital egalitarianism and commitment only an accident of history?

In two important respects, this opposition is not accidental. First, students of marriage and of relationships more generally, such as Julie Brines and Steven Nock, have found that task specialization is associated with higher levels of commitment.[42] Specialization in marriage allows partners to focus on a set of tasks that is more limited than the range of tasks each would otherwise encounter. This focus allows them to devote more time and energy to developing skills tailored to the tasks for which they are responsible. It also means that each spouse is more dependent on the other for the complementary skills the other has developed. This mutual dependency, in turn, is linked to higher levels of commitment to the relationship.[43]

Although specialization need not be organized along gendered lines, the pervasive cultural belief that gender is a useful way of organizing social life suggests that couples who choose to specialize will often do so along conventionally gendered lines.[44] Couples who specialize—regardless of whether they do so along gender-typical lines—will have less of the role homophily that the companionate theory of marriage links to positive marital emotion work. Accordingly, to the extent that commitment to the institution of marriage is linked to patterns of marital specialization, the institutional theory of marriage stands in tension with the companionate theory of marriage.

The second reason for the opposition between these two theoretical approaches is that the deliberate pursuit of marital equality stands in tension with the enchanted cultural logic found in marriages organized along more communitarian lines. Specifically, as Julie Brines and Kara Joyner have observed, spouses who hold egalitarian beliefs about marriage and consistently act upon them have to invest considerable energy in monitoring one another's contributions to ensure that both partners are doing their fair share.[45] Such account keeping runs counter to the enchanted logic of marriage, which depicts marital interaction as motivated by a spirit of unconditional love rather than a spirit of calculated exchange. Indeed, this account keeping can introduce a spirit of self-regard that undercuts the self-sacrificial ethic of communitarian marriage. Moreover, given differences in personal temperament, ability, and circumstance, it is difficult for spouses to make equal contributions day in and day out. But a failure to live up to this egalitarian ideology can call into question a spouse's commitment to the relationship itself. Thus, the deliberate pursuit of marital equality that most often guides couples who strongly embrace egalitarianism can introduce a self-interested spirit of account keeping that undercuts marital commitment.

SOFT PATRIARCHS AND GOOD GUYS

Church attendance may generically promote a family-oriented strategy of action for men irrespective of their religious tradition. With regard to men's marital emotion work, there are several ways in which church attendance may promote the various forms of positive marital emotion work—for example, affection, empathy, and attention to the emotional dynamics of the marital relationship—that contribute to higher rates of marital quality and lower rates of divorce. First, church attendance links men to family-oriented social networks that may encourage them to devote themselves more to their wives' emotional well-being and to avoid extramarital romantic attachments,[46] and they furnish men with tips on how to please their wives and may prompt them to be more attentive to marital emotion work when they appear negligent in their marital duties; thus they provide men with social support and sanctions that reinforce expressive "feeling rules" concerning their emotion work in contemporary marriage.[47]

Second, religious attendance is known to supply a range of psychological support mechanisms to individuals. By furnishing a "sacred canopy" of meaning over everyday events, as well as over more liminal experiences, religion supplies people with a sense of emotional security that helps them cope with the challenges of life. Likewise, this sacred canopy of meaning also can impart a sense of personal efficacy as persons come to believe that an omnipotent deity is helping guide them through life. And the social integration offered in and through the family-oriented networks in religious organizations also provides social support that fosters emotional well-being.[48] In these ways, religion can reduce stress, encourage personal efficacy, and improve global happiness. These psychological factors have been linked to higher levels of marital quality[49] and are, in all likelihood, associated with men's positive marital emotion work.

Third, the common religious and moral messages found in most congregations may spur men's emotion work. In contemporary liturgical and sermonic discourse, God is often depicted as a loving father, friend, or spouse who is greatly concerned about our emotional well-being.[50] This therapeutic model of God may help orient men's own emotion work in the family by encouraging them to devote themselves more fully to their wives. Likewise, the discursive stress given to common moral norms of caring, reciprocity, and compassion in many congregations may also prompt men to do more marital emotion work, especially since the family is seen as the primary venue for the enactment of religiously sanctioned values.[51] The hypothesis that religion generically fosters higher levels of emotion work on the part of married men with children is in keeping with a growing body of literature that finds religious attendance to be associated with higher levels of marital quality and lower levels of divorce.[52]

But what about the possibility that specific religious traditions, and the "world images" produced and legitimated by those traditions,[53] influence the marital emotion work of men with children? The research that has been conducted thus far on marital quality and stability suggests that differences in religious culture have little or no influence on the marital relationship.[54] These results have led some observers to conclude that cleavages in gender and family ideology between conservative Protestant institutions and progressive cultural institutions are more symbolic than real: that is, differences over gender and family matters serve more to mark off collective boundaries and signal commitment to distinctive ideological visions than to guide marital conduct.[55] This scholarship would lead us to expect few differences along religious, theological, or other ideological lines in men's marital emotion work. But what about the ideologies produced by conservative Protestant institutions on topics like marriage, gender roles, and men's emotion work in marriage? Do theological conservatism, familism, and gender-role traditionalism have no influence on men's emotion work in marriage?

Conservative Protestantism views the family as *the* foundational institution in society. The family is the repository of faith and virtue; it is the crucial arena where affection and support are most readily given and received. In this subculture, a healthy, happy, stable marriage is the linchpin of a strong family. The marital relationship is freighted with tremendous symbolic value for a range of religious and cultural reasons that in turn motivate discussions about male responsibilities that inhere in the institution of marriage. One of the key responsibilities husbands have is to demonstrate unconditional love toward their wives. In other words, the familistic ideology that pervades the conservative Protestant world furnishes to conservative Protestant married men the motivation and a template for marital behavior that should foster emotion work on their part.

The conservative Protestant dedication to marriage follows, in large part, from the biblically centered worldview that orients the religious ideology of this subculture. Drawing on creation accounts in Genesis and affirmed in the New Testament, especially the Pauline epistles, this perspective—as articulated by leaders like James Dobson—depicts marriage as a covenantal relationship ordained by God for a number of purposes.[56] First, marriage is designed to model the relationship between Christ and the church (Eph. 5:23–27): following Christ's example, the husband is supposed to provide for, protect, and lead his wife and family in a spirit of total self-sacrifice; following the church's example, the wife is to respond to her husband's sacrificial love with love of her own, as well as with respect and submission. Second, marriage is designed by God so that men and women can provide and receive spiritual, emotional, and economic support to one another (Gen. 1:28, 2:18, 2:21–24; Deut. 24:5). Finally, marriage is ordained for procreation and the rearing of children who should be brought up to love and serve God (Eph. 6:4; Gen. 1:28; Prov. 22:6; Ps. 78:4–8). And out of deference to all the parties vested in the relationship—God, spouses, and children, as well as church and community—married men and women are called to cultivate the virtues of self-sacrifice, fidelity, charity, and religious devotion in their marriages.[57]

But, of course, the conservative Protestant approach to marriage also grows out of particular historical developments. As we have seen, because key religious and cultural characteristics of conservative Protestantism were institutionalized in the nineteenth century, this religious tradition has been profoundly shaped by the bourgeois ethos and the social-structural differentiation that took hold in the nineteenth century.[58] The home came to be seen as a "haven in a heartless world"[59]—a place of rest and refuge where a feminine spirit of selflessness and sentiment prevails. As a consequence, intimacy and sentiment have been awarded a paramount position in the family ideals of conservative Protestantism.[60] Likewise, the ordering of work and family life along gendered lines that was institutionalized in this era also shapes contemporary conservative Protestant notions of femininity and masculinity, with women assigned primary responsibility for domestic life and men assigned primary responsibility for paid work outside of the home.[61]

The continuing influence of this bourgeois familism is clearly evident in contemporary conservative Protestant discussions of marriage. One family expert has this to say about family life and marriage: "The foundation upon which a society is constructed . . . is the family. And the most important component of the family is the husband-wife relationship. Any changes in that relationship will produce far-reaching effects upon the community as a whole. As long as the husband-wife tie is intact, an emotional cornerstone will be created upon which the happiness and satisfaction of everyone can be constructed."[62] This quote suggests how conservative Protestant views of the social world, the importance of the family, and the sentimental character of family life come together to focus attention on the stability and emotional health of marriage.

The conservative Protestant approach to marriage has also been shaped by the symbolic and practical challenges to the traditional family posed by developments in the second half of the twentieth century. In their effort to shore up this family model, conservative Protestant elites have vigorously asserted explicitly religious lines of argument in defense of the marital virtues of lifelong fidelity and self-sacrifice. For instance, in a clear challenge to more progressive understandings of intimate relationships, a committee of the Southern Baptist Convention recently issued a report defining and defending an explicitly biblical model of marriage: "Marriage, according to Scripture, is a covenant commitment to the exclusive, permanent, monogamous union of one man and one woman, and thus it cannot be defined as a flexible contract between consenting human beings. Rather, the strong and enduring bond of marriage, pledged in the presence of God Himself, is enriched by the couple's unconditional love for and acceptance of one another."[63] This report, which is replete with citations from Scripture, is emblematic of the way in which conservative Protestant elites and institutions have drawn on their biblical worldview to assert and reassert a familist approach to marriage. Family experts from this subculture have also relied upon a particular reading of the historical and the sociological record to make the Americanist argument that declines in the health and stability of marriage will seriously harm the commonweal and American civilization itself.[64]

Although conservative Protestantism has articulated a vision of marriage that is, in many ways, distinctively countercultural, it has in one crucial respect adopted and deepened the contemporary emphasis on emotional fulfillment in marriage. This expressive focus is readily apparent in the way that the voluminous marital advice literature that is produced and consumed in this subculture is overwhelmingly focused on the relational dynamics between husband and wife rather that the productive, consumptive, or child-rearing functions also associated with married life in the United States.[65] This expressive approach to marriage is motivated, on the one hand, by a desire to strengthen Christian marriages by adopting therapeutic techniques and goals in the hope that that will increase marital happiness and stability. It is also in keeping with the sentimental side of bourgeois familism. For instance, after decrying various indicators of family decline—rising rates of divorce, attacks on the institution of motherhood, and so on—James Dobson advises men to fight family decline by redoubling their emotion work through the "provision of emotional support . . . of conversation . . . of making her feeling like a lady . . . of building her ego."[66] What is striking about his comments is that this leading Christian family expert seems to think that the best answer to the challenges that beset contemporary marriage is a more expressive ethic centered around positive emotion work. Dobson devotes comparatively little attention to the role of faith and virtue in fostering good marriages.

This therapeutic focus also is motivated by more instrumental concerns. In the revealingly titled book *If Only He Knew: What No Woman Can Resist,* Gary Smalley details a host of feeling rules to guide men's marital emotion work. He exhorts men to listen, to comfort, to communicate, to praise, and to surprise their wives. He lists 122 ways in which husbands are insensitive to their wives—from "being easily distracted when she is trying to talk" to "not inviting her out on special romantic dates from time to time." He tells husbands to attend to their wives' "needs" and "potential" so that they grow as persons and feel cherished by their husbands.[67]

Smalley's perspective reflects the therapeutic assumption institutionalized in conservative Protestantism, as well as in the secular marital advice industry, that the key to a happy marriage is open, affirming communication and symbolic and verbal expressions of affection between two adults who are in touch with their own psychological needs and the needs of their partners. But what is also interesting about Smalley's work is that he is quite forthright about voicing the instrumentalist motivation that runs through much of conservative Protestant marital advice: namely, if men and women properly perform their roles in marriage, they will secure for themselves a happier, more fulfilling relationship. In Smalley's words, "Remember, *you* are the one who gains when you strive to have a loving relationship with your wife." Through-out the book he promises men that changes in their behavior will make their wives more understanding, appreciative, attentive, and sexually responsive. This is not to say that Smalley neglects to invoke Christian notions of self-sacrifice as he encourages men to attend to their wives' emotional well-being. At one point he writes, "You and I need to become more responsible, loving partners, no matter what our wives do. That is the basis for genuine love—*doing what is right no matter what the other person does or says.*"[68] But this book, like the conservative Protestant discourse on marriage more generally, offers an admixture of therapeutic, biblical, and instrumental rationales for increased levels of male marital emotion work.

Thus, the marital discourse produced by conservative Protestant institu-tions combines traditional cultural elements, biblical literalism and bourgeois familism, with more progressive cultural elements, therapeutic and instrumen-tal approaches to marriage, to detail feeling rules that call for married men to devote more time, affection, and empathy to their wives. In this area of family life, as in others, the conservative Protestant approach is characterized neither by resistance nor by accommodation but rather by an innovative form of expres-sive traditionalism that seeks to protect core religious values while incorporating some cultural elements from the broader social environment. If this discourse influences marital behavior, we can expect that, all other things being equal, conservative Protestant affiliation and theological conservatism are positively related to marital emotion work on the part of married men with children. Moreover, the strong familist arguments that are marshaled in support of mari-tal commitment and a marriage-centered lifestyle suggest that any positive reli-gious effects on male emotion work may be mediated by familism.

But, of course, all other things are not equal in considering the influence of conservative Protestant family culture on the emotion work of married men with children. As noted earlier, a number of scholars have argued that the largely traditional orientation toward gender found in conservative Protestant family discourse pushes men away from embracing positive marital emotion work and toward negative forms of emotion work like domestic violence.[69]

There are two important respects in which conservative Protestant family ideology takes a conservative approach to gender. First, conservative Protestant elites and laity generally support the principle of male headship in marriage. Recall, for instance, that the Southern Baptist Convention recently issued a state-ment calling upon the husband to "lead" his family and the wife "to submit herself graciously to the servant leadership of her husband."[70] This commitment to male authority is based upon a literal reading of biblical texts (Eph. 5:21–33; 1 Cor. 11:2–16; 1 Tim. 2:8–15.) and upon a broader conviction that God has established a divine order that extends to the ordering of the family along gendered lines.[71] Following the companionate theory of marriage, this endorsement of male authority would seem to promote distance between a husband and wife and, consequently, lower levels of male marital emotion work.

Evangelical and fundamentalist family ideology is also conservative insofar as it endorses a separate-spheres model of family and work, with men taking responsibility for breadwinning and women taking responsibility for homemaking. As we have seen, conservative Protestant support for this model has softened considerably in recent years, but a majority of key elites and laity continue to express support for this model. For instance, the Southern Baptist Convention recently called upon men to "provide" for their wives and for wives to act as a "helper in managing the household and nurturing the next generation."[72] The companionate theory of marriage would predict that role specialization would lead to lower levels of male marital emotion work since husbands and wives would have less in common to talk about.

However, in two crucial respects, the brand of gender-role traditionalism produced in the conservative Protestant world may not be associated with lower levels of men's marital emotion work. First, the conservative Protestant belief that gender differences are divinely ordained is paradoxically linked to a heightened awareness of the importance of encouraging men to do emotion work in their marriages. Sociologists have observed that men generally have to learn to act in ways counter to their gender socialization to perform the level of positive marital emotion work that their wives look for in the relationship.[73] Conservative Protestant family experts like Dobson and Smalley make similar claims prescriptively, though rooting their arguments in an essentialist understanding of gender.

For instance, after pointing to an array of biological and psychological evidence to show his readers that "God made" men and women "different," Dobson argues that women are more invested in relationships and family life and men are more invested in conquest and work. Operating with this essentialist logic, Dobson makes the point that men are naturally less inclined than women to attend to the emotional dynamics of their marriages. He does not use this line of argument to suggest that women should accept lower levels of emotion work, however. Instead, he says that a husband must work harder to "meet his wife's needs and longings"—including her desire for conversation, affirmation, affection, and so on—precisely because he is not as naturally inclined as his wife to attend to the marital relationship.[74]

Similarly, one of the central premises of Smalley's book *If Only He Knew* is that contemporary marital difficulties are rooted in men's ignorance of the fact that "men and women are TOTALLY DIFFERENT" and their concomitant blindness to the distinctive emotional needs of their wives. "What do you think is the major stumbling block for most husbands in developing a lasting love for their mates?" he asks. "I have found that it is failing to meet a woman's needs from *her viewpoint.*" Like Dobson, Smalley argues that men have a natural proclivity to focus more on their careers or hobbies than their marital relationships. Accordingly, a man must fight this inclination by frequently demonstrating to his wife that she is the most important person in his life. He can do this by planning romantic getaways, displaying frequent affection, and limiting the amount of time he spends on work or hobbies.[75] More generally, Smalley argues that men must recognize that God made women more attentive to relationships, and they must work harder in the emotional arena to make up for their comparative weakness in this arena. Dobson and Smalley's work is emblematic of the way in which conservative Protestant family ideology has adjusted its message to the increasingly expressive character of contemporary marriage by encouraging men to act in counterstereotypical ways without sacrificing their underlying belief that the world has been gendered by an omnipotent God.

The second reason the gender-role traditionalism of conservative Protestantism may not be associated with lower levels of men's marital emotion work is that the discourse around male headship has shifted markedly in the last three decades. Before feminism challenged patriarchal understandings of authority, conservative Protestantism asserted the ideal of male headship without equivocation or qualification. But since the feminist challenge of the 1970s, conservative Protestant supporters of male headship have increasingly stressed that male leadership is oriented toward service—hence, the near universal use of the term *servant-leadership* in conjunction with discussions of male authority.[76]

The Southern Baptist Convention, for instance, "calls the husband to a loving leadership in which he cares responsibly for his wife's spiritual, emotional, and physical needs."[77] Dobson says that male headship means that a husband should put "the best interests of his family above his own."[78] Moreover, the qualitative literature suggests that the notion of male headship has been redefined away from calling for men to occupy an encompassing and domineering position of authority and toward exhorting them to fulfill a more limited role that forces them to take responsibility for attending to the spiritual and emotional needs of their wives and children.[79] As one conservative Protestant man said, headship is a matter of

> providing for the emotional needs, for the sense of identity and security and so many things that men haven't even considered. It's to be the servant of, to make sure that the woman is provided and presented to Christ at his return as spotless and perfect or unblemished. And that's a huge task, a huge responsibility to nurture in such a way that that woman or that person is whole in every dimension in her life—in self-esteem, emotionally, spiritually, physically—that every area of her being is met by the husband.[80]

Notice that he does not say that headship entails making key family decisions or shouldering sole responsibility for breadwinning. His comments are indicative of the way in which headship has been reorganized along expressive lines, emptying the concept of virtually all of its authoritative character.

Indeed, research on marital decision making finds no relationship between conservative Protestantism and higher levels of male decision making.[81] It would appear that the world of conservative Protestantism is willing to dispense with the practice of male authority and to reorient notions of headship toward emotion work in the family so long as husbands can retain their symbolic leadership. Furthermore, the effects of conservative Protestant gender-role ideology may be complicated by this subculture's willingness to link notions of gender essentialism and male headship to prescriptive calls for more emotion work on the part of married men with children.

This review of conservative Protestant discourse on gender and marriage leads me to offer two competing hypotheses. If the theoretical mechanisms articulated by the companionate theory of marriage are correct and are applicable to the distinctive gender ideology of this subculture, conservative Protestant affiliation and theological conservatism—along with the conservative gender-role ideology produced and legitimated by conservative Protestant institutions—will be associated with lower levels of men's marital emotion work. On the other hand, conservative Protestantism's effort to link elements of its gender-role traditionalism with marital emotion work may offset any negative effects on such work associated with its approach to gender. Thus, the competing hypothesis is that conservative Protestant affiliation, theological conservatism, and gender-role traditionalism are not associated with lower levels of men's positive emotion work in marriage. Indeed, the kind of soft patriarchy endorsed by this subculture—a patriarchy denuded of real power and oriented, symbolically at least, to the service of wife and family—suggests that conservative Protestant men will be more attentive to the emotional needs of their wives than other men.

As with other domains of family life, mainline Protestantism has not dedicated as much attention to marriage as conservative Protestantism has. This reflects the mainline's tendency since the 1960s to shift attention away from the private world of family life and toward the public world of social justice;[82] it also reflects the ways in which the mainline approach to family and gender fails to support intense normative or practical attention to the marital relationship. The mainline rejects the crisis frame that conservative Protestantism has applied to the family in the United States. It is more inclined to take the view, also advanced by many leading cultural institutions, that the family is changing rather than declining.

For instance, in *Christian Marriage and Family: Caring for Our Generations,* mainline theologians John Patton and Brian Childs argue that a "revised norm for Christian family living" can lead the church "away from its grief over the idealized family . . . toward an inclusive view of the family as many different combinations of human beings who care for those before and after them."[83] The largest mainline denomination, the United Methodist Church, has underlined its support for "a wider range of options" than the nuclear family.[84] The mainline's inclusive approach to family life is heavily influenced by a therapeutic ethic that elevates the good of relationship quality over competing goods, including marital permanence; it is also shaped by a liberal Protestant ethic of divine love and acceptance that is based on a reading of the New Testament but seeks to follow the spirit rather than the letter of the biblical text.[85] This inclusive ethic is also shaped by mainline Protestantism's embrace of cultural liberalism, which has sought since the 1960s to throw off traditional family ideals that are seen as oppressive and discriminatory, especially toward women and minorities.[86]

This inclusive family ethic means that the mainline is less attached to the institution of marriage and more accepting of divorce than is conservative Protestantism. Patton and Childs write that the moral status of a divorce depends on the "relational circumstances" of a marriage. They explain that "it is more important to maintain and actualize the function of caring than to maintain the structure of marriage."[87] Thus, mainline Protestantism is less likely to foster a familist view of marriage that stresses the importance of virtues like fidelity and sacrifice.[88] If the institutional theory of marriage is correct, then, mainline Protestant men should be less committed than conservative

Protestant men to their marriages and, consequently, less likely to devote themselves to marital emotion work.

Mainline Protestantism also has fewer institutional and religious mechanisms that encourage men to attend to the relational dynamics of marriage. There is no mainline equivalent of Focus on the Family, which reaches millions of people with its messages about marriage, parenting, and other family matters through its radio and print media. Lower levels of religious practice and salience among mainline Protestant men mean that they are less likely to connect religious convictions and practices to their family life—including marriage.[89] For these reasons also, married mainline men with children should be less likely to perform positive marital emotion work than their conservative Protestant peers.

Although mainline Protestantism is less familist—at least culturally—than conservative Protestantism, this does not mean that mainline churches offer no cultural influences that push men to invest emotionally in their marriages. As Nancy Ammerman has observed, the Golden Rule Christianity found in many mainline congregations furnishes practices—rituals, family-oriented activities, and so on—that orient adherents to a generic ethic of caregiving and mutuality, especially in the family,[90] and the pastoral discourse that the mainline does produce regarding marriage also stresses the importance of fostering caring relationships. Caring tends to be defined along therapeutic lines: it means to help others grow as individuals, to see and fulfill their needs, and to communicate with greater honesty and authenticity. This therapeutic ethic of care is formulated in such a way as to stress that individuals should care for themselves as much as they care for others.[91] This leads me to a more nuanced hypothesis: the lower levels of familism found in mainline Protestantism, compared to conservative Protestantism, leads mainline men to do less emotion work than their conservative Protestant peers, but the generic ethic of caring found in mainline churches leads them to do more emotion work than their unchurched peers.

The foregoing discussion assumes that the institutional theory of marriage is more important than the companionate theory in predicting men's marital emotion work. But if the companionate theory of marriage is better able to predict men's emotion work, then the liberal gender culture institutionalized in mainline Protestant congregations may foster higher levels of marital emotion work by married men with children. As we have seen, mainline Protestant institutions clearly endorse an egalitarian vision of family life. Recall, for instance, that in 1988 the United Methodist Church affirmed "shared responsibility for parenting by men and women" and rejected "social norms that assume different standards for women than for men in marriage."[92] The egalitarian ethos found in mainline churches may be pushing men to embrace role homophily, egalitarian patterns of marital authority, and counterstereotypical forms of masculinity, all of which may be associated with higher levels of emotion work.

On the other hand, the effect of mainline institutional egalitarianism on men's emotion work may be limited. Because the mainline does not devote a great deal of attention to marriage per se and because mainline Protestants are less likely to see their family life through a religious lens, the laity may not be much affected by the egalitarian gender-role ideology found in mainline Protestantism. Indeed, my findings indicate that nominal mainline Protestant men are more egalitarian than active mainline Protestant men in belief and practice. Other research finds that mainline Protestant men are significantly less likely to think about their gender roles in religious terms than conservative Protestant men.[93] Accordingly, we can expect that any positive effects of mainline gender-role egalitarianism on marital emotion work will be weak.

MEN'S MARITAL EMOTION WORK

To measure men's marital emotion work, I relied on data taken from the second wave of the National Survey of Families and Households, which was conducted from 1992 to 1994 (NSFH2) (for methodological details see the appendix). I used the second wave of the survey because the first wave does not include any questions regarding marital emotion work.[94] Using data from a subset of 2,785 married men in NSFH2, I focused on five indicators of men's marital emotion work: affection and understanding, empathy, domestic violence, quality time together, and socializing together.

AFFECTION AND UNDERSTANDING

The first two dependent variables of interest here—husbands' affection and understanding—are taken from wives' reports of their husbands' emotion work. Specifically, wives were asked how happy they were with the "love and affection you get from your spouse" and with the "understanding you receive from your spouse." (See table A6.1 in the appendix.) Here, I rely upon spousal reports because the NSFH2 did not ask respondents directly about the marital emotion work they performed. As chapter 5 indicated, there are advantages and disadvantages to this empirical strategy. On the one hand, this measure does not suffer from self-report bias since it is derived from the partners of the men under study. On the other hand, wives' happiness with different dimensions of their husbands' emotion work may have more to do with their own standards

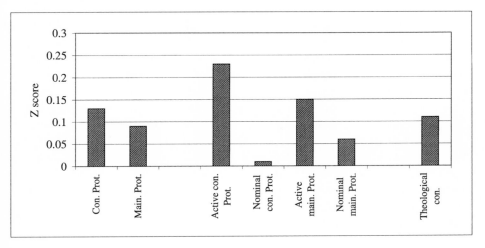

Figure 6.1   Wife's happiness with husband's love and affection

Source: NSFH2 (1992–1994).
Note: The comparison category for all religious affiliation effects is Unaffiliated, and for theological conservatives it is Non–theological conservative.

for spousal emotion work than with the actual amount of marital emotion work their husbands are doing. This is an especially important limitation in light of the fact that religious or ideological commitments may cause wives to lower their emotional standards. Accordingly, the results from these indirect measures of men's marital emotion work must be viewed in a more tentative light than results derived from direct reports of marital emotion work.

My findings indicate that the wives of both conservative and mainline Protestant family men are more likely to report happiness with the love and affection they receive from their husbands, compared to wives of unaffiliated men. However, only the conservative Protestant effect is statistically significant. The mean difference between the scores for wives of conservative Protestants and wives of unaffiliated husbands is about one-seventh of a standard deviation, a very modest effect size (see figure 6.1; see table A6.2 in the appendix for more details).

The wives of active conservative and mainline Protestants are more likely than their nominal counterparts to report happiness with the love and affection they receive from their husbands. Once again, however, in relation to the scores of wives of unaffiliated men, only the active conservative Protestant effect—

which is almost one-quarter of a standard deviation—is statistically significant. The effect size is not large, but standardized coefficient tests indicate that the active conservative Protestant effect is larger than that of sociocultural factors such as income, education, and region. Furthermore, wives of active conservative Protestants report higher levels of happiness for this outcome than the wives of all other groups of Protestants. The wives of theologically conservative men also report higher levels of happiness than the wives of men who are not theologically conservative; this effect is statistically significant. Adding theological conservatism to the model reduces the effect of active conservative Protestantism by more than 25 percent. This suggests that one of the reasons an active conservative Protestant affiliation is associated with wives' reports of love and affection is that the theologically conservative ideology of these men encourages them to invest in the marital relationship.

Adding familism to the model reduces the effect of theological conservatism by almost one-third, to nonsignificance, and of active conservative Protestantism by almost one-fifth, also to nonsignificance. Husbands' familism is strongly and significantly associated with wives' reports of happiness with the love and affection they receive from their partners. By contrast, the gender-role traditionalism of husbands is not related to this outcome and does not mediate any of the religious effects. Additional models looking at measures of marital equality—for example, the husband's share of household labor, the wife's share of the family's income, and the wife's labor-force participation—provide no indication that role homophily between husband and wife is associated with higher levels of men's emotion work on this outcome; indeed, women who work are less likely to report satisfaction with the love and affection they receive from their husbands. These results provide a good deal of support for the institutional theory of marriage and no support for the companionate theory of marriage.

As a whole, the wives of both conservative and mainline Protestant family men report higher levels of happiness with the understanding they receive from their husbands, compared to wives of unaffiliated men, but these effects are small and insignificant. There is a noteworthy difference, however, between the levels of happiness reported by wives of active Protestant men and those reported by wives of unaffiliated family men and of nominal Protestants. The difference between wives of active conservative Protestant men and wives of unaffiliated men on this outcome is about one-sixth of a standard deviation— a modest, but significant, effect size. Moreover, wives of active conservative and mainline Protestant men are significantly happier than the wives of nominal Protestant men (see figure 6.2). Thus, my findings suggest that religious attendance, especially for conservative Protestants, is associated with more

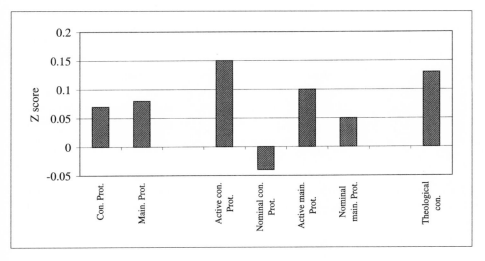

Figure 6.2   Wife's happiness with husband's understanding

Source: NSFH2 (1992–1994).
Note: The comparison category for all religious affiliation effects is Unaffiliated, and for theological conservatives it is Non–theological conservative.

empathetic behavior on the part of married men with children. (See table A6.3 in the appendix for details.)

Women who are married to theological conservatives are more likely to report happiness with the understanding they receive from their husbands than women who are married to men who are not theological conservatives. The difference between the two groups is about one-seventh of a standard deviation—a modest effect size. Theological conservatism also explains about one-half of the association between active religious affiliation and this outcome. Husbands' familism, in turn, mediates one-fourth of the association between theological conservatism and wives' reports of happiness with the understanding they receive from their husbands; it is a significant predictor of wives' reports of happiness with this outcome. By contrast, gender-role traditionalism is not associated with wives' reports of happiness with the understanding they receive from their husbands; nor does it mediate any of the religious effects. An additional model testing various measures of marital equality also provides no indication that equality is associated with higher levels of happiness in this regard for married women; indeed, part-time work is negatively associated with wives' reports of happiness for this outcome. Once again, we see that theological conservatism and familism seem to promote positive emotion work on the part of married men with children, and they help to explain why churchgoing Protestant men—especially active conservative Protestants—appear to be more empathetic than their peers. These results provide further support for the institutional, but not the companionate, theory of marriage.

Of course, since both of these outcomes are indirect measures of men's emotion work, we do not know whether they are indicative of husbands' actual emotion work or of their wives' expectations regarding emotion work. To explore this issue further, I ran an additional model for each outcome.[95] The model sorts couples into four categories on the basis of familism: couples in which both partners scored above the median on familism, couples in which only the husband scored above the median, couples in which only the wife scored above the median, and couples in which neither partner scored above the median. For both outcomes I find that couples who share high levels of familism are significantly more likely than couples who share low levels of familism to have wives who report high levels of happiness with the positive emotion work of their husbands. However, when just the husband reports high levels of familism, wives are *not* more likely to report happiness with the emotion work of their husbands. Finally, when just the wife reports high levels of familism, wives report greater happiness with the understanding they receive from their husbands, but they do not report greater happiness with the love and affection they receive from them. These findings largely parallel the results reported in chapter 5, which indicate that high dyadic levels of familism play a key role in predicting whether women are satisfied with the appreciation they receive from their husbands for their household labor.

All of this suggests that dyadic marital commitment is crucial in predicting whether women are happy with the emotion work they receive from their husbands. It is not enough for only husbands to be committed to marriage and the family. The dyadic nature of this process suggests two tentative conclusions. First, it may be that husbands do not put their familistic convictions into practice unless they perceive that their wives are equally committed to the marital relationship. Second, it may be that wives who hold familistic views are more likely to construct a family myth that their husbands are emotionally engaged in the marriage if they perceive that their husbands are equally committed to the marital relationship. I suspect that both dynamics are at work in contemporary marriages, but future research will be required to determine if dyadic familism has a greater impact on husbands' emotion work than on wives' perception of that work.

DOMESTIC VIOLENCE

Measures of the third dependent variable of interest—domestic violence—are based on both respondent and spousal reports. Husbands and wives were both asked whether they had had arguments that had gotten "physical" in the previous year. If they responded in the affirmative, they were then asked if they or their partner had "become physically violent." If the husband reported that he had become physically violent or if the wife reported that her husband had become physically violent on one or more occasion, I coded the husband as violent. By including wives' reports of violence, this strategy provides the most expansive categorization of domestic violence possible with NSFH2 and may help correct against husbands' tendency to underreport such incidents. Of course, given the sensitivity of the issue, this measure still probably underreports the true incidence of domestic violence among married couples. In any case, with this coding scheme I estimate that approximately seven percent of the husbands in this sample committed domestic violence in the year prior to the survey (see table A6.1 in the appendix). I view domestic violence as, among other things, an indicator that husbands have not been doing enough positive emotion work in their marriages and that, as a consequence, they are falling into a deeply destructive form of marital conflict.[96]

Very little empirical research has thus far been conducted on religion and domestic violence. A study on the subject by Christopher Ellison, John Bartkowski, and Kristin Anderson found that a conservative Protestant affiliation is not related to domestic violence and that weekly church attendance is associated with lower levels of such violence.[97] This study, however, did not break out affiliation by church attendance; nor did it look at the potential mediating role of familism and gender-role ideology on rates of domestic violence.

Figure 6.3 displays predicted means of husbands' domestic violence derived from logistic regression equations, with all the control variables set at the mean or mode. This figure indicates that 4.8 percent of conservative Protestant married men with children committed domestic violence in the year prior to NSFH2, compared to 4.3 percent of mainline Protestant married men with children and 3.2 percent of unaffiliated married men with children. The differences between the results for these groups, however, are not statistically significant.

Once religious affiliation is broken out by church attendance, however, the differences between religious groups become statistically significant. Nominal conservative Protestant husbands have a domestic violence rate of 7.2 percent and are significantly more abusive than unaffiliated husbands, active

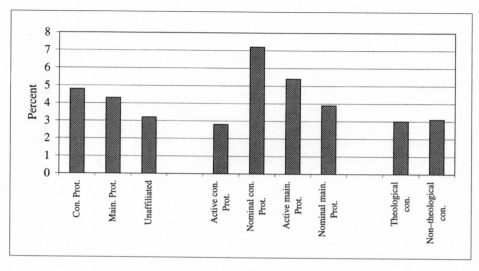

Figure 6.3   Husbands who commit domestic violence

Source: NSFH2 (1992–1994).

conservative Protestant husbands, and nominal mainline Protestant husbands. By contrast, active conservative Protestant husbands are significantly less likely to commit domestic violence compared to active mainline Protestant husbands as well as nominal conservative Protestant husbands. Thus, figure 6.3 depicts a surprising phenomenon: namely, that active conservative Protestant husbands are the group in this study least likely to commit domestic violence, and nominal conservative Protestant husbands are the group in this study most likely to commit domestic violence.

For this outcome, none of my ideological measures—theological conservatism, familism, or gender-role traditionalism—appears to be significant. Nor does any of them mediate the religious effects indicated above. An additional model testing various measures of marital equality provides no support for the companionate theory of marriage. No measures of marital equality are associated with lower levels of domestic violence on the part of husbands. Indeed, women who work part-time are more likely to be abused than women who do not work outside the home. (See table A6.4 in the appendix for complete details.)

How do we interpret these surprising differences in rates of domestic violence between active and nominal conservative Protestant husbands? I suspect, in keeping with the institutional theory of marriage, that active conservative Protestant husbands benefit from the intense focus on marriage and family life found in many conservative Protestant congregations. The family-centered ethos in these congregations probably promotes higher levels of marital emotion work, which protects against domestic violence, and strong social sanctions against spousal abuse. Furthermore, given the high rates of violence among their nominal conservative Protestant peers—who may be their friends, family members, or neighbors—it may also be that active conservative Protestant husbands wish to set clear moral boundaries against peers they see headed down the wrong path.

In turn, the high levels of physical abuse found among nominal conservative Protestant husbands may be a consequence of a lingering commitment to patriarchy that is not tempered by church participation. Or it may be related to social factors that my models cannot adequately address—for example, most nominal conservative Protestants hail from the working class. In any case, we have already seen that nominal conservative Protestant family men devote comparatively little effort to parenting and showing appreciation for their wives' household labor and that active conservative Protestant family men devote comparatively high levels of effort to the same, and here we have yet more evidence that nominal and active conservative Protestant men differ to a great degree when it comes to their approach to family life.

QUALITY TIME AND SOCIAL TIME TOGETHER

The NSFH2 asked married men with children, "About how often did you and your wife spend time alone with each other, talking, or sharing an activity" in the past month? This measure taps the extent to which a husband devotes himself to spending time specifically cultivating the marital relationship. I consider this to be an indicator of quality relationship time; it is an encompassing measure of the extent to which men do things like going with their wives on, in Gary Smalley's words, "special romantic dates."

Religious affiliation is not related to the amount of quality time husbands spend with their wives; neither does church attendance make a difference on this measure. I find no evidence that active mainline or conservative Protestant men are more involved in this way than their nominal and unaffiliated peers. Thus, we have no evidence that active conservative Protestant men are following the exhortations of their leaders to spend more intimate time with their wives. (For additional details, see table A6.5 in the appendix.)

Theological conservatism and gender-role traditionalism also do not affect the amount of quality time men spend with their wives. However, familism

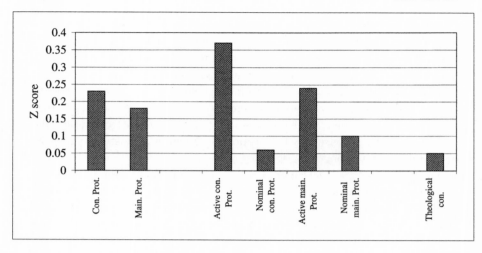

Figure 6.4 Couple's socializing time

Source: NSFH2 (1992–1994).
Note: The comparison category for all religious affiliation effects is Unaffiliated, and for theological conservatives it is Non–theological conservative.

is strongly and significantly associated with husbands' reports of marital quality time. The husbands with the highest familism scores were more than one-half a standard deviation higher on the index of quality time than the husbands with the lowest familism scores. This is a large effect, and standardized coefficient tests indicate that familism is more important in this domain than sociocultural factors such as age, education, income, and region. Thus, we again have evidence in support of the institutional theory rather than the companionate theory of marriage: a model testing the effects of marital equality finds no indication that it fosters higher levels of quality time. Indeed, wives who work part-time are less likely to enjoy special outings with their husbands, compared to wives who do not work outside the home.

NSFH2 also asked married men with children, "About how often did you and your wife spend time together in social activities with either friends or relatives" in the past month? I relied on this question to measure how much time husbands devote to socializing with their wives. I consider this another indicator of how emotionally invested a husband is in his marriage.

Figure 6.4 shows that both mainline and conservative Protestant family men are significantly more likely to socialize with their wives than are their unaffiliated peers. Mainline men are almost one-fifth of a standard deviation higher on this measure than unaffiliated men; conservative Protestant men are almost one-quarter of a standard deviation higher than unaffiliated men. Both of these effect sizes are modest. Effect sizes are larger, however, for active conservative and active mainline Protestant men. Active conservative Protestant husbands are more than one-third of a standard deviation higher than unaffiliated husbands in their score on the socializing index. This is a moderate effect size, and standardized coefficient tests reveal that the effect of an active conservative Protestant affiliation surpasses all other sociocultural factors in the model. Active mainline Protestant husbands are about one-quarter of a standard deviation higher on this measure than unaffiliated husbands. Furthermore, both groups of active Protestant husbands are significantly more likely than their nominal Protestant peers to spend time socializing with their wives.

Theological conservatives are slightly more likely to spend time with their wives than are husbands who are not theological conservatives. However, the effect of theological conservatism is not statistically significant and it does not mediate any of the denominational effects. Familism and gender-role traditionalism are also unrelated to this outcome. Finally, no measures of marital equality are associated with higher levels of socializing. (See table A6.6 in the appendix for details.)

Thus, on this outcome, we have modest support for the institutional theory and no support for the companionate theory of marriage. Family men who are integrated into the life of a religious institution—especially conservative Protestant men—spend more time socializing with their wives, compared to nominal Protestant and unaffiliated men. In all likelihood, the family-centered ethos and family-oriented social networks found in religious congregations—especially conservative Protestant ones—provide normative and social support for such socializing.

The results presented in this chapter provide three key sets of findings. First, we have clear evidence that ideology structures men's marital emotion work. Theological conservatism and familism, but not gender-role traditionalism, are both positively and significantly related to three out of five measures of men's marital emotion work. The addition of familism to each model where theological conservatism is significant consistently reduces theological conservatism to nonsignificance. Thus, consistent with the institutional theory of marriage, men who adhere to a familist ideology that stresses, among other things, the sanctity of marriage appear to be more likely to do positive marital emotion work. Moreover, the fact that familism consistently reduces the effect of theological conservatism to nonsignificance suggests that familism is produced and legitimated, at least in part, by religious institutions that, for religious and cultural reasons, stress the sanctity of marriage and the need for men's marital emotion work.

Second, consistent with the notion that religion has a generic influence on family life, religious attendance is associated with higher levels of marital socializing and, apparently, somewhat higher levels of affection and understanding on the part of married men with children. The family-oriented social networks, the common moral messages offered in religious congregations, and the psychological benefits associated with religious attendance probably account for the generic effect of religious attendance on men's marital emotion work.

Nevertheless, the findings reported in this chapter provide even stronger evidence that religion exercises tradition-specific influences on family behavior. Specifically, the third key set of findings is that conservative Protestant institutions appear to be uniquely capable of fostering positive emotion work on the part of married men with children. An active conservative Protestant affiliation is more consistently linked to a range of direct and indirect indicators of men's marital emotion work than an active mainline Protestant affiliation or no affiliation at all. The strong family orientation fostered by conservative Protestant institutions appears to push churchgoing men in the direction of an emotionally engaged approach to marital relations and away from a destructive approach marked by high levels of domestic violence. Curiously, nominal conservative Protestant family men take precisely the opposite approach to marriage: they are not emotionally engaged in their marriages and, perhaps partly as a consequence, they are the group in this study most likely to physically abuse their wives.

CONCLUSION

Given the increasingly expressive character of American marriages, the high importance that women, in particular, attach to the emotional quality of their marriages, and the leading role that women usually take in initiating divorces, men's emotion work in marriage and women's assessments of that work are two of the most important factors predicting contemporary marital quality and stability.[98] Accordingly, I have attempted to determine the role that religion and ideology play in structuring the marital emotion work of married men with school-age children. I also provide some suggestive evidence regarding the role religion and ideology play in structuring the assessments that women make of their husbands' emotion work. More particularly, in this chapter I provide answers to two competing but central theoretical and empirical questions: First, in keeping with the companionate theory of marriage, are conservative Protestantism and gender-role traditionalism associated with lower levels of male emotion work in marriage? And second, in keeping with the institutional theory of marriage, are religion and familism associated with higher levels of male emotion work in marriage?

The answer to the first question is no. None of the results reported in this chapter indicate that religion and gender-role traditionalism lead to lower levels of positive emotion work on the part of married men with children or to higher levels of domestic violence. Accordingly, we can conclude—at least for this sample of married men with children—that scholars of gender and the family who have charged, in the absence of any empirical evidence, that religious conservatism is one key force "pushing men toward authoritarian and stereotypical forms of masculinity" need to revisit their assumptions.[99] My findings not only fail to provide evidence that conservative Protestantism leads to stereotypical male insensitivity, they suggest precisely the opposite conclusion. Clearly, the expressive arena of marriage is one domain in which conservative Protestantism is not a force for reaction.

My findings offer no evidence in support of the companionate theory of marriage. None of the measures of gender equality in marriage—for example, equitable sharing of household labor, women's labor-force status, or earning parity—are associated with any of the five direct and indirect measures of men's marital emotion work examined in this chapter. This leads me to conclude that, at least with respect to men, egalitarian marriages are not characterized by higher levels of emotion work. One possible explanation for this is that egalitarian men may not accord marital emotion work the kind of salience that they accord to matters that have received more public attention—such as the division of household labor. The ideology of gender-role egalitarianism is associated with higher levels of housework on the part of men, but marital emotion work has not received the same level of public attention as a matter of gender justice, and, perhaps consequently, it also is not receiving the same level of private attention from men who have an egalitarian worldview.

The answer to the second question is more complex. My findings indicate that religious affiliation, particularly active conservative Protestant affiliation; theological conservatism; and familism are associated with higher levels of men's marital emotion work. These results are in keeping with the marriage-focused discourse produced by conservative Protestant institutions like Focus on the Family, which incorporate biblical, Americanist, therapeutic, and instrumental rationales into their calls for more marriage-centered behavior on the part of Christian men. This message is part and parcel of a larger familist ideology that is both produced and legitimated in religious institutions—especially conservative Protestant ones. Given the positive effects associated with theological conservatism and familism on three out of five outcomes regarding men's marital emotion work, it would appear that this message resonates most with theologically conservative men who identify with the sentimental and normative elements of the ideology of familism.

This discourse and practice regarding male emotion work is characteristic of the neotraditional approach to family life found in the conservative Protestant culture. While the vast majority of conservative Protestant institutions, leaders, and laity continue to maintain formal allegiance to the principle of male headship, it is an allegiance almost always softened by insistence on positive male emotion work, to a patriarchy that is rarely practiced. Husbands are urged to exercise servant-leadership by attending to their wives' needs for communication, emotional support, affection, and so on. Thus, in the marital domain, as in the parenting domain, conservative Protestantism appears to be fostering the ideal and practice of a soft patriarchy that is in keeping with the innovative cultural strategy of expressive traditionalism. According to this strategy, elements of modern life are incorporated into the religious tradition even as other elements are rejected so the tradition can maintain some degree of subcultural distinction and symbolically affirm continuity with its deepest impulses—in this case, biblical literalism, which is linked to patriarchal understandings of gender.

Mainline Protestantism, by contrast, does not appear to exert as much influence on men's marital emotion work, in part because church attendance is lower in this religious tradition. Accordingly, fewer men come in regular contact with the family-oriented ethos found in many mainline congregations. Another reason for this apparent lack of influence is that the mainline has not devoted a great deal of pastoral attention to cultivating strong and happy marriages, but has focused more attention to issues of social justice. Perhaps more importantly, in its effort to be inclusive, the mainline has shied away from addressing controversial family issues—including the state of marriage in general and marital relationship dynamics in particular. On the other hand, active mainline men do socialize often with their wives, and their wives report somewhat higher levels of happiness with the understanding they receive from their husbands, compared to wives of nominal Protestants. These outcomes can be attributed to the continuing emphasis that the mainline places on generic moral norms and the family-centered ethos that persists in many mainline congregations regardless of their official ideology. Thus, the Golden Rule liberalism found in mainline churches is associated with modestly higher levels of marital emotion work among active mainline Protestant family men than among their nominal counterparts.

My findings on husbands' emotion work provide support for the institutional theory of marriage. Men who embrace a familist ideology that sacralizes the institution of marriage appear to be more likely to invest themselves in the emotion work that is a crucial characteristic of happy and healthy marriages. Thus, the loyalty, trust, reciprocity, sense of obligation, and third party interest in the marital relationship that tend to inhere in a familist approach to marriage all combine to create an environment conducive to male investment in marital emotion work. In other words, commitment to the institution of marriage would seem to beget a willingness on the part of men to do more emotion work in their marriages.[100]

There is one major caveat to this support for institutional theory: usually wives report that they receive high levels of affection and understanding from their husbands only when both they and their husbands adhere to familist ideology. This may mean that men increase their marital emotion work only when they have wives who share their normative commitment to marriage, or it may mean that women with familist attitudes have lower expectations for the marital emotion work of their husbands when their husbands share their belief in the sanctity of marriage. Dyadic commitment to the institution of marriage, it would seem, is particularly valuable for the emotional health of contemporary marriages. These results suggest that the future of marital quality in the United States depends in part on the extent to which both spouses embrace a familist outlook that makes the husband more attentive to the emotional needs of his wife and the wife less likely to expect a great deal of emotion work from her husband.

CHAPTER SEVEN

CONCLUSION: FAMILY MODERNIZATION, THE DOMESTICATION OF MEN, AND THE FUTURES OF FATHERHOOD

Arguments over women in the pastorate and order in the Christian home (two years ago, the [Southern Baptist Convention] declared that wives should submit to their husbands) are not well understood by outside observers. For the vast majority of Southern Baptists, these issues are settled by the word of God. . . . Southern Baptists experience family trouble like everyone else, but at least they know how God intended to order the family. In essence, Southern Baptists are engaged in a battle against modernity, earnestly contending for the truth and authority of an ancient faith. To the cultured critics of religion, we are the cantankerous holdouts against the inevitable. But so far as the Southern Baptist Convention is concerned, the future is in God's hands. If faithfulness requires the slings and arrows of outraged opponents, so be it.

—R. Albert Mohler, president of Southern Baptist Seminary

MY FINDINGS paint a fairly stark picture of the growing moral polarization in the official family and gender ideologies produced by mainline and conservative Protestant institutions in response to the demographic and cultural changes that began in the late 1960s and early 1970s. This polarity has largely persisted into the present even though conservative Protestants have become more integrated into the modern world in the last three decades. As we have seen, at the ideological level, mainline Protestant churches have accommodated themselves to the family and gender changes that have marked the past half-century even as conservative Protestant churches and parachurch institutions have resisted central features of this family modernization.

But at the level of practice, the picture my findings paint of conservative and mainline Protestant family men is more nuanced. As might be expected, married men with children who are affiliated with conservative Protestant churches are in some ways traditional family patriarchs. They do a smaller share of household labor than most husbands, they are more likely than other fathers to use corporal punishment, and they affirm the importance of male headship in the family more than anyone else. But theirs is a very soft patriarchy. These family men are consistently the most active and emotionally engaged group of fathers and the most emotionally engaged group of husbands in this study. For these family men, the conservative Protestant commitment to the family largely outweighs their subculture's commitment to gender-role traditionalism. This family emphasis is found in conservative Protestant discourse, church social networks, and the ethos of most conservative Protestant congregations. This family focus helps to explain why so many of these men take an approach to family life that comes surprisingly close to the new man ideal of active and emotionally expressive familial involvement celebrated in the society at large.

At the same time, mainline Protestant married men with children are also more family focused than the official accommodationist ideology of their churches would suggest. They devote more affection to their wives and children compared to unaffiliated family men (but not conservative Protestant men), and they do more household labor than any other group in this study. Their relatively egalitarian approach to household labor, combined with their moderately high investments in child rearing and marriage, mean that they come closer than unaffiliated men to the new man ideal. I attribute their practical egalitarianism largely to the ideological commitments that motivate them to identify themselves as mainline Protestants. In other words, mainline Protestantism has not made them more egalitarian; rather, they have chosen to affiliate with or to remain affiliated with a mainline church because of their culturally progressive outlook. Their investments in parenting and marriage also seem to be derived in part from a progressive outlook that values male familial involvement. But in these latter two domains, church attendance seems to generate higher family investments. Here I think the family-oriented ethos and rituals and the Golden Rule ethical message and family-centered social networks found in many mainline Protestant churches all play a role in pushing mainline men in the direction of the new man ideal.

PERSISTENT POLARITIES IN THE FAMILY-RELATED IDEOLOGIES OF MAINLINE AND CONSERVATIVE PROTESTANTISM

In the last half of the twentieth century, the United States witnessed twin revolutions in the domains of gender and the family. Mainline and conservative Protestant institutions responded in markedly different fashion to these revolutions, with mainline institutions taking a largely accommodating stance and conservative Protestant institutions adopting a largely resistant posture. The resistance offered by conservative Protestantism to many of these changes has been particularly striking given that most major institutions in American life adopted a more accommodating stance—especially toward the changes in gender ideology and women's social status.

I have stressed four themes in the story of the emergence and persistence of family-related ideological polarity between these two religious traditions: their distinctive cultural orientations toward religious truth and morality, differences in social status and geographic concentration, variations in religious and institutional vitality, and the institutional imperatives of maintaining a distinctive sense of collective identity. Mainline Protestantism has had a progressive orientation toward religious and moral truth that is indebted to its emphasis on the spirit rather than the letter of the New Testament and to its embrace of the Enlightenment, which made it open to the changes in American family life and gender that occurred in the second half of the twentieth century. This orientation has shaped the mainline's embrace of a strategy of Golden Rule liberalism that combines an inclusive approach to family change with an abiding commitment to supporting generic moral norms.

Conservative Protestantism, by contrast, has maintained an orthodox orientation toward religious and moral truth—one characterized by the notion that this truth is the transcendent, absolute, and unchanging gift of a divine lawgiver. This orientation makes it skeptical of much of the modern project and, in this case, of the twin revolutions in gender and family in the second half of the twentieth century. Moreover, as these revolutions got under way in the late 1960s and early 1970s, mainline and conservative Protestantism occupied distinct positions in the American social structure. The majority of mainline Protestants hailed from middle and upper classes and from regions outside the South, and the majority of conservative Protestants hailed from the working and lower classes and from the South. These differences in social status and geography reflected and reinforced the distinct cultural orientations of these two religious traditions, with upwardly mobile and well-educated mainline Protestants inclined to identify with the "new morality" associated with the rise of a new social order and with less-educated, religiously traditional, Southern conservative Protestants inclined to reject the "new morality," which they associated with social disorder and Northern elites.

Since the 1970s the social and geographic position of conservative Protestants in American life has changed dramatically, with dramatic increases in education, female labor-force participation, and geographic dispersion outside the South. So why do the ideological polarities between mainline and conservative Protestant institutions continue to persist? All other things being equal, we might expect that these developments would have led to accommodation to family modernization and gender egalitarianism in ways that would have brought conservative Protestants closer to the mainline posture of openness to family modernization. But conservative Protestant institutions have continued to chart a path largely defined by resistance to family modernization, as illustrated by Southern Baptist pronouncements on marriage and gender. This is not to say that conservative Protestant institutions have not responded to changes in the broader social environment—indeed, we have seen a number of accommodations and innovations in their family-related ideologies. But what is striking about many of these changes, and especially the expressive strategy of encouraging men to be more engaged and affectionate with their families, is that they represent innovative efforts to shore up the family as an institution. Thus conservative Protestant institutions have adopted progressive means in the service of traditional ends.

The persistent institutional support for familism and gender-role traditionalism in the conservative Protestant world is a consequence essentially of two factors. First, conservative Protestantism enjoys high levels of religious and institutional vitality—measured by religious participation; religious giving; member support for large parachurch organizations; and a strong media presence in television, publishing, radio, and the Internet—that have allowed this subculture to maintain a measure of social and cultural distance from the broader society. Second, in this period support for the traditional family emerged as one of the central symbolic touchstones of conservative Protestant life: that is, as a crucial way of signaling conservative Protestant belief in the unchanging and inerrant truth articulated in the Bible and also of erecting cultural boundaries against liberal modernity.

In a word, support for familism and gender-role traditionalism has become a crucial dimension of conservative Protestant collective identity, and conservative Protestant institutions—especially multimillion-dollar organizations that aim to strengthen the traditional family, such as Focus on the Family, Concerned Women for America, and Promise Keepers—have an ongoing stake in the production and legitimacy of these ideologies. Conversely, one of the reasons mainline Protestant institutions have been so quick to publicly offer their support for family pluralism and gender equality is that they are thereby able to signal their progressive worldview and to assert cultural boundaries against fundamentalism—both of which are key to their sense of collective identity. Thus, the continuing ideological polarities over the family documented in this book provide some support for the notion that in American Protestantism there is a culture war over the family—at least at the institutional level.

LINKS BETWEEN THE FAMILY-RELATED IDEOLOGIES OF RELIGIOUS INSTITUTIONS AND THE FAMILY-RELATED BELIEFS AND PRACTICES OF THEIR MEMBERS

Mark Chaves has observed that the public ideologies espoused by a religious tradition and the practices of that tradition are often only "loosely coupled."[1] It could be that the formal positions staked out by mainline and conservative Protestant institutions have more to do with building collective identity than with guiding the beliefs and practices of the men and women who fill the church pews on Sundays. In other words, the disparate ideological positions staked out by, say, the Southern Baptist Convention and the United Methodist Church on women's issues and family pluralism may have more to do with these churches' effort to signal their symbolic position vis-à-vis liberal modernity than with their effort to influence the family behavior of their members.

Indeed, my findings based on data from the General Social Survey (GSS) and the National Survey of Families and Households (NSFH) show that there are gaps between the public ideologies of these religious groups and the family-related ideologies and practices of their members. Still, on a spectrum from loose to close coupling, the relationship between the beliefs and behaviors of mainline Protestants and the family and gender ideologies of mainline institutions is nearer to the loose end of the continuum, while the relationship between the beliefs and behaviors of conservative Protestants and the family and gender ideologies of conservative Protestant institutions is nearer to the close end of the continuum. Ideologically, 25 percent of mainline Protestant married men with children affirm progressive family and gender views (and 33 percent fall in the middle). By contrast, 54 percent of conservative Protestant married men with children hold traditional family and gender views (and 28 percent fall in the middle). Once we consider church attendance, the picture becomes even clearer. Less than 20 percent of active mainline Protestant family men affirm progressive family and gender views, and more than 60 percent of active conservative Protestant family men hold traditional family and gender views.[2] This means that church attendance is associated with a widening of the ideological gap between mainline institutions and their adherents and with a closing of the ideological gap between conservative Protestant institutions and their adherents.

Findings based on data from the NSFH and the Survey of Adults and Youth (SAY), reveal a similar picture when it comes to behavior. Compared to their unaffiliated and mainline counterparts, conservative Protestant married men with children are consistently the most active and expressive fathers and the most emotionally engaged husbands; they are also the strictest disciplinarians and the fathers least involved in household labor. Their neo-traditional family behavior largely corresponds to the strong note of familism and the accompanying gender-role traditionalism characteristic of the conservative Protestant subculture.

While mainline Protestant family men have the most egalitarian division of household labor, they are not significantly more involved with their children than are unaffiliated men. They are, however, somewhat more expressive with their children and wives than are unaffiliated men. Thus, the mainline's institutional support for egalitarianism and a Golden Rule ethic of family caring appears to be modestly associated with the family strategies of the married men with children who affiliate with mainline Protestant churches.

Once again, the coupling between ideology and practice is closest among conservative Protestant family men who attend church regularly. Active conservative Protestant family men consistently have the highest levels of practical and emotional engagement in fatherhood and marriage and the strictest approach to discipline of all the groups of men included in this study. By contrast, nominal conservative Protestant family men are not very different from their unaffiliated counterparts when it comes to their practical and emotional investments in family life, they are not strict disciplinarians, they invest the least amount of work in household labor, and they have the highest levels of domestic violence of any group in this study. Active mainline Protestant family men are somewhat more emotionally and practically engaged in their families than unaffiliated men, but they are less involved in housework than their nominal mainline peers. Indeed, it turns out that nominal mainline Protestant family men are the group in this study most committed to household labor; they are also more involved in one-on-one activities with their children than every other group except active conservative Protestants. Thus we see that in the practical domain, much as in the attitudinal domain, church attendance is associated with a closer coupling between institutional ideology and family practice among conservative Protestant family men than among their mainline counterparts.

Why does the coupling between institutional ideology and individual practice vary from one religious tradition to the next? First, the family is one of the central symbolic touchstones of conservative Protestant faith, so conservative Protestant institutions devote more attention than mainline institutions to underlining the religious and moral significance of their family-related ideals. Second, conservative Protestantism has devoted considerably more institutional and pastoral energy than mainline Protestantism to promoting its family and gender ideologies. Third, conservative Protestantism enjoys more religious vitality than mainline Protestantism, and consequently its social networks are better able to offer social support and exert social control on behalf of its family and gender norms. Finally, there is more ideological heterogeneity among active mainline men than among their active conservative Protestant counterparts. Almost half of active mainline Protestant married men identify themselves as theological conservatives, departing from the theologically progressive worldview endorsed by mainline institutions. These men are more inclined to hold conservative family and gender attitudes, to praise and hug their children, to spank their children, and to have wives who indicate that they feel their household labor is appreciated. In other words, many active mainline Protestant men resemble their active conservative Protestant peers and identify with the religious and family ideologies advocated by conservative Protestant institutions. By contrast, only about one-fifth of active conservative Protestant men fail to identify themselves as theological conservatives.

THE GENERIC AND TRADITION-SPECIFIC EFFECTS OF RELIGION ON FAMILY BEHAVIOR

The findings in this book also speak to recent debates about whether religion has generic or tradition-specific effects on family behavior. Religious participation is indeed associated with generic effects on male familial behavior in almost half of the outcomes examined herein, providing some evidence in support of the position that religion influences family behavior in a generic fashion. Religious participation is most likely to exert a generic effect on male family behavior in the parenting domain. Men who are regular churchgoers are more likely to spend time in youth-related activities, they hug and praise their children more often, they spank their kids more often, and they yell at their children less often than other fathers. This suggests that religion is most likely to exert a generic influence on family behavior when this behavior receives widespread social attention and approbation—as paternal involvement and emotional engagement now do.

But the findings in this book also lend strong support to the contention that religion has tradition-specific effects on family behavior. A conservative

Protestant affiliation, especially an active affiliation, is associated with virtually every behavioral outcome analyzed in this study. By contrast, a mainline Protestant affiliation is associated with only about half of the outcomes reviewed. Furthermore, the size of the conservative Protestant effect is consistently larger than any of the mainline effects, though the difference in effect sizes is not always statistically significant. Once again, the comparative advantages conservative Protestantism has over mainline Protestantism in its family focus, religious vitality, and ideological homogeneity help to explain why it has a larger and more consistent influence on the family behavior of married men with children. Thus, the cultural content and institutional strength of a particular religious tradition helps to determine how much that tradition influences the family behaviors of its adherents.

Of course, this argument assumes that religion is influencing family behavior, both in generic and tradition-specific ways, but the arrow of causality may run in the opposite direction. Given the symbolic and practical attention given the family by conservative Protestant institutions, it may be that family-oriented men and their families are actively affiliating with conservative Protestant churches that legitimate their neotraditional, family-centered lifestyle. It may also be that culturally progressive men and their families are nominally affiliating with mainline Protestant churches that legitimate their egalitarian lifestyle. Indeed, the "new religious voluntarism" that has developed in the United States since the 1960s suggests that some Americans are joining conservative religious denominations for their moral conservatism, just as other Americans are joining liberal religious denominations for their moral progressivism.[3]

In this case, I do not have sufficiently detailed longitudinal data on religion and family life to determine with any great precision how much the effects I document in this book are a product of selection. Previous work that I have done on religion and paternal involvement using both waves of the NSFH indicates that conservative Protestant affiliation in NSFH1 (1987–1988) is strongly associated with paternal involvement in one-on-one activities and youth-related activities five years later in NSFH2 (1992–1994).[4] Additional longitudinal analyses using these two waves of data indicate that paternal involvement in NSFH1 is not associated with increases in religious attendance in NSFH2.[5] These analyses provide some evidence that the findings in this book are not a consequence of selection bias where family-oriented men gravitate toward particular religious beliefs and practices.

However, at least some of the associations that my findings identify between religion and male familial involvement probably reflect, to one degree or another, the effect that men's family beliefs and practices have on their religious beliefs, practices, and affiliation. There is a growing body of literature that suggests that family behavior influences religious life and that religion and family have reciprocal effects on one another.[6] Future research, with access to longitudinal data that tracks religious and family behavior over the life course, will be needed to determine with greater accuracy the precise nature of the reciprocal relationship between religion and familial involvement among married men with children.

EFFECTS ON WOMEN AND CHILDREN

Future research also is necessary to determine precisely how these relationships between religion and family practices among married men with children influence the women and children in their lives. The literature on marriage and parenting suggests a few predictions. Women who are married to active conservative Protestant men probably enjoy high levels of marital quality and are less likely to experience a marital breakup, given the comparatively high levels of appreciation, affection, and understanding, and the low levels of domestic violence, they report. By contrast, women who are married to nominal conservative Protestant men are likely to experience low levels of marital quality and high rates of marital breakup, given the comparatively low levels of appreciation, affection, and understanding, and the high levels of domestic violence, they report. Indeed, the distinctively poor marital behavior of nominal conservative Protestant men may account for the fact that some studies find that conservative Protestants divorce at a higher rate than the population at large.[7]

The experiences of women who are married to nominal and active mainline Protestant men probably fall somewhere in between those of women married to nominal and active conservative Protestants. Compared to their peers married to conservative Protestants, they enjoy slightly higher levels of equality in the division of household labor, especially if they are married to nominal mainline Protestants. Compared to the wives of active conservative Protestants, they report only slightly lower levels of happiness with the appreciation, affection, and understanding they receive from their husbands. Thus, we can expect that the wives of mainline Protestant family men experience somewhat higher levels of marital quality and marital stability, compared to women whose husbands are unaffiliated or are nominal conservative Protestants.

For the most part, we can expect similar outcomes among children. The children of active conservative Protestant men experience high levels of paternal support and control. Their fathers are consistently the most active and expressive. When it comes to discipline, their fathers are the most likely to spank and the least likely to yell, as well as the most likely to monitor their behavior. For the most part, we can expect that these children are more likely to experience positive social and psychological outcomes than their peers. The big question is whether the strict parenting style—especially the tendency to spank—among active conservative Protestant fathers offsets any positive effects associated with their distinctively active and expressive orientation to parenting, given that corporal punishment and excessive parental control are associated with negative child outcomes.[8] One possibility is that the distinctive neotraditional parenting style of active conservative Protestant fathers is associated with both positive outcomes (e.g., global happiness) and negative outcomes (e.g., lack of independence) for their children. For the most part, the children of nominal conservative Protestant fathers experience comparatively low levels of both parental support and parental control; we can expect them to be at greater risk of negative psychological and social outcomes—especially compared to the children of active conservative Protestant fathers.

Once again, results for the children of mainline Protestant fathers probably fall somewhere between those for the children of active and nominal conservative Protestant fathers. Active mainline Protestant fathers are highly involved in youth-related activities, they praise and hug their children more than many fathers, and they are more likely than many fathers to spank their children but less likely to yell at them. These fathers come closest to active conservative Protestant fathers in their behavioral profile, and their children probably experience outcomes that parallel those of children of active conservative Protestants, but to a lesser degree. Nominal mainline fathers are highly involved in one-on-one activities with their children and they are slightly more likely than unaffiliated fathers to both spank and yell at their children, but they exhibit only average levels of affection and monitoring. Thus, children of nominal mainline Protestant fathers experience a moderately high level of support and control from their parents; we can expect that they will do slightly better than average on outcomes that are influenced specifically by paternal involvement (e.g., educational achievement) but not on those influenced by paternal warmth (e.g., self-esteem).

Overall, then, these findings paint a striking picture. Churchgoing conservative Protestant men family are soft patriarchs. Contrary to the assertions of feminists, many family scholars, and public critics, these men cannot be fairly described as "abusive" and "authoritarian" family men wedded to "stereotypical forms of masculinity." They outpace mainline Protestant and unaffiliated family men in their emotional and practical dedication to their children and wives and in their commitment to familism, and they are the least likely to physically abuse their wives. Still, their critics have a point. Conservative Protestant family men's support for gender traditionalism, their commitment to a puritanical form of discipline, and their lesser dedication to household labor continue to mark them as patriarchs, albeit soft patriarchs who are more expressive and active than most fathers. By contrast, their nominal conservative Protestant peers bear all the marks of what is called backsliding in much of the conservative Protestant world: compared to the other men in this study, they are not highly invested in the emotional and practical lives of their families, they do the least household labor, and they are the most likely to physically abuse their wives. Clearly, these nominal conservative Protestant men tend to be less invested in life of their families; perhaps this is because they hail overwhelmingly from poor and working-class communities that are often characterized by lower levels of emotional and practical investment in family life.[9]

In their own ways, churchgoing and nominal mainline Protestant family men display some of the attributes of the iconic new man. Churchgoing mainline men are more affectionate with their wives and children and more involved in youth-related activities than most of the men in this study. Nominal mainline Protestant family men hold the most egalitarian views of any group of religious men in this study. They are more involved in one-on-one activities with their children than most groups, and they also do the most household labor of any group in this study. Taken together, these findings suggest that mainline Protestant fathers and husbands can, in certain respects, be viewed as new men.

FAMILY MODERNIZATION AND ITS DISCONTENTS

Modernity has generally undercut traditional, taken-for-granted religious life. But the loss of meaning and the depersonalization associated with some aspects of modernization—for example, the cultural and political disestablishment of traditional religious beliefs; the dissolution of paternalist-style working relations in favor of impersonal, bureaucratic working relations; and the erosion of stable ties to persons and places—can, under certain conditions, fuel the rise of new religious movements and stimulate innovation and revival among traditional religious movements throughout entire societies or in subcultures within societies. These movements can serve as vehicles for protest against government corruption, sources of social welfare and work for the unemployed and underemployed, carriers of collective identity in regions wracked by religio-ethnic conflict, and guardians of "traditional" lifestyles threatened by the modern state and market.[10] More fundamentally, as Martin Riesebrodt has observed, these movements often succeed "in identifying certain structural problems in modern societies that can by no means be characterized as resolved."[11] The revival of Islam throughout portions of North Africa, the Middle East, and South Asia; of Hinduism in South Asia; and of conservative Protestantism in North America; and the rise of Roman Catholicism in sub-Saharan Africa and Pentecostalism in Latin America, sub-Saharan Africa, and China all attest to the ways in which these movements have made a place for the sacred in the modern world by capitalizing on the discontents of modernity.[12]

Rapid changes in the meaning and practice of family life; increases in divorce and out-of-wedlock births that break or hinder the formation of intimate social ties between partners, parents, and children; and the erosion of financial and practical ties of dependence between the generations create anomic tendencies that encourage some to turn to religious communities for psychic and social stability. State support for sexual liberalism and gender equality can generate a backlash among status groups with a traditional moral orientation that crystallizes around "profamily" religious movements. Similarly, market offerings, especially media-related ones, that promote sexual expression and, more generally, an ethic of hedonism can also prompt religiously centered reactions. Another factor fueling these reactive movements can be the success of state- and market-led family modernization in penetrating the life worlds of traditional status groups. That is, when beliefs and behaviors associated with family modernization—for example, divorce and out-of-wedlock births and support for gender equality and sexual expression—begin to be manifested in status groups that support moral traditionalism, strenuous efforts are often launched to restore the traditional moral order.[13]

THE UNINTENDED CONSEQUENCES OF FAMILY MODERNIZATION IN THE UNITED STATES AND AROUND THE WORLD

Many of these dynamics apply to the case at hand. One factor driving the increase in the size of conservative Protestant groups in the United States is that a growing number of men and women have experienced divorce or entry into a stepfamily. These men and women typically experience more difficulties with children and partners and are hence more likely to seek out the moral guidance and social support found in conservative Protestant congregations—especially the guidance and support they offer for families.[14] More importantly, however, the process that José Casanova calls the "third disestablishment"—the delegitimization of Protestant morality and the rise of the "new morality" in American public life and the broader culture—prompted a flurry of political and pastoral organization building and activism among conservative Protestants in defense of the traditional family and their absolute moral code. As we have seen, the 1970s witnessed the founding of groups like Focus on the Family, Concerned Women for America, and the Moral Majority. These groups, and the religiously grounded profamily movement in general, offered a political and pastoral response to developments in the political arena such as *Roe v. Wade* (1973) and congressional passage of the Equal Rights Amendment (1972), which they saw as threatening to their way of life.[15] They were also reacting to developments in the wider culture—from the surge in mass-produced pornography to the dramatic increase in divorce over the course of the 1970s—that were hostile to their vision of family and morality.

The religiously grounded profamily movement experienced a substantial measure of organizational, pastoral, and political success because a large minority of Americans—many of whom were conservative Protestants—were disturbed, angered, or unsettled by the pace and direction of the family and gender revolutions that got under way in the latter half of the twentieth century. Part of their concern was with developments in the broader society. But developments closer to home also appear to have played a role in driving conservative Protestant mobilization on behalf of the family. One of the most striking findings in this study is that nominal conservative Protestant family men appear to be singularly disengaged from family life—especially in comparison to their active conservative Protestant brethren. If my findings about domestic violence are any indication, these backsliding men and their female peers are probably leading the way in the types of family behaviors—divorce, marital trouble, child neglect—that conservative Protestants see as the poisonous fruits of family modernization. Thus, another reason conservative Protestants became so concerned about the family and morality is that they saw family members and friends succumbing to the logic of family modernization. Accordingly, conservative Protestantism's ongoing support for the profamily movement is rooted not only in its distinctive religious outlook and its antimodern collective identity, but also in its commitment to a family-centered lifestyle that continues to face both external and internal threats.

There are obvious parallels with other religious movements around the world—especially those associated with Islam. The Islamic revolution in Iran in the 1970s was motivated in part by concerns about rising female labor-force participation rates, Western-inspired patterns of leisure and media that ran counter to traditional familial and sexual norms, and public policies elevating the status of women.[16] More recently, the Islamist movement in Egypt has capitalized on public concerns about the "degenerate" influence of Western tourism and popular culture on the nation's moral fiber, the state's liberalization of censorship laws that had curtailed sexually suggestive media offerings, and gains in women's public status that threaten Islamic understandings of patriarchal authority.[17] Islamic revivalist movements have capitalized on such concerns about family modernization among status groups with a traditional moral orientation to launch reactive strategies that engender heightened religious commitment, build new institutions, and seek political change.

INNOVATIVE FAMILY STRATEGIES IN RELIGIOUS MOVEMENTS IN THE UNITED STATES AND AROUND THE WORLD

Religious movements that pursue only a strategy of resistance to family modernization are not likely to succeed in the long term. As the broader literature on religion suggests, "fundamentalist," or "orthodox," religious movements need to innovate in response to "the changing sociocultural environments they confront" if they are to maintain their viability in the contemporary world. But this literature also suggests that these innovations must not threaten core religious beliefs and practices, lest they end up as "self-defeating accommodations" that weaken the distinctive components of the group's religious identity.[18] Applying these insights specifically to the relationship between religion and family modernization, I argue that religious movements must develop innovative family strategies that respond to social and cultural changes in family life, but these strategies must not weaken the functions and moral salience of the family if the movements wish to maintain a high level of commitment to family life.

In the case at hand, conservative Protestantism has pursued strategies that can be viewed as innovative in important respects. First, it has put a wide range of contemporary media—from radio to the Internet—in the service of its family agenda. Second, partly because of its long-standing tradition of pietistic subjectivism, conservative Protestantism has embraced therapeutic and more broadly expressive approaches to marriage and parenting that respond to the increasingly emotional character of contemporary family life. Third, the movement has recently begun to push homeschooling, which returns a range of social and cultural functions to the family, but does so in a way that inscribes the domestic world of work with a level of sophistication and challenge that can be attractive to conservative Protestant women who are well-educated and might otherwise find domestic work limiting.[19] Most importantly, as we have seen, conservative Protestantism has sought to shore up the family by encouraging men to connect their traditional theological, familist, and patriarchal beliefs to an active and expressive style of familial involvement. This subculture seems to recognize that in the face of dramatic changes in women's labor-force participation and social status the only way to secure the stability and quality of family life, and a largely symbolic patriarchy, is to encourage men to act in ways that are more congruent with the ideals and aspirations of women. In so doing, it has succeeded in driving up the investments that men make in family life.

Similar types of innovation can be seen in other family-oriented religious movements around the globe—especially Pentecostalism. Pentecostalism is particularly strong among poor and working-class citizens of developing countries who seek moral order, social solidarity, and upward mobility in the face of a disorganized economic life and social anomie.[20] Economic and cultural modernization—for example, the migration of men away from their families in rural areas to seek work in growing cities—leads to family modernization, including erosion of the stability, functions, and moral salience of family life, in many parts of the developing world. For instance, in much of the developing world, out-of-wedlock birth and divorce rates are on the rise.[21] These developments, especially when overlaid on long-standing traditions that celebrate hypermasculinity, such as Latin American machismo, often mean that men are only loosely connected to family life, with detrimental consequences for women and children.[22]

With respect to the family, Pentecostalism may be viewed as innovative in that it provides a range of strategies for domesticating men: that is, for linking men to their families in ways that promote the economic and emotional welfare of women and children. First, the Pentecostal faith is strongly linked to an ethos of moral asceticism that encompasses the repudiation of alcohol and adultery and the embrace of hard work. This typically means both that Pentecostal men earn more money and that more of the money they earn actually supports their wives and children; this, of course, is particularly important in developing countries with high levels of poverty and economic disorganization. Second, the expressive ethos and the family-centered message of Pentecostalism encourages men to be affectionate and attentive to the needs of their wives and children. Third, Pentecostalism connects its moral asceticism and its strong family orientation to a biblically based headship ideology that suggests male family leadership and entails an ethic of sacrifice on behalf of the family. As Jorge Maldonado has observed, the "patriarchal ideology of family relations is a welcome corrective to the problem of male absence from the family. Teaching men about family management includes a new discipline, an emphasis on seriousness, cooperation, demonstration of affection, compassion, and above all 'responsibility'—meaning economic support and fidelity."[23] In all these ways, then, Pentecostalism promotes the economic and emotional welfare of the family, and of women and children in particular, by pursuing innovative strategies that address some of the key economic and cultural challenges facing families in the developing world.

The key question, of course, is whether these new and revivalist religious movements around the globe will have long-term success in resisting family modernization—or at least those elements of family modernization that touch directly on their religious doctrine, such as divorce and nonmarital cohabitation. Family scholars often point to the contemporary experience of Europe to argue that the changes associated with family modernization are irreversible and that resistance to these changes is futile, even among family-oriented religious movements. They assume that no group will be able to respond to larger changes in the sociocultural environment—for example, the emergence of a postindustrial economy, the decline in men's real wages, increases in women's social status, and the rise of expressive individualism—in ways that preserve the functions, stability, and moral salience of the family against the pressures of family modernization.[24] In my view, however, the long-term success of religious movements in resisting family modernization is an open question.

Certainly in places where religious institutions are currently weak, society is relatively homogenous, and the state is strong and well-developed—such as Europe—the family scholars' view seems quite plausible. In societies like this, religious institutions and families need not and are not likely to serve as bulwarks of meaning, economic support, and social solidarity.[25] But in societies where religious institutions are vital—where the state is relatively weak, disorganized, or unpopular; or where there is a substantial measure of ethnic or religious pluralism—religious movements are more likely to foster family-oriented strategies that successfully resist those aspects of family modernization that touch most centrally on their religious worldview.[26] They will be able to capitalize on discontentment with family modernization, the weakness of the state, or tensions with other religious groups or a secular society, as well as their own institutional strengths, to build religiously based family strategies that combine elements of resistance and innovation to shore up the family.[27]

In the United States, the institutional vitality of religion, the comparative weakness of the federal government, the substantial measure of ethnic and religious pluralism, and the discontentment with family modernization experienced by some Americans translate into fertile ground for religiously based movements on behalf of the family. One sign that conservative Protestantism may continue to foster family-oriented beliefs and practices even as its membership experiences marked gains in social status is that education—which is usually seen as an indicator of modernization—is positively associated with familism from 1972 to 1999 among conservative Protestants and negatively associated with familism among other Americans over this same period of time. Thus, we can expect that conservative Protestantism (like some other religious traditions, such as Mormonism) will experience at least a modicum of success in its ongoing effort to resist the logic of family modernization with its strategy of expressive traditionalism.

THE DOMESTICATION OF MEN AND THE FUTURES OF FATHERHOOD

RELIGION AND THE GENDER REVOLUTION

The gender revolution ushered in by the second half of the twentieth century dramatically transformed the opportunities and responsibilities that women take on in the public worlds of work and political life. Although men have moved in recent years to take up a larger share of the emotional and practical work associated with the private world of family life, they have not come close to taking up an equal share of that work. Consequently, women with children at home still do the lion's share of child care, household labor, and emotion work in American families and are therefore less able than similarly situated men to devote themselves to public life. This helps explain why marriage and parenthood are associated with lower earnings and opportunities for women but not for men.[28] Thus, men have helped to slow, if not to stall, the gender revolution.[29]

One of the central questions addressed by this book is the role that religion, especially conservative Protestantism, may have played in slowing the gender revolution. In the domains of marital emotion work and fatherhood we have found no evidence that religion, or conservative Protestantism in particular, is a force for reaction. Instead, we see that churchgoing family men—especially conservative Protestant family men—are more progressive than their peers: they spend more time with their children; they are more likely to hug and praise their children; their wives report higher levels of satisfaction with the appreciation, affection, and understanding their receive from their husbands; and they spend more time socializing with their wives. We have also seen that, contrary to the predictions of their critics, churchgoing conservative Protestant men register the lowest rates of domestic violence of any group in this study. Indeed, as table A6.4 in the appendix reveals, churchgoing conservative Protestant family men have the lowest rates of domestic violence of any major religious group in the United States. In all of these family domains, the influence of the family-oriented values and social networks found in conservative Protestant congregations clearly outweighs the impact of the gender-role traditionalism also found in this subculture. So in many respects religion and conservative Protestantism have not been a force for gender reaction.

However, in two respects conservative Protestantism does appear to be a force for gender reaction. First, when it comes to household labor, conservative Protestantism—but not necessarily religion generally—does appear to be slowing the gender revolution. Conservative Protestant family men do less household labor than their mainline and unaffiliated peers—in terms of both the actual hours they devote to housework and their overall share of the household labor. Perhaps more importantly, we see evidence that conservative Protestant family men are casting a veil of enchantment over this inequality. For the wives of theologically conservative, churchgoing Protestant family men are significantly more likely to report that their household labor is appreciated than are the wives of secular or less religious men. This probably means that these women are less likely to view the division of household labor as unfair, even though it is manifestly more unequal. So in the domain of household labor, conservative Protestantism not only fosters inequality, it also appears to play an important role in legitimating that inequality.

Second, conservative Protestantism plays a signal role in promoting gender-role traditionalism in the cultural domain. A conservative Protestant affiliation, especially an active one, is consistently one of the most important predictors of gender-role traditionalism in the population at large and among married men with children in particular. So given that conservative Protestant institutions are the only major institutional players in American life to publicly challenge the egalitarian impulse of the gender revolution and that they appear to have achieved some success in retarding the movement of public opinion on this issue, we have some additional evidence that conservative Protestantism has been a force for gender reaction.

In sum, then, conservative Protestantism clearly has played a role in slowing the gender revolution; nevertheless, given its attentiveness to the emotional domain of family life, its role has been a curious one in that the women most affected by its traditional influence seem to be enchanted, rather than alienated, by their encounter with this family strategy.

THE PLURALISTIC FUTURE OF FAMILIES

When we look at the more general failure of men to respond to the gender revolution with sufficient vigor, we see a different picture. Men's failure in this regard is implicated in the trends associated with family modernization—such as increases in divorce and declines in fertility. Because women's expectations and needs for more practical and emotional support in the home have risen more quickly than men's provision of such support, many women have become disenchanted with their husbands in particular and with marriage more generally.[30] This helps to explain why the quality and stability of marriage has declined since the late 1960s.[31] It also helps to explain declining fertility rates since women are now less likely to have children if they are not assured of considerable help from their male partner. Thus, as Frances Goldscheider and Linda Waite argue, the rise of "no families"—characterized by greater numbers of childless couples, lifetime singles, and mother-only families that result from divorce or nonmarital birth—has been driven to a large degree by the failure of men to take up a significant share of the work associated with the home.[32] Women are less likely to want to marry, stay married to, and bear children with men who are not committed to taking on a large share of the domestic responsibilities. In Goldscheider and Waite's view, without significant changes on the part of men, a "no families" future could come to dominate the American family system.

But Goldscheider and Waite argue that a second possibility for the future is a "new families" scenario in which men (and children) take up more of the responsibilities of family life. In this scenario, the emotional and practical work of family life is divided equally between men and women. This egalitarian family model is more likely to accommodate women's desire to combine work and family, thereby shoring up their commitment to marriage, childbearing, and child rearing. Goldscheider and Waite point to recent gains in men's contributions to child care and housework to argue that this scenario could also come to dominate the American family system. The future of the this system thus depends in large part on the domestication of men: "It seems increasingly that the road to 'new families' will lead through men, who must decide whether they want homes, families, and children enough to share responsibility for them."[33] In other words, men must do more to conform to the family aspirations and ideals of women who wish to balance work and family life.

Goldscheider and Waite dismiss a third scenario for the future: the return of "old families" with a strongly gendered division of family labor in which men focus on provisioning and women focus on homemaking and nurturing. They argue, along with other family scholars, that the sociocultural foundations of this model have largely collapsed due to changes in fertility, women's work patterns, men's real income, and the status of women.[34] They are right.

But Goldscheider and Waite overlook a fourth possibility suggested by my findings, namely, that the United States will see the rise of a neotraditional family order that succeeds in domesticating men while retaining a measure of traditionalism in the division of labor and authority in the home. This order is appealing to men and women who are discontented with the anomic tendencies of family modernization, the lack of clarity in gender roles and identity associated with the gender revolution, and the pressures associated with combining family and two full-time careers. It is also appealing to women who continue to identify primarily with the domestic sphere, who wish to see homemaking and nurturing accorded high value, and who wish to have husbands who share their commitment to family life and act upon that commitment. Men who continue to seek status as domestic patriarchs who have the primary earning responsibility and at least titular authority over their families are also attracted to this order.[35] The neotraditional order not only is promoted and legitimated by conservative Protestant institutions; it also receives support from Orthodox Judaism, traditional Catholicism, and Mormonism.[36]

Given the socioeconomic, ethnic, and religious pluralism in the United States, it is unlikely that any of these family models will come to dominate the American family system. Current demographic trends suggest that the "no family" model has become entrenched among large swaths of poor, working-class, and minority communities, as evidenced by high rates of divorce and nonmarital births, and in portions of the upper-middle-class in the urban United States, as reflected in comparatively high rates of childlessness and lifetime singleness.[37] Men and women in this family category tend to be nominally religious or unaffiliated, in part because they are less welcome in religious congregations, in part because they have less reason to seek out the family-oriented ethos of American religious life, and in part because they have a low level of religious interest.[38]

Men and women who come closer to exemplifying the "new family" model are more likely to be found in middle- and upper-class communities in inner suburbs and some urban enclaves and to have high levels of education.

This study suggests that their religious profile is mainline Protestant, nominally Catholic, and Jewish (see the tables in the appendix for results for nominal Catholic and Jewish family men) but not nominally conservative Protestant or unaffiliated.[39] The religious profile of the men and women who come closest to the "new family" model suggests that these Americans are religious in a conventional way—attending services for major holidays and enough to send their children to religious education on a semiregular basis.

The "neotraditional family" model is most strongly institutionalized among working- and middle-class residents of outer suburbs; it also competes with the "no family" model in large portions of the working- and middle-class rural United States.[40] My findings suggest that this group is drawn largely from the ranks of active conservative Protestants, though traditional Catholics and Mormons probably make up a large minority.[41] As we have seen, this group has the deepest levels of religious commitment and is most intent on establishing moral boundaries against those who fit the "no families" model—in part, it would seem, because a large percentage of "no families" are their family members, neighbors, or friends in the rural and suburban United States who are divorced, cohabiting, or never-married parents.[42]

The pluralistic character of American family life is likely to be with us for some time. Scholars who are proponents of family modernization correctly note that widespread sociocultural changes have undercut the old family model in which the vast majority of men could earn enough to support a family on a single income and the extrafamilial and individual interests of family members—especially women—were subordinated to the imperatives of a bourgeois family order. As a consequence of these changes, "no families" emerged among a large minority of the American population—especially in lower- and working-class communities affected by the economic and cultural shifts of the 1960s and 1970s that undercut the viability of male breadwinning and the necessity of morally upright living, and in those sectors of the middle and upper class where a strong career orientation and an ethic of expressive individualism took hold, especially among women.[43] "New families" have emerged in response to these same trends (though, as we have seen, very few men actually take up an equal share of domestic labor). The difference, of course, between "no families" and "new families" is that the men and women in the latter group have a commitment to marriage and childbearing and possess the requisite socioeconomic resources to chart a family strategy that combines work and family for both men and women.[44] Because the sociocultural dynamics underlying these trends are not likely to disappear anytime soon, we can expect both of these models to persist into the near future.

But the discontentment associated with these trends in some quarters, and the continuing institutional and cultural vitality of conservative Protestantism and other orthodox religious traditions in the United States, suggest that the ranks of neotraditional families will also continue to remain strong in the near future. We will continue to see religious leaders decrying the latest developments in American family life. We will continue to see political and religious efforts to save or revive marriage and the family—witness the George W. Bush administration's efforts to promote marriage.[45] And we will continue to see religious groups pursuing innovative strategies, such as the domestication of men, in their efforts to reinvigorate the functions and moral significance of family life in the United States in ways that allow them to respond to sociocultural change. All of these efforts give adherents to the neotraditional model an institutional and ideological plausibility structure for their family-centered way of life that will enable it to survive and even thrive amid family modernization.

RELIGION AND THE FUTURES OF FATHERHOOD

What, then, does this mean for the future of religion and fatherhood? In my view, three models of fatherhood that correspond to the three family models just discussed will come to dominate the social landscape. Of course, many fathers will combine elements of more than one of these models, and some fathers will continue to follow the old model of fatherhood that focuses on provisioning at the expense of familial involvement. But the following three models of fatherhood will have especially high profiles in the United States.

First, we can expect to see a large minority of fathers who do not live with their children, due to either divorce or nonmarriage. These men will typically have only infrequent contact with their children—especially as the years go by—and for obvious reasons they will make only minimal contributions to the practical and emotional labor associated with the everyday care of their children.[46] These men will be distant from religious institutions and from the wider range of civic institutions associated with a conventional, family-oriented lifestyle.[47] Their ties to the labor force will also be more marginal, in part because they lack social ties to familial, religious, and civic institutions that would otherwise bind them to a providership ethic, and in part because they face fewer economic opportunities than their recent forefathers did.[48]

Second, we can expect to see a large minority of fathers, most of them married, who pursue the new fatherhood model by taking on an increasing share of family responsibilities, though the day when they take on an equal share of those responsibilities still seems distant. These new men will be active and expressive fathers, and they will be more attentive to housework than other fathers.[49] But my findings also suggest that they will be less committed to their marriages and less invested in responding to the ideals and aspirations of their wives than neotraditional fathers. Consequently, their marriages will be less stable than those of neotraditional fathers. They will be attracted to the conventional forms of religious life found in mainline Protestant, liberal Catholic, and Reform Jewish congregations. These congregations are known for their progressive orientation toward social issues and their commitment to a Golden Rule religiosity centered around childrearing and community partici-pation.[50] But if the results reported here are any indication, these new men's commitment to religious life will often be a nominal affair, tied largely to that window of time in their lives when their children are in need of the religious and moral formation afforded by participation in a religious congregation.[51]

Finally, we can expect that a large minority of fathers, the vast majority of them married, will pursue a neotraditional model of fatherhood that com-bines a moderate providership ethic with a strong commitment to family life. Motivated by a desire to both transmit their faith to the next generation and protect their children from a society they see as degraded and degrading, these soft patriarchs will combine involvement and affection with strict discipline and vigilant oversight. They will also have a strong commitment to marriage and will be unusually attentive to the emotional and familial ideals and aspira-tions of their wives. However, they will do less household labor than men committed to new fatherhood, partly because they wish to signal their commit-ment to gender differences. Neotraditional couples will also have the lowest levels of divorce, both because of their moral traditionalism and because of their emotional investment in their wives and children.

These soft patriarchs will be found in conservative Protestant churches, traditional Catholic parishes, Mormon temples, and Orthodox synagogues. They will abide by an absolutist vision of the family that they believe to be divinely ordained and that attempts to articulate universal moral principles that govern family life in all times and places. This vision will be closely con-nected to the religious and family-related ideologies they encounter in their places of worship and the family strategies they practice in their homes. These soft patriarchs will be ever in search of new strategies in their effort to defend traditional ends. Their continuing "battle against modernity" in the service of "the truth and authority of an ancient faith" will undoubtedly look increasingly quixotic to many as the twenty-first century proceeds, but as far as they are concerned, "the future is in God's hands."[52]

APPENDIX: DATA, METHODS, AND TABLES

THE ANALYSES conducted in this book are based on data from three different data sets: the General Social Survey (GSS), the National Survey of Families and Households (NSFH), and the Survey of Adults and Youth (SAY). The GSS, conducted by the National Opinion Research Center, is one of the most widely used surveys of national attitudes and behaviors in the United States. It is a nationally representative sample survey of U.S. households and has been conducted on an annual or biannual basis since 1972.[1] I rely on data from 1972 to 1998, when more than 30,000 adults were surveyed by the GSS. Specifically, my logistic regression analyses in tables A3.2–A3.5 focus on a subset of 24,099 GSS respondents who answered questions dealing with their religious affiliation, religious attendance, family attitudes, gender attitudes, and a range of other sociodemographic factors. The GSS analyses are based on unweighted data.

The NSFH is a nationally representative survey of more than 13,000 adults age nineteen and over. The survey was conducted for the Center for Demography at the University of Wisconsin–Madison. It covers a range of family attitudes and behaviors, religious beliefs and behaviors, and other socio-demographic factors. The first wave of the survey, NSFH1, was conducted in 1987–1988. The second wave of the survey, NSFH2, was conducted in 1992–1994, with a response rate of 82 percent. In both waves the spouses of the respondents were interviewed if they were available.[2] I focus on a subset of 3,539 married men with children age eighteen and under at home from NSFH1 and a subset of 2,785 married men with children age eighteen and under at home from NSFH2. I rely on ordinary least squares (OLS) and logistic regression analyses of these data for tables A3.6–A3.8, A4.2, A4.4–A4.9, A5.2–A5.4, and A6.2–A6.6. The analyses are based on weighted data and adjusted for oversamples of blacks, Hispanics, and families with stepchildren.

The SAY is a national telephone survey that was conducted from 1998 to 1999 by Schulman, Ronca, and Buccuvalas, Inc. (SRBI) for researchers at the Wagner Graduate School of Public Service of New York University, the Office of Population Research of Princeton University, and the Social Indicators Survey Center of Columbia University. It was administered both to a nationally representative sample and to representative samples in five cities (Baltimore; Detroit; Philadelphia; Oakland, California; and Richmond, Virginia) of 13,852 adults and 6,675 youth. The survey questioned respondents about, among other things, their parenting beliefs and behaviors, their religious beliefs, and their socioeconomic status.[3] I rely on a subset of 2,309 married fathers with children ages ten to eighteen at home for the OLS regression analyses in tables A4.3–A4.10.

Table A3.1

Summary of GSS (1972–1998) and NSFH1 (1987–1988) Attudinal Measures

Variable	Item Wording/Codes	N	Mean	SD	Alpha
Divorce	Should divorce in this country be easier or more difficult to obtain than it is now? (0 = easier or stay as is; 1 = more difficult)	23,451	0.51	0.49	
Premarital sex	There's been a lot of discussion about the way morals and attitudes about sex are changing in this country. If a man and a woman have sexual relations before marriage, do you think it is always wrong, almost always wrong, wrong only sometimes, or not wrong at all? (0 = not always wrong; 1 = always wrong)	24,099	0.29	0.45	
Separate spheres	It is much better for everyone involved if the man is the achiever outside the home and the woman takes care of the home and family. (0 = do not agree; 1 = agree or strongly agree)	15,428	0.43	0.49	
Mom working	A preschool child is likely to suffer if his or her mother works. (0 = do not agree; 1 = agree or strongly agree)	15,411	0.49	0.49	
Theological conservative[a]	(1) The Bible is God's word and everything happened or will happen exactly as it says; (2) The Bible is the answer to all important human problems. (0 = do not agree with one or both statements; 1 = agree with both statements)	3,251	0.36	0.48	
Familism[a]	The familism index is based on respondents' level of disapproval of (1) "women who have a child with out getting married"; (2) "a couple with an unhappy marriage getting a divorce if their youngest child is under 5." (1 = strongly approve; 5 = strongly disapprove) It is also based on their level of agreement with the following five statements (3) "It's better for a person to get	3,539	3.58	0.54	0.60

Table A3.1
(*continued*)

Variable	Item Wording/Codes	N	Mean	SD	Alpha
	married than to go through life being single"; (4) "Marriage is a lifetime relationship and should never be ended except under extreme circumstances"; (5) "Children ought to let aging parents live with them when the parents can no longer live by themselves"; (6) "Children ought to provide financial help to aging parents when their parents are having financial difficulty"; and (7) "It's better for a person to have a child than to go through life childless." (1 = strongly disagree; 5 = strongly agree)				
Gender-role traditionalism[a]	The gender role traditionalism index is based on respondents' level of disapproval of (1) "mothers who work full-time when their youngest child is under age 5." (1 = strongly approve; 5 = strongly disapprove) It is also based on their level of agreement with the following three statements: (2) "It is much better for everyone if the man earns the main living and the woman takes care of the home and family"; (3) "If a husband and wife both work full-time, they should share housework tasks equally"; and, (4) "Preschool children are likely to suffer if their mother is employed." Responses were averaged and, where necessary, reverse-coded so that higher scores indicate agreement with gender-role traditionalism. (1 = strongly disagree; 5 = strongly agree)	3,539	3.07	0.71	0.61

[a]These items are derived from NSFH1 (1987–1988).

Table A3.2

Coefficients from Logistic Regressions on Support for Anti-divorce Legislation

	Model 1	Model 2	Model 3	Model 4
Controls				
Age	0.01***	0.01***	0.01***	0.01***
Gender	0.12***	0.12***	0.05	0.05
Cohort	−0.12**	−0.12**	−0.11*	−0.12*
Year	0.02***	0.02***	0.02***	0.02***
Black	−0.64***	−0.65***	−0.76***	−0.75***
Education	−0.06***	−0.06***	−0.11***	−0.11***
South	0.15***	0.15***	0.10**	0.10**
Northeast	−0.13**	−0.13**	−0.14**	−0.14**
Midwest	0.34***	0.34***	0.30***	0.30***
Religious tradition[a]				
Black Protestant	0.38***	0.38***		
Catholic	0.77***	0.76***		
Jewish	−0.05	−0.05		
Other	0.70***	0.70***		
Conservative Protestant	1.10***$_H$	1.09***		
Mainline Protestant	0.65***$_L$	0.66***		
Conservative Protestant × year		0.00		
Mainline Protestant × year		0.00		
Religious tradition by attendance[a]				
Frequently attending BP			0.65***	0.65***
Infrequently attending BP			0.26*	0.26*
Frequently attending RC			1.14***	1.14***
Infrequently attending RC			0.42***	0.42***
Frequently attending Jew			0.34	0.34
Infrequently attending Jew			−0.05	−0.05
Frequently attending other			1.22***	1.22***
Infrequently attending other			0.25*	0.25*
Frequently attending CP			1.64***$_H$	1.64***
Infrequently attending CP			0.57***$_L$	0.57***
Frequently attending MP			1.09***$_L$	1.09***
Infrequently attending MP			0.44***$_L$	0.44***
Frequently attending CP × year				0.00
Frequently attending MP × year				0.00
.2 Log likelihood	30,475.67	30,474.86	29,753.59	29,753.55

Note: Data are from GSS (1974–1998). $N = 23,451$. Significance tests are two-tailed. BP = black Protestant; RC = Roman Catholic; CP = conservative Protestant; MP = mainline Protestant.
[a]The comparison category is Unaffiliated.
*$p < .05$. **$p < .01$. ***$p < .001$.
H, L = Coefficients with different subscripts are significantly different ($p < .05$).

Table A3.3

Coefficients from Logistic Regressions on Opposition to Premarital Sex

	Model 1	Model 2	Model 3	Model 4
Controls				
Age	0.04***	0.04***	0.04***	0.04***
Gender	0.41***	0.42***	0.30***	0.30***
Cohort	0.01	0.01	0.04	0.03
Year	−0.02***	−0.02***	−0.02***	−0.03***
Black	0.04	0.05	−0.16	−0.16
Education	−0.10***	−0.10***	−0.19***	−0.19***
South	0.53***	0.54***	0.49***	0.50***
Midwest	0.18***	0.18***	0.12*	0.12*
Northeast	−0.15**	−0.15**	−0.16**	−0.16**
Religious tradition[a]				
Black Protestant	0.68***	0.68***		
Catholic	0.76***	0.76***		
Jewish	−0.39*	−0.39*		
Other	1.68***	1.68***		
Conservative Protestant	1.69***$_H$	1.69***		
Mainline Protestant	0.56***$_L$	0.52***		
Conservative Protestant × year		0.01*		
Mainline Protestant × year		−0.02**		
Religious tradition by attendance[a]				
Frequently attending BP			1.21***	1.20***
Infrequently attending BP			0.19	0.18
Frequently attending RC			1.23***	1.23***
Infrequently attending RC			−0.03	−0.03
Frequently attending Jew			0.74*	0.74*
Infrequently attending Jew			−0.64**	−0.64**
Frequently attending other			2.72***	2.73***
Infrequently attending other			0.41**	0.41**
Frequently attending CP			2.40***$_H$	2.39***
Infrequently attending CP			0.78***$_L$	0.78***
Frequently attending MP			1.14***$_L$	1.10***
Infrequently attending MP			0.10$_L$	0.10
Frequently attending CP × year				0.02***
Frequently attending MP × year				−0.01
−2 Log likelihood	24,509.22	24,488.63	22,847.36	22,822.29

Note: Data are from GSS (1972–1998). $N = 24,099$. Significance tests are two-tailed. BP = black Protestant; RC = Roman Catholic; CP = conservative Protestant; MP = mainline Protestant.
[a]The comparison category is Unaffiliated.
*$p < .05$. **$p < .01$. ***$p < .001$.
H, L = Coefficients with different subscripts are significantly different ($p < .05$).

Table A3.4

Coefficients from Logistic Regressions on Support for Separate-Spheres Ideology

	Model 1	Model 2	Model 3	Model 4
Controls				
Age	0.04^{***}	0.04^{***}	0.03^{***}	0.03^{***}
Gender	-0.38^{***}	-0.38^{***}	-0.43^{***}	-0.43^{***}
Cohort	-0.16^{**}	-0.16^{**}	-0.17^{**}	-0.17^{**}
Year	-0.05^{***}	-0.05^{***}	-0.05^{***}	-0.05^{***}
Black	0.10	0.10	0.03	0.04
Education	-0.33^{***}	-0.33^{***}	-0.36^{***}	-0.36^{***}
South	0.17^{**}	0.17^{**}	0.17^{**}	0.17^{**}
Midwest	-0.09	-0.09	-0.10	-0.10
Northeast	-0.06	-0.06	-0.05	-0.05
Religious tradition[a]				
Black Protestant	0.19	0.19		
Catholic	0.44^{***}	0.44^{***}		
Jewish	-0.09	-0.09		
Other	0.92^{***}	0.92^{***}		
Conservative Protestant	0.75^{***}_{H}	0.67^{***}		
Mainline Protestant	0.21^{**}_{L}	0.27^{***}		
Conservative Protestant $\times$ year		0.02^{*}		
Mainline Protestant $\times$ year		-0.02^{*}		
Religious tradition by attendance[a]				
Frequently attending BP			0.25^{*}	0.25^{*}
Infrequently attending BP			0.23	0.23
Frequently attending RC			0.60^{***}	0.60^{***}
Infrequently attending RC			0.30^{***}	0.30^{***}
Frequently attending Jew			0.23	0.23
Infrequently attending Jew			-0.12	-0.12
Frequently attending other			1.43^{***}	1.43^{***}
Infrequently attending other			0.48^{***}	0.48^{***}
Frequently attending CP			1.16^{***}_{H}	1.04^{***}
Infrequently attending CP			0.31^{***}_{L}	0.31^{***}
Frequently attending MP			0.35^{***}_{L}	0.41^{***}
Infrequently attending MP			0.14_{L}	0.14
Frequently attending CP $\times$ year				0.03^{**}
Frequently attending MP $\times$ year				-0.02
-2 Log likelihood	$17,821.61$	$17,805.14$	$17,613.61$	$17,602.54$

Note: Data are from GSS (1977–1998). $N = 15,428$. Significance tests are two-tailed. BP = black Protestant; RC = Roman Catholic; CP = conservative Protestant; MP = mainline Protestant.
[a]The comparison category is Unaffiliated.
$^{*}p < .05.$ $^{**}p < .01.$ $^{***}p < .001.$
H, L = Coefficients with different subscripts are significantly different ($p < .05$).

Table A3.5

Coefficients from Logistic Regressions on Opposition to Working Mothers

	Model 1	Model 2	Model 3	Model 4
Controls				
Age	0.03***	0.03***	0.02***	0.02***
Gender	−0.64***	−0.64***	−0.68***	−0.68***
Cohort	−0.06	−0.06	−0.07	−0.07
Year	−0.04***	−0.04***	−0.04***	−0.04***
Black	−0.37***	−0.37***	−0.41***	−0.41***
Education	−0.10***	−0.10***	−0.12***	−0.12***
South	−0.10	−0.09	−0.10*	−0.10*
Midwest	−0.13*	−0.13*	−0.14**	−0.14**
Northeast	−0.04	−0.05	−0.04	−0.04
Religious tradition[a]				
Black Protestant	0.08	0.08		
Catholic	0.19**	0.19**		
Jewish	−0.15	−0.15		
Other	0.62***	0.62***		
Conservative Protestant	0.38***$_H$	0.32***		
Mainline Protestant	0.12$_L$	0.16*		
Conservative Protestant × year		0.01*		
Mainline Protestant × year		−0.01		
Religious tradition by attendance[a]				
Frequently attending BP			0.12	0.12
Infrequently attending BP			0.12	0.12
Frequently attending RC			0.32***	0.31***
Infrequently attending RC			0.08	0.08
Frequently attending Jew			−0.10	−0.10
Infrequently attending Jew			−0.14	−0.14
Frequently attending other			0.97***	0.97***
Infrequently attending other			0.33**	0.33**
Frequently attending CP			0.67***$_H$	0.59***
Infrequently attending CP			0.07$_L$	0.06
Frequently attending MP			0.21**$_L$	0.24**
Infrequently attending MP			0.08$_L$	0.08
Frequently attending CP × year				0.02*
Frequently attending MP × year				−0.01
.2 Log likelihood	19,677.60	19,668.54	19,563.44	19,577.67

Note: Data are from GSS (1977–1998). $N = 15,411$. Significance tests are two-tailed. BP = black Protestant; RC = Roman Catholic; CP = conservative Protestant; MP = mainline Protestant.
[a]The comparison category is Unaffiliated.
*$p < .05$. **$p < .01$. ***$p < .001$.
H, L = Coefficients with different subscripts are significantly different ($p < .05$).

Table A3.6

Odds Ratios from Logistic Regressions on Theological Conservatism of Married Men with Children

	Model 1	Model 2
Controls		
Age	1.01	1.00
Couple's income (in $10,000s, logged)	0.96	0.97
Education	0.89*	0.78***
Black	1.14	1.07
Hispanic	2.64***	2.31***
South	1.77***	1.72***
Midwest	1.16	1.03
Northeast	0.82	0.83
Religious tradition[a]		
Catholic	1.45*	
Jewish	0.21*	
Other	4.33***	
Conservative Protestant	7.40***$_H$	
Mainline Protestant	2.45***$_L$	
Religious tradition by attendance[a]		
Frequently attending RC		2.24***
Infrequently attending RC		0.94
Frequently attending Jew		0.76
Infrequently attending Jew		0.20*
Frequently attending other		8.17***
Infrequently attending other		1.24
Frequently attending CP		17.56***$_H$
Infrequently attending CP		3.93***$_L$
Frequently attending MP		6.16***$_L$
Infrequently attending MP		1.39*$_L$
.2 Log likelihood	3,972.65	3,711.21

Note: Data are from NSFH1 (1987–1988). $N = 3,251$. Significance tests are two-tailed. RC = Roman Catholic; CP = conservative Protestant; MP = mainline Protestant.
[a]The comparison category is Unaffiliated.
*$p < .05$. **$p < .01$. ***$p < .001$.
H, L = Coefficients with different subscripts are significantly different ($p < .05$).

Table A3.7

Coefficients from OLS Regression Models on Familism of Married Men with Children

	Model 1	Model 2	Model 3
Controls			
Age	0.01***	0.01***	0.01***
Couple's income (in $10,000s, logged)	0.00	0.01	0.01
Education	0.01	−0.01	0.00
Black	−0.06	−0.07*	−0.07*
Hispanic	0.18***	0.15***	0.09**
South	0.17***	0.16***	0.12***
Midwest	0.01	−0.02	−0.02
Northeast	0.04	0.04	0.05
Religious tradition[a]			
Catholic	0.22***		
Jewish	0.10		
Other	0.51***		
Conservative Protestant	0.28***$_H$		
Mainline Protestant	0.17***$_L$		
Religious tradition by attendance[a]			
Frequently attending RC		0.33***	0.28***
Infrequently attending RC		0.11**	0.11**
Frequently attending Jew		0.52***	0.51***
Infrequently attending Jew		0.05	0.07
Frequently attending other		0.69***	0.54***
Infrequently attending other		0.18**	0.17**
Frequently attending CP		0.39***$_H$	0.19***
Infrequently attending CP		0.18***$_L$	0.09*
Frequently attending MP		0.30***$_L$	0.18***
Infrequently attending MP		0.10**$_L$	0.09**
Religious ideology			
Theological conservative[b]			0.35***
Intercept	3.07	3.11	3.02
R^2	0.08	0.12	0.20

Note: Data are from NSFH1 (1987–1988). N = 3,539. Significance tests are two-tailed. RC = Roman Catholic; CP = conservative Protestant; MP = mainline Protestant.

[a]The comparison category is Unaffiliated.

[b]The comparison category is Non–theological conservative.

*$p < .05$. **$p < .01$. ***$p < .001$.

H, L = Coefficients with different subscripts are significantly different ($p < .05$).

Table A3.8

Coefficients from OLS Regression Models on Gender-Role Traditionalism of Married Men with Children

	Model 1	Model 2	Model 3
Controls			
Age	0.01***	0.01***	0.01***
Couple's income (in $10,000s, logged)	−0.03*	−0.03*	−0.02*
Education	−0.05***	−0.07***	−0.06***
Black	−0.26***	−0.27***	−0.28***
Hispanic	0.23***	0.21***	0.17***
South	0.10**	0.09**	0.06
Midwest	0.08*	0.07	0.07
Northeast	0.10**	0.10**	0.11**
Religious tradition[a]			
Catholic	0.07		
Jewish	−0.13		
Other	0.55***		
Conservative Protestant	0.21***$_H$		
Mainline Protestant	0.07$_L$		
Religious tradition by attendance[a]			
Frequently attending RC		0.16**	0.12**
Infrequently attending RC		−0.02	−0.01
Frequently attending Jew		−0.09	−0.10
Infrequently attending Jew		−0.12	−0.11
Frequently attending other		0.69***	0.59***
Infrequently attending other		0.29**	0.28**
Frequently attending CP		0.28***$_H$	0.13**
Infrequently attending CP		0.14**$_L$	0.07
Frequently attending MP		0.18***$_L$	0.09
Infrequently attending MP		0.01$_L$	0.00
Religious ideology			
Theological conservative[b]			0.26***
Intercept	2.90	2.94	2.87
R^2	0.08	0.09	0.12

Note: Data are from NSFH1 (1987–1988). $N = 3,539$. Significance tests are two-tailed. RC = Roman Catholic; CP = conservative Protestant; MP = mainline Protestant.

[a] The comparison category is Unaffiliated.

[b] The comparison category is Non–theological conservative.

*$p < .05$. **$p < .01$. ***$p < .001$.

H, L = Coefficients with different subscripts are significantly different ($p < .05$).

Table A4.1
Summary of NSFH1 Paternal Involvement and Style Measures (1987–1988)

Variable	Item Wording/Codes	N	Mean	SD	Alpha
One-on-one involvement	How often do you spend time with the children in leisure activities away from home (e.g., picnics, sports, movies)? At home working on a project or playing together? Having private talks? Helping with reading or homework? (1 = never or rarely; 6 = almost every day)	2,478	3.59	1.13	0.76
Activities[a]	Now let's talk about the activities that you and [focal child] do together. Please tell me if you do these at least once a week, several times a month, several times a year, or less often than that: Homework or school projects when school is in session? Attend a party or a family gathering? Do volunteer work together to help other people or improve your neighborhood? Play a game or sport? Read a book or discuss a book with your child? (1 = less than several times a year; 4 = at least once a week)	2,195	3.04	0.57	0.65
Youth-related activities	During the past 12 months, how much time did you spend in an average week in . . . the following organized youth activities as a participant, advisor, coach or leader? Parent-teacher organization or other school activities; religious youth group; community youth group; team sports or youth athletic clubs. (0 to 40 hours)	1,998	2.40	5.05	
Praising and hugging	Please indicate how often you praise child? Hug child? (0 = never to sometimes; 1 = very often)	2,192	0.43	0.49	
Spanking	Spank or slap child? (1 = never; 4 = very often)	2,540	1.83	0.80	

Table A4.1
(*continued*)

Variable	Item Wording/Codes	N	Mean	SD	Alpha
Yelling	Yell at child? (1 = never; 4 = very often)	2,548	2.60	0.80	
Television rules	Do you restrict the amount of television that [focal child] watches? Do you restrict the type of programs that he/she watches? (0 = no restrictions; 1 = some restrictions)	1,068	0.68	0.47	
Whereabouts of child	When [focal child] is away from home, is he/she supposed to let you know where he/she is? (0 = never to sometimes; 1 = all of the time)	1,060	0.84	0.37	
Bedtime[a]	Does [focal child] have a regular bedtime? (0 = no; 1 = yes)	2,309	0.78		

[a]These items are derived from the Survey of Adults and Youth (1998–1999).

Table A4.2

Coefficients from OLS Regression Models on Paternal One-on-One Involvement

	Model 1	Model 2	Model 3	Model 4	Model 5
Controls					
Primary respondent	0.28***	0.28***	0.28***	0.28***	0.27***
Focal child's age	−0.03***	−0.03***	−0.03***	−0.03***	−0.03***
Father's age	−0.01*	−0.01*	−0.01*	−0.01*	−0.01*
Couple's income	0.13***	0.13***	0.13***	0.13***	0.12***
(in $10,000s, logged)					
Education	0.12***	0.12***	0.12***	0.12***	0.12***
Black	0.09	0.10	0.10	0.10	0.06
Hispanic	0.20*	0.18*	0.17*	0.17*	0.18*
All male children	0.31***	0.31***	0.31***	0.31***	0.30***
Mixed gender children	0.22***	0.22***	0.23***	0.23***	0.23***
All biological children	0.33***	0.33***	0.32***	0.32***	0.33***
Biological and stepchildren	0.24*	0.24*	0.25**	0.25**	0.26**
Age of youngest child	−0.07***	−0.07***	−0.07***	−0.07***	−0.07***
Number of preschool children	−0.32***	−0.33***	−0.33***	−0.33***	−0.31***
Number of school-age children	−0.06*	−0.06*	−0.06*	−0.06*	−0.06*
South	−0.01	−0.01	−0.02	−0.02	−0.01
Midwest	−0.02	−0.02	−0.02	−0.02	−0.01
Northeast	0.00	0.00	0.01	0.01	0.02
Employed	0.30*	0.28*	0.29*	0.29*	0.28*
Work hours	−0.01**	−0.01**	−0.01**	−0.01**	−0.01**
Shift work	−0.11*	−0.12*	−0.12*	−0.12*	−0.12*
Religious tradition[a]					
Catholic	0.07				
Jewish	0.28				
Other	0.33**				
Conservative Protestant	0.19**				
Mainline Protestant	0.14				
Religious tradition by attendance[a]					
Frequently attending RC		0.13	0.12	0.12	0.12
Infrequently attending RC		0.01	0.01	0.01	0.01
Frequently attending Jew		0.45	0.46	0.46	0.42
Infrequently attending Jew		0.26	0.26	0.26	0.25
Frequently attending other		0.32**	0.29*	0.29*	0.33**
Infrequently attending other		0.35*	0.34*	0.34*	0.36*
Frequently attending CP		0.27**_H	0.21*	0.21*	0.22*
Infrequently attending CP		0.11_L	0.09	0.09	0.10

Table A4.2

(*continued*)

	Model 1	Model 2	Model 3	Model 4	Model 5
Frequently attending MP		0.09$_L$	0.06	0.06	0.06
Infrequently attending MP		0.16*	0.16*	0.16*	0.16
Religious, family, and gender ideologies					
Theological conservative[b]			0.09	0.09	0.11*
Familism				−0.00	0.06
Gender-role traditionalism					−0.14***
Intercept	2.73	2.76	2.75	2.75	2.93
R^2	0.22	0.22	0.22	0.22	0.23

Note: Data are from NSFH1 (1987–1988). $N = 2,487$. Significance tests are two-tailed. RC = Roman Catholic; CP = conservative Protestant; MP = mainline Protestant.

[a]The comparison category is Unaffiliated.

[b]The comparison category is Non–theological conservative.

*$p < .05$. **$p < .01$. ***$p < .001$.

H, L = Coefficients with different subscripts are significantly different ($p < .05$).

Table A4.3
Coefficients from OLS Regression Models on Paternal Involvement in One-on-One Activities (1998–1999)

	Model 1	Model 2
Controls		
Focal child's age	−0.06***	−0.06***
Father's age	−0.01*	−0.01**
Family income	0.02	0.02
Education	0.05***	0.04***
Black	0.09**	0.07*
Hispanic	−0.16**	−0.17***
Stepchildren	−0.18***	−0.17**
Age of youngest child	0.00	0.00
Number of preteen children	0.00	−0.01
Number of teenage children	0.03	0.02
South	0.06	0.05
Northeast	−0.03	−0.04
Midwest	−0.02	−0.03
Employed	0.07	0.05
Work hours	0.00	0.00
Religious tradition[a]		
Catholic	0.14***	
Jewish	0.03	
Other	0.10*	
Conservative Protestant	0.10*	
Mainline Protestant	0.07	
Religious tradition by attendance[a]		
Frequently attending RC		0.17***
Infrequently attending RC		0.07
Frequently attending Jew		0.07
Infrequently attending Jew		0.07
Frequently attending other		0.20***
Infrequently attending other		−0.01
Frequently attending CP		0.14**$_H$
Infrequently attending CP		0.00$_L$
Frequently attending MP		0.13**$_H$
Infrequently attending MP		0.00$_L$
Intercept	3.60	3.66
R^2	0.14	0.16

Note: Data are from SAY (1998–1999). $N = 2,195$. Significance tests are two-tailed. RC = Roman Catholic; CP = conservative Protestant; MP = mainline Protestant.
[a]The comparison category is Unaffiliated.
*$p < .05$. **$p < .01$. ***$p < .001$.
H, L = Coefficients with different subscripts are significantly different ($p < .05$).

Table A4.4

Coefficients from Tobit Regression Models on Paternal Involvement in Youth-Related
Activities

	Model 1	Model 2	Model 3	Model 4	Model 5
Controls					
Father's age	−0.06	−0.07	−0.07	−0.07	−0.07
Couple's income	0.76*	0.77*	0.77*	0.77*	0.77*
(in $10,000s, logged)					
Education	1.32***	1.17***	1.18***	1.18***	1.18***
Black	−0.29	−0.36	−0.35	−0.35	−0.34
Hispanic	−0.56	−0.54	−0.58	−0.58	−0.59
All male children	2.29**	2.30**	2.29**	2.29**	2.30**
Mixed gender children	0.85	0.89	0.89	0.89	0.89
All biological children	1.77*	1.87*	1.86*	1.86*	1.86*
Biological and stepchildren	0.32	0.53	0.52	0.52	0.52
Age of youngest child	−0.16	−0.15	−0.16	−0.16	−0.16
Number of preschool children	−1.15	−1.27*	−1.29*	−1.29*	−1.29*
Number of school-age children	0.96**	0.87**	0.86**	0.87**	0.86**
South	0.66	0.61	0.58	0.58	0.58
Midwest	0.27	0.22	0.22	0.22	0.21
Northeast	0.30	0.43	0.43	0.43	0.42
Employed	0.02	0.05	0.11	0.11	0.11
Work hours	−0.02	−0.01	−0.02	−0.02	−0.02
Religious tradition[a]					
Catholic	1.13				
Jewish	−0.52				
Other	3.21**				
Conservative Protestant	1.99*				
Mainline Protestant	1.29				
Religious tradition by attendance[a]					
Frequently attending RC		1.70	1.66	1.66	1.66
Infrequently attending RC		0.56	0.56	0.56	0.56
Frequently attending Jew		0.63	0.64	0.65	0.66
Infrequently attending Jew		−0.41	−0.39	−0.38	−0.39
Frequently attending other		4.74***	4.63***	4.64***	4.63**
Infrequently attending other		0.14	0.26	0.26	0.25
Frequently attending CP		3.75***H	3.57***	3.58***	3.57***
Infrequently attending CP		0.30L	0.23	0.23	0.23
Frequently attending MP		2.08*	1.98	1.98	1.98
Infrequently attending MP		0.91L	0.89	0.89	0.89

Table A4.4
(*continued*)

	Model 1	Model 2	Model 3	Model 4	Model 5
Religious, family, and gender ideologies					
Theological conservative[b]			0.29	0.30	0.29
Familism				−0.02	−0.04
Gender-role traditionalism					0.04
Intercept	−14.50***	−13.91***	−13.97***	−13.92***	−13.98***
Pseudo R^2	0.02	0.02	0.02	0.02	0.02

Note: Data are from NSFH (1987–1988). N = 2,487. Significance tests are two-tailed. RC = Roman Catholic; CP = conservative Protestant; MP = mainline Protestant.
[a]The comparison category is Unaffiliated.
[b]The comparison category is Non–theological conservative.
*p < .05. **p < .01. ***p < .001.
H, L = Coefficients with different subscripts are significantly different (p < .05).

Table A4.5
Odds Ratios from Logistic Regressions on Paternal Praising and Hugging

	Model 1	Model 2	Model 3	Model 4	Model 5
Controls					
Primary respondent	1.13	1.13	1.15	1.13	1.12
Focal child's age	0.95**	0.95**	0.95**	0.95**	0.95**
Father's age	1.13*	1.01*	1.01	1.01	1.01
Couple's income (in $10,000s, logged)	1.31***	1.32***	1.33***	1.32***	1.31***
Education	1.23***	1.21***	1.23***	1.22***	1.22***
Black	1.02	1.01	1.00	1.01	0.97
Hispanic	0.92	0.90	0.86	0.84	0.85
All male children	0.83	0.83	0.84	0.84	0.83
Mixed gender children	1.06	1.08	1.08	1.08	1.09
All biological children	1.66**	1.66**	1.65**	1.62**	1.63**
Biological and stepchildren	1.49	1.48	1.49	1.45	1.48
Age of youngest child	0.87***	0.87***	0.87***	0.87***	0.87***
Number of preschool children	0.61***	0.60***	0.60***	0.59***	0.61***
Number of school-age children	0.73***	0.72***	0.72***	0.71***	0.72***
South	0.92	0.90	0.88	0.85	0.86
Midwest	0.70**	0.69**	0.68**	0.68**	0.70**
Northeast	0.74*	0.74*	0.74*	0.73*	0.75
Employed	0.76	0.75	0.78	0.78	0.77
Work hours	1.00	1.00	1.00	1.00	1.00
Religious tradition[a]					
Catholic	1.50*				
Jewish	1.67				
Other	2.02**				
Conservative Protestant	1.65**				
Mainline Protestant	1.40*				
Religious tradition by attendance[a]					
Frequently attending RC		1.77**	1.73**	1.64**	1.64**
Infrequently attending RC		1.23	1.23	1.21	1.21
Frequently attending Jew		3.36	3.40	3.02	2.90
Infrequently attending Jew		1.52	1.55	1.51	1.49
Frequently attending other		2.04**	1.84*	1.63*	1.72*
Infrequently attending other		1.99*	1.96*	1.93*	1.97*
Frequently attending CP		1.66**	1.43	1.38	1.39
Infrequently attending CP		1.65**	1.55*	1.53*	1.54*
Frequently attending MP		1.59*	1.46	1.41	1.41
Infrequently attending MP		1.30	1.29	1.27	1.28

Table A4.5
(continued)

Religious, family, and gender ideologies	Model 1	Model 2	Model 3	Model 4	Model 5
Theological conservative[b]			1.29*	1.19	1.21
Familism				1.27**	1.35**
Gender-role traditionalism					0.86*
.2 Log likelihood		3,125.52	3,119.23	3,113.20	3,106.32

Note: Data are from NSFH (1987–1988). N = 2,192. Significance tests are two-tailed. RC = Roman Catholic; CP = conservative Protestant; MP = mainline Protestant.

[a]The comparison category is Unaffiliated.

[b]The comparison category is Non–theological conservative.

*p < .05. **p < .01. ***p < .001.

Table A4.6

Coefficients from OLS Regression Models on Paternal Use of Corporal Punishment

	Model 1	Model 2	Model 3	Model 4	Model 5
Controls					
Primary respondent	−0.04	−0.04	−0.03	−0.03	−0.03
Focal child's age	−0.01	−0.01	−0.01	−0.01	−0.01
Father's age	−0.02***	−0.02***	−0.02***	−0.02***	−0.02***
Couple's income (in $10,000s, logged)	−0.03*	−0.03*	−0.03*	−0.03*	−0.03*
Education	−0.01	−0.02	−0.01	−0.01	−0.01
Black	−0.02	−0.02	−0.02	−0.02	−0.02
Hispanic	−0.16**	−0.16**	−0.19**	−0.19**	−0.19**
All male children	0.17***	0.17***	0.17***	0.17***	0.17***
Mixed gender children	0.10**	0.10**	0.10**	0.10**	0.10**
All biological children	0.03	0.03	0.03	0.03	0.03
Biological and stepchildren	0.05	0.06	0.06	0.05	0.05
Age of youngest child	−0.05***	−0.05***	−0.05***	−0.05***	−0.05***
Number of preschool children	0.05	0.04	0.04	0.04	0.04
Number of school-age children	0.04*	0.03*	0.03	0.03	0.03
South	0.07	0.07	0.05	0.05	0.05
Midwest	0.01	0.01	0.01	0.01	0.01
Northeast	−0.05	−0.05	−0.05	−0.05	−0.05
Employed	0.05	0.04	0.05	0.06	0.06
Work hours	−0.00	−0.00	−0.00	−0.00	−0.00
Religious tradition[a]					
Catholic	−0.00				
Jewish	0.02				
Other	0.17*				
Conservative Protestant	0.16**				
Mainline Protestant	0.13**				
Religious tradition by attendance[a]					
Frequently attending RC		0.01	−0.00	−0.01	−0.01
Infrequently attending RC		−0.01	−0.02	−0.02	−0.02
Frequently attending Jew		−0.39	−0.38	−0.40	−0.40
Infrequently attending Jew		0.11	0.11	0.11	0.11
Frequently attending other		0.24**	0.20*	0.18*	0.17*
Infrequently attending other		0.00	−0.00	−0.01	−0.01
Frequently attending CP		0.24***ₕ	0.17**	0.16**	0.16**
Infrequently attending CP		0.08ₗ	0.05	0.05	0.05
Frequently attending MP		0.14*	0.10	0.09	0.09
Infrequently attending MP		0.12*ₗ	0.12*	0.11*	0.11*

Table A4.6
(*continued*)

Religious, family, and gender ideologies	Model 1	Model 2	Model 3	Model 4	Model 5
Theological conservative[b]			0.12***	0.10**	0.10**
Familism				0.04	0.04
Gender-role traditionalism					0.01
Intercept	2.99	3.01	2.99	2.89	2.88
R^2	0.25	0.25	0.26	0.26	0.26

Note: Data are from NSFH (1987–1988). $N = 2{,}540$. Significance tests are two-tailed. RC = Roman Catholic; CP = conservative Protestant; MP = mainline Protestant.

[a]The comparison category is Unaffiliated.

[b]The comparison category is Non–theological conservative.

*$p < .05$. **$p < .01$. ***$p < .001$.

H, L = Coefficients with different subscripts are significantly different ($p < .05$).

Table A4.7

Coefficients from OLS Regression Models on Paternal Yelling

	Model 1	Model 2	Model 3	Model 4	Model 5
Controls					
Primary respondent	−0.00	0.00	−0.00	−0.00	0.00
Focal child's age	0.01	0.01	0.01	0.01	0.01
Father's age	−0.02***	−0.02***	−0.02***	−0.02***	−0.02***
Couple's income (in $10,000s, logged)	0.04**	0.04*	0.04*	0.04*	0.04*
Education	−0.02	−0.01	−0.01	−0.01	−0.01
Black	−0.14*	−0.13*	−0.13*	−0.13*	−0.13*
Hispanic	−0.38***	−0.36***	−0.35***	−0.35***	−0.35***
All male children	0.07	0.07	0.07	0.07	0.07
Mixed gender children	0.11**	0.10*	0.10*	0.10*	0.10*
All biological children	0.20**	0.20**	0.20**	0.20**	0.20**
Biological and stepchildren	0.19**	0.20**	0.19**	0.20**	0.20**
Age of youngest child	−0.01**	−0.01	−0.01	−0.01	−0.01
Number of preschool children	0.03	0.04	0.04	0.05	0.04
Number of school-age children	0.08***	0.09***	0.09***	0.09***	0.09***
South	−0.00	0.01	0.02	0.02	0.02
Midwest	0.17***	0.18***	0.18***	0.18***	0.18***
Northeast	0.09	0.08	0.08	0.08	0.08
Employed	0.08	0.09	0.08	0.08	0.08
Work hours	−0.00	−0.00	−0.00	−0.00	−0.00
Religious tradition[a]					
Catholic	0.08				
Jewish	0.05				
Other	−0.12				
Conservative Protestant	−0.06$_L$				
Mainline Protestant	0.04$_H$				
Religious tradition by attendance[a]					
Frequently attending RC		−0.05	−0.04	−0.03	−0.03
Infrequently attending RC		0.23***	0.23***	0.24***	0.24***
Frequently attending Jew		−0.19	−0.19	−0.17	−0.17
Infrequently attending Jew		0.07	0.07	0.07	0.07
Frequently attending other		−0.19*	−0.16	−0.14	−0.14
Infrequently attending other		0.02	0.02	0.03	0.02
Frequently attending CP		−0.12$_L$	−0.08	−0.08	−0.08
Infrequently attending CP		−0.01	0.01	0.01	0.01
Frequently attending MP		−0.05$_L$	−0.03	−0.03	−0.03
Infrequently attending MP		0.10$_H$	0.10	0.11	0.11

Table A4.7
(*continued*)

	Model 1	Model 2	Model 3	Model 4	Model 5
Religious, family, and gender ideologies					
Theological conservative[b]			−0.07	−0.05	−0.06
Familism				−0.03	−0.04
Gender-role traditionalism					0.01
Intercept	2.46	2.38	2.40	2.49	2.48
R^2	0.10	0.11	0.12	0.12	0.12

Note: Data are from NSFH (1987–1988). $N = 2,548$. Significance tests are two-tailed. RC = Roman Catholic; CP = conservative Protestant; MP = mainline Protestant.

[a]The comparison category is Unaffiliated.

[b]The comparison category is Non–theological conservative.

*$p < .05$. **$p < .01$. ***$p < .001$.

H, L = Coefficients with different subscripts are significantly different ($p < .05$).

Table A4.8
Odds Ratios from Logistic Regressions on Television Rules

	Model 1	Model 2	Model 3	Model 4	Model 5
Controls					
Focal child's age	0.74***	0.74***	0.74***	0.74***	0.74***
Father's age	0.99	0.99	0.99	0.98	0.99
Couple's income (in $10,000s, logged)	1.02	1.02	1.01	1.01	1.01
Education	1.11	1.06	1.08	1.09	1.08
Black	1.07	1.10	1.05	1.06	1.02
Hispanic	0.93	0.84	0.78	0.77	0.79
All male children	1.13	1.09	1.05	1.06	1.03
Mixed gender children	1.02	1.01	1.01	1.01	1.00
All biological children	0.82	0.86	0.85	0.81	0.83
Biological and stepchildren	0.72	0.70	0.71	0.69	0.72
Age of youngest child	0.92**	0.92**	0.91**	0.92**	0.92**
Number of preschool children	0.69	0.64	0.65	0.65	0.66
Number of school-age children	1.16	1.12	1.11	1.11	1.12
South	1.23	1.22	1.16	1.11	1.12
Midwest	0.97	1.01	1.01	1.01	1.03
Northeast	1.01	1.02	1.06	1.04	1.06
Employed	0.60	0.52	0.53	0.54	0.54
Work hours	1.01	1.01	1.01	1.01	1.01
Religious tradition[a]					
Catholic	1.17				
Jewish	0.87				
Other	2.78**				
Conservative Protestant	2.25**$_H$				
Mainline Protestant	1.31$_L$				
Religious tradition by attendance[a]					
Frequently attending RC		1.73	1.60	1.52	1.53
Infrequently attending RC		0.84	0.85	0.84	0.83
Frequently attending Jew		0.73	0.76	0.66	0.64
Infrequently attending Jew		1.04	1.05	1.04	1.07
Frequently attending other		6.29***	5.31***	4.62**	4.79**
Infrequently attending other		0.92	0.93	0.90	0.94
Frequently attending CP		3.80***$_H$	3.04**	2.96**	2.97**
Infrequently attending CP		1.39$_L$	1.32	1.30	1.32
Frequently attending MP		1.25$_L$	1.12	1.10	1.09
Infrequently attending MP		1.39$_L$	1.38	1.36	1.37

Table A4.8
(continued)

	Model 1	Model 2	Model 3	Model 4	Model 5
Religious, family, and gender ideologies					
Theological conservative[b]			1.58*	1.46*	1.48*
Familism				1.23	1.34
Gender-role traditionalism					0.82
.2 Log likelihood	1,206.97	1,180.95	1,174.68	1,172.85	1,170.18

Note: Data are from NSFH (1987–1988). N = 1,068. Significance tests are two-tailed. RC = Roman Catholic; CP = conservative Protestant; MP = mainline Protestant.

[a]The comparison category is Unaffiliated.

[b]The comparison category is Non–theological conservative.

*p < .05. **p < .01. ***p < .001.

H, L = Coefficients with different subscripts are significantly different (p < .05).

Table A4.9

Odds Ratios from Logistic Regressions on Children's Whereabouts

	Model 1	Model 2	Model 3	Model 4	Model 5
Controls					
Focal child's age	0.82***	0.82***	0.82***	0.81***	0.82***
Father's age	1.02	1.02	1.02	1.01	1.01
Couple's income (in $10,000s, logged)	1.05	1.06	1.05	1.04	1.04
Education	1.00	0.98	1.00	1.00	1.00
Black	1.73	1.78	1.69	1.69	1.66
Hispanic	3.16**	3.09*	2.80*	2.78*	2.85*
All male children	0.54**	0.55**	0.53**	0.53**	0.52**
Mixed gender children	0.87	0.87	0.87	0.87	0.86
All biological children	0.62	0.65	0.64	0.62	0.63
Biological and stepchildren	0.41**	0.41**	0.42**	0.41**	0.42**
Age of youngest child	0.99	0.99	0.98	0.99	0.99
Number of preschool children	1.01	0.96	0.96	0.96	0.98
Number of school-age children	1.07	1.06	1.04	1.04	1.05
South	1.38	1.35	1.28	1.24	1.24
Midwest	2.13**	2.30**	2.32**	2.32**	2.36**
Northeast	2.15**	2.13**	2.21**	2.18**	2.20**
Employed	0.37*	0.34*	0.35*	0.37*	0.36*
Work hours	1.01	1.01	1.02	1.02	1.02
Religious tradition[a]					
Catholic	1.29				
Jewish	5.68*				
Other	3.78**				
Conservative Protestant	2.09**				
Mainline Protestant	1.37				
Religious tradition by attendance[a]					
Frequently attending RC		1.34	1.26	1.20	1.19
Infrequently attending RC		1.28	1.31	1.29	1.27
Frequently attending Jew		0.43	0.45	0.40	0.38
Infrequently attending Jew		482.67	498.72	496.30	497.02
Frequently attending other		11.44**	9.89**	8.68**	8.91**
Infrequently attending other		1.36	1.41	1.33	1.36
Frequently attending CP		2.94**$_H$	2.35*	2.30*	2.30*
Infrequently attending CP		1.52$_L$	1.45	1.43	1.42
Frequently attending MP		1.19$_L$	1.08	1.06	1.05
Infrequently attending MP		1.48$_L$	1.49	1.47	1.47

Table A4.9
(continued)

	Model 1	Model 2	Model 3	Model 4	Model 5
Religious, family, and gender ideologies					
Theological conservative[b]			1.54*	1.43	1.44
Familism				1.19	1.26
Gender-role traditionalism					0.88
.2 Log likelihood	1,026.39	1,006.34	1,001.95	1,000.85	1,000.05

Note: Data are from NSFH (1987–1988). $N = 1,060$. Significance tests are two-tailed. RC = Roman Catholic; CP = conservative Protestant; MP = mainline Protestant.

[a]The comparison category is Unaffiliated.

[b]The comparison category is Non–theological conservative.

*$p < .05$. **$p < .01$. ***$p < .001$.

H, L = Coefficients with different subscripts are significantly different ($p < .05$).

Table A4.10

Odds Ratios from Logistic Regressions on Existence of Regular Bedtime for Child

	Model 1	Model 2
Controls		
Focal child's age	0.74***	0.74***
Father's age	1.02*	1.02
Family income	0.90	0.89
Education	0.94	0.92
Black	1.41*	1.36*
Hispanic	1.52	1.44
Stepchildren	1.24	1.32
Age of youngest child	0.99	0.99
Number of preteen children	1.01	0.98
Number of teenage children	1.21**	1.19*
South	1.17	1.08
Northeast	1.04	0.99
Midwest	1.13	1.10
Employed	1.51	1.43
Work hours	1.00	1.00
Religious tradition[a]		
Catholic	1.34	
Jewish	0.87	
Other	1.36	
Conservative Protestant	1.65**	
Mainline Protestant	1.25	
Religious tradition by attendance[a]		
Frequently attending RC		1.60*
Infrequently attending RC		0.96
Frequently attending Jew		1.08
Infrequently attending Jew		0.58
Frequently attending other		2.50**
Infrequently attending other		0.79
Frequently attending CP		2.25***$_H$
Infrequently attending CP		0.72$_L$
Frequently attending MP		1.36$_L$
Infrequently attending MP		1.14$_L$
.2 Log likelihood	2,153.26	2,114.83

Note: Data are from SAY (1998–1999). $N = 2,309$. Significance tests are two-tailed. RC = Roman Catholic; CP = conservative Protestant; MP = mainline Protestant.

[a] The comparison category is Unaffiliated.

*$p < .05$. **$p < .01$. ***$p < .001$.

H, L = Coefficients with different subscripts are significantly different ($p < .05$).

Table A5.1

Summary of NSFH1 Household Labor Measures (1987–1988)

Variable	Item Wording/Codes	N	Mean	SD
Husband's hours of household labor	The approximate number of hours per week that you . . . normally spend preparing meals? Washing dishes and cleaning up after meals? Cleaning house? Doing outdoor and other household maintenance tasks? Shopping for groceries and other household goods? Washing, ironing, mending? Paying bills . . . ? Automobile maintenance and repair? Driving other household members to work, school, or other activities?	3,366	17.52	15.03
Husband's percentage of household labor	Husband's hours of household labor divided by sum of husband's and wife's hours of household labor.	3,179	0.32	0.16
Wife feels household labor appreciated	How would you describe the work you do around the house? Would you say it is appreciated? (1 = unappreciated; 7 = appreciated)	1,499	4.59	1.77

Table A5.2

Coefficients from OLS Regression Models on Husband's Weekly Hours of Household Labor

	Model 1	Model 2	Model 3	Model 4	Model 5	Model 6
Controls						
Primary respondent	2.60***	2.59***	2.57***	2.65***	2.57***	2.32***
Father's age	−0.12**	−0.12**	−0.12**	−0.11**	−0.09**	−0.09**
Couple's income (in $10,000s, logged)	0.26	0.26	0.26	0.28	0.23	0.16
Education	−0.17	−0.16	−0.18	−0.19	−0.28	−0.17
Black	4.78***	4.80***	4.81***	4.70***	4.26***	3.78***
Hispanic	−0.24	−0.23	−0.15	−0.01	0.19	0.10
All biological children	−2.46*	−2.47*	−2.45*	−2.32*	−2.21*	−2.14*
Biological and step-children	−2.31	−2.28	−2.29	−2.21	−1.90	−1.94
Number of preschool children	1.13**	1.14**	1.15**	1.22**	1.35**	1.78***
Number of school-age children	0.44	0.45	0.46	0.48	0.61*	0.75**
South	−1.25	−1.23	−1.18	−1.01	−0.96	−1.02
Midwest	0.30	0.32	0.32	0.29	0.41	0.49
Northeast	−0.75	−0.76	−0.78	−0.70	−0.55	−0.44
Employed	0.71	0.71	0.66	0.55	0.45	0.59
Work hours	−0.10***	−0.10***	−0.10***	−0.10***	−0.09**	−0.08**
Religious tradition[a]						
Catholic	0.33					
Jewish	−0.98					
Other	−1.68					
Conservative Protestant	−1.43$_L$					
Mainline Protestant	0.30$_H$					
Religious tradition by attendance[a]						
Frequently attending RC		0.11	0.17	0.51	0.44	0.34
Infrequently attending RC		0.56	0.56	0.70	0.61	0.71
Frequently attending Jew		0.84	0.86	1.54	1.04	1.96

Table A5.2

(*continued*)

	Model 1	Model 2	Model 3	Model 4	Model 5	Model 6
Infrequently attending Jew		−1.32	−1.33	−1.23	−1.44	−1.27
Frequently attending other		−2.08	−1.90	−1.17	−0.69	−0.77
Infrequently attending other		−0.95	−0.95	−0.76	−0.48	−0.37
Frequently attending CP		−1.22	−0.96	−0.70	−0.64	−0.68
Infrequently attending CP		−1.66$_L$	−1.54	−1.44	−1.36	−1.34
Frequently attending MP		0.11	0.27	0.53	0.55	0.74
Infrequently attending MP		0.41$_H$	0.44	0.53	0.48	0.57
Religious, family, and gender ideologies						
Theological conservative[b]			−0.44	0.03	0.18	0.20
Familism				−1.41**	−0.72	−0.83
Gender-role traditionalism					−1.59***	−0.88*
Spousal factors						
Wife employed						−1.57
Wife's work hours						0.09**
Wife's percentage of income						3.29**
Intercept	23.05	22.95	23.06	27.05	29.08	28.57
R^2	0.04	0.04	0.04	0.04	0.04	0.05

Note: Data are from NSFH1 (1987–1988). N = 3,366. Significance tests are two-tailed. RC = Roman Catholic; CP = conservative Protestant; MP = mainline Protestant.

[a]The comparison category is Unaffiliated.

[b]The comparison category is Non–theological conservative.

*p < .05. **p < .01. ***p < .001.

H, L = Coefficients with different subscripts are significantly different (p < .05).

Table A5.3
Coefficients from OLS Regression Models on Husband's Percentage of Household Labor

	Model 1	Model 2	Model 3	Model 4	Model 5	Model 6
Controls						
Primary respondent	0.020**	0.020**	0.019**	0.020**	0.017**	0.010
Father's age	−0.001*	−0.001*	−0.001*	−0.001	−0.000	−0.000
Couple's income (in $10,000s, logged)	0.005	0.005	0.005	0.005	0.004	0.000
Education	0.006*	0.006*	0.005*	0.005	0.002	0.006*
Black	0.070***	0.070***	0.071***	0.069***	0.056***	0.042***
Hispanic	0.022	0.022	0.027*	0.029*	0.035**	0.034**
All biological children	−0.013	−0.013	−0.013	−0.011	−0.007	−0.005
Biological and step-children	−0.032*	−0.032*	−0.033*	−0.032*	−0.022	−0.022
Number of preschool children	−0.010*	−0.010*	−0.010*	−0.009	−0.004	0.008
Number of school-age children	−0.009**	−0.008**	−0.008**	−0.008*	−0.004	0.000
South	−0.013	−0.012	−0.010	−0.008	−0.007	−0.007
Midwest	0.004	0.005	0.005	0.005	0.008	0.009
Northeast	−0.010	−0.010	−0.011	−0.010	−0.006	−0.003
Employed	0.056**	0.056**	0.052**	0.051**	0.048**	0.048**
Work hours	−0.002***	−0.002***	−0.002***	−0.002***	−0.002***	−0.002***
Religious tradition[a]						
Catholic	0.008					
Jewish	0.045*					
Other	−0.010					
Conservative Protestant	−0.007L					
Mainline Protestant	0.007H					
Religious tradition by attendance[a]						
Frequently attending RC		0.003	0.007	0.012	0.009	0.005
Infrequently attending RC		0.013	0.013	0.015	0.013	0.017
Frequently attending Jew		0.001	0.002	0.013	−0.001	0.029
Infrequently attending Jew		0.053*	0.052*	0.054**	0.046*	0.050*
Frequently attending other		−0.008	0.001	0.012	0.026	0.023
Infrequently attending other		−0.014	−0.013	−0.010	−0.003	−0.001

Table A5.3

(continued)

	Model 1	Model 2	Model 3	Model 4	Model 5	Model 6
Frequently attending CP		−0.003	0.011	0.015	0.016	0.015
Infrequently attending CP		−0.011$_L$	−0.005	−0.003	−0.001	0.002
Frequently attending MP		0.002	0.010	0.015	0.015	0.021
Infrequently attending MP		0.010$_H$	0.011	0.013	0.011	0.014
Religious, family, and gender ideologies						
Theological conservative[b]			−0.023**	−0.016*	−0.011	−0.010
Familism				−0.023***	−0.002	−0.006
Gender-role traditionalism					−0.047***	−0.028***
Spousal factors						
Wife employed						−0.017
Wife's work hours						0.002***
Wife's percentage of income						0.070***
Intercept	0.34	0.34	0.35	0.41	0.47	0.45
R^2	0.05	0.05	0.06	0.06	0.09	0.15

Note: Data are from NSFH1 (1987–1988). $N = 3,179$. Significance tests are two-tailed. RC = Roman Catholic; CP = conservative Protestant; MP = mainline Protestant.

[a]The comparison category is Unaffiliated.

[b]The comparison category is Non–theological conservative.

*$p < .05$. **$p < .01$. ***$p < .001$.

H, L = Coefficients with different subscripts are significantly different ($p < .05$).

Table A5.4

Coefficients from OLS Regression Models on Wife's Reports That Household Labor Is Appreciated

	Model 1	Model 2	Model 3	Model 4	Model 5	Model 6	Model 7
Controls							
Father's age	−0.00	−0.00	−0.00	−0.00	−0.00	−0.00	−0.00
Couple's income (in $10,000s, logged)	−0.00	0.01	0.03	0.03	0.02	0.03	0.05
Education	0.01	−0.01	−0.01	−0.01	−0.02	−0.02	−0.03
Black	0.39*	0.38*	0.39*	0.40*	0.37	0.37	0.40*
Hispanic	0.72***	0.72***	0.69***	0.68***	0.69***	0.67***	0.67**
All biological children	0.04	0.03	0.01	0.01	0.02	0.04	0.05
Biological and stepchildren	−0.28	−0.27	−0.28	−0.26	−0.25	−0.22	−0.22
Number of preschool children	0.04	0.03	0.02	0.01	0.02	0.02	−0.01
Number of school-age children	−0.15**	−0.17***	−0.17***	−0.18***	−0.17***	−0.17***	−0.18***
South	0.08	0.07	0.05	0.03	0.04	0.06	0.07
Midwest	0.14	0.10	0.10	0.11	0.12	0.14	0.15
Northeast	0.18	0.16	0.17	0.16	0.18	0.21	0.21
Employed	−0.34	−0.36	−0.33	−0.30	−0.32	−0.34	−0.31
Work hours	0.00	0.00	0.00	0.00	0.00	0.00	0.01
Religious tradition[a]							
Catholic	0.07						
Jewish	0.37						
Other	−0.00						
Conservative Protestant	0.19						
Mainline Protestant	0.05						
Religious tradition by attendance[a]							
Frequently attending RC		0.22	0.18	0.12	0.12	0.16	0.18
Infrequently attending RC		−0.06	−0.07	−0.10	−0.11	−0.10	−0.10
Frequently attending Jew		0.77	0.78	0.70	0.67	0.71	0.63
Infrequently attending Jew		0.38	0.39	0.40	0.37	0.38	0.38
Frequently attending other		0.10	−0.00	−0.11	−0.07	−0.09	−0.07
Infrequently attending other		−0.22	−0.24	−0.26	−0.25	−0.20	−0.22
Frequently attending CP		0.41*$_H$	0.27	0.23	0.23	0.25	0.25
Infrequently attending CP		−0.01$_L$	−0.09	−0.11	−0.10	−0.06	−0.05
Frequently attending MP		0.38*$_H$	0.30	0.25	0.25	0.28	0.25
Infrequently attending MP		−0.13$_L$	−0.15	−0.17	−0.17	−0.14	−0.14
Religious, family, and gender ideologies							
Theological conservative[b]			0.23*	0.16	0.17	0.17	0.17
Familism				0.22*	0.27**	−0.62	−0.61

Table A5.4
(*continued*)

	Model 1	Model 2	Model 3	Model 4	Model 5	Model 6	Model 7
Gender-role traditionalism					−0.12	−1.15**	−1.20**
Gender-role traditionalism × familism						0.29*	0.29*
Spousal factors							
Wife employed							0.18
Wife's work hours							−0.01*
Wife's percentage of income							0.28
Intercept	4.66	4.68	4.55	3.87	4.04	7.15	7.32
R^2	0.03	0.04	0.04	0.05	0.05	0.05	0.06

Note: Data are from NSFH1 (1987–1988). $N = 1,499$. Significance tests are two-tailed. RC = Roman Catholic; CP = conservative Protestant; MP = mainline Protestant.

[a] The comparison category is Unaffiliated.

[b] The comparison category is Non–theological conservative.

*$p < .05$. **$p < .01$. ***$p < .001$.

H, L = Coefficients with different subscripts are significantly different ($p < .05$).

Table A6.1
Summary of NSFH2 Marital Emotion Work Measures (1992–1994)

Variable	Item Wording/Codes	N	Mean	SD
Affection	How happy are you with the love and affection you get from your spouse? (1 = very unhappy; 7 = very happy)	2,695	5.55	1.61
Understanding	How happy are you with the understanding you receive from your spouse? (1 = very unhappy; 7 = very happy)	2,695	5.19	1.59
Domestic violence	Sometimes arguments between partners become physical. (Asked of the wife:) During the past year, in how many of these arguments did your husband become physically violent with you? (Asked of the husband:) During the past year, in how many of these arguments did you become physically violent with your wife? (0 = none; 1 = one or more occasions)	2,769	0.07	0.25
Quality time	During the past month, about how often did you and your wife spend time alone with each other, talking or sharing an activity? (1 = never; 6 = almost every day)	2,785	4.26	1.39
Social time	During the past month, about how often did you and your wife spend time together in social activities with either friends or relatives? (1 = never; 6 = almost every day)	2,785	3.04	1.14

Table A6.2

Coefficients from OLS Regression Models on Wife's Reports of Happiness with Husband's Love and Affection

	Model 1	Model 2	Model 3	Model 4	Model 5	Model 6
Controls						
Focal child's age	0.00	0.00	0.00	−0.00	−0.00	−0.00
Length of marriage	−0.00	−0.01	−0.00	−0.01	−0.01	−0.01
Husband ever divorced	−0.18	−0.16	−0.16	−0.15	−0.15	−0.17
Wife ever divorced	0.05	0.06	0.07	0.07	0.07	0.07
Couple's income (in $10,000s, logged)	−0.07*	−0.07*	−0.07*	−0.07*	−0.07*	−0.06*
Education	0.02	0.00	0.01	0.02	0.02	0.02
Black	−0.49***	−0.49***	−0.49***	−0.46***	−0.46***	−0.34**
Hispanic	−0.15	−0.18	−0.20	−0.21	−0.21	−0.19
Biological and step-children	−0.41**	−0.41**	−0.40**	−0.42**	−0.42**	−0.37*
All biological children	−0.37**	−0.37**	−0.36**	−0.37**	−0.37**	−0.37**
Age of youngest child	−0.02*	−0.02*	−0.02*	−0.02*	−0.02*	−0.01
Number of children	0.03	0.01	0.01	0.01	0.01	−0.01
South	−0.11	−0.11	−0.14	−0.14	−0.14	−0.14
Northeast	−0.20	−0.19	−0.19	−0.19	−0.19	−0.16
Midwest	−0.07	−0.08	−0.07	−0.07	−0.07	−0.06
Husband employed	0.20	0.20	0.21	0.24	0.24	0.23
Husband's work hours	−0.00	−0.00	−0.00	−0.00	−0.00	−0.00
Religious tradition[a]						
Catholic	0.14					
Jewish	0.32					
Other	0.30					
Conservative Protestant	0.21*					
Mainline Protestant	0.15					
Religious tradition by attendance[a]						
Frequently attending RC		0.26*	0.24	0.20	0.19	0.18
Infrequently attending RC		0.04	0.04	0.01	0.00	−0.08
Frequently attending Jew		0.75	0.75	0.72	0.71	0.56
Infrequently attending Jew		0.26	0.27	0.26	0.26	0.17
Frequently attending other		0.31	0.25	0.13	0.13	0.15

Table A6.2

(*continued*)

	Model 1	Model 2	Model 3	Model 4	Model 5	Model 6
Infrequently attending other		0.29	0.30	0.26	0.25	0.22
Frequently attending CP		0.37^{**}_{H}	0.27^{*}	0.22	0.22	0.19
Infrequently attending CP		0.02_{L}	−0.03	−0.04	−0.04	−0.08
Frequently attending MP		0.24	0.18	0.13	0.13	0.10
Infrequently attending MP		0.09_{L}	0.09	0.08	0.07	0.02
Religious, family, and gender ideologies						
Theological conservative[b]			0.18^{**}	0.13	0.13	0.07
Familism				0.17^{**}	0.16^{**}	0.17^{**}
Gender-role traditionalism					0.01	−0.03
Measures of marital equality						
Wife's gender-role traditionalism						−0.02
Wife employed full-time						-0.20^{*}
Wife employed part-time						-0.23^{**}
Wife's percentage of income						−0.34
Husband's percentage of household labor						−0.02
Intercept	6.60	6.69	6.62	6.16	6.13	6.60
R^2	0.03	0.03	0.03	0.04	0.04	0.04

Note: Data are from NSFH2 (1992–1994). $N = 2,695$. Significance tests are two-tailed. RC = Roman Catholic; CP = conservative Protestant; MP = mainline Protestant.

[a]The comparison category is Unaffiliated.

[b]The comparison category is Non–theological conservative.

$^{*}p < .05.$ $^{**}p < .01.$ $^{***}p < .001.$

H, L = Coefficients with different subscripts are significantly different ($p < .05$).

Table A6.3

Coefficients from OLS Regression Models on Wife's Happiness with Husband's
Understanding

	Model 1	Model 2	Model 3	Model 4	Model 5	Model 6
Controls						
Focal child's age	0.01	0.01	0.01	0.01	0.01	0.01
Length of marriage	−0.00	−0.00	−0.00	−0.00	−0.00	−0.00
Husband ever divorced	−0.32**	−0.30**	−0.30**	−0.29**	−0.29**	−0.31**
Wife ever divorced	0.00	0.00	0.02	0.02	0.02	0.02
Couple's income (in $10,000s, logged)	−0.10**	−0.10**	−0.10**	−0.10**	−0.10**	−0.09**
Education	0.07*	0.05	0.06*	0.07*	0.06*	0.06*
Black	−0.42***	−0.43***	−0.43***	−0.40***	−0.41***	−0.33***
Hispanic	−0.10	−0.13	−0.15	−0.16	−0.16	−0.16
Biological and step-children	−0.53***	−0.53***	−0.52***	−0.54***	−0.54***	−0.49***
All biological children	−0.47***	−0.46***	−0.46***	−0.46***	−0.47***	−0.47***
Age of youngest child	−0.03**	−0.02**	−0.03**	−0.02**	−0.02**	−0.02**
Number of children	−0.01	−0.02	−0.02	−0.03	−0.02	−0.05
South	−0.17	−0.17	−0.20*	−0.20*	−0.20*	−0.21*
Northeast	−0.24*	−0.24*	−0.23*	−0.23*	−0.22*	−0.20
Midwest	−0.11	−0.11	−0.11	−0.10	−0.10	−0.09
Husband employed	0.06	0.06	0.07	0.09	0.09	0.10
Husband's work hours	0.00	0.00	0.00	0.00	0.00	0.00
Religious tradition[a]						
Catholic	0.06					
Jewish	0.07					
Other	0.05					
Conservative Protestant	0.11					
Mainline Protestant	0.12					
Religious tradition by attendance[a]						
Frequently attending RC		0.10	0.08	0.04	0.04	0.02
Infrequently attending RC		0.03	0.03	0.00	0.01	−0.08
Frequently attending Jew		0.43	0.43	0.40	0.40	0.25
Infrequently attending Jew		0.02	0.03	0.02	0.02	−0.05

Table A6.3

(continued)

	Model 1	Model 2	Model 3	Model 4	Model 5	Model 6
Frequently attending other		0.10	0.03	−0.08	−0.07	−0.06
Infrequently attending other		−0.01	0.00	−0.03	−0.03	−0.05
Frequently attending CP		0.24^*_H	0.12	0.08	0.09	0.07
Infrequently attending CP		$−0.06_L$	−0.12	−0.13	−0.13	−0.18
Frequently attending MP		0.16_H	0.09	0.06	0.06	0.03
Infrequently attending MP		0.08_L	0.09	0.07	0.07	0.03
Religious, family, and gender ideologies						
Theological conservative[b]			0.21^{**}	0.16^*	0.17^*	0.11
Familism				0.15^*	0.17^*	0.17^*
Gender-role traditionalism					−0.04	−0.10
Measures of marital equality						
Wife's gender-role traditionalism						0.04
Wife employed full-time						−0.15
Wife employed part-time						$−0.22^{**}$
Wife's percentage of income						−0.29
Husband's percentage of household labor						0.04
Intercept	6.39	6.46	6.38	5.97	6.04	6.32
R^2	0.03	0.03	0.04	0.04	0.04	0.04

Note: Data are from NSFH2 (1992–1994). $N = 2,695$. Significance tests are two-tailed. RC = Roman Catholic; CP = conservative Protestant; MP = mainline Protestant.

[a] The comparison category is Unaffiliated.

[b] The comparison category is Non–theological conservative.

$^*p < .05.$ $^{**}p < .01.$ $^{***}p < .001.$

H, L = Coefficients with different subscripts are significantly different $(p < .05)$.

Table A6.4

Odds Ratios from Logistic Regressions on Husband's Domestic Violence in Previous Year

	Model 1	Model 2	Model 3	Model 4	Model 5	Model 6
Controls						
Focal child's age	0.96*	0.96*	0.96*	0.96*	0.96*	0.96*
Length of marriage	0.94**	0.94**	0.94**	0.95**	0.95**	0.94**
Husband ever divorced	1.28	1.28	1.28	1.27	1.27	1.26
Wife ever divorced	0.91	0.91	0.91	0.90	0.90	0.85
Couple's income (in $10,000s, logged)	1.09	1.10	1.10	1.09	1.10	1.09
Education	0.87	0.88	0.88	0.88	0.88	0.88
Black	1.71*	1.73*	1.74*	1.65	1.66	1.61
Hispanic	0.74	0.79	0.79	0.81	0.81	0.87
Biological and step-children	1.43	1.49	1.49	1.49	1.50	1.47
All biological children	1.16	1.15	1.14	1.15	1.15	1.10
Age of youngest child	1.01	1.01	1.01	1.01	1.01	1.00
Number of children	1.14	1.14	1.14	1.15	1.14	1.14
South	1.10	1.11	1.11	1.12	1.13	1.06
Northeast	1.10	1.14	1.14	1.13	1.13	1.11
Midwest	1.17	1.16	1.16	1.15	1.15	1.12
Husband employed	0.74	0.74	0.74	0.72	0.72	0.75
Husband's work hours	1.00	1.00	1.00	1.00	1.00	1.00
Religious tradition[a]						
Catholic	1.67					
Jewish	2.03					
Other	2.86**					
Conservative Protestant	1.53					
Mainline Protestant	1.36					
Religious tradition by attendance[a]						
Frequently attending RC		1.97	1.98	2.09*	2.08*	2.19*
Infrequently attending RC		1.50	1.50	1.55	1.54	1.67
Frequently attending Jew		1.26	1.26	1.36	1.35	1.70
Infrequently attending Jew		2.23	2.22	2.22	2.23	2.21
Frequently attending other		3.04**	3.06*	3.64*	3.57**	3.97**
Infrequently attending other		2.92*	2.91*	3.06*	3.03*	3.06*

Table A6.4

(*continued*)

	Model 1	Model 2	Model 3	Model 4	Model 5	Model 6
Frequently attending CP		0.88_L	0.89	0.97	0.96	1.05
Infrequently attending CP		$2.36^{**}{}_H$	2.38^{**}	2.43^{**}	2.44^{**}	2.63^{**}
Frequently attending MP		1.74	1.76	1.88	1.88	2.07^*
Infrequently attending MP		1.23_L	1.23	1.27	1.27	1.38
Religious, family, and gender ideologies						
Theological conservative[b]			0.97	1.02	1.01	1.03
Familism				0.79	0.77	0.79
Gender-role traditionalism					1.07	1.09
Measures of marital equality						
Wife's gender-role traditionalism						0.99
Wife employed full-time						1.21
Wife employed part-time						1.60^*
Wife's percentage of income						1.99
Husband's percentage of household labor						0.51
.2 Log likelihood	1,220.15	1,207.67	1,207.65	1,205.38	1,205.16	1,168.39

Note: Data are from NSFH2 (1992–1994). $N = 2,769$. Significance tests are two-tailed. RC = Roman Catholic; CP = conservative Protestant; MP = mainline Protestant.

[a]The comparison category is Unaffiliated.

[b]The comparison category is Non–theological conservative.

$^*p < .05.$ $^{**}p < .01.$ $^{***}p < .001.$

H, L = Coefficients with different subscripts are significantly different ($p < .05$).

Table A6.5

Coefficients from OLS Regression Models on Husband's Quality Time with Wife

	Model 1	Model 2	Model 3	Model 4	Model 5	Model 6
Controls						
Focal child's age	0.01	0.01	0.01	0.01	0.01	0.01
Length of marriage	−0.01	−0.01	−0.01	−0.01	−0.01	−0.01
Husband ever divorced	−0.21*	−0.20*	−0.20*	−0.19*	−0.19*	−0.20*
Wife ever divorced	0.06	0.06	0.07	0.08	0.08	0.08
Couple's income (in $10,000s, logged)	−0.01	−0.01	−0.01	−0.01	−0.01	−0.01
Education	0.09***	0.08***	0.08***	0.09***	0.09***	0.10***
Black	−0.33**	−0.33**	−0.33**	−0.28**	−0.28**	−0.32**
Hispanic	0.54***	0.54***	0.53***	0.52***	0.52***	0.53***
Biological and step-children	−0.32**	−0.31*	−0.31*	−0.32*	−0.31*	−0.31*
All biological children	−0.31**	−0.31**	−0.31**	−0.32**	−0.31**	−0.28**
Age of youngest child	0.01	0.01	0.01	0.01	0.01	0.02
Number of children	−0.05	−0.06*	−0.06*	−0.07*	−0.07*	−0.07*
South	−0.05	−0.06	−0.06	−0.08	−0.08	−0.10
Northeast	−0.03	−0.02	−0.02	−0.01	−0.02	−0.02
Midwest	−0.04	−0.04	−0.04	−0.03	−0.03	−0.03
Husband employed	−0.21	−0.21	−0.21	−0.18	−0.18	−0.19
Husband's work hours	−0.00	−0.00	−0.00	−0.00	−0.00	−0.00
Religious tradition[a]						
Catholic	0.05					
Jewish	0.08					
Other	0.20					
Conservative Protestant	0.16					
Mainline Protestant	0.11					
Religious tradition by attendance[a]						
Frequently attending RC		0.14	0.13	0.08	0.08	0.12
Infrequently attending RC		−0.03	−0.03	−0.07	−0.07	−0.03
Frequently attending Jew		0.22	0.22	0.19	0.19	0.13
Infrequently attending Jew		0.05	0.05	0.05	0.05	0.19
Frequently attending other		0.27	0.25	0.10	0.10	0.12

Table A6.5

(*continued*)

	Model 1	Model 2	Model 3	Model 4	Model 5	Model 6
Infrequently attending other		0.11	0.12	0.07	0.06	0.14
Frequently attending CP		0.16	0.12	0.05	0.05	0.06
Infrequently attending CP		0.15	0.14	0.12	0.12	0.21
Frequently attending MP		0.18	0.16	0.11	0.11	0.13
Infrequently attending MP		0.07	0.07	0.05	0.05	0.07
Religious, family, and gender ideologies						
Theological conservative[b]			0.06	0.01	0.00	0.02
Familism				0.20^{***}	0.19^{**}	0.17^{***}
Gender-role traditionalism					0.02	−0.02
Measures of marital equality						
Wife's gender-role traditionalism						0.08
Wife employed full-time						−0.04
Wife employed part-time						-0.17^{*}
Wife's percentage of income						−0.08
Husband's percentage of household labor						0.11
Intercept	4.33	4.35	4.33	3.80	3.76	3.72
R^2	0.04	0.04	0.04	0.04	0.04	0.05

Note: Data are from NSFH2 (1992–1994). $N = 2,785$. Significance tests are two-tailed. RC = Roman Catholic; CP = conservative Protestant; MP = mainline Protestant.

[a] The comparison category is Unaffiliated.

[b] The comparison category is Non–theological conservative.

$^*p < .05.$ $^{**}p < .01.$ $^{***}p < .001.$

Table A6.6

Coefficients from OLS Regression Models on Husband's Time Socializing with Wife

	Model 1	Model 2	Model 3	Model 4	Model 5	Model 6
Controls						
Focal child's age	−0.00	−0.00	−0.00	−0.00	−0.00	−0.00
Length of marriage	−0.00	−0.00	−0.00	−0.00	−0.00	−0.00
Husband ever divorced	−0.06	−0.04	−0.04	−0.03	−0.03	−0.05
Wife ever divorced	−0.04	−0.04	−0.04	−0.03	−0.03	0.01
Couple's income (in \$10,000s, logged)	−0.01	−0.00	−0.00	−0.01	−0.01	−0.00
Education	0.04*	0.02	0.02	0.03	0.03	0.03
Black	−0.20*	−0.20*	−0.20*	−0.19*	−0.19*	−0.20*
Hispanic	0.33***	0.30***	0.29***	0.30***	0.30***	0.35***
Biological and step-children	−0.15	−0.15	−0.15	−0.16	−0.16	−0.15
All biological children	0.00	0.01	0.01	0.01	0.01	0.04
Age of youngest child	−0.00	−0.00	−0.00	−0.00	−0.00	−0.00
Number of children	−0.07**	−0.09***	−0.09***	−0.09***	−0.09***	−0.08**
South	0.12	0.11	0.10	0.10	0.10	0.13*
Northeast	0.14	0.14*	0.14*	0.14	0.14	0.15*
Midwest	0.11	0.10	0.10	0.10	0.10	0.13
Husband employed	0.01	0.01	0.01	0.04	0.03	0.10
Husband's work hours	−0.00	−0.00	−0.00	−0.00	−0.00	−0.00
Religious tradition[a]						
Catholic	0.10					
Jewish	0.20					
Other	0.50***					
Conservative Protestant	0.26***					
Mainline Protestant	0.21**					
Religious tradition by attendance[a]						
Frequently attending RC		0.17	0.17	0.15	0.15	0.16
Infrequently attending RC		0.05	0.05	0.03	0.03	0.04
Frequently attending Jew		0.66*	0.66*	0.65*	0.65*	0.56*
Infrequently attending Jew		0.11	0.12	0.12	0.11	0.09
Frequently attending other		0.64***	0.62***	0.58***	0.59***	0.61***

Table A6.6

(*continued*)

	Model 1	Model 2	Model 3	Model 4	Model 5	Model 6
Infrequently attending other		0.32*	0.32*	0.31*	0.31*	0.36*
Frequently attending CP		0.43***_H	0.40***	0.38***	0.38***	0.35***
Infrequently attending CP		0.06_L	0.05	0.05	0.05	0.05
Frequently attending MP		0.30**_H	0.28***	0.27**	0.27**	0.25**
Infrequently attending MP		0.14_L	0.14	0.14	0.14	0.11
Religious, family, and gender ideologies						
Theological conservative[b]			0.05	0.04	0.04	0.05
Familism				0.05	0.06	0.01
Gender-role traditionalism					−0.01	−0.02
Measures of marital equality						
Wife's gender-role traditionalism						0.03
Wife employed full-time						−0.00
Wife employed part-time						−0.01
Wife's percentage of income						−0.11
Husband's percentage of household labor						0.15
Intercept	3.14	3.20	3.18	3.04	3.07	2.98
R^2	0.03	0.04	0.04	0.04	0.04	0.04

Note: Data are from NSFH (1992–1994). $N = 2,785$. Significance tests are two-tailed. RC = Roman Catholic; CP = conservative Protestant; MP = mainline Protestant.
[a]The comparison category is Unaffiliated.
[b]The comparison category is Non–theological conservative.
*$p < .05$. **$p < .01$. ***$p < .001$.
H, L = Coefficients with different subscripts are significantly different ($p < .05$).

NOTES

CHAPTER ONE

1. For an overview of the rise and fall of Promise Keepers, see James A. Mathisen, "The Strange Decade of the Promise Keepers."
2. For overviews of the gender revolution and its consequences, see Robert Max Jackson, *Destined for Equality: The Inevitable Rise of Women's Status;* and Daphne Spain and Suzanne Bianchi, *Balancing Act: Motherhood, Marriage, and Employment among American Women.*
3. Spain and Bianchi, *Balancing Act*, 82, 152, 183.
4. U.S. Census Bureau, *Population Profile of the United States*, 23.
5. See Paula England, "Marriage, the Costs of Children, and Gender Inequality," and Arlie Hochschild with Ann Machung, *The Second Shift: Working Parents and the Revolution at Home.*
6. Hochschild with Machung, *Second Shift*, 3–13.
7. Arlie Hochschild, "Emotion Work, Feeling Rules, and Social Structure," 561.

8. Of course, families with children headed by single mothers, which make up 23 percent of all families and 82 percent of single-parent families (U.S. Census Bureau, *Population Profile*), are typically characterized by much greater gender inequality than married families, insofar as single mothers are responsible for virtually all domestic and parental responsibilities (see also England, "Marriage").

9. Suzanne M. Bianchi, "Maternal Employment and Time with Children: Dramatic Change or Surprising Continuity?" 411.

10. Suzanne M. Bianchi, Melissa A. Milkie, Liana C. Sayer, and John P. Robinson, "Is Anyone Doing the Housework? Trends in the Gender Division of Household Labor," 209.

11. For a discussion of emotion work in relationships, see several works by Arlie Hochschild: "Emotion Work," "The Economy of Gratitude," and (with Ann Machung), *Second Shift*. My definition of emotion work is slightly more expansive than the one offered by Hochschild.

12. Julia McQuillan and Myra Marx Ferree, "The Importance of Variation among Men and the Benefits of Feminism for Families," 217.

13. Frances K. Goldscheider and Linda J. Waite, *New Families, No Families? The Transformation of the American Home*, 195.

14. Paul R. Amato, "More Than Money? Men's Contributions to Their Children's Lives," 268; David Popenoe, *Life without Father: Compelling New Evidence That Fatherhood and Marriage Are Indispensable for the Good of Children and Society*, 139–63; Paul R. Amato and Fernando Rivera, "Paternal Involvement and Children's Behavior Problems."

15. McQuillan and Ferree, "Importance of Variation among Men"; W. Bradford Wilcox and Steven L. Nock, "What's Love Got to Do with It? Gender Role Ideology, Men's Emotion Work, and Women's Marital Quality."

16. Wilcox and Nock, "What's Love Got to Do with It?"

17. Margaret F. Brinig and Douglas W. Allen, "These Boots Are Made for Walking: Why Most Divorce Filers Are Women"; John M. Gottman, "Toward a Process Model of Men in Marriages and Families"; Steven L. Nock, "The Marriages of Equally Dependent Spouses."

18. Wilcox and Nock, "What's Love Got to Do with It?"

19. Larry L. Bumpass and James A. Sweet, *Cohabitation, Marriage, and Union Stability*.

20. Alfred DeMaris and Monica Longmore, "Ideology, Power, and Equity: Testing Competing Expectations for the Perception of Fairness in Household Labor"; Beth Anne Shelton and Daphne John, "The Division of Household Labor."

21. Wilcox and Nock, "What's Love Got to Do with It?"

22. Larry L. Bumpass, "What's Happening to the Family? Interactions between Demographic and Institutional Change"; Larry L. Bumpass, "Family-Related Attitudes, Couple Relationships, and Union Stability"; Stephanie Coontz, *The Way We Never Were: American Families and the Nostalgia Trap;* Scott Coltrane, "Fatherhood and Marriage in the 21st Century"; William J. Goode, *World Changes in Divorce Patterns;* Ron Lesthaeghe, "The Second Demographic Transition in Western Countries: An Interpretation"; David Popenoe, *Disturbing the Nest: Family Change and Decline in Modern Societies;* Arlene S. Skolnick, *Embattled Paradise: The American Family in an Age of Uncertainty.*

23. Bumpass, "Family-Related Attitudes," 178.

24. Scott Coltrane, "Marketing the Marriage 'Solution': Misplaced Simplicity in the Politics of Fatherhood," 391; Coltrane, "Fatherhood and Marriage in the 21st Century."

25. See, for instance, Michael A. Messner, *Politics of Masculinities: Men in Movements.*

26. Karen McCarthy Brown, "Fundamentalism and the Control of Women"; Coltrane, "Marketing the Marriage 'Solution'"; Gottman, "Toward a Process Model"; McQuillan and Ferree, "Importance of Variation"; Messner, *Politics of Masculinities.*

27. James Davison Hunter, *Culture Wars: The Struggle to Define America.*

28. Cokie Roberts and Steven V. Roberts, "Southern Baptists Have a Distorted View of the Family."

29. Marcia Slacum Greene, "Promise Keepers Evoke Strong Emotions; Some Women Praise Its Influence; Others Fear Effect on Rights"; W. Bradford Wilcox and John P. Bartkowski, "The Conservative Protestant Family: Traditional Rhetoric, Progressive Practice," 33.

30. Gottman, "Toward a Process Model," 183.

31. McQuillan and Ferree, "Importance of Variation," 223.

32. John P. Bartkowski, *Remaking the Godly Marriage: Gender Negotiation in Evangelical Families;* Brenda Brasher, *Godly Women: Fundamentalism and Female Power;* R. Marie Griffith, *God's Daughters: Evangelical Women and the Power of Submission;* Christian Smith, *Christian America? What Evangelicals Really Want;* Judith Stacey, *Brave New Families: Stories of Domestic Upheaval in Late Twentieth Century America.*

33. A growing literature on conservative Protestantism and the "reformation of machismo" in Latin America strongly suggests this conclusion (Elizabeth E. Brusco, *The Reformation of Machismo: Evangelical Conversion and Gender in Colombia*). As Brusco (*Reformation of Machismo*) and Jorge E. Maldonado

("Building 'Fundamentalism' from the Family in Latin America") argue, conservative Protestantism in Latin America often succeeds in making men better and more financially responsible parents and more affectionate husbands compared to when they were nominal Roman Catholics.

34. I am indebted to Connie Anderson and Michael A. Messner, authors of "The Political Is Personal: Masculinity Therapy and Patriarchal Bargains among the Promise Keepers," for the concept of a patriarchal bargain.

35. Bartkowski, *Remaking the Godly Marriage*, 162.

36. See, for instance, ibid., 161–71 and Stacey, *Brave New Families*, 144.

37. The first part of the book specifically draws on the theoretical arguments made by Robert Wuthnow in *Communities of Discourse: Ideology and Structure in the Reformation, the Enlightenment, and European Socialism;* Pierre Bourdieu in *Distinction: A Social Critique of the Judgement of Taste* and *The Field of Cultural Production;* and Christian Smith in *American Evangelicalism: Embattled and Thriving* to make claims about the ways in which institutional resources, collective identities, and distinctive ideologies influence the cultural responses of religious communities to changes in their sociocultural environment. My goal is to explain why conservative and mainline Protestant institutions responded so differently to the family and gender changes of the late twentieth century.

38. Mark Chaves, *Ordaining Women: Culture and Conflict in Religious Organizations.*

39. See ibid.; Paul J. DiMaggio and Walter W. Powell, "Introduction"; W. Richard Scott, John W. Meyer, and associates, *Institutional Environments and Organizations: Structural Complexity and Individualism.*

40. For divergent classical approaches that stress the effect that institutions and the culture they produce have on action, see Émile Durkheim, *Suicide;* Émile Durkheim, *The Elementary Forms of Religious Life;* Max Weber, "The Social Psychology of the World Religions"; and Max Weber, *The Protestant Ethic and the Spirit of Capitalism.* For cultural approaches that stress moral culture, see Michael Schudson, "How Culture Works: Perspectives from Media Studies on the Efficacy of Symbols"; Smith, *American Evangelicalism;* Robert Wuthnow, *Meaning and Moral Order: Explorations in Cultural Analysis;* and Wuthnow, *Communities of Discourse.* For cultural approaches that emphasize the importance of cultural repertoires, or the "logic of practice," see Pierre Bourdieu, *The Logic of Practice;* Ann Swidler, "Culture in Action: Symbols and Strategies."

41. James Davison Hunter, *American Evangelicalism: Conservative Religion and the Quandary of Modernity;* Lyman A. Kellstedt and John C. Green,

"Knowing God's Many People: Denominational Preference and Political Behavior"; Brian Steensland, Jerry Z. Park, Mark D. Regnerus, Lynn D. Robinson, W. Bradford Wilcox, and Robert D. Woodberry, "The Measure of American Religion: Toward Improving the State of the Art"; Smith, *Christian America?*

42. Data from the National Survey of Families and Households and pre-1984 data from the General Social Survey do not allow me to distinguish between conservative and mainline Presbyterians, Lutherans, and Baptists because respondents' denominational affiliations were not coded with sufficient specificity. Hence, all Presbyterians and Lutherans (including, for instance, members of the conservative Presbyterian Church in America and Lutheran Church–Missouri Synod) are coded as mainline Protestants. Likewise, all Baptists (including, for instance, members of the mainline American Baptist Church) are coded as conservative Protestants. This coding strategy introduces a degree of bias into my empirical analyses. Nevertheless, because a clear majority of Lutherans and Presbyterians are mainline Protestants and the vast majority of Baptists are conservative Protestants, I am confident that this coding scheme does not pose a serious threat to the validity of my findings.

43. Nancy Tatom Ammerman, "Golden Rule Christianity: Lived Religion in the American Mainstream."

44. Robert Wuthnow, *The Restructuring of American Religion.*

45. Smith, *American Evangelicalism;* and Wuthnow, *Restructuring of American Religion.*

CHAPTER TWO

1. Biographical information on James Dobson and organizational information about Focus on the Family were accessed at www.family.org/welcome/ on September 26, 2002.

2. James Davison Hunter, *Evangelicalism: The Coming Generation;* Christian Smith, *American Evangelicalism: Embattled and Thriving.*

3. Larry L. Bumpass, "What's Happening to the Family? Interactions between Demographic and Institutional Change"; William J. Goode, *World Changes in Divorce Patterns;* Ron Lesthaeghe, "The Second Demographic Transition in Western Countries: An Interpretation"; David Popenoe, *Disturbing the Nest: Family Change and Decline in Modern Societies.*

4. Bumpass, "What's Happening to the Family?" 493.

5. Pierre Bourdieu, *Distinction: A Social Critique of the Judgement of Taste;* Pierre Bourdieu, *The Field of Cultural Production;* Smith, *American Evangelicalism;*

Robert Wuthnow, *Communities of Discourse: Ideology and Structure in the Reformation, the Enlightenment, and European Socialism.*

6. Wuthnow, *Communities of Discourse.*

7. Wuthnow, *Meaning and Moral Order: Explorations in Cultural Analysis.*

8. Bourdieu, *Distinction;* Bourdieu, *Field of Cultural Production;* Smith, *American Evangelicalism.*

9. Smith, *American Evangelicalism,* 97.

10. Wuthnow, *Communities of Discourse.*

11. William H. Sewell Jr., "A Theory of Structure: Duality, Agency, and Transformation," 13; see also Swidler, "Culture in Action: Symbols and Strategies," and Wuthnow, *Communities of Discourse.*

12. See Paul J. DiMaggio and Walter W. Powell, "Introduction," and Mark Chaves, *Ordaining Women: Culture and Conflict in Religious Organizations.*

13. Bumpass, "What's Happening to the Family?"

14. Wade Clark Roof and William McKinney, *American Mainline Religion: Its Changing Shape and Future.*

15. Dean R. Hoge, Benton Johnson, and Donald A. Luidens, *Vanishing Boundaries: The Religion of Mainline Protestant Baby Boomers.*

16. E. Brooks Holifield, *A History of Pastoral Care in America: From Salvation to Self-Realization;* Roof and McKinney, *American Mainline Religion.*

17. John Murray Cuddihy, *No Offense: Civil Religion and Protestant Taste;* Holifield, *History of Pastoral Care;* Roof and McKinney, *American Mainline Religion.*

18. James Davison Hunter, *American Evangelicalism: Conservative Religion and the Quandary of Modernity;* George Marsden, *Reforming Fundamentalism: Fuller Seminary and the New Evangelicalism.*

19. See Robert Wuthnow, *The Restructuring of American Religion.*

20. Smith, *American Evangelicalism.*

21. Hunter, *American Evangelicalism;* Roof and McKinney, *American Mainline Religion.*

22. Smith, *American Evangelicalism.*

23. Andrew J. Cherlin, *Marriage, Divorce, Remarriage.*

24. Elaine Tyler May, *Homeward Bound: American Families in the Cold War.*

25. Alan Ehrenhalt, *The Lost City: The Forgotten Virtues of Community in America;* May, *Homeward Bound;* Wuthnow, *Restructuring of American Religion.*

26. Wuthnow, *Restructuring of American Religion.*

27. Roof and McKinney, *American Mainline Religion,* 209–17; Robert Wuthnow, *After Heaven: Spirituality in America since the 1950s.*

28. Jessie Bernard, "The Good-Provider Role: Its Rise and Fall."

29. Janet Saltzman Chafetz, "Chicken or Egg? A Theory of the Relationship between Feminist Movements and Family Change."

30. Spain and Bianchi, *Balancing Act: Motherhood, Marriage, and Employment among American Women*, 25–34, 81; David Popenoe and Barbara Dafoe Whitehead, 29.

31. Jeffrey Hadden, *The Gathering Storm in the Churches;* Wade Clark Roof, *A Generation of Seekers: The Spiritual Journeys of the Baby Boom Generation.*

32. Richard W. Reifsnyder, "Transformations in Administrative Leadership in the United Presbyterian Church in the U.S.A., 1920–1983."

33. W. Bradford Wilcox, "For the Sake of the Children? Family-Related Discourse and Practice in the Mainline."

34. Robert Booth Fowler, *A New Engagement: Evangelical Political Thought, 1966–1976.*

35. Wuthnow, *Restructuring of American Religion.*

36. Fowler, *New Engagement.*

37. Hunter, *American Evangelicalism.*

38. Hunter, *Culture Wars: The Struggle to Define America;* and Wuthnow, *Restructuring of American Religion.*

39. Hunter, *American Evangelicalism*, 59.

40. Bourdieu, *Distinction.*

41. Ibid., 371; see also Kristen Luker, *Abortion and the Politics of Motherhood.*

42. Roof and McKinney, *American Mainline Religion.*

43. Holifield, *History of Pastoral Care*, 287, 296–98.

44. Wilcox, "For the Sake of the Children?"

45. Holifield, *History of Pastoral Care;* Wuthnow, *After Heaven.*

46. William Smith, "Evangelicalism and the Therapeutic," 11.

47. David Powlison, "Integration or Inundation?"

48. Marsden, *Reforming Fundamentalism*, 233.

49. Smith, "Evangelicalism and the Therapeutic," 15–18.

50. Hunter, *American Evangelicalism.*

51. John P. Bartkowski and W. Bradford Wilcox, "Conservative Protestant Child Discipline: The Case of Parental Yelling."

52. DiMaggio and Powell, "Introduction"; Sewell, "A Theory of Structure."

53. Wuthnow, *Restructuring of American Religion*, 209.

54. Bartkowski and Wilcox, "Conservative Protestant Child Discipline"; W. Bradford Wilcox, "Conservative Protestant Childrearing: Authoritarian or Authoritative?"

55. For broader discussions of the rise of public reason and the importance of elites in that process, see Steven Brint, *In an Age of Experts;* Christopher Lasch, *The Revolt of the Elites.*

56. Brian Steensland, "The Hydra and the Swords: Social Welfare and Mainline Advocacy, 1964–2000"; Wilcox, "For the Sake of the Children?"

57. Sharon Hays, *The Cultural Contradictions of Motherhood;* Christopher Lasch, *Haven in a Heartless World: The Family Besieged.*

58. Peter Berger cited in Kevin J. Christiano, "Religion and the Family in Modern American Culture."

59. For a history of family ideologies in the West, see Edward Shorter, *The Making of the Modern Family;* and Lawrence Stone, *The Family, Sex, and Marriage: In England 1500–1800.* For recent studies of family ideologies in the United States, see Marjorie L. DeVault, *Feeding the Family: The Social Organization of Caring as Gendered Work;* Hays, *Cultural Contradictions of Motherhood;* and Viviana Zelizer, *Pricing the Priceless Child: The Changing Social Value of Children.*

60. Joanna Bowen Gillespie, "Episcopal: Family as the Nursery of Church and Society."

61. *Journal of the 1956 General Conference of the Methodist Church,* 205.

62. Hays, *Cultural Contradictions of Motherhood,* 49.

63. Margaret Lamberts Bendroth, *Fundamentalism and Gender: 1875 to the Present,* 112, 104.

64. Chafetz, "Chicken or Egg?"; Cherlin, *Marriage, Divorce, Remarriage.*

65. I do not mean to suggest that gender-role ideology is now unrelated to familism. Clearly familism is still linked to gender inequality in practice and belief, especially insofar as the logic of sentimental domesticity generally focuses on women's roles as mothers and wives. Nonetheless, dramatic gains in women's socioeconomic status since the 1960s have contributed to a dramatic liberalization of gender-role attitudes without commensurately large shifts in family-related attitudes on other matters like abortion and homosexuality (Paul J. DiMaggio, John H. Evans and Bethany Bryson, "Have Americans' Social Attitudes Become More Polarized?"; Arland Thornton, "Changing Attitudes toward Family Issues in the United States"). For instance, in the conservative Protestant world, there is increased institutional and popular support for gender equality but comparatively little support for abortion, homosexuality, and family pluralism. In society at large, familism—as measured, for instance, by attitudes against divorce—has gained popularity while gender-role traditionalism has lost support (see chapter 3). Moreover, the historical trajectories of familism and the separate-spheres ideology are distinct. The emergence of familism preceded the onset of the separate-spheres ideology by at least a century in the West, and hence it is not necessarily connected to the rise of industrial capitalism, which provided

the social practices and resources that anchored the separate-spheres ideology (Peter Laslett, *Family Life and Illicit Love in Earlier Generations;* Stone, *Family, Sex, and Marriage*). Thus, familism may continue to thrive in modified form after the separate-spheres ideology has fallen out of favor. Therefore, I treat the two ideologies as analytically distinct from one another.

66. United Methodist Church, *United Methodist Church Book of Discipline,* 71.

67. Richard Lyon Morgan, *Is There Life after Divorce in the Church?*

68. John Patton and Brian H. Childs, *Christian Marriage and Family: Caring for Our Generations,* 12, 154.

69. Ibid., 99.

70. Presbyterian Panel, "Public Role of Presbyterians."

71. Penny Edgell Becker, "The Family Orientations of Local Congregations," 20.

72. Laura Olson, *Filled with Spirit and Power.*

73. Lois Gehr Livezey, "The Fourth Presbyterian Church of Chicago: One Congregation's Response to the Challenges of Family Life in Urban America."

74. Ibid.

75. Becker, "Family Orientations of Local Congregations."

76. Olson, *Filled with Spirit and Power.*

77. Wilcox, "For the Sake of the Children?"

78. With the assistance of Sarah Curran and Niall Fagan, I surveyed issues of the *Christian Century* from 1970 to 1990 at five-year intervals. All articles dealing with race and civil rights, poverty, the Vietnam War, Central America, the peace movement, environmentalism, sexism, and gender inclusive language were coded as *social justice* articles. All articles dealing with sexual practices and ethics (for example, family planning and premarital sex), abortion, and homosexuality were coded as *sex-related family* articles. Articles addressing marriage, parenting, divorce, day care, gender roles in the family, family/ work balance, domestic violence, single parenting, housework, youth groups, Sunday school, and children's issues were coded as *other family-related* articles. See Wilcox, "For the Sake of the Children?" 306, for more details.

79. Wilcox, "For the Sake of the Children?" 306–7.

80. James M. Wall, "The New Right Exploits Abortion."

81. John H. Evans and Bethany Bryson, "Locating Actual Cultural Conflict: Polarization over Abortion in Protestant Denominations, 1972–1996."

82. Special Committee on Human Sexuality, *Keeping Body and Soul Together: Sexuality, Spirituality, and Social Justice.*

83. Wilcox, "For the Sake of the Children?"

84. Marsha Grace Witten, *All Is Forgiven: The Secular Message in American Protestantism,* 37.

85. Peter Berger, *The Sacred Canopy*.

86. Nancy Tatom Ammerman, "Golden Rule Christianity: Lived Religion in the American Mainstream," 198; Wuthnow, *After Heaven*.

87. Wilcox, "For the Sake of the Children?" 301.

88. Robert L. Browning and Roy A. Reed, "Families and Worship," 261.

89. Becker, "Family Orientations of Local Congregations," 20.

90. Hays, *Cultural Contradictions of Motherhood;* Duane F. Alwin, "Religion and Parental Child-Rearing Orientations: Evidence of a Catholic-Protestant Convergence."

91. "America on Its Knees."

92. "Getting God's Kingdom into Politics."

93. Conservative Protestantism has a long tradition of large and powerful parachurch ministries—organizations with no formal church affiliation and supported by grassroots members—dedicated to particular evangelical and social reform tasks (Hunter, *Evangelicalism*). These special-purpose organizations allow conservative Protestants to respond to religious and social needs with creativity, speed, and flexibility. However, the proliferation of independent organizations also contributes to ideological polarization, concentrations of power in charismatic leaders who are unaccountable to churches, and the use of attention-grabbing rhetorical and presentational tactics (Wuthnow, *Restructuring of American Religion*). In any case, because parachurch organizations are so prominent in this subculture, my survey of conservative Protestant discourse on the family draws heavily from the pronouncements of the leaders of these groups.

94. Jerry Falwell, *Listen America!* 210.

95. James C. Dobson, *Love Must Be Tough,* 235.

96. Becker, "Family Orientations of Local Congregations," 20.

97. I surveyed *Christianity Today* at five-year intervals from 1970 to 1990, using the same criteria I used in my survey of the *Christian Century* to count sex-related family articles and other family-related articles.

98. Fowler, *New Engagement,* 196–97. For an evangelical view of abortion, see Randy Alcorn, *ProLife Answers to ProChoice Arguments*.

99. Jerry Falwell cited in Wuthnow, *Restructuring of American Religion,* 212.

100. Hunter, *Culture Wars;* Luker, *Abortion and the Politics of Motherhood*.

101. Southern Baptist Convention, "Resolution on Abortion," June 1971, at www.sbc.net/resolutions/amResolution.asp?ID=13 and "Resolution on Abortion," June 1980, www.sbc.net/resolutions/amResolution.asp?ID=19, accessed April 4, 2002.

102. "Homosexuality: Biblical Guidance Through a Moral Morass," 12.

103. Bill J. Leonard, "Southern Baptist: Family as Witness of Grace in the Community," 17.

104. William M. Kinnaird, "Divorce and Remarriage: Ministers in the Middle," 27; Norskov Olsen, "Divorce and Remarriage."

105. Dobson, *Love Must Be Tough,* 142–45.

106. Kinnaird, "Divorce and Remarriage," 27.

107. Rev. Steven Brown cited in Kinnaird, "Divorce and Remarriage," 26.

108. See, for example, Diana Garland, *Family Ministry: A Comprehensive Guide,* 551–57.

109. Kinnaird, "Divorce and Remarriage," 27.

110. Rus Walton, *One Nation under God,* 45.

111. Ibid., 48.

112. Charles R. Swindoll, *You and Your Child,* 53.

113. James C. Dobson, *The New Dare to Discipline,* 16, 92.

114. Hays, *The Cultural Contradictions of Motherhood.*

115. James C. Dobson, *Dare to Discipline,* 11.

116. J. Richard Fugate, *What the Bible Says about Child Training,* 40–41.

117. Ibid., 154.

118. Becker, "Family Orientations of Local Congregations," 20.

119. Here, I include sex-related family articles and other family articles in one family category for both *Christianity Today* and the *Christian Century.*

120. Don S. Browning, Bonnie J. Miller-McLemore, Pamela D. Couture, K. Brynoff Lyon, and Robert M. Franklin, *From Culture Wars to Common Ground: Religion and the American Family Debate,* 319 (emphasis in original).

121. Becker, "Family Orientations of Local Congregations," 20.

122. Bendroth, *Fundamentalism and Gender;* Browning et al., *From Culture Wars to Common Ground.*

123. Shorter, *Making of the Modern Family.*

124. Browning et al., *From Culture Wars to Common Ground,* 85.

125. Support for patriarchal authority was already weakening by mid-century, except in the conservative Protestant world, where it remained a mark of orthodoxy, a sign of fidelity to the doctrine of biblical inerrancy (Bendroth, *Fundamentalism and Gender*).

126. Joan Wallach Scott, *Gender and the Politics of History,* 45.

127. Wilcox, "For the Sake of the Children?"

128. Chaves, *Ordaining Women,* 19; Thomas Reeves, *The Empty Church: The Suicide of Liberal Christianity,* 146.

129. Jean Miller Schmidt and Gail E. Murphy-Geiss, "Methodist: 'Tis Grace Will Lead Us Home."

130. J. Gordon Melton, *The Churches Speak on Sex and Family Life,* 173.

131. Becker, "Family Orientations of Local Congregations," 20.

132. Reeves, *Empty Church;* Wuthnow, *Restructuring of American Religion.*

133. For the 1979 *Book of Common Prayer,* which is published by Oxford University Press, see justus.anglican.org/resources/bcp/bcp.htm#1979 (accessed January 26, 2003). Andy Langford, ed., *The United Methodist Book of Worship; Book of Common Worship.*

134. Max L. Stackhouse, "The Free-Church Tradition and Social Ministry."

135. Special Committee on Human Sexuality, *Keeping Body and Soul Together: Sexuality, Spirituality, and Social Justice,* 52.

136. Chaves, *Ordaining Women,* 83.

137. James Dobson, *Straight Talk to Men and Their Wives,* 128–29.

138. Falwell, *Listen America!* 124.

139. Eileen W. Lindner, "Ecumenical and Interdenominational: Private and Public Approaches to Family Issues."

140. Chaves, *Ordaining Women,* 89.

141. Donald G. Bloesch, "The Father and the Goddess"; Elisabeth Elliot, "Why I Oppose the Ordination of Women"; Institute on Religion and Democracy, "Women of Renewal: A Statement."

142. Larry Christenson, *The Christian Family,* 14–17.

143. For example, see Dobson, *Straight Talk;* W. Peter Blitchington, *Sex Roles for the Christian Family.*

144. Bendroth, *Fundamentalism and Gender.*

145. Elliot, "Why I Oppose the Ordination of Women," 14.

146. Dobson, *Straight Talk,* 177, 23, 178, 183–34.

147. Carl F. H. Henry, "Further Thoughts about Women"; Carl F. H. Henry, "The Battle of the Sexes"; Hunter, *Evangelicalism,* 103.

148. Henry, "Battle of the Sexes."

149. Anthony L. Jordan, et al., *Report of the Baptist Faith and Message Study Committee to the Southern Baptist Convention,* 2; cf. Ephesians 5:22.

150. Hunter, *Evangelicalism,* 92.

151. Dobson, *Straight Talk,* 22.

152. Blitchington, *Sex Roles,* 66.

153. Christians for Biblical Equality, "Men, Women, and Biblical Equality," 36.

154. Melinda Lundquist and Christian Smith, "Christian Participation"; Tracey Scott, "What's God Got to Do with It? Protestantism, Gender, and the Meaning of Work."

155. Bartkowski, *Remaking the Godly Marriage: Gender Negotiation in Evangelical Families;* Hunter, *Evangelicalism.*

156. Experts cited in Hunter, *Evangelicalism,* 104.

157. Gary Smalley, *If Only He Knew: What No Woman Can Resist,* 27, 30.

158. Mary Stewart Van Leeuwen, "Servanthood or Soft Patriarchy? A Christian Feminist Looks at the Promise Keepers Movement," 38 (emphasis in original).

159. Bill McCartney, ed., *What Makes a Man?* 64, 82.

160. Smalley, *If Only He Knew,* 17, 137.

161. Becker, "Family Orientations of Local Congregations," 20.

162. Richard Land and Barret Duke, "Fatherhood in the Evangelical Tradition."

163. James A. Mathisen, "The Strange Decade of the Promise Keepers"; William H. Lockhart, "'We Are One Life,' but Not of One Gender Ideology: Unity, Ambiguity, and the Promise Keepers."

164. Smith, *American Evangelicalism,* 89.

165. R. Albert Mohler Jr., "Against an Immoral Tide."

166. Wuthnow, *Communities of Discourse.*

167. My estimates of institutional resources are based upon Hunter's work on evangelicalism (*American Evangelicalism; Evangelicalism*) and Mark Chaves and his colleagues' overview of U.S. congregations (Mark Chaves, Mary Ellen Konieczny, Kraig Beyerlien, and Emily Barman, "The National Congregations Study: Background, Methods, and Selected Results").

168. DiMaggio and Powell, "Introduction."

169. Smith, *American Evangelicalism;* Wuthnow, *Restructuring of American Religion;* Robert Wuthnow, "Mobilizing Civic Engagement: The Changing Impact of Religious Involvement."

170. Robert Putnam, *Bowling Alone: The Collapse and Revival of American Community.*

171. Wilcox, "Conservative Protestant Childrearing"; W. Bradford Wilcox, "Conservative Protestantism and the Family: Resisting, Engaging, or Accommodating Modernity?"

172. Berger, *Sacred Canopy.*

173. This estimate is based upon my analysis of the National Congregation Survey (NCS) (Chaves, Konieczny, Beyerlien, and Barman, "National Congregations Study"). Of NCS respondents who reported attending a church with more than nine hundred members, 75 percent were located in the Midwest or the South.

174. Wilcox, "Conservative Protestant Childrearing."

175. Smith, *American Evangelicalism;* Brian Steensland, Jerry Z. Park, Mark D. Regnerus, Lynn D. Robinson, W. Bradford Wilcox, and Robert D. Woodberry, "The Measure of American Religion: Toward Improving the State of the Art"; Wuthnow, "Mobilizing Civic Engagement."

176. Mark Chaves, "Family Structure and Protestant Church Attendance: The Sociological Basis of Cohort and Age Effects"; Penny Long Marler, "Lost in the Fifties: The Changing Family and the Nostalgic Church"; Ross M. Stolzenberg, Mary Blair-Loy, and Linda J. Waite, "Religious Participation in Early Adulthood: Age and Family Life Cycle Effects on Church Membership"; Wilcox, "For the Sake of the Children?"

177. Reifsnyder, "Transformations in Administrative Leadership," 245–46.

178. W. Bradford Wilcox, "The Presbyterian Church (USA): A Profile," 5.

179. Nancy Tatom Ammerman, *Congregation and Community,* 256.

180. Smith, *American Evangelicalism,* 148.

181. Ammerman, "Golden Rule Christianity"; Chaves, *Ordaining Women;* Mark Chaves, Helen Giesel, and William Tsitsos, "Religious Variations in Public Presence: Evidence from the National Congregations Study."

182. James M. Wall, "Purity and Single-Issue Politics."

183. Sally Geis, "Gay and Christian: Two Stories."

184. See Livezey, "The Fourth Presbyterian Church of Chicago"; Olson, *Filled with Spirit and Power.*

185. Peter Brimelow, "Who Has Abortions?"; Chaves, "Family Structure and Protestant Church Attendance"; Wilcox, "For the Sake of the Children?"

186. United Methodist Church, *United Methodist Church Book of Discipline* 71.

187. Sewell, "A Theory of Structure," 13 (emphasis in original). I recognize that Sewell views resources as potentially both social and cultural. Nevertheless, for the sake of analytical clarity, I distinguish between social and cultural resources here.

188. Vaughn R. A. Call and Tim B. Heaton, "Religious Influence on Marital Stability"; Timothy T. Clydesdale, "Family Behaviors among Early U.S. Baby Boomers: Exploring the Effects of Religion and Income Change, 1965–1982"; Wilcox, "Conservative Protestants and the Family."

189. Although religious affiliation is not related to marital stability, church attendance is a significant predictor: people who attend church more are less likely to divorce (Call and Heaton, "Religious Influence"; Clydesdale, "Family Behaviors").

190. Lundquist and Smith, "Christian Participation."

191. Brian C. Robertson, *There's No Place Like Work,* 103.

192. Wilcox, "For the Sake of the Children?"

193. Bumpass, "What's Happening to the Family?"; Goode, *World Changes in Divorce Patterns;* Lesthaeghe, "Second Demographic Transition"; Popenoe, *Disturbing the Nest;* Shorter, *Making of the Modern Family.*

194. Swidler, "Culture in Action"; see also Paul J. DiMaggio, "Culture and Cognition," 272.

195. Stacey, *Brave New Families;* Darren E. Sherkat, "Religious Socialization and the Family: An Examination of Religious Influence in the Family over the Life Course"; Stolzenberg, Blair-Loy, and Waite, "Religious Participation in Early Adulthood."

CHAPTER THREE

1. See "Baptist Faith and Message, XVIII: The Family," at www.sbc.net/bfm/bfm2000.asp#xviii, accessed October 18, 2002.

2. United Methodist Church, United Methodist Church Book of Discipline, 71; J. Gordon Melton, The Churches Speak on Sex and Family Life, 173.

3. Mark Chaves, *Ordaining Women.*

4. For discussions of the ways in which persons do and do not internalize the formal ideologies produced by collectivities, see Pierre Bourdieu, *The Logic of Practice;* Paul DiMaggio, "Culture and Cognition"; William H. Sewell Jr., "A Theory of Structure: Duality, Agency, and Transformation"; Ann Swidler, "Culture in Action: Symbols and Strategies"; and Dennis H. Wrong, "The Oversocialized Conception of Man in Modern Sociology."

5. From 1972 to 1998, the GSS randomly surveyed more than thirty-eight thousand respondents in semiannual samples, each of which comprised about one thousand to three thousand people from around the continental United States. See www.icpsr.umich.edu:8080/GSS/about/gss/about.htm.

6. I used the classification scheme developed by Brian Steensland and his colleagues to classify GSS respondents as mainline Protestants, conservative Protestants, black Protestants, Roman Catholics, Jews, Others (primarily Mormons), and unaffiliated Americans. Most nondenominational Protestants were categorized as conservative (Brian Steensland, Jerry Z. Park, Mark D. Regnerus, Lynn D. Robinson, W. Bradford Wilcox, and Robert D. Woodberry, "The Measure of American Religion: Toward Improving the State of the Art").

7. I dichotomized the outcome for each of the four measures from the GSS to indicate whether respondents held familistic and traditional gender views on these four questions (see table A3.1 in the appendix).

8. I do not include the results of this second, ancillary set of models in the tables in the appendix. The analyses are available from the author upon request.

9. See, for instance, Larry Bumpass, "What's Happening to the Family? Interactions between Demographic and Institutional Change," and David Popenoe, *Disturbing the Nest: Family Change and Decline in Modern Societies.*

10. The divorce item was first asked in 1974 and has been regularly repeated since then. Respondents were asked, "Should divorce in this country be easier or more difficult to obtain than it is now?" Those who indicated that it should be "more difficult to obtain" were coded as familistic. (See table A3.1 in the appendix.)

11. Denese Ashbaugh Vlosky and Pamela A. Monroe, "The Effective Dates of No-Fault Divorce Laws in the Fifty States."

12. Christian Smith, *Christian America? What Evangelicals Really Want*, 164.

13. The difference between mainline attitudes to divorce in the 1970s and the 1990s is statistically significant.

14. The GSS item on premarital sex was first asked in 1972 and has been repeated consistently since then. Respondents were asked, "If a man and a woman have sexual relations before marriage, do you think it is always wrong, almost always wrong, wrong, wrong only sometimes, or not wrong at all?" Those who answered that premarital sex is "always wrong" were coded as familistic. (See table A3.1 in the appendix.)

15. The GSS item on the gendered division of family labor was first asked in 1977 and has been repeated regularly since then. The item reads, "It is much better for everyone involved if the man is the achiever outside the home and the woman takes care of the home and family." Respondents who indicated they agreed or strongly agreed with this statement were coded as gender traditionalists. (See table A3.1 in the appendix.)

16. John P. Bartkowski, *Remaking the Godly Marriage: Gender Negotiation in Evangelical Families*, 137.

17. Beginning in 1977, the GSS asked respondents if they agreed with this statement. Respondents who indicated agreement or strong agreement were coded as gender traditionalists. (See table A3.1 in the appendix.)

18. Smith, *Christian America?* 160–91; and Bartkowski, *Remaking the Godly Marriage*, 136–60.

19. See Wilcox, "For the Sake of the Children? Family-Related Discourse and Practice in the Mainline."

20. Melinda Lundquist Denton, "Gender Roles and Marital Decision Making: Negotiating Religious Ideology and Practice."

CHAPTER FOUR

1. See Ralph LaRossa, "Fatherhood and Social Change."

2. See Liana Sayer, "Gender, Time, and Inequality: Trends in Women's and Men's Paid Work, Unpaid Work, and Free Time."

3. John M. Gottman, "Toward a Process Model of Men in Marriages and Families."

4. Julia McQuillan and Myra Marx Ferree, "The Importance of Variation among Men and the Benefits of Feminism for Families," 223.

5. Glen Elder, Tri Van Nguyen, and Avshalom Caspi, "Linking Family Hardship to Children's Lives"; Eleanor E. Maccoby and John A. Martin, "Socialization in the Context of the Family: Parent-Child Interaction." For the seminal work on authoritarian and authoritative parenting, see Diana Baumrind, "Current Patterns of Parental Authority." For a discussion of parental support and parental control, see Paul R. Amato and Alan Booth, *A Generation at Risk: Growing Up in an Era of Family Upheaval*, 17.

6. Amato and Booth, *Generation at Risk;* Baumrind, "Current Patterns of Parental Authority"; Maccoby and Martin, "Socialization in the Context of the Family"; Elizabeth Thomson, Thomas L. Hanson, and Sara S. McLanahan, "Family Structure and Child Well-Being: Economic Resources vs. Parental Behaviors."

7. Donald Capps, "Religion and Child Abuse: Perfect Together," 2.

8. Gottman, "Toward a Process Model"; Philip Greven, *Spare the Child: The Religious Roots of Punishment and the Psychological Impact of Abuse;* Murray A. Straus, *Beating the Devil Out of Them: Corporal Punishment in American Families;* for reviews, see John P. Bartkowski, "Spare the Rod . . . , or Spare the Child? Divergent Perspectives on Conservative Protestant Child Discipline."

9. Amato and Booth, *Generation at Risk;* Paul R. Amato and Fernando Rivera, "Paternal Involvement and Children's Behavior Problems"; Nan Marie Astone and Sara McLanahan, "Family Structure, Parental Practices, and High School Completion"; Henry B. Biller, *Fathers and Families: Paternal Factors in Child Development;* Marcia J. Carlson, "Family Structure, Father Involvement and Adolescent Behavioral Outcomes"; Kathleen Mullan Harris, Frank F. Furstenberg Jr., and Jeremy K. Marmer, "Paternal Involvement with Adolescents in Intact Families: The Influence of Fathers Over the Life Course"; Michael E. Lamb, "Fathers and Child Development: An Integrative Overview"; Ross D. Parke, *Fatherhood.* For a review, see Amato, "More Than Money? Men's Contributions to Their Children's Lives."

10. Amato, "More Than Money?" 268.

11. For research that suggests that religion has generic effects on parenting, see Duane F. Alwin, "Religion and Parental Child-Rearing Orientations: Evidence of a Catholic-Protestant Convergence"; Timothy T. Clydesdale, "Family Behaviors among Early U.S. Baby Boomers; Exploring the Effects of Religion and Income Change, 1965–1982"; and Lisa D. Pearce and William G.

Axinn, "The Impact of Family Religious Life on the Quality of Mother-Child Relations."

12. For research indicating that particular religious traditions have distinctive effects on child rearing, see Christopher G. Ellison and Darren E. Sherkat, "Conservative Protestantism and Support for Corporal Punishment"; Christopher G. Ellison and Darren E. Sherkat, "Obedience and Autonomy: Religion and Parental Values Reconsidered"; Christopher G. Ellison, John P. Bartkowski, and Michelle L. Segal, "Conservative Protestantism and the Parental Use of Corporal Punishment"; W. Bradford Wilcox, "Conservative Protestant Childrearing: Authoritarian or Authoritative?"

13. Some studies of religion and family behavior do develop a clear and cogent theoretical model of the institutional and cultural mechanisms through which religion influences family behavior. See, for instance, Clydesdale, "Family Behaviors."

14. Émile Durkheim, *Suicide,* 170.

15. See Pearce and Axinn, "Impact of Family Religious Life," and W. Bradford Wilcox, *Sacred Vows, Public Purposes: Religion, the Marriage Movement, and Public Policy.*

16. Arland Thornton, "Reciprocal Influences of Family and Religion in a Changing World."

17. See, for instance, Nancy Tatom Ammerman, "Golden Rule Christianity: Lived Religion in the American Mainstream."

18. For the coping functions of religion, see Kenneth I. Pargament, *The Psychology of Religion and Coping: Theory, Research, Practice.* For one study showing the negative effects of stress on family life, see Elder, Nguyen, and Caspi, "Linking Family Hardship."

19. For studies suggesting a generic relationship between religious beliefs and positive family outcomes, see Howard M. Bahr and Bruce A. Chadwick, "Religion and Family in Middletown, USA"; Annette Mahoney, Kenneth Pargament, Aaron Murray-Swank, and Nichole Murray-Swank, "Religion and the Sanctification of Family Relationships"; and Pearce and Axinn, "Impact of Family Religious Life."

20. Pearce and Axinn, "Impact of Family Religious Life."

21. Penny Edgell, "In Rhetoric and Practice: Defining 'The Good Family' in Local Congregations."

22. Ross M. Stolzenberg, Mary Blair-Loy, and Linda J. Waite, "Religious Participation in Early Adulthood: Age and Family Life Cycle Effects on Church Membership"; W. Bradford Wilcox, "For the Sake of the Children? Family-Related Discourse and Practice in the Mainline."

23. Émile Durkheim, *Suicide,* 170.

24. Christian Smith, *American Evangelicalism: Embattled and Thriving,* 21; see also Rodney Stark and Roger Finke, *Acts of Faith: Explaining the Human Side of Religion.*

25. Christopher G. Ellison, "Religion, the Life Stress Paradigm, and the Study of Depression."

26. Pierre Bourdieu, *The Logic of Practice.*

27. Robert Wuthnow, *Meaning and Moral Order: Explorations in Cultural Analysis.*

28. Ann Swidler, "Culture in Action: Symbols and Strategies"; Wuthnow, *Meaning and Moral Order.*

29. Loren D. Marks and David C. Dollahite, "Religion, Relationships, and Responsible Fathering in Latter-Day Saint Families of Children with Special Needs," 628–29.

30. Ann Swidler, "Cultural Power and Social Movements," 320.

31. This discussion of the generic effects of religious participation on fatherhood is indebted to W. Bradford Wilcox, "Religion, Convention, and Paternal Involvement."

32. See Peter Berger, *The Sacred Canopy.*

33. Ibid.; John P. Bartkowski and Xiaohe Xu, "Distant Patriarchs or Expressive Dads? The Discourse and Practice of Fathering in Conservative Protestant Families"; Marks and Dollahite, "Religion, Relationships, and Responsible Fathering."

34. I focus on these particular conservative Protestant leaders for two reasons. First, all of the elites that I cite have published books or head key ministries in the world of conservative Protestantism. Many of them also appear regularly on Christian radio and television or have their own shows. This gives them significant cultural authority among conservative Protestants. Second, I take their popularity in this subculture to be an indication that their views are representative, to some degree, of the attitudes of average evangelical and fundamentalist Christians.

35. Beverly LaHaye, *How to Develop Your Child's Temperament,* 69.

36. Larry Christenson, *The Christian Family,* 100.

37. James Dobson, *Straight Talk to Men and Their Wives,* 79 (emphasis in original).

38. W. Peter Blitchington, *Sex Roles for the Christian Family,* 39–40.

39. Dobson, *Straight Talk,* 76, 93; Stu Weber, *Tender Warrior: God's Intention for a Man.*

40. Richard Land and Barret Duke, "Fatherhood in the Evangelical Tradition," 98.

41. Dobson, *Straight Talk,* 76, 61, 49.

42. Gary Smalley and John Trent, *The Blessing,* 18.

43. James Dobson, *The New Dare to Discipline;* LaHaye, *How to Develop Your Child's Temperament;* Charles Swindoll, *You and Your Child.*

44. Dobson, *New Dare to Discipline;* LaHaye, *How to Develop Your Child's Temperament;* Smalley and Trent, *Blessing.*

45. See, for example, Dobson, *New Dare to Discipline.*

46. Dobson, *Straight Talk,* 106; LaHaye, *How to Develop Your Child's Temperament;* Swindoll, *You and Your Child.*

47. Blitchington, *Sex Roles for the Christian Family;* Dobson, *Straight Talk;* Rus Walton, *One Nation under God;* for a review, see John P. Bartkowski, "Changing of the Gods: The Gender and Family Discourse of American Evangelicalism in Historical Perspective."

48. Jessie Bernard, "The Good-Provider Role: Its Rise and Fall."

49. William Marsiglio, "Paternal Engagement Activities with Minor Children."

50. Arlie Hochschild, "Emotion Work, Feeling Rules, and Social Structure," 561.

51. Swindoll, *You and Your Child,* 53, 114 (emphasis in original).

52. Dobson, *New Dare to Discipline,* 94.

53. LaHaye, *How to Develop Your Child's Temperament,* 141.

54. Gottman, "Toward a Process Model"; McQuillan and Ferree, "The Importance of Variation among Men."

55. Hochschild, "Emotion Work," 566.

56. Greven, *Spare the Child.*

57. Dobson, *New Dare to Discipline;* LaHaye, *How to Develop Your Child's Temperament;* Swindoll, *You and Your Child.*

58. Swindoll, *You and Your Child,* 91.

59. James C. Dobson, *The Strong-Willed Child: Birth through Adolescence,* 172–73.

60. Dobson, *New Dare to Discipline,* 20, 79; LaHaye, *How to Develop Your Child's Temperament,* 127; Swindoll, *You and Your Child,* 98.

61. Dobson, *Strong-Willed Child; New Dare to Discipline;* LaHaye, *How to Develop Your Child's Temperament;* Swindoll, *You and Your Child.*

62. LaHaye, *How to Develop Your Child's Temperament,* 147, 145.

63. Dobson, *New Dare to Discipline,* 36.

64. Wilcox, "Conservative Protestant Childrearing."

65. Ammerman, "Golden Rule Christianity."

66. Presbyterian Panel, "Public Role of Presbyterians."

67. Marsha Grace Witten, *All Is Forgiven,* 37.

68. Livezey, "The Fourth Presbyterian Church of Chicago," 119.

69. Witten, *All Is Forgiven,* 39.

70. Livezey, "Fourth Presbyterian Church."

71. Becker, "The Family Orientations of Local Congregations," 20.

72. Ellison and Sherkat, "Conservative Protestantism and Support for Corporal Punishment"; Ellison and Sherkat, "Obedience and Autonomy."

73. Alwin, "Religion and Parental Child-Rearing Orientations"; Ellison and Sherkat, "Conservative Protestantism and Support for Corporal Punishment."

74. Wilcox, "Conservative Protestant Childrearing"; James Davison Hunter, *Evangelicalism: The Coming Generation.*

75. My ancillary analyses of the nature of paternal involvement in youth activities do reveal religious differences in the kinds of activities fathers pursue. Conservative Protestant fathers are more likely to volunteer for religious youth groups, while mainline Protestant fathers are more likely to volunteer for scouting groups and sports teams. This finding is consistent with Robert Wuthnow's research showing that conservative Protestants direct their civic engagement in more insular, religious directions, while mainline Protestants direct their civic engagement in more encompassing, secular directions ("Mobilizing Civic Engagement: The Changing Impact of Religious Involvement"). Thus, although differences in religious affiliation do not much influence the amount of time Protestant fathers invest in youth activities, they do structure the types of activities fathers participate in.

76. Alwin, "Religion and Parental Child-Rearing Orientations"; Pearce and Axinn, "Impact of Family Religious Life"; Clydesdale, "Family Behaviors."

77. Thornton, "Reciprocal Influences"; Stolzenberg, Blair-Loy and Waite, "Religious Participation."

78. Timothy T. Clydesdale, "Money and Faith in America: Exploring Effects of Religious Restructuring and Income Inequality on Social Attitudes and Family Behavior"; Robert Griswold, *Fatherhood in America: A History;* Wilcox, "Religion, Convention, and Paternal Involvement"; Robert Wuthnow, *After Heaven: Spirituality in America since the 1950s.*

79. See also Ellison, Bartkowski, and Segal, "Conservative Protestantism."

80. Amato and Booth, *Generation at Risk;* Baumrind, "Current Patterns of Parental Authority"; Maccoby and Martin, "Socialization in the Context of the Family"; Thomson, Hanson, and McLanahan, "Family Structure and Child Well-Being."

81. Amato, "More Than Money?"; Harris, Furstenberg, and Marmer, "Paternal Involvement"; Michael E. Lamb, ed., *The Role of the Father in Child Development.*

82. Greven, *Spare the Child;* Murray A. Straus, David Sugarman, and Jean Giles-Sims, "Spanking by Parents and Subsequent Antisocial Behavior of Children."

83. Diana Baumrind, "Necessary Distinctions"; Robert E. Larzelere, "A Review of the Outcomes of Parental Use of Nonabusive or Customary Physical Punishment"; Ronald L. Simons, Christine Johnson, and Rand D. Conger, "Harsh

Corporal Punishment versus Quality of Parental Involvement as an Explanation of Adolescent Maladjustment."

84. See Marsiglio, "Paternal Engagement Activities."

85. LaRossa, "Fatherhood and Social Change."

86. Frank F. Furstenberg Jr., "Good Dads—Bad Dads: Two Faces of Fatherhood."

CHAPTER FIVE

1. For a discussion of moral order, see Robert Wuthnow, *Meaning and Moral Order: Explorations in Cultural Analysis.*

2. Sarah Fenstermaker Berk, *The Gender Factory,* 201

3. Ibid.; Steven L. Nock, *Marriage in Men's Lives;* Candace West and Don H. Zimmerman, "Doing Gender."

4. Marjorie DeVault, *Feeding the Family: The Social Organization of Caring as Gendered Work;* Sharon Hays, *The Cultural Contradictions of Motherhood;* Louise A. Tilly and Joan Wallach Scott, *Women, Work, and Family;* Viviana Zelizer, *Pricing the Priceless Child: The Changing Social Value of Children.*

5. Arlie Hochschild, "The Economy of Gratitude."

6. Daphne Spain and Suzanne Bianchi, *Balancing Act: Motherhood, Marriage, and Employment among American Women,* 152.

7. Janet Saltzman Chafetz, "Chicken or Egg? A Theory of the Relationship between Feminist Movements and Family Change."

8. Spain and Bianchi, *Balancing Act,* 182–83.

9. Frances K. Goldscheider and Linda J. Waite, *New Families, No Families? The Transformation of the American Home;* Arlie Hochschild with Ann Machung, *The Second Shift: Working Parents and the Revolution at Home;* Nock, *Marriage in Men's Lives.*

10. Hochschild with Machung, *Second Shift.*

11. Spain and Bianchi, *Balancing Act;* Suzanne M. Bianchi, Melissa A. Milkie, Liana C. Sayer, and John P. Robinson, "Is Anyone Doing the Housework? Trends in the Gender Division of Household Labor."

12. Hochschild with Machung, *Second Shift;* Laura Sanchez and Emily W. Kane, "Women's and Men's Constructions of Perceptions of Housework Fairness."

13. Paula England, "Marriage, the Costs of Children, and Gender Inequality"; Beth Anne Shelton and Daphne John, "The Division of Household Labor."

14. Ralph LaRossa, "Fatherhood and Social Change"; Arland Thornton, "Changing Attitudes toward Family Issues in the United States."

15. Nancy Tatom Ammerman and Wade Clark Roof, "Introduction: Old Patterns, New Trends, Fragile Experiments"; Peter Berger, "Religious Institutions"; Kevin J. Christiano, "Religion and the Family in Modern American Culture."

16. Rosalind C. Barnett and Grace K. Baruch, "Determinants of Fathers' Participation in Family Work"; Bianchi, Milkie, Sayer, and Robinson, "Is Anyone Doing the Housework?"; Goldscheider and Waite, *New Families, No Families?*; Harriet B. Presser, "Employment Schedules among Dual-Earner Spouses and the Division of Household Labor by Gender"; Beth Anne Shelton, "The Distribution of Household Tasks: Does Wife's Employment Status Make a Difference?"

17. Sampson Lee Blair and Daniel T. Lichter, "Measuring the Division of Household Labor: Gender Segregation among American Couples"; Julie Brines, "Economic Dependency, Gender, and the Division of Labor at Home"; Myra Marx Ferree, "The Gender Division of Labor in Two-Earner Marriages: Dimensions of Variability and Change"; Yoshinori Kamo, "Determinants of Household Division of Labor: Resources, Power, and Ideology."

18. Kathleen Gerson, *Hard Choices: How Women Decide about Work, Career, and Motherhood*; Kathleen Gerson, *No Man's Land: Men's Changing Commitments to Family and Work.*

19. For an excellent account of this process, see Scott Coltrane, *Family Man.*

20. Gerson, *No Man's Land.*

21. Myra Marx Ferree, "Feminism and Family Research."

22. I recognize that the gender perspective is attentive to both the cultural and social-structural sources of gender but I focus here on the way this perspective illuminates the manner in which culture influences household labor (Ferree, "Feminism and Family Research").

23. Berk, *The Gender Factory*; Brines, "Economic Dependency"; Coltrane, *Family Man*; Theodore N. Greenstein, "Gender Ideology and the Perceptions of the Fairness of the Division of Household Labor: Effects on Marital Quality"; Theodore N. Greenstein, "Husbands' Participation in Domestic Labor: Interactive Effects of Wives' and Husbands' Gender Ideologies"; Theodore N. Greenstein, "Economic Dependence, Gender, and the Division of Labor in the Home: A Replication and Extension"; Hochschild with Machung, *Second Shift.*

24. Brines, "Economic Dependency"; see also Greenstein, "Economic Dependence."

25. Greenstein, "Husbands' Participation"; Greenstein, "Economic Dependence."

26. Berk, *Gender Factory.*

27. DeVault, *Feeding the Family*; Hays, *Cultural Contradictions of Motherhood.*

28. For an exception to this general trend see Goldscheider and Waite's discussion of gender-role attitudes and social context in *New Families, No Families?* 31–33.

29. Cf. Bianchi, Milkie, Sayer, and Robinson, "Is Anyone Doing the Housework?"; Coltrane, *Family Man;* Greenstein, "Gender Ideology"; Greenstein, "Husbands' Participation."

30. Margaret Lamberts Bendroth, *Fundamentalism and Gender: 1875 to the Present;* Christiano, "Religion and the Family"; James Davison Hunter, *Evangelicalism: The Coming Generation;* Charles W. Peek, George D. Lowe, and L. Susan Williams, "Gender and God's Word: Another Look at Religious Fundamentalism and Sexism"; W. Bradford Wilcox and John P. Bartkowski, "The Conservative Protestant Family: Traditional Rhetoric, Progressive Practice." Another important social source of gender-role traditionalism in the United States is immigration.

31. Hochschild with Machung, *Second Shift;* Hochschild, "Economy of Gratitude."

32. Hochschild with Machung, *Second Shift,* 18.

33. Hochschild, "Economy of Gratitude."

34. Hochschild with Machung, *Second Shift;* Margaret F. Brinig and Steven L. Nock, "Weak Men and Disorderly Women: Divorce and the Division of Labor"; Rebecca J. Erickson, "Reconceptualizing Family Work: The Effect of Emotion Work on Perceptions of Marital Quality."

35. Julie Brines and Kara Joyner, "The Ties That Bind: Principles of Cohesion in Cohabitation and Marriage"; Brinig and Nock, "Weak Men and Disorderly Women."

36. Anthony Giddens, *The Transformation of Intimacy;* Christopher Lasch, *Haven in a Heartless World: The Family Besieged;* Edward Shorter, *The Making of the Modern Family.*

37. Marcel Mauss, *The Gift;* Kurt H. Wolff, *The Sociology of George Simmel.*

38. Pierre Bourdieu, *The Logic of Practice.*

39. Here Bourdieu is following in a distinguished sociological tradition that runs from Marx to Simmel in arguing that the logic of gift exchange is distinguished from the logic of the market by its value-laden and intimate character (*Logic of Practice,* 114–15). This tradition has recently been contested, however, by insights from contemporary economic sociology (see, for instance, Zelizer, *Pricing the Priceless Child;* Viviana Zelizer, *The Social Meaning of Money*).

40. Bourdieu, *Logic of Practice,* 126.

41. Mary Douglas, "Foreword"; Hochschild, "Economy of Gratitude"; Viviana Zelizer, "Intimate Transactions."

42. Hochschild, "Economy of Gratitude."

43. Hochschild with Machung, *Second Shift,* 18.

44. Hochschild, "The Economy of Gratitude," 108–9.

45. Hochschild with Machung, *Second Shift,* 59–74; Hochschild, "Economy of Gratitude," 98–100.

46. Hochschild, "Economy of Gratitude," 100.

47. Hochschild, *Second Shift,* 61.

48. John P. Bartkowski, "Beyond Biblical Literalism and Inerrancy: Conservative Protestants and the Hermeneutic Interpretation of Scripture"; John P. Bartkowski, "Debating Patriarchy: Discursive Disputes over Spousal Authority among Evangelical Family Commentators," 393–410; Christopher G. Ellison and John P. Bartkowski, "Conservative Protestantism and the Division of Household Labor among Married Couples"; Sally K. Gallagher and Christian Smith, "Symbolic Traditionalism and Pragmatic Egalitarianism: Contemporary Evangelicals, Family, and Gender"; Hunter, *Evangelicalism.*

49. Ellison and Bartkowski, "Conservative Protestantism and the Division of Household Labor."

50. Beverly LaHaye, *The Spirit-Controlled Woman;* Elisabeth Elliot, *Let Me Be a Woman;* Marilee Horton, *Free to Stay at Home: A Woman's Alternative.*

51. Horton, *Free to Stay at Home,* 15.

52. James Dobson, *Straight Talk to Men and Their Wives;* Gary Smalley, *If Only He Knew: What No Woman Can Resist.*

53. Smalley, *If Only He Knew,* 114, 111.

54. Hunter, *Evangelicalism;* Christian Smith, *Christian America? What Evangelicals Really Want;* W. Bradford Wilcox, "Conservative Protestant Childrearing: Authoritarian or Authoritative?"; Robert Wuthnow, *The Restructuring of American Religion;* see also chapter 2.

55. LaHaye, *Spirit-Controlled Woman;* Elliot, *Let Me Be a Woman.*

56. Ellison and Bartkowski, "Conservative Protestantism and the Division of Household Labor"; Charles Hall, "Entering the Labor Force: Ideals and Realities among Evangelical Women"; Smith, *Christian America?*

57. Gilbert Bilezikian, *Beyond Sex Roles: What the Bible Says about a Woman's Place in Church and Family;* Rebecca M. Groothuis, *Women Caught in the Conflict: The Culture War between Traditionalism and Feminism;* Mary Stewart Van Leeuwen, *Gender and Grace: Love, Work, and Parenting in a Changing World;* for a review of this debate about women's roles, see Bartkowski, "Debating Patriarchy."

58. Melinda Lundquist Denton, "Gender Roles and Marital Decision Making: Negotiating Religious Ideology and Practice."

59. John P. Bartkowski, *Remaking the Godly Marriage: Gender Negotiation in Evangelical Families;* Gallagher and Smith, "Symbolic Traditionalism"; Smith, *Christian America?*

60. Wilcox and Bartkowski, "The Conservative Protestant Family."

61. Anne Carr and Mary Stewart Van Leeuwen, eds. *Religion, Feminism, and the Family;* Thomas C. Reeves, *The Empty Church: The Suicide of Liberal Christianity;* Wuthnow, *Restructuring of American Religion.*

62. Mark Chaves, *Ordaining Women: Culture and Conflict in Religious Organizations,* 192.

63. Jean Miller Schmidt and Gail Murphy-Geiss, "Methodist: 'Tis Grace Will Lead Us Home."

64. United Methodist Church, *The Book of Discipline of the United Methodist Church.*

65. Laura Olson, *Filled with Spirit and Power;* Robert Wuthnow, *Christianity in the Twenty-First Century: Reflections on the Challenges Ahead.*

66. Phyllis D. Airhart and Margaret Lamberts Bendroth, *Faith Traditions and the Family.*

67. Ibid.; Wade Clark Roof, *A Generation of Seekers: The Spiritual Journeys of the Baby Boom Generation;* Christian Smith, *American Evangelicalism: Embattled and Thriving.*

68. Tracey Scott, "What's God Got to Do with It? Protestantism, Gender, and the Meaning of Work."

69. Peter Berger, "Protestantism and the Quest for Certainty"; Lyn Gesch, "Responses to Changing Lifestyles: 'Feminists' and 'Traditionalists' in Mainstream Religion"; Roof and McKinney, *American Mainline Religion: Its Changing Shape and Future.*

70. Goldscheider and Waite, *New Families, No Families?;* Presser, "Employment Schedules among Dual-Earner Spouses"; Scott J. South and Glenna Spitze, "Housework in Marital and Nonmarital Households"; Greenstein, "Gender Ideology."

71. Ellison and Bartkowski, "Conservative Protestantism and the Division of Household Labor among Married Couples."

72. Analyses available from the author upon request.

73. Sampson Lee Blair and Michael P. Johnson, "Wives' Perceptions of the Fairness of the Division of Household Labor: The Intersection of Housework and Ideology"; Hochschild with Machung, *Second Shift;* Linda Thompson, "Family Work: Women's Sense of Fairness."

74. Berk, *Gender Factory;* Hochschild with Machung, *Second Shift.*

75. Blair and Johnson, "Wives' Perceptions."

76. Hochschild, "Economy of Gratitude."

77. Hochschild with Machung, *Second Shift,* 43.

78. Analyses available from the author upon request.

79. Weber, "The Social Psychology of the World Religions," 280.

80. Alfred DeMaris and Monica Longmore, "Ideology, Power, and Equity: Testing Competing Expectations for the Perception of Fairness in Household Labor"; Shelton and John, "The Division of Household Labor."

81. See Blair and Johnson, "Wives' Perceptions," in which the authors rely on the same NSFH measures used in this study.

82. Hochschild with Machung, *Second Shift,* 46.

83. Gallagher and Smith, "Symbolic Traditionalism"; Marie R. Griffith, *God's Daughters: Evangelical Women and the Power of Submission;* Smith, *Christian America?;* Wilcox and Bartkowski, "The Conservative Protestant Family."

84. Bourdieu, *Logic of Practice,* 128–29.

CHAPTER SIX

1. David Popenoe and Barbara Dafoe Whitehead, *The State of Our Unions.*

2. Janet Saltzman Chafetz, "Chicken or Egg? A Theory of the Relationship between Feminist Movements and Family Change"; Linda Thompson and Alexis Walker, "Gender in Families: Women and Men Marriage, Work, and Parenthood."

3. William J. Goode, *World Changes in Divorce Patterns;* Christopher Lasch, *Haven in a Heartless World: The Family Besieged;* Edward Shorter, *The Making of the Modern Family.*

4. Larry L. Bumpass, "What's Happening to the Family? Interactions between Demographic and Institutional Change"; Andrew J. Cherlin, *Marriage, Divorce, Remarriage.*

5. Rebecca J. Erickson, "Reconceptualizing Family Work: The Effect of Emotion Work on Perceptions of Marital Quality"; W. Bradford Wilcox and Steven L. Nock, "What's Love Got to Do with It? Gender Role Ideology, Men's Emotion Work, and Women's Marital Quality"; Jane R. Wilkie, Myra M. Ferree, and Kathryn S. Ratcliff, "Gender and Fairness: Marital Satisfaction in Two-Earner Couples."

6. Paula England and George Farkas, *Households, Employment, and Gender;* Thompson and Walker, "Gender in Families."

7. Walter R. Gove, Michael Hughes, and Carolyn Briggs Style, "Does Marriage Have Positive Effects on the Psychological Well Being of the Individual?"

8. John M. Gottman, "Toward a Process Model of Men in Marriages and Families"; Gay C. Kitson with William M. Holmes, *Portrait of Divorce: Adjustment to Marital Breakdown.*

9. Margaret F. Brinig and Douglas W. Allen, "These Boots Are Made for Walking: Why Most Divorce Filers Are Women"; Wilcox and Nock, "What's Love Got to Do with It?"

10. Paul R. Amato, "More Than Money? Men's Contributions to Their Children's Lives"; Paul R. Amato and Alan Booth, *A Generation at Risk: Growing Up in an Era of Family Upheaval;* Gottman, "Toward a Process Model."

11. Brinig and Allen, "These Boots Are Made for Walking"; Arlie Hochschild, *The Managed Heart: Commercialization of Human Feeling;* Thompson and Walker, "Gender in Families."

12. Julia McQuillan and Myra Marx Ferree, "The Importance of Variation among Men and the Benefits of Feminism for Families," 223; see also Gottman, "Toward a Process Model"; Messner, *Politics of Masculinities: Men in Movements.*

13. The sociological and theological literature on religion and wife abuse is large. For representative samples, see James Alsdurf and Phyllis Alsdurf, *Battered into Submission: The Tragedy of Wife Abuse in the Christian Home;* Joanne Carlson Brown and Carole R. Bohn, *Christianity, Patriarchy, and Abuse: A Feminist Critique;* R. Emerson Dobash and Russell Dobash, *Violence against Wives: A Case against the Patriarchy;* Catherine Clark Kroeger and James R. Beck, *Women, Abuse, and the Bible;* and Nancy Nason-Clark, *The Battered Wife: How Christians Confront Family Violence.*

14. Dobash and Dobash, *Violence against Wives,* 33–34.

15. James R. Beck, "Theology for the Healthy Family," 221.

16. Alsdurf and Alsdurf, *Battered into Submission,* 152.

17. Cokie Roberts and Steven V. Roberts, "Southern Baptists Have a Distorted View of the Family."

18. See also John Scanzoni and C. Arnett, "Enlarging the Understanding of Marital Commitment via Religious Devoutness, Gender-Role Preferences, and Locus of Marital Control."

19. Paul R. Amato and Stacy Rogers, "Do Attitudes toward Divorce Affect Marital Quality?"; Vaughn R. A. Call and Tim B. Heaton, "Religious Influence on Marital Stability."

20. Scanzoni and Arnett, "Enlarging the Understanding of Marital Commitment."

21. Chafetz, "Chicken or Egg?"

22. Arlie Hochschild with Ann Machung, *The Second Shift: Working Parents and the Revolution at Home,* 44.

23. Philip Blumstein and Pepper Schwartz, *American Couples: Money, Work, Sex;* England and Farkas, *Households, Employment, and Gender;* Frances K.

Goldscheider and Linda J. Waite, *New Families, No Families? The Transformation of the American Home;* Gottman, "Toward a Process Model."

24. Max Weber, *Economy and Society,* vol. 1.

25. Robert O. Blood and Donald M. Wolfe, *Husbands and Wives;* Francesca M. Cancian, *Love in America;* Thompson and Walker, "Gender in Families."

26. McQuillan and Ferree, "Importance of Variation."

27. Nancy Chodorow, *The Reproduction of Mothering;* David D. Gilmore, *Manhood in the Making: Cultural Concepts of Masculinity.*

28. McQuillan and Ferree, "Importance of Variation," 223.

29. Goldscheider and Waite, *New Families, No Families?* 4.

30. Andrew J. Cherlin, "Toward a New Home Socioeconomics of Union Formation"; Paula England and Barbara Stanek Kilbourne, "Markets, Marriages, and Other Mates: The Problem of Power"; Shelly Lundberg and Robert A. Pollak, "Bargaining and Distribution in Marriage."

31. Pierre Bourdieu, *The Logic of Practice,* 126.

32. See also Julie Brines and Kara Joyner, "The Ties That Bind: Principles of Cohesion in Cohabitation and Marriage"; Margaret F. Brinig, *From Contract to Covenant: Beyond the Law and Economics of the Family.* Of course, in some marriages one spouse takes a more communitarian approach and the other spouse takes a more contractual approach.

33. Thompson and Walker, "Gender in Families."

34. Brinig, *From Contract to Covenant;* Ross M. Stolzenberg, Mary Blair-Loy, and Linda J. Waite, "Religious Participation in Early Adulthood: Age and Family Life Cycle Effects on Church Membership."

35. Brines and Joyner, "Ties That Bind"; Steven L. Nock, "Commitment and Dependency in Marriage"; Linda Waite and Maggie Gallagher, *The Case for Marriage: Why Married People are Happier, Healthier, and Better Off Financially.*

36. Durkheim cited in Steven L. Nock, *Marriage in Men's Lives,* 11–12.

37. Arland Thornton, "Changing Attitudes toward Family Issues in the United States."

38. See Albert O. Hirschman, *Exit, Voice, and Loyalty: Responses to Decline in Firms, Organizations, and States.*

39. Blumstein and Schwartz, *American Couples;* Brines and Joyner, "Ties That Bind."

40. Bourdieu, *Logic of Practice,* 126.

41. Nancy Folbre and Thomas E. Weisskopf, "Did Father Know Best? Families, Markets, and the Supply of Caring Labor."

42. Gary Becker, *A Treatise on the Family;* Brines and Joyner, "Ties That Bind"; Nock, *Marriage in Men's Lives.*

43. Nock, "Commitment and Dependency in Marriage."

44. Maxine P. Atkinson and Jacqueline Boles, "WASP (Wives as Senior Partners)"; Candace West and Don H. Zimmerman, "Doing Gender."

45. Brines and Joyner, "Ties That Bind."

46. Stolzenberg, Blair-Loy, and Waite, "Religious Participation in Early Adulthood."

47. Arlie Hochschild, "Emotion Work, Feeling Rules, and Social Structure," 551, 564.

48. Peter Berger, *The Sacred Canopy;* Christopher G. Ellison, "Religious Involvement and Subjective Well-Being."

49. Norval D. Glenn, "Quantitative Research on Marital Quality in the 1980s: A Critical Review"; Scott M. Myers and Alan Booth, "Marital Strains and Marital Quality: The Role of High and Low Locus of Control."

50. Marsha Grace Witten, *All Is Forgiven: The Secular Message in American Protestantism.*

51. Nancy Tatom Ammerman, "Golden Rule Christianity: Lived Religion in the American Mainstream"; Peter Berger, "Religious Institutions."

52. Call and Heaton, "Religious Influence on Marital Stability"; Timothy T. Clydesdale, "Family Behaviors among Early U.S. Baby Boomers: Exploring the Effects of Religion and Income Change, 1965–1982"; Tim B. Heaton and Edith L. Pratt, "The Effects of Religious Homogamy on Marital Satisfaction and Stability."

53. Max Weber, "The Social Psychology of the World Religions," 280.

54. Call and Heaton, "Religious Influence on Marital Stability"; Clydesdale, "Family Behaviors"; Heaton and Pratt, "Effects of Religious Homogamy."

55. Clydesdale, "Family Behaviors," 628–29.

56. W. Peter Blitchington, *Sex Roles for the Christian Family;* Larry Christenson, *The Christian Family;* James Dobson, *Straight Talk to Men and Their Wives.*

57. Christenson, *Christian Family.*

58. James Davison Hunter, *Evangelicalism: The Coming Generation;* George Marsden, *Fundamentalism and American Culture.*

59. Lasch, *Haven in a Heartless World.*

60. Hunter, *Evangelicalism.*

61. Margaret Lamberts Bendroth, *Fundamentalism and Gender: 1875 to the Present.*

62. Blitchington, *Sex Roles for the Christian Family,* 49.

63. Anthony L. Jordan et al., *Report of the Baptist Faith and Message Study Committee to the Southern Baptist Convention,* 2.

64. Blitchington, *Sex Roles for the Christian Family;* Dobson, *Straight Talk;* Rus Walton, *One Nation under God.*

65. E.g., Gary Smalley, *If Only He Knew: What No Woman Can Resist.*

66. Dobson, *Straight Talk,* 129.

67. Smalley, *If Only He Knew,* 30, 42, 95–96, 25, 30.

68. Ibid., 16, 173–86, 108.

69. Gottman, "Toward a Process Model"; McQuillan and Ferree, "Importance of Variation"; Messner, *Politics of Masculinities.*

70. Jordan et al., *Report of the Baptist Faith and Message Study Committee,* 2.

71. Christenson, *Christian Family,* 18.

72. Jordan et al., *Report of the Baptist Faith and Message Study Committee,* 2.

73. Thompson and Walker, "Gender in Families"; McQuillan and Ferree, "Importance of Variation."

74. Dobson, *Straight Talk,* 179, 182–84, 121–23, 125.

75. Smalley, *If Only He Knew,* 7, 27, 46–54.

76. Bendroth, *Fundamentalism and Gender.*

77. Jordan et al., *Report of the Baptist Faith and Message Study Committee,* 3.

78. Dobson, *Straight Talk,* 184.

79. R. Marie Griffith, *God's Daughters: Evangelical Women and the Power of Submission,* 169–85; Christian Smith, *Christian America?* 170–82.

80. Christian Smith, *Christian America?* 179–80.

81. Melinda Lundquist Denton, "Gender Roles and Marital Decision Making: Negotiating Religious Ideology and Practice"; John P. Bartkowski, *Remaking the Godly Marriage: Gender Negotiation in Evangelical Families;* Sally K. Gallagher, *Evangelical Identity and Gendered Family Life;* Smith, *Christian America?*

82. W. Bradford Wilcox, "For the Sake of the Children? Family-Related Discourse and Practice in the Mainline."

83. John Patton and Brian H. Childs, *Christian Marriage and Family: Caring for Our Generations,* 210.

84. United Methodist Church, *United Methodist Church Book of Discipline,* 71.

85. Wilcox, "For the Sake of the Children?"

86. Don S. Browning, Bonnie J. Miller-McLemore, Pamela D. Couture, K. Brynoff Lyon, and Robert M. Franklin, *From Culture Wars to Common Ground: Religion and the American Family Debate.*

87. Patton and Childs, *Christian Marriage and Family,* 169.

88. Chapter 2; Browning, Miller-McLemore, Couture, Lyon, and Franklin, *From Culture Wars to Common Ground,* 20, 281.

89. Tracey Scott, "What's God Got to Do with It?"

90. Ammerman, "Golden Rule Christianity."

91. Patton and Childs, *Christian Marriage and Family,* 30–31.

92. J. Gordon Melton, *The Churches Speak on Sex and Family Life,* 173.

93. Scott, "What's God Got to Do with It?"

94. The results I report in this chapter apply to a group of men who are slightly different from the men in NSFH1 (1987–1988), whose beliefs and behaviors I analyze in chapters 3 through 5. First, NSFH2 men were sampled—on

average—five years after those in NSFH1, which means that there may be differences in period effects from NSFH1 to NSFH2. Nevertheless, since Promise Keepers was not a national force until the latter half of the 1990s, I do not expect that any major period effects influenced the primary religious, ideological, and family variables of interest here. Second, the composition of the sample changed: some of the men interviewed in NSFH1 were no longer in the sample by the time of NSFH2 because they divorced, their children were no longer under the age of eighteen, or they were not reinterviewed; on the other hand, the NSFH2 sample picks up additional men, whose children were not yet school-age at the time of NSFH1. The primary concern here is sample attrition due to divorce. Because divorce is, in all likelihood, negatively related to men's marital emotion work, I suspect that my sample under-represents men who did lower levels of marital emotion work at the time of NSFH1. This suggests that the size of any religious or ideological effects in NSFH2 may be smaller than they would have been in NSFH1, but I do not think sample attrition will bias the direction of regression coefficients.

95. Analyses are available from the author upon request.

96. Gottman, "Toward a Process Model."

97. Christopher G. Ellison, John P. Bartkowski, and Kristin L. Anderson, "Are There Religious Variations in Domestic Violence?"

98. Brinig and Allen, "These Boots Are Made for Walking"; Wilcox and Nock, "What's Love Got to Do with It?"

99. McQuillan and Ferree, "Importance of Variation," 223; see also Gottman, "Toward a Process Model"; Messner, *Politics of Masculinities.*

100. See also Amato and Rogers, "Do Attitudes toward Divorce Affect Marital Quality?"

CHAPTER SEVEN

1. Mark Chaves, *Ordaining Women: Culture and Conflict in Religious Organizations.*

2. To obtain these estimates, I averaged attitudes among mainline Protestant, active mainline Protestant, conservative Protestant, and active conservative Protestant men who are married with children on the following to the following family and gender topics in NSFH1 (1987–1988): the gendered division of labor, mothers of preschoolers working, the advisability of divorce for couples with children, and unwed childbearing.

3. R. Stephen Warner, "Work in Progress toward a New Paradigm for the Sociological Study of Religion in the United States," 1078, 1076–77.

4. W. Bradford Wilcox, "Religion, Convention, and Paternal Involvement."

5. David Sikkink, Department of Sociology, University of Notre Dame, personal correspondence, February 4, 2002.

6. See, for instance, Ross M. Stolzenberg, Mary Blair-Loy, and Linda Waite, "Religious Participation in Early Adulthood: Age and Family Life Cycle Effects on Church Membership," and Arland Thornton, "Reciprocal Influences of Family and Religion in a Changing World."

7. See, for instance, W. Bradford Wilcox, "Conservative Protestantism and the Family: Resisting, Engaging, or Accommodating Modernity?"

8. On the negative effects of spanking, see Murray A. Straus, David Sugarman, and Jean Giles-Sims, "Spanking by Parents and Subsequent Antisocial Behavior of Children." On the negative effects of excessive parental control, see Eleanor E. Maccoby and John A. Martin, "Socialization in the Context of the Family: Parent-Child Interaction."

9. For a recent discussion of social class that suggests middle-class parents are more emotionally and practically engaged than lower-class parents, see Annette Lareau, *Unequal Childhood: The Importance of Social Class in Family Life.* See also Melvin L. Kohn, *Class and Conformity: A Study in Values.*

10. For accounts of the persistence of religion in modern and modernizing societies, see José Casanova, *Public Religions in the Modern World;* Martin Riesebrodt, *Pious Passion: The Emergence of Modern Fundamentalism in the United States and Iran;* and Warner, "Work in Progress toward a New Paradigm."

11. Riesebrodt, *Pious Passion,* 208.

12. For coverage of Islamic revivalism, see Riesebrodt, *Pious Passion;* and Said Amir Arjomand, ed., *From Nationalism to Revolutionary Islam.* For a consideration of the relationship between late modernity and conservative Protestantism in Northern America, see Christian Smith, *American Evangelicalism: Embattled and Thriving.* For a discussion of the recent politicization of Hinduism in India, see Thomas Blom Hansen, *The Saffron Wave: Democracy and Hindu Nationalism in Modern India.* For a wide-ranging discussion of recent developments in Roman Catholicism and Pentecostalism in the global South, see Philip Jenkins, *The Next Christendom: the Rise of Global Christianity.*

13. Three important treatments of the relationship between family modernization and religion around the world are Sharon K. Houseknecht and Jerry G. Pankhurst, eds. *Family, Religion, and Social Change in Diverse Societies;* Riesebrodt, *Pious Passion;* and Casanova, *Public Religions.*

14. For an ethnographic account of this phenomenon, see Judith Stacey, *Brave New Families: Stories of Domestic Upheaval in Late Twentieth Century America.* For empirical evidence of the phenomenon, see Darren E. Sherkat,

"Religious Socialization and the Family: An Examination of Religious Influence in the Family over the Life Course."

15. Casanova, *Public Religions in the Modern World,* 145–66.

16. Riesebrodt, *Pious Passion,* 126–28, 167–73.

17. Sharon Houseknecht, "Social Change in Egypt: The Roles of Religion and Family."

18. A number of observers of contemporary religious movements have made the point that religious movements with a "fundamentalist" or "orthodox" orientation must incorporate some aspects of the broader society if they wish to continue to draw resources and recruits from the social environment, and to keep the rising generation in the fold. See Riesebrodt, *Pious Passion;* Smith, *American Evangelicalism;* Warner, "Work in Progress toward a New Paradigm." These quotes are taken from Smith, *American Evangelicalism,* 97–102.

19. Mitchell L. Stevens, *Kingdom of Children: Culture and Controversy in the Homeschooling Movement.*

20. For a discussion of the sociocultural sources of Pentecostalism in Latin America, see David Martin, *Tongues of Fire: the Explosion of Protestantism in Latin America.* Also see Jenkins, *Next Christendom.*

21. William J. Goode, *World Changes in Divorce Patterns.*

22. Jorge E. Maldonado, "Building 'Fundamentalism' from the Family in Latin America."

23. Ibid., 230.

24. For discussions that assume the triumph of family modernization, see Larry L. Bumpass, "What's Happening to the Family? Interactions between Demographic and Institutional Change"; Larry Bumpass, "Family-Related Attitudes, Couple Relationships, and Union Stability"; Scott Coltrane, "Marketing the Marriage 'Solution': Misplaced Simplicity in the Politics of Fatherhood"; and Goode, *World Changes in Divorce Patterns.*

25. For example, see Alan Wolfe's *Whose Keeper? Social Science and Moral Obligation,* 132–58, for a discussion of the ways in which the strong states in Scandinavia have eroded the functions and vitality of civil society and the family.

26. For my assertions about the comparative strength or weakness of religion and the state I am indebted to Casanova, *Public Religions in the Modern World;* and Warner, "Work in Progress toward a New Paradigm."

27. This discussion draws on the theoretical discussion of the relationship between religion and the family in Jerry G. Pankhurst and Sharon K. Houseknecht, "Introduction: The Religion-Family Linkage and Social Change—A Neglected Area of Study."

28. For the effect of marriage and parenthood on women, see Paula England, "Marriage, the Costs of Children, and Gender Inequality." For the effect of marriage and parenthood on men, see Steven L. Nock, *Marriage in Men's Lives*.

29. In *The Second Shift: Working Parents and the Revolution at Home*, Arlie Hochschild argues that men's behavior helps to account for the "stalled" gender revolution.

30. Janet Saltzman Chafetz, "Chicken or Egg? A Theory of the Relationship between Feminist Movements and Family Change"; Andrew J. Cherlin, *Marriage, Divorce, Remarriage*, 48–65.

31. Norval Glenn, "Values, Attitudes, and the State of American Marriage."

32. Frances K. Goldscheider and Linda J. Waite, *New Families, No Families?* 192–209. Note that I include mother-only families under the rubric of "no families."

33. Ibid., 200, 204–5, 195.

34. Ibid., 202–4. See also Bumpass, "What's Happening to the Family?" and Daphne Spain and Suzanne Bianchi, *Balancing Act: Motherhood, Marriage, and Employment among American Women*.

35. For studies that explain the attractiveness of a neotraditional family order for women, see Lynn Davidman, *Tradition in a Rootless World*; Sally K. Gallagher, *Evangelical Identity and Gendered Family Life*; Christel J. Manning, *God Gave Us the Right*; Christian Smith, *Christian America? What Evangelicals Really Want*; and Stacey, *Brave New Families*. For studies that do the same thing for men, see John P. Bartkowski, *Remaking the Godly Marriage: Gender Negotiation in Evangelical Families*; Smith, *Christian America?* and W. Bradford Wilcox and John P. Bartkowski, "The Conservative Protestant Family: Traditional Rhetoric, Progressive Practice."

36. See Davidman, *Tradition in a Rootless World*; and Manning, *God Gave Us the Right*.

37. For evidence of "no families" in poor, working-class, and minority communities, see Robert D. Mare and Christopher Winship, "Socioeconomic Change and the Decline of Marriage for Blacks and Whites," and Joshua Goldstein and Catherine Kenney, "Marriage Delayed or Marriage Foregone? New Cohort Forecasts of First Marriage for U.S. Women." For evidence of high levels of childlessness and lifetime singleness in the upper-middle-class metropolitan United States, see Amaru Bachu and Martin O'Connell, *Fertility of American Women: June 1998*.

38. For a discussion of the links between religion and nonmarital births in the urban United States, see W. Bradford Wilcox, *Then Comes Marriage?*

Religion, Race, and Marriage in Urban America. For a discussion of the reciprocal influences of family and religion, see Stolzenberg, Blair-Loy, and Waite,
"Religious Participation in Early Adulthood."

39. For instance, table A5.3 in the appendix indicates that highly educated couples
and African American couples have higher levels of equality in the division
of household labor—one key measure of the "new family" model. Annette
Lareau's *Unequal Childhood* also suggests that both men and women in the
middle and upper classes are more engaged as parents, even if women still
take on the majority of child-rearing responsibilities.

40. David Brooks, "One Nation, Slightly Divisible."

41. For evidence that traditional Catholics exhibit distinctively high levels of paren-
tal involvement, see W. Bradford Wilcox, "Religion, Parenting, and Child
Well-Being." For evidence that Mormons fit the neotraditional model, see
David Dollahite, *Strengthening Our Families.*

42. Wilcox, "Conservative Protestantism and the Family."

43. For coverage of "no families" in lower-class and minority communities, see
Elijah Anderson, *Code of the Street;* Paul E. Peterson, "The Urban Underclass
and the Poverty Paradox"; William Julius Wilson, *When Work Disappears:
The World of the New Urban Poor.* For coverage of "no families" in middle-
class and upper-class communities, see Kathleen Gerson, *Hard Choices: How
Women Decide about Work, Career, and Motherhood;* and Carolyn M. Morell,
Unwomanly Conduct: The Challenges of Intentional Childlessness.

44. Goldscheider and Waite, *New Families, No Families?* Scott Coltrane, *Family Man.*

45. W. Bradford Wilcox, *Sacred Vows, Public Purposes: Religion, the Marriage
Movement, and Public Policy.*

46. Judith Seltzer and Suzanne Bianchi, "Children's Contact with Absent Parents."

47. Nock, *Marriage in Men's Lives;* David Eggebeen and Christopher Knoester,
"Does Fatherhood Matter for Men?"

48. Nock, *Marriage in Men's Lives;* Elizabeth Gorman, "Bringing Home the Bacon:
Marital Allocation of Income-Earning Responsibility, Job Shifts, and Men's
Wage"; Anderson, *Code of the Street;* William Julius Wilson, *When Work
Disappears.*

49. For new evidence that suggests that married men's contributions to family
work are increasing at a marked pace, see Liana Sayer, "Gender, Time, and
Inequality: Trends in Women's and Men's Paid Work, Unpaid Work, and
Free Time."

50. Ammerman, "Golden Rule Christianity."

51. W. Bradford Wilcox, "For the Sake of the Children?"

52. R. Albert Mohler Jr., "Against an Immoral Tide."

APPENDIX

1. See www.icpsr.umich.edu:8080/GSS/about/gss/about.htm.
2. See James Sweet, Larry Bumpass, and Vaughan Call, *The Design and Content of the National Survey of Families and Households;* and Larry Bumpass and James Sweet, *Cohabitation, Marriage, and Union Stability.*
3. Personal correspondence with Julien Teitler, Social Indicators Survey Center, Columbia University, December 23, 2002.

WORKS CITED

Airhart, Phyllis D., and Margaret Lamberts Bendroth. *Faith Traditions and the Family.* Louisville, Ky.: Westminster/John Knox Press, 1996.

Alcorn, Randy. *ProLife Answers to ProChoice Arguments.* Sisters, Ore.: Multnomah, 1992.

Alsdurf, James, and Phyllis Alsdurf. *Battered into Submission: The Tragedy of Wife Abuse in the Christian Home.* Downer's Grove, Ill.: InterVarsity Press, 1989.

Alwin, Duane F. "Religion and Parental Child-Rearing Orientations: Evidence of a Catholic-Protestant Convergence." *American Journal of Sociology* 92 (1986): 412–40.

Amato, Paul R. "More Than Money? Men's Contributions to Their Children's Lives." In *Men in Families: When Do They Get Involved? What Difference*

Does It Make? ed. Alan Booth and Ann Crouter. Mahwah, N.J.: Lawrence Erlbaum Associates, 1998.

Amato, Paul R., and Alan Booth. *A Generation at Risk: Growing Up in an Era of Family Upheaval.* Cambridge, Mass.: Harvard University Press, 1997.

Amato, Paul R., and Fernando Rivera. "Paternal Involvement and Children's Behavior Problems." *Journal of Marriage and the Family* 61 (1999): 375–84.

Amato, Paul R., and Stacy Rogers. "Do Attitudes toward Divorce Affect Marital Quality." *Journal of Family Issues* 20 (1999): 69–86.

"America on Its Knees." *Christianity Today,* June 19, 1970, 20–21.

Ammerman, Nancy Tatom. *Congregation and Community.* New Brunswick, N.J.: Rutgers University Press, 1997.

———. "Golden Rule Christianity: Lived Religion in the American Mainstream." In *Lived Religion in America: Toward a History of Practice,* ed. David D. Hall. Princeton, N.J.: Princeton University Press, 1997.

Ammerman, Nancy Tatom, and Wade Clark Roof. "Introduction: Old Patterns, New Trends, Fragile Experiments." In *Work, Family, and Religion in Contemporary Society,* ed. Nancy Ammerman and Wade Clark Roof. New York: Routledge, 1995.

Anderson, Connie, and Michael A. Messner. "The Political Is Personal: Masculinity Therapy and Patriarchal Bargains among the Promise Keepers." Paper presented at the annual meeting of the Pacific Sociological Association, San Francisco, 1997.

Anderson, Elijah. *Code of the Street.* New York: Norton, 1999.

Arjomand, Said Amir, ed. *From Nationalism to Revolutionary Islam.* London: Macmillan, in association with St. Anthony's College, Oxford, 1984.

Astone, Nan Marie, and Sara McLanahan. "Family Structure, Parental Practices, and High School Completion." *American Sociological Review* 56 (1991): 309–20.

Atkinson, Maxine P., and Jacqueline Boles. "WASP (Wives as Senior Partners)." *Journal of Marriage and the Family* 46 (1984): 861–70.

Bachu, Amaru, and Martin O'Connell. *Fertility of American Women: June 1998.* Current Population Reports. P20–526. Washington, D.C.: U.S. Census Bureau, 1998.

Bahr, Howard M., and Bruce A. Chadwick. "Religion and Family in Middletown, USA." Pp. 51–65 in *The Religion and Family Connection: Social Science Perspectives,* ed. D. L. Thomas. Provo, Utah: Religious Studies Center, Brigham Young University, 1988.

Barnett, Rosalind C., and Grace K. Baruch. "Determinants of Fathers' Participation in Family Work." *Journal of Marriage and the Family* 49 (1987): 29–40.

Bartkowski, John P. "Beyond Biblical Literalism and Inerrancy: Conservative Protestants and the Hermeneutic Interpretation of Scripture." *Sociology of Religion* 57 (1996): 259–72.

———. "Changing of the Gods: The Gender and Family Discourse of American Evangelicalism in Historical Perspective." *The History of the Family: An International Quarterly* 3 (1998): 95–115.

———. "Debating Patriarchy: Discursive Disputes over Spousal Authority among Evangelical Family Commentators." *Journal for the Scientific Study of Religion* 36 (1997): 393–410.

———. *Remaking the Godly Marriage: Gender Negotiation in Evangelical Families.* New Brunswick, N.J.: Rutgers University Press, 2001.

———. "Spare the Rod . . . , or Spare the Child? Divergent Perspectives on Conservative Protestant Child Discipline." *Review of Religious Research* 37 (1995): 97–116.

Bartkowski, John P., and W. Bradford Wilcox. "Conservative Protestant Child Discipline: The Case of Parental Yelling." *Social Forces* 79 (2000): 265–90.

Bartkowski, John P., and Xiaohe Xu. "Distant Patriarchs or Expressive Dads? The Discourse and Practice of Fathering in Conservative Protestant Families." *Sociological Quarterly* 41 (2000): 465–85.

Baumrind, Diana. "Current Patterns of Parental Authority." *Developmental Psychology Monographs* 4 (1971): 1–103.

———. "Necessary Distinctions." *Psychological Inquiry* 8 (1997): 176–82.

Beck, James R. "Theology for the Healthy Family." In *Women, Abuse, and the Bible,* eds. Catherine Clark Kroeger and James R. Beck. Grand Rapids, Mich.: Paternoster, 1996.

Becker, Gary. *A Treatise on the Family.* Cambridge, Mass.: Harvard University Press, 1981.

Becker, Penny Edgell. "The Family Orientations of Local Congregations." Unpublished manuscript. Department of Sociology, Cornell University, 2000.

Bendroth, Margaret Lamberts. *Fundamentalism and Gender: 1875 to the Present.* New Haven, Conn.: Yale University Press, 1993.

Berger, Peter. "Protestantism and the Quest for Certainty." *Christian Century,* August 26, 1998, 782–85, 792–96.

———. "Religious Institutions." Pp. 329–79 in *Sociology: An Introduction,* ed. Neil J. Smelser. New York: John Wiley & Sons, 1967.

———. *The Sacred Canopy.* Garden City, N.Y.: Doubleday, 1967.

Berger, Peter, and Thomas Luckmann. *The Social Construction of Reality: A Treatise in the Sociology of Knowledge.* Garden City, N.Y.: Doubleday, 1966.

Berk, Sarah Fenstermaker. *The Gender Factory.* New York: Plenum, 1985.

Bernard, Jessie. "The Good-Provider Role: Its Rise and Fall." *American Psychologist* 36 (1981): 1–12.

Bianchi, Suzanne M. "Maternal Employment and Time with Children: Dramatic Change or Surprising Continuity?" *Demography* 37 (2000): 401–14.

Bianchi, Suzanne M., Melissa A. Milkie, Liana C. Sayer, and John P. Robinson. "Is Anyone Doing the Housework? Trends in the Gender Division of Household Labor." *Social Forces* 79 (2000): 191–228.

Bilezikian, Gilbert. *Beyond Sex Roles: What the Bible Says about a Woman's Place in Church and Family,* 2nd ed. Grand Rapids, Mich.: Baker, 1985.

Biller, Henry B. *Fathers and Families: Paternal Factors in Child Development.* Westport, Conn.: Auburn House, 1993.

Blair, Sampson Lee, and Michael P. Johnson. "Wives' Perceptions of the Fairness of the Division of Household Labor: The Intersection of Housework and Ideology." *Journal of Marriage and the Family* 54 (1992): 570–81.

Blair, Sampson Lee, and Daniel T. Lichter. "Measuring the Division of Household Labor: Gender Segregation among American Couples." *Journal of Family Issues* 12 (1991): 91–113.

Blitchington, W. Peter. *Sex Roles for the Christian Family.* Wheaton, Ill.: Tyndale House, 1980.

Bloesch, Donald G. "The Father and the Goddess." *Christianity Today,* October 8, 1990, 74–76.

Blood, Robert O., and Donald M. Wolfe, *Husbands and Wives.* New York: Free Press, 1960.

Blumstein, Philip, and Pepper Schwartz. *American Couples: Money, Work, Sex.* New York: Morrow, 1983.

Book of Common Prayer. New York: Oxford University Press, 1979.

Book of Common Worship. Compiled by the Presbyterian Church (U.S.A.), Theology and Ministry Unit, and the Cumberland Presbyterian Church. Louisville, Ky.: Westminster/John Knox, 1993.

Bourdieu, Pierre. *Distinction: A Social Critique of the Judgement of Taste.* Cambridge, Mass.: Harvard University Press, 1984.

———. *The Field of Cultural Production.* New York: Columbia University Press, 1993.

———. *The Logic of Practice.* Stanford, Calif.: Stanford University Press, 1990.

Brasher, Brenda. *Godly Women: Fundamentalism and Female Power.* New Brunswick, N.J.: Rutgers University Press, 1998.

Brimelow, Peter. "Who Has Abortions?" *Forbes,* October 18, 1999. Accessed July 3, 2000, at www.forbes.com/forbes/99/1018/6410110a.htm.

Brines, Julie. "Economic Dependency, Gender, and the Division of Labor at Home." *American Journal of Sociology* 100 (1994): 652–88.

Brines, Julie, and Kara Joyner. "The Ties That Bind: Principles of Cohesion in Cohabitation and Marriage." *American Sociological Review* 64 (1999): 333–55.

Brinig, Margaret F. *From Contract to Covenant: Beyond the Law and Economics of the Family.* Cambridge, Mass.: Harvard University Press, 2000.

Brinig, Margaret F., and Douglas W. Allen. "These Boots Are Made for Walking: Why Most Divorce Filers Are Women." *American Law and Economics Review* 2 (2000): 126–69.

Brinig, Margaret F., and Steven L. Nock. "Weak Men and Disorderly Women: Divorce and the Division of Labor." Annual Meetings, American Law and Economics Association and Canadian Law and Economics Association, 1999.

Brint, Steven. *In an Age of Experts.* Princeton, N.J.: Princeton University Press, 1994.

Brooks, David. "One Nation, Slightly Divisible," *Atlantic Monthly* 288 (2001): 53–65. www.theatlantic.com/issues/2001/12/brooks.htm.

Brown, Joanne Carlson, and Carole R. Bohn. *Christianity, Patriarchy, and Abuse: A Feminist Critique.* Cleveland, Ohio: Pilgrim, 1989.

Brown, Karen McCarthy. "Fundamentalism and the Control of Women." Pp. 175–201 in *Fundamentalism and Gender,* ed. John Stratton Hawley. New York: Oxford University Press, 1994.

Browning, Don S., Bonnie J. Miller-McLemore, Pamela D. Couture, K. Brynoff Lyon, and Robert M. Franklin. *From Culture Wars to Common Ground: Religion and the American Family Debate.* Louisville, Ky.: Westminster/John Knox Press, 1997.

Browning, Robert L., and Roy A. Reed. "Families and Worship." In *The Family Handbook,* ed. Herbert Anderson, Don Browning, Ian Evison, and Mary Stewart Van Leeuwen. Louisville, Ky.: Westminster/John Knox, 1998.

Brusco, Elizabeth E. *The Reformation of Machismo: Evangelical Conversion and Gender in Colombia.* Austin: University of Texas Press, 1995.

Bumpass, Larry L. "Family-Related Attitudes, Couple Relationships, and Union Stability." In *Meaning and Choice: Value Orientations and Life Cycle*

Decisions, ed. Ron Lesthaeghe. The Hague, Netherlands: Netherlands Interdisciplinary Demographic Institute, 2001.

———. "What's Happening to the Family? Interactions between Demographic and Institutional Change." *Demography* 27 (1990): 483–98.

Bumpass, Larry L., and James A. Sweet. *Cohabitation, Marriage, and Union Stability.* Madison: Center for Demography and Ecology, University of Wisconsin–Madison, 1995.

Call, Vaughn R. A., and Tim B. Heaton. "Religious Influence on Marital Stability." *Journal for the Scientific Study of Religion* 36 (1997): 382–92.

Cancian, Francesca M. *Love in America.* New York: Cambridge University Press, 1987.

Capps, Donald. "Religion and Child Abuse: Perfect Together." *Journal for the Scientific Study of Religion* 31 (1992): 1–14.

Carlson, Marcia J. "Family Structure, Father Involvement, and Adolescent Behavioral Outcomes." Ph.D. diss., Department of Sociology, University of Michigan, 1999.

Carr, Anne, and Van Leeuwen, Mary Stewart, eds. *Religion, Feminism, and the Family.* Louisville, Ky.: Westminster/John Knox, 1996.

Casanova, José. *Public Religions in the Modern World.* Chicago: University of Chicago Press, 1994.

Chafetz, Janet Saltzman. "Chicken or Egg? A Theory of the Relationship between Feminist Movements and Family Change." In *Gender and Family Change in Industrialized Countries,* ed. Karen Oppenheim Mason and An-Magritt Jensen. Oxford: Clarendon, 1995.

Chaves, Mark. "Family Structure and Protestant Church Attendance: The Sociological Basis of Cohort and Age Effects." *Journal for the Scientific Study of Religion* 39 (1991): 329–40.

———. *Ordaining Women: Culture and Conflict in Religious Organizations.* Cambridge, Mass.: Harvard University Press, 1997.

Chaves, Mark, Helen Giesel, and William Tsitsos. "Religious Variations in Public Presence: Evidence from the National Congregations Study." Pp. 108–28 in *Quietly Influential: The Public Role of Mainline Protestantism,* ed. Robert Wuthnow and John H. Evans. Berkeley: University of California Press, 2002.

Chaves, Mark, Mary Ellen Konieczny, Kraig Beyerlien, and Emily Barman. "The National Congregations Study: Background, Methods, and Selected Results." *Journal for the Scientific Study of Religion* 38 (1999): 458–76.

Cherlin, Andrew J. *Marriage, Divorce, Remarriage.* Cambridge, Mass.: Harvard University Press, 1992.

————. "Toward a New Home Socioeconomics of Union Formation." In *The Ties That Bind: Perspectives on Marriage and Cohabitation*, ed. Linda Waite. New York: Aldine de Gruyter, 2000.

Chodorow, Nancy. *The Reproduction of Mothering*. Berkeley: University of California Press, 1978.

Christenson, Larry. *The Christian Family*. Minneapolis, Minn.: Bethany Fellowship, 1970.

Christiano, Kevin J. "Religion and the Family in Modern American Culture." In *Family, Religion, and Social Change in Diverse Societies*, ed. Sharon K. Houseknecht and Jerry G. Pankhurst. Oxford: Oxford University Press, 2000.

Christians for Biblical Equality. "Men, Women, and Biblical Equality." *Christianity Today*, April 9, 1990, 36–37.

Clydesdale, Timothy T. "Family Behaviors among Early U.S. Baby Boomers: Exploring the Effects of Religion and Income Change, 1965–1982." *Social Forces* 76 (1997): 605–35.

————. "Money and Faith in America: Exploring Effects of Religious Restructuring and Income Inequality on Social Attitudes and Family Behavior." Ph.D. diss., Department of Sociology, Princeton University, 1994.

Coltrane, Scott. *Family Man*. New York: Oxford University Press, 1996.

————. "Fatherhood and Marriage in the 21st Century." *National Forum* 80 (2000): 25–28.

————. "Marketing the Marriage 'Solution': Misplaced Simplicity in the Politics of Fatherhood." *Sociological Perspectives* 44 (2001): 387–418.

Coontz, Stephanie. *The Way We Never Were: American Families and the Nostalgia Trap*. New York: Basic Books, 1992.

Cuddihy, John Murray. *No Offense: Civil Religion and Protestant Taste*. New York: Scribner, 1978.

Davidman, Lynn. *Tradition in a Rootless World*. Berkeley: University of California Press, 1991.

DeMaris, Alfred, and Monica Longmore. "Ideology, Power, and Equity: Testing Competing Expectations for the Perception of Fairness in Household Labor." *Social Forces* 74 (1996): 1043–71.

Denton, Melinda Lundquist. "Gender Roles and Marital Decision Making: Negotiating Religious Ideology and Practice." Unpublished manuscript, Department of Sociology, University of North Carolina at Chapel Hill, 2002.

DeVault, Marjorie L. *Feeding the Family: The Social Organization of Caring as Gendered Work*. Chicago: University of Chicago Press, 1991.

DiMaggio, Paul J. "Culture and Cognition." *Annual Review of Sociology* 23 (1997): 263–87.

DiMaggio, Paul J., John H. Evans, and Bethany Bryson. "Have Americans' Social
    Attitudes Become More Polarized?" *American Journal of Sociology* 102
    (1996): 690–755.
DiMaggio, Paul J., and Walter W. Powell. "Introduction." In *The New Institu-
    tionalism in Organizational Analysis,* ed. Walter W. Powell and Paul J.
    DiMaggio. Chicago: University of Chicago Press, 1991.
Dobash, R. Emerson, and Russell Dobash. *Violence against Wives: A Case
    against the Patriarchy.* New York: Free Press, 1983.
Dobson, James C. *Dare to Discipline.* 1970. Reprint, Wheaton, Ill.: Tyndale
    House, 1977.
———. *Love Must Be Tough.* Nashville, Tenn.: Word, 1983.
———. *The New Dare to Discipline.* Wheaton, Ill.: Tyndale House, 1992.
———. *Straight Talk to Men and Their Wives.* 1982. Reprint, Nashville, Tenn.:
    Word, 1995.
———. *The Strong-Willed Child: Birth through Adolescence.* Wheaton, Ill.: Tyn-
    dale House, 1976.
Dollahite, David. *Strengthening Our Families.* Salt Lake City: Bookcraft, 2000.
Douglas, Mary. "Foreword." In *The Gift,* by Marcel Mauss. New York: Norton,
    1990.
Durkheim, Émile. *The Elementary Forms of Religious Life.* Translated by Karen
    Fields. New York: Free Press, 1995.
———. *Suicide.* 1897. Reprint, New York: Free Press, 1951.
Edgell, Penny. "In Rhetoric and Practice: Defining 'The Good Family' in Local
    Congregations." In *The Handbook of the Sociology of Religion,* ed.
    Michelle Dillon. New York: Cambridge University Press, 2003.
Eggebeen, David and Christopher Knoester. "Does Fatherhood Matter for
    Men?" *Journal of Marriage and Family* 63 (2001): 381–93.
Ehrenhalt, Alan. *The Lost City: The Forgotten Virtues of Community in America.*
    New York: Basic Books, 1995.
Elder, Glen, Tri Van Nguyen, and Avshalom Caspi. "Linking Family Hardship
    to Children's Lives." *Child Development* 56 (1985): 361–75.
Elliot, Elisabeth. *Let Me Be a Woman.* Wheaton, Ill.: Tyndale House, 1976.
———. "Why I Oppose the Ordination of Women." *Christianity Today,* June 6,
    1975, 12–16.
Ellison, Christopher G. "Religion, the Life Stress Paradigm, and the Study of De-
    pression." In *Religion in Aging and Health: Theoretical Foundations and
    Methodological Frontiers,* ed. J. S. Levin. Newbury Park, Calif.: Sage, 1994.
———. "Religious Involvement and Subjective Well-Being." *Journal of Health
    and Social Behavior* 32 (1991): 80–99.

Ellison, Christopher G. and John P. Bartkowski. "Conservative Protestantism
and the Division of Household Labor among Married Couples." *Journal of
Family Issues* 23 (2002): 950–85.

Ellison, Christopher G., John P. Bartkowski, and Kristin L. Anderson. "Are
There Religious Variations in Domestic Violence?" *Journal of Family Issues* 20 (1999): 87–113.

Ellison, Christopher G., John P. Bartkowski, and Michelle L. Segal. "Conservative Protestantism and the Parental Use of Corporal Punishment." *Social
Forces* 74 (1996): 1003–29.

Ellison, Christopher G., and Darren E. Sherkat. "Conservative Protestantism and
Support for Corporal Punishment." *American Sociological Review* 58
(1993): 131–44.

———. "Obedience and Autonomy: Religion and Parental Values Reconsidered." *Journal for the Scientific Study of Religion* 32 (1993): 313–29.

England, Paula. "Marriage, the Costs of Children, and Gender Inequality." In
The Ties That Bind: Perspectives on Marriage and Cohabitation, ed. Linda
Waite. Hawthorne, N.Y.: Aldine de Gruyter, 2000.

England, Paula, and George Farkas. *Households, Employment, and Gender.* Hawthorne, N.Y.: Aldine de Gruyter, 1986.

England, Paula, and Barbara Stanek Kilbourne. "Markets, Marriages, and Other
Mates: The Problem of Power." In *Beyond the Marketplace,* ed. Roger
Friedland and A. F. Robertson. New York: Aldine de Gruyter, 1990.

Erickson, Rebecca J. "Reconceptualizing Family Work: The Effect of Emotion
Work on Perceptions of Marital Quality." *Journal of Marriage and the
Family* 55 (1993): 888–900.

Evans, John H., and Bethany Bryson. "Locating Actual Cultural Conflict: Polarization over Abortion in Protestant Denominations, 1972–1996." Unpublished manuscript, Department of Sociology, University of California–Los
Angeles, 2000.

Evans, Tony. "Spiritual Purity." In *Seven Promises of a Promise Keeper,* ed.
Randy Philips. Colorado Springs, Colo.: Focus on the Family Publishing,
1994.

Falwell, Jerry. *Listen America!* New York: Doubleday, 1980.

Ferree, Myra Marx. "Feminism and Family Research." Pp. 103–21 in *Contemporary Families,* ed. Alan Booth. Minneapolis: National Council of Family
Relations, 1991.

———. "The Gender Division of Labor in Two-Earner Marriages: Dimensions
of Variability and Change." *Journal of Family Issues* 12 (1991): 158–80.

Folbre, Nancy, and Thomas E. Weisskopf. "Did Father Know Best? Families,

Markets, and the Supply of Caring Labor." In *Economics, Values, and Organization*, ed. Avner Ben-Ner and Louis Putterman. New York: Cambridge University Press, 1998.

Fowler, Robert Booth. *A New Engagement: Evangelical Political Thought, 1966–1976*. Grand Rapids, Mich.: Eerdmans, 1982.

Fugate, J. Richard. *What the Bible Says about Child Training*. Tempe, Ariz.: Aletheia, 1980.

Furstenberg, Frank F., Jr. "Good Dads—Bad Dads: Two Faces of Fatherhood." In *The Changing American Family and Public Policy*, ed. Andrew Cherlin. Washington, D.C.: Urban Institute Press, 1988.

Gallagher, Sally K. *Evangelical Identity and Gendered Family Life*. New Brunswick, N.J.: Rutgers University Press, 2003.

Gallagher, Sally K., and Christian Smith. "Symbolic Traditionalism and Pragmatic Egalitarianism: Contemporary Evangelicals, Family, and Gender." *Gender and Society* 13 (1999): 211–33.

Garland, Diana R. *Family Ministry: A Comprehensive Guide*. Downer's Grove, Ill.: InterVarsity Press, 1999.

Geis, Sally. "Gay and Christian: Two Stories." *Christian Century*, January 18, 1995, 55–57.

Gerson, Kathleen. *Hard Choices: How Women Decide about Work, Career, and Motherhood*. Berkeley: University of California Press, 1985.

———. *No Man's Land: Men's Changing Commitments to Family and Work*. New York: Basic Books, 1993.

Gesch, Lyn. "Responses to Changing Lifestyles: 'Feminists' and 'Traditionalists' in Mainstream Religion." In *Work, Family, and Religion in Contemporary Society*, ed. Nancy Tatom Ammerman and Wade Clark Roof. New York: Routledge, 1995.

"Getting God's Kingdom into Politics." *Christianity Today*, September 19, 1980, 10–11.

Giddens, Anthony. *The Transformation of Intimacy*. Stanford, Calif.: Stanford University Press, 1992.

Gillespie, Joanna Bowen. "Episcopal: Family as the Nursery of Church and Society." Pp. 143–56 in *Faith Traditions and the Family*. Louisville, Ky.: Westminster/John Knox, 1996.

Gilmore, David D. *Manhood in the Making: Cultural Concepts of Masculinity*. New Haven, Conn.: Yale University Press, 1990.

Glenn, Norval D. "Quantitative Research on Marital Quality in the 1980s: A Critical Review." *Journal of Marriage and the Family* 52 (1990): 818–31.

———. "Values, Attitudes, and the State of American Marriage." In *Promises* to Keep: Decline and Renewal of Marriage in America, ed. David Popenoe, Jean Bethke Elshtain, David Blankenhorn. Lanham, Md.: Rowman and Littlefield, 1996.

Goldscheider, Frances K., and Linda J. Waite. New Families, No Families? The Transformation of the American Home. Berkeley: University of California Press, 1991.

Goldstein, Joshua, and Catherine Kenney. "Marriage Delayed or Marriage Foregone? New Cohort Forecasts of First Marriage for U.S. Women." American Sociological Review 66 (2001): 506–19.

Goode, William J. World Changes in Divorce Patterns. New Haven, Conn.: Yale University Press, 1993.

Gorman, Elizabeth. "Bringing Home the Bacon: Marital Allocation of Income-Earning Responsibility, Job Shifts, and Men's Wages." Journal of Marriage and the Family 61 (1999): 110–12.

Gottman, John M. "Toward a Process Model of Men in Marriages and Families." In Men in Families: When Do They Get Involved? What Difference Does it Make? ed. Alan Booth and Ann Crouter. Mahway, N.J.: Lawrence Erlbaum, 1998.

Gove, Walter R., Michael Hughes, and Carolyn Briggs Style. "Does Marriage Have Positive Effects on the Psychological Well Being of the Individual?" Journal of Health and Social Behavior 24 (1983): 122–31.

Greene, Marcia Slacum. "Promise Keepers Evoke Strong Emotions; Some Women Praise Its Influence; Others Fear Effect on Rights." Washington Post, September 27, 1997.

Greenstein, Theodore N. "Economic Dependence, Gender, and the Division of Labor in the Home: A Replication and Extension." Journal of Marriage and the Family 62 (2000): 322–35.

———. "Gender Ideology and the Perceptions of the Fairness of the Division of Household Labor: Effects on Marital Quality." Social Forces 74 (1996): 1029–42.

———. "Husbands' Participation in Domestic Labor: Interactive Effects of Wives' and Husbands' Gender Ideologies." Journal of Marriage and the Family 58 (1996): 585–95.

Greven, Philip. Spare the Child: The Religious Roots of Punishment and the Psychological Impact of Abuse. New York: Alfred Knopf, 1990.

Griffith, R. Marie. God's Daughters: Evangelical Women and the Power of Submission. Berkeley: University of California Press, 1997.

Griswold, Robert. Fatherhood in America: A History. New York: Basic Books, 1993.

Groothuis, Rebecca M. *Women Caught in the Conflict: The Culture War between Traditionalism and Feminism.* Grand Rapids, Mich.: Baker, 1994.

Hadden, Jeffrey. *The Gathering Storm in the Churches.* New York: Doubleday, 1969.

Hall, Charles. "Entering the Labor Force: Ideals and Realities among Evangelical Women." Pp. 137–55 in *Work, Family, and Religion in Contemporary Society,* ed. Nancy Tatom Ammerman and Wade Clark Roof. New York: Routledge, 1995.

Hansen, Thomas Blom. *The Saffron Wave: Democracy and Hindu Nationalism in Modern India.* Princeton, N.J.: Princeton University Press, 1999.

Harris, Kathleen Mullan, Frank F. Furstenberg, Jr., and Jeremy K. Marmer. "Paternal Involvement with Adolescents in Intact Families: The Influence of Fathers over the Life Course." *Demography* 35 (1998): 201–16.

Hays, Sharon. *The Cultural Contradictions of Motherhood.* New Haven, Conn.: Yale University Press, 1996.

Heaton, Tim B., and Edith L. Pratt. "The Effects of Religious Homogamy on Marital Satisfaction and Stability." *Journal of Family Issues* 11 (1990): 191–207.

Henry, Carl F. H. "The Battle of the Sexes." *Christianity Today,* July 4, 1975, 45–46.

———. "Further Thoughts about Women." *Christianity Today,* June 6, 1975, 36–37.

Hirschman, Albert O. *Exit, Voice, and Loyalty: Responses to Decline in Firms, Organizations, and States.* Cambridge, Mass.: Harvard University Press, 1970.

Hochschild, Arlie. "The Economy of Gratitude." Pp. 95–113 in *The Sociology of Emotions: Original Essays and Research Papers,* ed. Thomas Hood. Greenwich, Conn.: JAI Press, 1989.

———. "Emotion Work, Feeling Rules, and Social Structure." *American Journal of Sociology* 85 (1979): 551–75.

———. *The Managed Heart: Commercialization of Human Feeling.* Berkeley: University of California Press, 1983.

Hochschild, Arlie, with Ann Machung. *The Second Shift: Working Parents and the Revolution at Home.* New York: Viking, 1989.

Hoge, Dean R., Benton Johnson, and Donald A. Luidens. *Vanishing Boundaries: The Religion of Mainline Protestant Baby Boomers.* Louisville, Ky.: Westminster/John Knox, 1994.

Holifield, E. Brooks. *A History of Pastoral Care in America: From Salvation to Self-Realization.* Nashville, Tenn.: Abingdon, 1983.

"Homosexuality: Biblical Guidance through a Moral Morass." *Christianity Today,* April 18, 1980, 12–13.

Horton, Marilee. *Free to Stay at Home: A Woman's Alternative.* Waco: Word, 1982.

Houseknecht, Sharon K. "Social Change in Egypt: The Roles of Religion and Family." Pp. 79–106 in *Family, Religion, and Social Change in Diverse Societies,* ed. Sharon K. Houseknecht and Jerry G. Pankhurst. New York: Oxford University Press, 2000.

Houseknecht, Sharon K., and Jerry G. Pankhurst, eds. *Family, Religion, and Social Change in Diverse Societies.* New York: Oxford University Press, 2000.

Howard, Judith, and Hollander, Jocelyn. *Gendered Situations, Gendered Selves: A Gender Lens on Social Psychology.* Thousand Oaks, Calif.: Sage, 1997.

Hunter, James Davison. *American Evangelicalism: Conservative Religion and the Quandary of Modernity.* New Brunswick, N.J.: Rutgers University Press, 1983.

———. *Culture Wars: The Struggle to Define America.* New York: Basic Books, 1992.

———. *Evangelicalism: The Coming Generation.* Chicago: University of Chicago Press, 1987.

Institute on Religion and Democracy. "Women of Renewal: A Statement." *First Things* (February 1998): 36–40.

Jackson, Robert Max. *Destined for Equality: The Inevitable Rise of Women's Status.* Cambridge, Mass.: Harvard University Press, 1998.

Janssen, Al, ed. *Seven Promises of a Promise Keeper.* Colorado Springs, Colo.: Promise Keepers, 1994.

Jenkins, Philip. *The Next Christendom: The Rise of Global Christianity.* New York: Oxford University Press, 2002.

Jordan, Anthony L., et al. *Report of the Baptist Faith and Message Study Committee to the Southern Baptist Convention.* Salt Lake City, Utah: Southern Baptist Convention, 1998.

Journal of the 1956 General Conference of the Methodist Church. Nashville, Tenn.: Board of Publications of the Methodist Church, 1956.

Kamo, Yoshinori. "Determinants of Household Division of Labor: Resources, Power, and Ideology." *Journal of Family Issues* 9 (1988): 177–200.

Kellstedt, Lyman A., and John C. Green. "Knowing God's Many People: Denominational Preference and Political Behavior." In *Rediscovering the Religious Factor in American Politics,* ed. David Leege and Lyman Kellstedt. Armonk, N.Y.: M. E. Sharpe, 1993.

Kinnaird, William M. "Divorce and Remarriage: Ministers in the Middle." *Christianity Today,* June 6, 1980, 24–27.

Kitson, Gay C., with William M. Holmes, *Portrait of Divorce: Adjustment to Marital Breakdown.* New York: Guilford, 1992.

Kohn, Melvin L. *Class and Conformity: A Study in Values.* Chicago: University of Chicago Press, 1977.

Kroeger, Catherine Clark, and James R. Beck. *Women, Abuse, and the Bible.* Grand Rapids, Mich.: Paternoster, 1996.

LaHaye, Beverly. *How to Develop Your Child's Temperament.* Eugene, Ore.: Harvest House, 1977.

———. *The Spirit-Controlled Woman.* Eugene, Ore.: Harvest House, 1977.

Lamb, Michael E. "Fathers and Child Development: An Integrative Overview." In *The Role of the Father in Child Development,* ed. Michael Lamb. New York: John Wiley & Sons, 1997.

———, ed. *The Role of the Father in Child Development.* New York: John Wiley & Sons, 1997.

Land, Richard, and Barret Duke. "Fatherhood in the Evangelical Tradition." In *The Faith Factor in Fatherhood,* ed. Don E. Eberly. Lanham, Md.: Lexington, 1999.

Langford, Andy, ed. *United Methodist Book of Worship.* Nashville, Tenn.: Abingdon, 1992.

Lareau, Annette. *Unequal Childhood: The Importance of Social Class in Family Life.* Berkeley: University of California Press, 2003.

LaRossa, Ralph. "Fatherhood and Social Change." *Family Relations* 37 (1988): 451–57.

Larzelere, Robert E. "A Review of the Outcomes of Parental Use of Nonabusive or Customary Physical Punishment." *Pediatrics* 98 (1996): 824–28.

Lasch, Christopher. *Haven in a Heartless World: The Family Besieged.* New York: Norton, 1977.

———. *The Revolt of the Elites.* New York: Norton, 1995.

Laslett, Peter. *Family Life and Illicit Love in Earlier Generations.* Cambridge: Cambridge University Press, 1977.

Leonard, Bill J. "Southern Baptist: Family as Witness of Grace in the Community." In *Faith Traditions and the Family,* ed. Phyllis D. Airhart and Margaret Lamberts Bendroth. Louisville, Ky.: Westminster/John Knox, 1996.

Lesthaeghe, Ron. "The Second Demographic Transition in Western Countries: An Interpretation." In *Gender and Family Change in Industrialized Countries,* ed. Karen Oppenheim Mason and An-Magritt Jensen. Oxford: Oxford University Press, 1995.

Lindner, Eileen W. "Ecumenical and Interdenominational: Private and Public Approaches to Family Issues." In *Faith Traditions and the Family,* ed. Phyllis D. Airhart and Margaret Lamberts Bendroth. Louisville, Ky.: Westminster/John Knox, 1996.

Livezey, Lois Gehr. "The Fourth Presbyterian Church of Chicago: One Congregation's Response to the Challenges of Family Life in Urban America." In *Tending the Flock: Congregations and Family Ministry,* ed. Brynolf Lyon and Archie Smith. Louisville, Ky.: Westminster/John Knox, 1998.

Lockhart, William H. "'We Are One Life,' but Not of One Gender Ideology: Unity, Ambiguity, and the Promise Keepers." *Sociology of Religion* 61 (2000): 73–92.

Luker, Kristen. *Abortion and the Politics of Motherhood.* Berkeley: University of California Press, 1984.

Lundberg, Shelly, and Robert A. Pollak. "Bargaining and Distribution in Marriage." *Journal of Economic Perspectives* 10 (1996): 139–58.

Lundquist, Melinda, and Christian Smith. "Christian Participation." Paper presented at the annual meeting of the Society for the Scientific Study of Religion, Boston, November 1999.

Maccoby, Eleanor E., and John A. Martin. "Socialization in the Context of the Family: Parent-Child Interaction." Pp. 1–101 in *Handbook of Child Psychology,* ed. E. M. Hetherington. New York: Wiley, 1983.

Mahoney, Annette, and Kenneth Pargament, Aaron Murray-Swank, and Nichole Murray-Swank. "Religion and the Sanctification of Family Relationships." *Review of Religious Research* 40 (2003): 220–36.

Maldonado, Jorge E. "Building 'Fundamentalism' from the Family in Latin America." Pp. 214–39 in *Fundamentalisms and Society: Reclaiming the Sciences, the Family, and Education,* ed. Martin E. Marty and R. Scott Appleby. Chicago: University of Chicago Press, 1993.

Manning, Christel J. *God Gave Us the Right.* New Brunswick, N.J.: Rutgers University Press, 1999.

Mare, Robert D., and Christopher Winship. "Socioeconomic Change and the Decline of Marriage for Blacks and Whites." In *The Urban Underclass,* ed. Christopher Jencks and Paul Peterson. Washington, D.C.: Brookings Institution, 1991.

Marks, Loren D., and David C. Dollahite. "Religion, Relationships, and Responsible Fathering in Latter-Day Saint Families of Children with Special Needs." *Journal of Social and Personal Relationships* 18 (2001): 625–50.

Marler, Penny Long. "Lost in the Fifties: The Changing Family and the Nostalgic Church." In *Work, Family, and Religion in Contemporary Society,* ed.

Nancy Tatom Ammerman and Wade Clark Roof. New York: Routledge, 1995.

Marsden, George. *Fundamentalism and American Culture*. New York: Oxford University Press, 1980.

———. *Reforming Fundamentalism: Fuller Seminary and the New Evangelicalism*. Grand Rapids, Mich.: Eerdmans, 1987.

Marsiglio, William. "Paternal Engagement Activities with Minor Children." *Journal of Marriage and the Family* 53 (1991): 973–86.

Martin, David. *Tongues of Fire: The Explosion of Protestantism in Latin America*. Cambridge, Mass.: Blackwell, 1989.

Mathisen, James A. "The Strange Decade of the Promise Keepers." *Books and Culture* 7 (2001): 36–39.

Mauss, Marcel. *The Gift*. New York: Norton, 1990.

May, Elaine Tyler. *Homeward Bound: American Families in the Cold War*. New York: Basic Books, 1988.

McCartney, Bill, ed. *What Makes a Man?* Colorado Springs, Colo.: Navigator Press, 1992.

McQuillan, Julia, and Myra Marx Ferree. "The Importance of Variation among Men and the Benefits of Feminism for Families." In *Men in Families: When Do They Get Involved? What Difference Does It Make?* ed. Alan Booth and Ann Crouter. Mahway, N.J.: Lawrence Erlbaum, 1998.

Melton, J. Gordon. *The Churches Speak on Sex and Family Life*. Detroit: Gale Research, 1991.

Messner, Michael A. *Politics of Masculinities: Men in Movements*. Thousand Oaks, Calif.: Sage Publications, 1997.

Mohler, R. Albert, Jr. "Against an Immoral Tide." *New York Times*, June 19, 2000.

Morell, Carolyn M. *Unwomanly Conduct: The Challenges of Intentional Childlessness*. New York: Routledge, 1994.

Morgan, Richard Lyon. *Is There Life after Divorce in the Church?* Atlanta: John Knox, 1985.

Myers, Scott M., and Alan Booth. "Marital Strains and Marital Quality: The Role of High and Low Locus of Control." *Journal of Marriage and the Family* 61 (1999): 423–36.

Nason-Clark, Nancy. *The Battered Wife: How Christians Confront Family Violence*. Louisville, Ky.: Westminster/John Knox, 1997.

Nock, Steven L. "Commitment and Dependency in Marriage." *Journal of Marriage and the Family* 57 (1995): 503–14.

———. *Marriage in Men's Lives*. New York: Oxford University Press, 1998.

————. "The Marriages of Equally Dependent Spouses." *Journal of Family Issues* 22 (2001): 755–75.

Olsen, Norskov. "Divorce and Remarriage." *Christianity Today,* December 13, 1985, 42–44.

Olson, Laura. *Filled with Spirit and Power.* Albany: State University of New York Press, 2000.

Pankhurst, Jerry G., and Sharon K. Houseknecht. "Introduction: The Religion-Family Linkage and Social Change—A Neglected Area of Study." In *Family, Religion, and Social Change in Diverse Societies,* ed. Sharon K. Houseknecht and Jerry G. Pankhurst. New York: Oxford University Press, 2000.

Pargament, Kenneth I. *The Psychology of Religion and Coping: Theory, Research, Practice.* New York: Guilford Press, 1997.

Parke, Ross D. *Fatherhood.* Cambridge, Mass.: Harvard University Press, 1996.

Patton, John, and Brian H. Childs. *Christian Marriage and Family: Caring for Our Generations.* Nashville, Tenn.: Abingdon, 1988.

Pearce, Lisa D., and William G. Axinn. "The Impact of Family Religious Life on the Quality of Mother-Child Relations." *American Sociological Review* 63 (1998): 810–28.

Peek, Charles W., George D. Lowe, and L. Susan Williams. "Gender and God's Word: Another Look at Religious Fundamentalism and Sexism." *Social Forces* 69 (1991): 1205–21.

Peterson, Paul E. "The Urban Underclass and the Poverty Paradox." In *The Urban Underclass,* ed. Christopher Jencks and Paul Peterson. Washington, D.C.: Brookings Institution Press.

Popenoe, David. *Disturbing the Nest: Family Change and Decline in Modern Societies.* Hawthorne, N.Y.: Aldine de Gruyter, 1988.

————. *Life without Father: Compelling New Evidence that Fatherhood and Marriage are Indispensable for the Good of Children and Society.* New York: Martin Kessler Books, 1996.

Popenoe, David, and Barbara Dafoe Whitehead. *The State of Our Unions.* New Brunswick: National Marriage Project, 2000.

Powlison, David. "Integration or Inundation?" In *Power Religion: The Selling Out of the Evangelical Church.* Chicago: Moody Press, 1992.

Presbyterian Panel. "Public Role of Presbyterians." Louisville, Ky.: Office of Research, Presbyterian Church (U.S.A.), 1999.

Presser, Harriet B. "Employment Schedules among Dual-Earner Spouses and the Division of Household Labor by Gender." *American Sociological Review* 59 (1994): 348–64.

Putnam, Robert. *Bowling Alone: The Collapse and Revival of American Community.* New York: Simon and Schuster, 2000.

Reeves, Thomas C. *The Empty Church: The Suicide of Liberal Christianity.* New York: Free Press, 1996.

Reifsnyder, Richard W. "Transformations in Administrative Leadership in the United Presbyterian Church in the U.S.A., 1920–1983." In *The Pluralistic Vision: Presbyterians and Mainstream Protestant Education and Leadership,* ed. Milton Coalter, John Mulder, and Louis Weeks. Louisville, Ky.: Westminster/John Knox, 1996.

Riesebrodt, Martin. *Pious Passion: The Emergence of Modern Fundamentalism in the United States and Iran.* Translated by Don Reneau. Berkeley: University of California Press, 1993.

Roberts, Cokie, and Steven V. Roberts. "Southern Baptists Have a Distorted View of the Family." *Denver Rocky Mountain News,* June 21, 1998.

Robertson, Brian C. *There's No Place Like Work.* Dallas: Spence, 2000.

Roof, Wade Clark. *A Generation of Seekers: The Spiritual Journeys of the Baby Boom Generation.* San Francisco: Harper, 1993.

Roof, Wade Clark, and William McKinney. *American Mainline Religion: Its Changing Shape and Future.* New Brunswick, N.J.: Rutgers University Press, 1987.

Sanchez, Laura, and Emily W. Kane. "Women's and Men's Constructions of Perceptions of Housework Fairness." *Journal of Family Issues* 17 (1996): 358–87.

Sayer, Liana. "Gender, Time, and Inequality: Trends in Women's and Men's Paid Work, Unpaid Work, and Free Time." Unpublished manuscript. Population Studies Center, University of Pennsylvania, 2002.

Scanzoni, John, and C. Arnett. "Enlarging the Understanding of Marital Commitment via Religious Devoutness, Gender-Role Preferences, and Locus of Marital Control." *Journal of Family Issues* 8 (1987): 136–56.

Schmidt, Jean Miller, and Gail E. Murphy-Geiss. "Methodist: 'Tis Grace Will Lead Us Home." In *Faith Traditions and the Family,* ed. Phyllis D. Airhart and Margaret Lamberts Bendroth. Louisville, Ky.: Westminster/John Knox, 1996.

Schudson, Michael. "How Culture Works: Perspectives from Media Studies on the Efficacy of Symbols." *Theory and Society* 18 (1989): 153–80.

Scott, Joan Wallach. *Gender and the Politics of History.* New York: Columbia University Press, 1988.

Scott, Tracey. "What's God Got to Do with It? Protestantism, Gender, and the Meaning of Work." Ph.D. diss., Department of Sociology, Princeton University, 1999.

Scott, W. Richard, John W. Meyer, and associates. *Institutional Environments and Organizations: Structural Complexity and Individualism.* Thousand Oaks, Calif.: Sage, 1994.

Seltzer, Judith, and Suzanne Bianchi. "Children's Contact with Absent Parents." *Journal of Marriage and the Family* 50 (1988): 666–78.

Sewell, William H., Jr. "A Theory of Structure: Duality, Agency, and Transformation." *American Journal of Sociology* 98 (1992): 1–29.

Shelton, Beth Anne. "The Distribution of Household Tasks: Does Wife's Employment Status Make a Difference?" *Journal of Family Issues* 11 (1990): 115–35.

Shelton, Beth Anne, and Daphne John. "The Division of Household Labor." *Annual Review of Sociology* 22 (1996): 299–322.

Sherkat, Darren E. "Religious Socialization and the Family: An Examination of Religious Influence in the Family over the Life Course." Ph.D. diss., Department of Sociology, Duke University, 1991.

Shorter, Edward. *The Making of the Modern Family.* New York: Basic Books, 1977.

Simons, Ronald L., Christine Johnson, and Rand D. Conger. "Harsh Corporal Punishment versus Quality of Parental Involvement as an Explanation of Adolescent Maladjustment." *Journal of Marriage and the Family* 56 (1994): 591–607.

Skolnick, Arlene S. *Embattled Paradise: The American Family in an Age of Uncertainty.* New York: Basic Books.

Smalley, Gary. *If Only He Knew: What No Woman Can Resist.* New York: HarperCollins, 1988.

Smalley, Gary, and John Trent. *The Blessing.* Nashville, Tenn.: Thomas Nelson, 1986.

Smith, Christian. *American Evangelicalism: Embattled and Thriving.* Chicago: University of Chicago Press, 1998.

———. *Christian America? What Evangelicals Really Want.* Berkeley: University of California Press, 2000.

Smith, William. "Evangelicalism and the Therapeutic." Unpublished manuscript. Department of Sociology, Rutgers University, 1998.

South, Scott J., and Glenna Spitze. "Housework in Marital and Nonmarital Households." *American Sociological Review* 59 (1994): 327–47.

Spain, Daphne, and Suzanne Bianchi. *Balancing Act: Motherhood, Marriage, and Employment among American Women.* New York: Russell Sage Foundation, 1996.

Special Committee on Human Sexuality. *Keeping Body and Soul Together: Sexuality, Spirituality, and Social Justice.* Baltimore, Md.: Presbyterian Church (U.S.A.), 1991.

Stacey, Judith. *Brave New Families: Stories of Domestic Upheaval in Late Twenti-eth Century America.* New York: Basic Books, 1991.

Stackhouse, Max L. "The Free-Church Tradition and Social Ministry." *Christian Century,* November 6, 1985, 995–97.

Stark, Rodney, and Roger Finke. *Acts of Faith: Explaining the Human Side of Religion.* Berkeley: University of California Press, 2000.

Steensland, Brian. "The Hydra and the Swords: Social Welfare and Mainline Advocacy, 1964–2000." Pp. 213–36 in *The Quiet Hand of God: Faith-Based Activism and the Public Role of Mainline Protestantism,* ed. Robert Wuthnow and John H. Evans. Berkeley: University of California Press, 2002.

Steensland, Brian, Jerry Z. Park, Mark D. Regnerus, Lynn D. Robinson, W. Bradford Wilcox, and Robert D. Woodberry. "The Measure of American Religion: Toward Improving the State of the Art." *Social Forces* 79 (2000): 291–318.

Stevens, Mitchell L. *Kingdom of Children: Culture and Controversy in the Homeschooling Movement.* Princeton, N.J.: Princeton University Press, 2001.

Stolzenberg, Ross M., Mary Blair-Loy, and Linda J. Waite. "Religious Participa-tion in Early Adulthood: Age and Family Life Cycle Effects on Church Membership." *American Sociological Review* 60 (1995): 84–103.

Stone, Lawrence. *The Family, Sex, and Marriage: In England 1500–1800.* New York: Harper & Row, 1977.

Straus, Murray A. *Beating the Devil Out of Them: Corporal Punishment in Ameri-can Families.* San Francisco: Jossey-Bass, 1994.

Straus, Murray A., David Sugarman, and Jean Giles-Sims. "Spanking by Parents and Subsequent Antisocial Behavior of Children." *Archives of Pediatric Ad-olescent Medicine* 151 (1997): 761–67.

Sweet, James, Larry Bumpass, and Vaughan Call. *The Design and Content of the National Survey of Families and Households.* Madison: Center for Demog-raphy and Ecology, University of Wisconsin–Madison, 1988.

Swidler, Ann. "Cultural Power and Social Movements." Pp. 311–23 in *Cultural Sociology,* ed. Lyn Spillman. Oxford, U.K.: Blackwell, 2002.

———. "Culture in Action: Symbols and Strategies." *American Sociological Re-view* 51 (1986): 273–86.

Swindoll, Charles R. *You and Your Child.* Nashville, Tenn.: Thomas Nelson, 1977.

Thompson, Linda. "Family Work: Women's Sense of Fairness." *Journal of Fam-ily Issues* 12 (1991): 181–96.

Thompson, Linda, and Alexis Walker. "Gender in Families: Women and Men in Marriage, Work, and Parenthood." *Journal of Marriage and the Family* 51 (1989): 845–71.

Thomson, Elizabeth, Thomas L. Hanson, and Sara S. McLanahan. "Family Structure and Child Well-Being: Economic Resources vs. Parental Behaviors." *Social Forces* 73 (1994): 221–42.

Thornton, Arland. "Changing Attitudes toward Family Issues in the United States." *Journal of Marriage and the Family* 47 (1989): 381–94.

———. "Reciprocal Influences of Family and Religion in a Changing World." *Journal of Marriage and the Family* 47 (1985): 381–94.

Tilly, Louise A., and Joan Wallach Scott. *Women, Work, and Family.* New York: Holt, Rinehart and Winston, 1978.

United Methodist Church. *The Book of Discipline of the United Methodist Church.* Nashville, Tenn.: United Methodist Publishing House, 1996.

———. *United Methodist Church Book of Discipline.* Nashville, Tenn.: Cokesbury, 1976.

U.S. Census Bureau. *Population Profile of the United States.* Current Population Reports, Series P-23, No. 205. Washington, D.C.: Government Printing Office, 2001.

Van Leeuwen, Mary Stewart. *Gender and Grace: Love, Work, and Parenting in a Changing World.* Downers Grove, Ill.: InterVarsity Press, 1990.

———. "Servanthood or Soft Patriarchy? A Christian Feminist Looks at the Promise Keepers Movement." *Priscilla Papers* 11 (1997): 28–40.

Vlosky, Denese Ashbaugh, and Pamela A. Monroe. "The Effective Dates of No-Fault Divorce Laws in the Fifty States." *Family Relations* 51 (2002): 317–24.

Waite, Linda, and Maggie Gallagher. *The Case for Marriage: Why Married People are Happier, Healthier, and Better Off Financially.* New York: Doubleday, 2000.

Wall, James M. "The New Right Exploits Abortion." *Christian Century,* July 30–August 6, 1980, 747–48.

———. "Purity and Single-Issue Politics." *Christian Century,* April 9, 1980, 395–96.

Walton, Rus. *One Nation under God.* Nashville, Tenn.: Thomas Nelson, 1987.

Warner, R. Stephen. "Work in Progress toward a New Paradigm for the Sociological Study of Religion in the United States." *American Journal of Sociology* 98 (1993): 1044–93.

Weber, Max. *Economy and Society.* Vol. 1. Berkeley: University of California Press, 1968.

————. *The Protestant Ethic and the Spirit of Capitalism.* New York: Charles Scribner's Sons, 1958.

————. "The Social Psychology of the World Religions." In *From Max Weber: Essays in Sociology,* ed. H. H. Gerth and C. Wright Mills. New York: Oxford University Press, 1946.

Weber, Stu. *Tender Warrior: God's Intention for a Man.* Sisters, Ore.: Multnomah, 1993.

West, Candace, and Don H. Zimmerman. "Doing Gender." *Gender and Society* 1 (1987): 125–51.

Wilcox, W. Bradford. "Conservative Protestant Childrearing: Authoritarian or Authoritative?" *American Sociological Review* 63 (1998): 796–809.

————. "Conservative Protestantism and the Family: Resisting, Engaging, or Accommodating Modernity?" In *A Public Faith: Evangelicals and Civic Engagement,* ed. Michael Cromartie. Lanham, Md.: Rowman and Littlefield, 2003.

————. "For the Sake of the Children? Family-Related Discourse and Practice in the Mainline." Pp. 287–316 in *The Quiet Hand of God: Faith-Based Activism and the Public Role of Mainline Protestantism,* ed. Robert Wuthnow and John H. Evans. Berkeley: University of California Press, 2002.

————. "The Presbyterian Church (USA): A Profile." Unpublished manuscript. Department of Sociology, Princeton University, 1999.

————. "Religion, Convention, and Paternal Involvement." *Journal of Marriage and Family* 64 (2002): 780–92.

————. "Religion, Parenting, and Child Well-Being." Paper presented before the Commission on Children at Risk, Dartmouth Medical School, Hanover, N.H., June 25, 2002.

————. *Sacred Vows, Public Purposes: Religion, the Marriage Movement, and Public Policy.* Washington, D.C.: The Pew Forum on Religion and Public Life, 2002.

————. *Then Comes Marriage? Religion, Race, and Marriage in Urban America.* Philadelphia: Center for Research on Religion and Urban Civil Society, University of Pennsylvania, 2002.

Wilcox, W. Bradford, and John P. Bartkowski. "The Conservative Protestant Family: Traditional Rhetoric, Progressive Practice." In *What's God Got to Do with the American Experiment? Essays on Religion and Politics,* ed. E. J. Dionne and John J. DiIulio. Washington, D.C.: Brookings Institution Press, 2000.

Wilcox, W. Bradford, and Steven L. Nock. "What's Love Got to Do with It? Gender Role Ideology, Men's Emotion Work, and Women's Marital Quality."

Population Association of America Annual Meeting, Washington, D.C., March 31, 2001.

Wilkie, Jane R., Myra M. Ferree, and Kathryn S. Ratcliff. "Gender and Fairness: Marital Satisfaction in Two-Earner Couples." *Journal of Marriage and the Family* 60 (1998): 577–94.

Wilson, William Julius. *When Work Disappears: The World of the New Urban Poor.* New York: Knopf, 1996.

Witten, Marsha Grace. *All Is Forgiven: The Secular Message in American Protestantism.* Princeton, N.J.: Princeton University Press, 1993.

Wolfe, Alan. *Whose Keeper? Social Science and Moral Obligation.* Berkeley: University of California Press, 1989.

Wolff, Kurt H. *The Sociology of George Simmel.* New York: Free Press, 1950.

Wrong, Dennis H. "The Oversocialized Conception of Man in Modern Sociology." *American Sociological Review* 26 (1961): 183–93.

Wuthnow, Robert. *After Heaven: Spirituality in America since the 1950s.* Berkeley: University of California Press, 1998.

———. *Christianity in the Twenty-First Century: Reflections on the Challenges Ahead.* New York: Oxford University Press, 1993.

———. *Communities of Discourse: Ideology and Structure in the Reformation, the Enlightenment, and European Socialism.* Cambridge, Mass.: Harvard University Press, 1989.

———. *Meaning and Moral Order: Explorations in Cultural Analysis.* Berkeley: University of California Press, 1987.

———. "Mobilizing Civic Engagement: The Changing Impact of Religious Involvement." In *Civic Engagement in American Democracy,* ed. Theda Skocpol and Morris Fiorina. Washington, D.C.: Brookings Institution Press, 1999.

———. *The Restructuring of American Religion.* Princeton, N.J.: Princeton University Press, 1988.

Zelizer, Viviana. "Intimate Transactions." In *Economic Sociology for the Next Millennium.* New York: Russell Sage Foundation, 2000.

———. *Pricing the Priceless Child: The Changing Social Value of Children.* New York: Basic Books, 1985.

———. *The Social Meaning of Money.* New York: Basic Books, 1994.

INDEX